Agrarian Reform
and Grassroots Development

A Policy Study by the Curry Foundation

Agrarian Reform and Grassroots Development

Ten Case Studies

edited by

Roy L. Prosterman
Mary N. Temple
Timothy M. Hanstad

Lynne Rienner Publishers   •   Boulder & London

Published in the United States of America in 1990 by

Lynne Rienner Publishers, Inc.
1800 30th Street, Boulder, Colorado 80301

and in the United Kingdom by
Lynne Rienner Publishers, Inc.
3 Henrietta Street, Covent Garden, London WC2E 8LU

Library of Congress Cataloging-in-Publication Data
Agrarian reform and grassroots development:
ten case studies / edited by Roy L. Prosterman, Mary N. Temple, Timothy M. Hanstad.
    Includes bibliographical references and index.
    ISBN 1-55587-231-X
    1. Land reform—Case studies. 2. Sustainable agriculture.
3. Family farms. I. Prosterman, Roy L. II. Temple, Mary N.
III. Hanstad, Timothy M.
HD1332.L34 1990
333.3'1—dc20   90-8493
                                                               CIP

British Cataloguing in Publication Data
A Cataloguing in Publication record for this book
is available from the British Library.

Printed and bound in the United States of America

The paper used in this publication meets the requirements
of the American National Standard for Permanence of
Paper for Printed Library Materials Z39.48-1984.

Contents

Part 3 The Soviet Union and Eastern Europe

Part 4 Southern Africa

Part 5 Conclusion

Figures and Tables

Figure

Foreword

The relationship of the producer to the land—in the developing world and in collectivized farming—is the subject of this seventh Curry Foundation study of U.S. policies toward agricultural development.

In the developing world, exclusive of China, about 1.4 billion people—over 250 million families—make their living from agriculture. About 100 million of them are landless, farming land they do not own—as tenants on small plots or hired laborers on large plantations or smaller holdings. Besides ownership of the land, nearly all these poverty-stricken families also lack access to credit, inputs, marketing, extension, and other services essential to success.

In addition, collectivized agriculture presently involves some 14 million families in the Soviet Union and Eastern Europe; and while China's 1980s decollectivization gave use rights to its 150 million peasant families, they still lack the secure tenure necessary to motivate them to make the long-term improvements essential to further increased production.

This study examines the land tenure patterns and considers the prospects for reforms in areas as different as China and Central America, the Philippines and the Soviet Union, India and Mexico, Brazil and Southern Africa, Bangladesh and Eastern Europe.

The authors of this unique, ground-breaking volume are among the world's best-informed scholars on this issue, representing, in aggregate, well over a century of experience in fieldwork, research, and writing on land tenure and agrarian reform in these crucial areas of the world. They recount successes and failures, analyze policies, and make recommendations—to the leaders of the international development aid community, to U.S. policymakers, and to the leaders and farmers of the countries studied.

We expect this book—the first of its kind—to stimulate policymakers to look again at the successes of our development aid programs after World War II, when land reform was enacted with U.S.

support in Japan, Taiwan, and South Korea, establishing their system of owner-operated agriculture and laying much of the foundation for the economic progress they have achieved.

The editors and I would like to express our gratitude to the authors, to my fellow members of the foundation's Board of Trustees, to the Advisory Committee, and to the Joyce Mertz-Gilmore Foundation for their support and guidance.

Charles E. Curry
Chairman
Curry Foundation

Introduction

Roy L. Prosterman
Mary N. Temple
Timothy M. Hanstad

It is easy for those in the First World, having progressed over the past century from agrarian to industrial economies, to forget how important the issue of land is today in less developed countries. In the developing world, land continues to constitute the principal source of livelihood, security, and status. About six families out of ten are still engaged in agriculture. Yet roughly 100 million agricultural families—over half-a-billion people—make their living principally from land they do not own. Some work as tenant farmers, paying rent to a landlord, as in the Philippines, Bangladesh, and large parts of India. Others work as agricultural laborers on large plantations or medium-sized farms, as in Latin America or parts of southern Africa. Still others work for a wage or a share of the crop in the small-holding sector, as on Java. Together, these insecure and impoverished nonlandowning agricultural families—the poorest of the poor—are sometimes referred to as the "landless," and there are tens of millions more who are near-landless.

Such landlessness is at the root of some of the world's most serious and persisting problems, with consequences frequently extending to severe exploitation and deprivation of minimal political rights and basic human needs. Yet, for decades this problem, an issue that should be at the heart of the development process, has been neglected or ignored.

Landlessness is a cause of low productivity on lands farmed by poorly compensated and poorly motivated tenants and laborers. Farmers with insecure tenure lack incentives to make capital improvements to the land or to invest the "sweat equity" needed to produce high yields. Where the mass of the population is unproductive, poor, and hungry, and has little income with which to purchase basic goods and services, the village economy stagnates. Where landless families form a significant part of the population, their low productivity and lack of purchasing power in turn become a drag on the entire process of economic development. Although not included in the classification of landless, many of the tens of millions of workers on collective or state farms have similar motivation problems, contributing greatly to the notoriously poor performance of such farms.

Landlessness is a cause of social and political instability. In this century the grievances of landless agriculturalists have played a major role in the revolutionary upheavals in Mexico, Russia, Spain, China, Vietnam, Cuba, Bolivia, Ethiopia, and Nicaragua. Tenants and agricultural laborers, desperate for land of their own, currently provide rank-and-file support for ongoing insurgencies in such settings as El Salvador (where land reform, although significant, is still incomplete) and the Philippines.

Continued landlessness is implicated in both excessive urbanization and large-scale deforestation and erosion. Landlessness leaves each succeeding generation rootless and desperate, forcing more people into already overcrowded cities. Or they have to move onto steep hillsides and other marginal farmland where they cut down forests and contribute to the environmental degradation already under way because of policies that encourage large-scale cattle ranching and logging. Finally, landless farmers lack the dignity, status, and economic stake in their society that accompanies landownership, limiting the prospects for the development of democratic institutions.

Land-tenure reform is the most direct and effective approach to addressing the problems raised by landlessness. Throughout the world, experience demonstrates that the farmer who owns the land he tills will make the long-term investments essential to increasing production, prospering and becoming a real participant in the local, and ultimately in the global, economy. The owner-operated family farm remains the most productive of all agricultural systems. Furthermore, land reform is probably the most important, and sometimes the only, means of altering inequitable power structures for effective development of participatory institutions, local and national, and thus for strengthening democracy.

This was recognized by U.S. policymakers in the decade after World War II, when land reform was promulgated in Japan by General Douglas MacArthur and was at the heart of the development programs in both Taiwan and South Korea. But later—because of both McCarthyism and changes in development fashion that relegated agricultural development to a secondary role—it fell out of favor, and such foreign-aid policies gave way to programs for large-scale industrialization and infrastructure. It was hoped that benefits of these projects would "trickle down" to help the poor. In the 1970s, interest in agriculture revived, but development planners pinned their hopes on Green Revolution technology. Now, as macroeconomic policy reforms and price adjustments are being tried, landlessness increases and Third World poverty stubbornly persists.

The term "land reform" is variously understood and frequently misunderstood by the public and by officials in the aid-giving institutions and in the developing world. In brief, land reform in these discussions is used to refer to the transfer of agricultural landholdings to landless tenants or laborers—those who actually till the soil—to bring about broad-based ownership (or equivalent owner-like rights) of farmholdings, together with essential support for the new owner-operators. This encourages the long-term investment necessary for increased agricultural production and sustained economic growth, as well as altering inequitable power structures, which impede democratization. The transfer of land to the tillers is quintessential, but redistribution of land assets is incomplete without other complementary programs. Support for credit, inputs, and marketing, together with extension advice, are vital to assure the beneficiaries' early success. The ex-owners need not be left out of a land-reform plan. In a number of successful examples some form of compensation was paid to the ex-owners to encourage investment in the broader economy. Various aspects of land-reform policies and experience are explored in depth in this volume.

The concept of land reform is not a new one. Since Biblical times, the land and its accumulation by the few at the expense of the many—slaves, serfs, and peasants—has created inequities and discontent, political and social instability. In the Old Testament, the Book of Leviticus describes the Year of Jubilee, occurring every fifty years, when accumulations of land were required to be relinquished and redistributed.

The problem of landlessness and its relationship to economic development, social equity, and political stability faced today by leaders in the Philippines and Central America, in Bangladesh and Zimbabwe, were faced in sixth century B.C. Athens by Solon and Pisistratus, in second century B.C. Rome by the Gracchi brothers (who were assassinated as a result of their attempts at land reform), and in ancient China, where land was periodically redivided on an equitable basis.

In more modern times, the eighteenth century brought the French Revolution's dismantling of the feudal estates and distribution of the land to the peasants. The nineteenth century brought other European reforms, the Homestead Act in the United States, and similar policies in

Canada, creating the widespread owner-operated family-farm system that prevails today. As the masses of farmers gained economic and political power in Europe and North America, the way was opened for the development of what are now the industrialized democracies. Throughout recent European history, relatively egalitarian agrarian systems have been associated with democracy and development, and inegalitarian systems with instability and antidemocratic forces.

Since 1900, some twenty-five countries containing two-fifths of the world's population have carried out major redistributions of land. Such redistributions followed violent upheavals in Mexico, Russia, China, Bolivia, and Cuba. "Land to the tiller" was Lenin's and Mao's promise to the masses of peasants for their support of the Russian and Chinese revolutions. That promise, betrayed by forced collectivization, may yet be fulfilled as the Soviet Union and China struggle toward economic reforms.

Waves of land redistribution occurred in Eastern Europe both before and after World War II. Significant redistribution occurred in Romania, Bulgaria, Poland, and Yugoslavia.

In Asia after World War II, Japan, Taiwan, and South Korea carried out land-reform programs with massive United States aid, including assistance in implementation, which redistributed land to their tenant farmers. As owner-operators of family farms, these ex-tenants began investing in improvements, prospered, and created effective demand for goods and services. The ex-tenants paid for their land, and the former landlords were compensated and encouraged to invest in other enterprises. These reforms laid the foundation for the postwar process of economic and industrial development in these countries, leaving nearly all of Asia far behind.

In the last twenty years alone, land redistribution has altered significantly the structure of society in South Vietnam, Ethiopia, Kerala state in India, Nicaragua, El Salvador, and China.

Yet, despite the important role that land reform has played through the ages—and notably in the twentieth century—land tenure issues often have been ignored, even in settings where landlordism or large plantations are rife, and a high proportion of agricultural families do not own the land they till.

Why is land reform not the subject of consistent or coherent attention by aid donors or policymakers for those countries where landlessness remains acute? Perhaps it is because the poor are invisible, and the issue arises in conspicuous form in only a handful of countries each decade where revolt or famine grabs the attention of media, the public, and governments. Yet, awareness that it remains a problem simmering beneath the surface in many settings could avoid last-minute panic and help develop programs and remedies that would replace this institutional inattention.

Perhaps those concerned with the future of developing countries do not recognize the extent of the landlessness problem. Yet much of the data on the prevalence and patterns of landlessness is readily available, and appropriate concern could lead to additional data-gathering.

Or perhaps the complexity of the problem and the tangled web of political, economic, social, agronomic, and legal issues it involves cause policymakers, academics, and other observers to turn their attention from the land issue in favor of other, "easier" issues. Yet we seek to address other very complex problems such as the Third World debt.

Perhaps it is easier to choose the palliative solutions, such as "trickle-down," rapid industrialization, and price adjustments, in order to avoid disturbing relationships with land-owning elites who exercise power and influence in these countries. Yet such "easy" solutions have proven inadequate, whereas land-reform programs that are well planned and supported have brought economic benefits to all sectors in societies where they have been undertaken, acheiving a non-zero-sum result in which all participants gain.

Or perhaps the land issue in developing countries is downplayed for the oft-cited reason that such consideration would be futile—a mere academic exercise—in the absence of any political possibility that a given country would undertake a land-reform program.

In response to this last reason, one should never underestimate the potential for rapidly shifting winds in the political and economic climate. Who would have predicted, even in 1988, that Solidarity would be heading a government in Poland in 1989, that the Berlin Wall would crumble, that Ceausescu would be overthrown in Romania, or that free elections would be taking place in the Soviet Union and Nicaragua? Who could have foreseen that, less than ten years after Mao's Cultural Revolution, China's agriculture would be dominated by individual family farms? In most countries where sweeping land reforms have been implemented in the twentieth century, the prospects for such reforms, even a year or two before they took place, appeared very doubtful. In sum, political possibilities are difficult to judge.

Furthermore, there may not be time, when the political moment of truth arrives, to design hastily an adequate land-reform program. Well-designed land reform must be thought through carefully in order to address the myriad of problems involved. When land reform does become politically feasible in a particular setting, there is often only a narrow window of time in which it remains politically possible to enact a reform. Particularly in the case of such reform, justice delayed is justice denied. If development experts and policymakers have not studied the problems and thought through prospective solutions in detail beforehand, the opportunity to implement a reform may slip by.

Finally, a new, well-designed solution to a recognized, but seemingly insurmountable problem of landlessness sometimes can create the necessary political will.

Effectively addressing the problem of landlessness anywhere involves a multitude of issues, and each individual setting provides its own array of unique problems. Solving the landlessness dilemma is no easy task. Yet, although no land reform will be a panacea for all of the ills of a country, an appropriately designed and well-implemented program can address an array of fundamental social problems while laying the foundation for broad-based economic growth.

Convinced that landlessness is at the heart of agricultural development problems in many Third World countries, this Curry Foundation study has brought together the thinking, analysis, and research of a dozen of the leading scholars in this field. Each has spent years, if not decades, of study and field research in the areas being considered. They have examined the problems in ten different country (or regional) settings and the prospects for solving those problems in the 1990s and beyond.

In beginning this study, we included a chapter on the Soviet Union, Poland, and Hungary to illustrate the land-tenure patterns that have prevailed in the centrally planned economies, little realizing the extent to which the Soviet Union and some of the Eastern European societies would be considering change in their land-tenure systems today.

This study aims to help acquaint policymakers, legislators, and others concerned about development and land-tenure problems with current issues and to offer policy recommendations concerning landlessness and land-tenure problems in each setting. The case studies include:

The Philippines. Jeffrey Riedinger looks at one of the worst land-tenure problems in the developing world. In a country that lags behind its East Asian neighbors in terms of development success, 2.9–3.1 million agricultural families make their living farming land they do not own. Altogether, one-quarter or more of the entire population consists of such impoverished landless peasants, either as tenant farmers or agricultural laborers. The Philippines produces agricultural yields far below those of Japan, Taiwan, and South Korea, where small owner-operated farms flourish due to postwar land reforms. The land problem is implicated in the countryside's stagnation and poverty and in the growth of the Communist insurgency of the New People's Army. After the election of President Aquino in 1986, expectations were high for sweeping land reform. Yet those expectations have not been met. Riedinger examines the various forces pressing for effective land reform in the Philippines and those that have blocked it. He discusses whether and how progress may still be possible, and what the consequences are for Philippine development and democracy.

Kerala state, India. Ronald Herring writes about Kerala, an Indian state with a population about equal to that of Kenya or all of Central America, which undertook a land-to-the-tiller program in the 1970s. The Keralan reform is an interesting model because, unlike many other settings, a sweeping land reform was accomplished by peaceful and democratic means and was not initiated in either the midst or wake of a major political crisis. The reforms emerged from the organized demands and decades of agitation of the peasantry.

Herring's analysis centers on the conditions that made such a program possible and the political constraints on further progress. The Keralan model illustrates the potential of a highly politicized agrarian system in which militant, but nonviolent, grassroots mobilization has played a major role in the land-reform process.

Kerala also illustrates concretely a potential implicitly or explicitly denied in the growth-first and trickle-down models of development. For example, there have been significant reductions in human misery and advances in welfare for the bottom of society despite extreme aggregate poverty and an income level well below the national mean for India.

Bangladesh. F. Tomasson Jannuzi and James Peach write on the issue of agrarian reform in Bangladesh, which, for the Indian subcontinent, presents a contrast in failure to the success story of Kerala. Bangladesh possesses one of the richest agricultural bases on the planet, yet two decades after the start of Green Revolution strategies of rural development, its crop yields remain among the lowest in Asia and its rural areas are characterized by extreme poverty. The authors suggest that the primary impediment to economic progress in Bangladesh is the traditional system of relationships of people to the land. They examine the role of land tenure in Bangladesh's thwarted development process and the possible land-reform solutions. Jannuzi and Peach also look at the 1984 land-reform law, and discuss why it is poorly conceived and why it remains unimplemented.

China. After a quarter century of sluggish growth under various forms of collectivized agriculture, the Chinese started at the beginning of the 1980s to decollectivize under the household responsibility system. They have now carried out one of the largest land reforms of this century by distributing individual parcels, benefiting some 750 million Chinese engaged in farming. Crop production surged dramatically in response to increased incentives associated with decollectivization, but the increases have plateaued since 1984. Roy Prosterman and Timothy Hanstad discuss these developments and explore both the explanation for the initial dramatic production increases and the potential for further increases.

The Soviet Union, Poland, and Hungary. While focusing on the Soviet Union, Karen Brooks also explores the land-tenure issue in the settings of Hungary and Poland. The experience of collectivized agriculture in the Soviet Union has proved to be a dismal failure, and the government is searching for means of reform. A crucial component of successful reform in the Soviet Union will be new forms of landholding and management embodying incentives for efficient use of land and labor. Brooks points out that the attractiveness and the productivity advantages of newer forms of tenure depend on changes made in the markets for other agricultural inputs.

In Hungary, collective farms since 1965 have been given relatively more freedom to produce and market as they choose. Although their economic performance exceeds that of agriculture in other countries of Eastern Europe, recent rising costs of production are increasing the pressure for tenurial change.

The Polish case holds a lesson for Soviet reformers: privatization of landholdings is a crucial step toward maximum productivity in the agricultural sector, but it is not enough. Even though private ownership has been tolerated in Poland, the profitability and productivity of private agriculture in Poland has been constrained by past government policies, which starved the private sector of modern inputs, sufficient credit, and efficient marketing.

Central America. Central America has experienced a turbulent decade during which both violence and social reforms were tried as means of redressing long-standing social inequities. Rupert Scofield looks at the land-tenure issue in the five Central American countries, where a three-way comparison emerges from the experiences of the past decade.

El Salvador and Nicaragua both undertook widespread land

redistribution, but with different approaches. In 1980, El Salvador enacted two major phases of a sweeping land-reform program with U.S. support: large farms became peasant cooperatives, and tenants on small-holdings became owner-operators. Scofield discusses a number of factors that have combined in recent years to blunt the reform's momentum. Only about one-third of the intended landless beneficiaries have been reached, leaving significant issues unresolved.

In Nicaragua, land reform following the Sandinista victory substantially reduced landlessness; however, the disastrous economic situation, coupled with an adherence to discredited collective forms of farming, have combined to prevent the reform from realizing its productive potential.

In neighboring Guatemala, Honduras, and Costa Rica—all countries where landlessness remains a significant problem and a hindrance to development—nothing more than token distribution programs have been accomplished.

Mexico. Land reform has been a long, protracted process in Mexico during this century, but today about half of Mexico's farm area and 70 percent of its farm units are in the reformed sector. The reform has contributed greatly to political stability in Mexico, but its economic results have been less efficacious: underproductivity and marginality still characterize much of the rural population. Merilee Grindle writes about the Mexican reform and its results, tracing current rural conditions to government policies that gave little or no support to reform beneficiaries. Grindle looks to the creation of nonagricultural jobs in the rural sector as essential in overcoming Mexico's rural poverty. She concludes that Mexico's experience teaches that in the absence of credit, extension, infrastructure, human capital formation, and a supportive policy environment, and in the absence of a capacity of reform beneficiaries to make sustained political and economic demands on the government, agrarian reform cannot realize its economic potential or resolve deep-seated problems of rural poverty, underproductivity, and inequity.

Brazil. Brazil's agrarian structure is characterized by extreme concentration of landownership, high landlessness, and rural violence arising from conflicts over access to land as well as worsening environmental destruction, much of which is traceable to land-tenure conditions. In a situation where the stakes are especially high, Brazil's leaders still have not addressed adequately the politically sensitive issue of agrarian reform. Anthony Hall traces the roots of the current agrarian situation, analyzes the agrarian reform record of the post-1985 civilian government, and examines further policy options to address the growing landlessness problem in a country that, paradoxically, possesses vast land resources that could be utilized without environmental destruction.

Zimbabwe. Since political independence in 1980, the government of Zimbabwe has responded in an ambiguous and halting fashion to a widespread problem of landlessness. Relatively large areas of commercial land have been redistributed to peasant small-holders, but most are in ecological zones of intermediate or marginal agricultural potential. Even so, redistribution of land in Zimbabwe has not led to national economic decline or collapse, and the dire predictions that it would do so no longer seem plausible. In particular, the family-farm model of resettlement has shown signs of promising economic potential. Michael Bratton summarizes the history of land distribution and the current debates on land reform in Zimbabwe. He also analyzes the extent of landlessness in Zimbabwe, the reemergence of the land issue in the late 1980s, the factors constraining the land-redistribution program to date, and policy proposals that can be implemented under a revised constitutional order after April 1990.

South Africa. Daniel Weiner explores the land-tenure issue in South Africa, where legislation has solidified white control of 87 percent of the country's territory, including the prime agricultural land, and transformed Africans into suppliers of cheap labor to the white economy. To this day, apartheid legislation forbids black ownership of land in white areas and perpetuates mass poverty in designated black "homelands."

The successful transition to a multiracial and democratic South Africa will require dramatic changes in current patterns of land use and control. Weiner presents relevant empirical information, focuses on the issues that are emerging concerning the land question in South Africa, and outlines important objectives for future policy formulation.

These ten chapters serve to highlight the importance of land tenure issues in each of the countries discussed, to underline the multifarious elements and issues encompassed by the concept of land reform, and to help explain the role land reform has played in the recent past and can play in the 1990s. Possible ways in which the United States and the other industrialized democracies can contribute to the solution of important land-tenure problems through foreign aid and technical assistance also are considered.

This book does not include discussions of every country where land-tenure issues still loom large. The countries and regions covered were chosen for two reasons: First, they are countries where land reform is currently an issue of great importance or has played a significant role in the country's recent past. Second, the countries chosen are illustrative of the varied models of land reform, the diverse and complex issues involved in attacking land-tenure problems, and the possible functions land reform can serve in a country's development process.

But the potential role of land reform in successfully addressing numerous political, social, and economic problems in a variety of countries cannot be realized until the concept of land reform and the problems presented by landlessness are well understood. We hope this book will contribute to the greater understanding of land reform, landlessness, and land-tenure issues, both in general and in each country or region covered, in order to further effective solutions to land-tenure problems around the globe.

As Ronald Herring concludes in his chapter on Kerala state in India, "Land reforms are neither easy nor costless; nor are they a panacea. But it is difficult to find a more direct route to creating some security and opportunity for those whose labor makes it possible for the rest of us to eat."

part one

Asia

chapter one

Philippine Land Reform in the 1980s

Jeffrey Riedinger

Summary

The Philippine "People Power Revolution" of February 1986 was accompanied by heightened rural expectations concerning comprehensive agrarian reform. (Agrarian reform is here defined to include both redistribution of land ownership—land reform—and complementary credit, extension, infrastructure, pricing, and research.) The law that emerged after more than two years of deliberations, although the "centerpiece" of the Aquino government's development program, is considerably short of being comprehensive. Most of the reform, as it is likely to be implemented, could have been accomplished under a combination of previous legislation, bank foreclosures, and "voluntary" land transfers, the latter occasioned in some instances by the activities of the insurgent New People's Army (NPA). Unless the shortcomings of the new law are redressed through administrative action, and this seems unlikely, the problem of landlessness will remain acute (to be exacerbated by rapid population growth), agricultural productivity will remain low by Asian and world standards, and civil unrest will continue to be fueled by tenure-related peasant grievances.

Correcting the flaws of the new law will require strong administrative action on numerous fronts. Program implementation must be rapidly accelerated. Retention limits should be set well below the present five-hectare maximum. A consistent and simplified valuation procedure, such as the value of crops produced, appropriately capitalized, should be established. In the case of corporate farms, the government must insist that all stock of a separate corporate entity having full ownership of the land assets be distributed to the farmworker beneficiaries. Penalties for landowner evasion and efforts to sabotage the reform program must be strengthened and coupled with forceful presidential leadership and education and mobilization of

*beneficiaries concerning their rights. Finally, responsible financial
support from the donor community should be conditional upon
verifiable progress in land redistribution and improvements in the
human rights situation in the Philippines.*

National Setting

With 64.9 million people (roughly 11.6 million families averaging 5.6 persons each) living in a country of 297,410 square kilometers, the Philippine population has a density of 218 people per square kilometer. Population growth continues to be rapid (currently 2.8 percent per year), with a doubling time of twenty-five years. The 41 percent of the population now under the age of fifteen underscores the employment and family-planning tasks confronting the government in the years ahead. The infant mortality rate of 48 per 1,000 live births, although low by developing country standards, reflects continuing problems of poverty, malnutrition, and inadequate health care.

Sixty percent of the Philippine population is rural. Over 40 percent (some 5 million households) of all Filipinos make their living directly from agricultural cultivation. (Families engaged in forestry or fisheries are *excluded* from the agricultural population figures throughout this study.) As of 1980, some 7.85 million hectares (1 hectare = 2.47 acres) were planted in annual or permanent crops, out of a total farm area of 9.73 million hectares. Most of the remainder was equally divided between temporarily idle, but arable, land (0.84 million hectares) and nonarable meadows or forests (0.87 million hectares). The result is a current ratio of 1.58 cropped hectares per farm family; inclusion of idle arable land raises the ratio to 1.74 hectares. These ratios are significantly higher than in countries like China or South Korea, but are much lower than is typical in most Latin American or African settings.

The 1980 agricultural census confirmed the trends of growing population pressure and diminishing availability of land suitable for agricultural expansion. While there were increases in both the number of farms (from 2.4 million to 3.4 million) and the total area in farms (from 8.5 million to 9.7 million hectares), average farm size declined from 3.6 to 2.8 hectares over the 1971–1980 period.

The Philippines' acute and growing landlessness is explained by limited land resources relative to population and a highly skewed distribution of land resources. Table 1.1 details the national pattern of farm holding size as of 1980, giving evidence of persisting concentration of landownership. Farms of less than two hectares account for 50.9 percent of Filipino farms, yet their aggregate area is only 16 percent of total farm area. Farms of ten hectares and above include 26 percent of the land in farms, yet represent a mere 3.4 percent of all farms.

Table 1.1   Distribution of Philippine Farms by Number and Size, 1980

Farm Size (ha)	Number	Percent	Area (1,000 ha)	Percent
Under 0.5	289,962	8.5	68.9	0.7
0.5–0.99	485,829	14.2	300.1	3.1
1.00–1.99	964,220	28.2	1,189.9	12.2
2.00–2.99	613,824	17.9	1,332.3	13.7
3.00–4.99	588,151	17.2	2,066.7	21.3
5.00–7.00	283,585	8.3	1,612.1	16.6
7.01–9.99	76,421	2.2	630.8	6.5
10.00–24.99	103,723	3.0	1,406.4	14.5
25.00 and over	14,608	0.4	1,117.8	11.5
Totals	3,420,323	100.0	9,725.2	100.0

Source: *1980 Census of Agriculture* (Manila: National Census and Statistics Office, 1985).
Notes: Numbers may not add to total due to rounding. Data are for operational holdings.

The continuing skewed distribution of land is evidence of the ineffectiveness and limited scope of previous land-reform initiatives. By focusing on reform of tenanted rice and corn holdings, these earlier programs created incentives for large owners to displace tenant farmers in favor of hired laborers while shifting out of rice or corn production. Other policies, such as subsidized credit for imported farm machinery and the high costs of supervising hired labor, compounded such distortions by fostering a substitution of capital for labor. Production was biased toward capital-intensive operations with few hired laborers.

Landlessness in the Philippines
Although data on landlessness in the Philippines is imprecise, there is general agreement that landlessness is extensive and growing. (The term "landless" refers throughout to *all* cultivating relationships in which the cultivator works land without having ownership or ownership-like rights in that land, whether he is denominated "tenant," "agricultural laborer," or otherwise.) It appears that of the now roughly 5 million agricultural families, some 2.9–3.1 million make their living wholly or primarily from land they do not own. Of these, some 1.1–1.3 million families are on holdings wholly or predominantly rented and another 1.6–2.0 million families are wholly or primarily dependent on performing agricultural labor for hire without simultaneously farming land as tenants. (The higher estimate for each group correlates with the lower estimate for the other group.) That is, landless families represent roughly 58–64 percent of the agricultural population and 25–27 percent

of the total population.

It is probably appropriate to use the higher landlessness figure for present planning purposes, particularly in light of the projected 10-year time frame for implementation of the new reform program. However, more accurate data on landlessness are essential for rational planning. Such data might be provided by a rapid national sample survey using the framework of the pending 1990 population and agricultural censuses.

Agricultural Performance

Rice and corn are the primary staple crops in the Philippines; coconuts and sugarcane, the principal cash crops. In 1980, some 3.65 million hectares were devoted to rice production (inclusive of multiple cropping). Corn production accounted for another 2.47 million hectares (again inclusive of multiple cropping). Sugarcane cultivation occupied a further 0.3 million hectares. Coconut data are reported in terms of trees rather than cultivated area; the total area of farms devoted primarily to coconut production was 2.84 million hectares (29.2 percent of the 9.73 million hectares in farms).

Historically, cheap food imports from the United States, an urban-biased food-pricing policy, and relatively abundant land (at least into the 1950s) all served as disincentives to intensification of Philippine agriculture. The import and pricing-related disincentives persisted until well into the 1970s. The modest nature of improvements in Philippine rice and corn yields in more recent years, and the decline in sugarcane yields, suggest the existence of other, continuing structural impediments to production, including land-tenure arrangements.

Although the debate among economists is far from settled, farm-level studies generally sustain the proposition that, other things being equal, share and fixed-rent tenancy are less efficient than owner-operated farming. The relative efficiency of owner-operated farms is fairly clear in terms of crop mix and output value per hectare. On balance, the evidence in terms of output for a given crop—although more ambiguous—points to the same finding, particularly in the absence of efficient mechanisms for contract enforcement.[1] There are surprisingly few studies of the relationships between tenurial status, technology choice, and productivity in the Philippines, particularly studies that control for land quality and access to support services. This is an area in which better data are urgently needed.

Table 1.2 provides comparative productivity data for the major Philippine crops, which illustrate the poor performance of Philippine agriculture. The Philippines is home to the International Rice Research Institute (IRRI), the source of most Green Revolution hybrid rice varieties, making Philippine rice yields all the more disappointing. The primarily tenant-operated rice farms of the Philippines produce only two-fifths to one-half as much rice per hectare, on average, as the owner-operated rice farms of Japan, South Korea, or Taiwan, or the owner-like farms of China (operated under the household responsibility system).

Table 1.2   Comparative Crop Yields for Selected Asian Countries
(Yields in Metric Tons per Hectare)

Country	Rice	Corn	Sugarcane
Bangladesh	2.24	—	45.15
China, People's Republic of	5.33	3.66	53.79
India	2.23	1.33	58.98
Indonesia	3.94	1.79	75.15
Japan	6.32	—	—
Philippines	2.64	1.10	47.57
South Korea	6.38	4.72	—
Taiwan	4.81	3.76	87.14
Thailand	2.01	2.52	39.98
Vietnam	2.79	1.46	39.91
World	3.26	3.67	58.57

Sources: *1986 FAO Production Yearbook*, vol. 40 (Rome: UN Food and Agriculture Organization, 1987); Foreign Agricultural Service, U.S. Department of Agriculture, History of Sugarcane computer printout (August 16, 1989) and Rice: Area, Yield and Production computer printout (September 15, 1988).
Notes: Yields are weighted average of crop years 1984–1986. Yield data are included for countries planting 25,000 hectares or more of that crop.

Similarly, the predominantly tenant-operated Philippine corn farms produce less than one-third as much corn per hectare, on average, as in South Korea, Taiwan, or China. Finally, average Philippine sugarcane yields, with plantations accounting for much of the production, are less than two-thirds those of Indonesia. More importantly, in light of often-heard arguments about economies of scale in sugarcane production, Philippine sugarcane yields are, on average, little more than one-half those of the small (one to two hectare) owner-operated farms of Taiwan, and only one-quarter of the yields obtained on small owner-operated farms in Maharashtra state in western India.

Rural Poverty
Assessed against social welfare criteria, the performance of Philippine agriculture is equally disappointing. Philippine agricultural gross domestic product (GDP) growth for the period 1965–1984, although calculated from a low base, compared favorably with that for all middle-income countries, particularly in the years after 1973. Yet

despite this growth the government estimates that 64 percent of the rural population was living below the poverty threshold in 1987. Annual unemployment and underemployment increased in the 1978–1986 period. Among the rural poor, underemployment is extreme, with estimates of 40–60 percent. The pressures of high population growth rates and limited rural employment opportunities (agricultural or nonagricultural) are also reflected in stagnant or declining real wage levels for most agricultural laborers during the 1960s and 1980s (with perhaps some improvement during the 1970s). In some sectors, notably sugar, periodic sharp downturns in world and domestic prices in the 1970s and 1980s have led to massive unemployment and to permanent labor displacement through mechanization or diversification to alternate, capital-intensive products. In turn, the high incidence of landlessness, underemployment, and poverty is heavily implicated in the nationwide growth of rural insurgency.

Land Tenure and Rural Unrest

Philippine history is replete with peasant uprisings, with tenure-related grievances providing much of the impetus for revolt. Ileto argues that Catholicism, as adopted by rural Filipinos, nurtured an undercurrent of millennial beliefs.[2] This facilitated organization of peasant protest movements in times of economic and political crisis, particularly in the late Spanish and early American colonial eras.

Philippine uprisings in which agrarian issues played a central role date from 1745. This early revolt in the provinces around Manila was primarily directed against land usurpation for the haciendas of the Spanish friars. The concentration of landownership in the religious orders and the often illegal means by which that land was acquired made the friar estates a repeated focal point for agrarian unrest.

Landgrabbing was by no means the exclusive preserve of the religious orders, however. Land registration laws established as a means of promoting commercial agriculture were abused by the politico-economic elites, which allowed them to usurp vast tracts of theretofore untitled communal or individual farmlands. The Spanish land registration acts of 1880 and 1894 and U.S. introduction of cadastral surveys and the Torrens land registration system in 1913 afforded opportunities for massive landgrabbing. Other cultivators lost their lands through a money-lending system known as *pacto de retroventa*, under which lands were often forfeited for failure to repay loans amounting to only a fraction of the value of the land. The enmity engendered by these and other land-related injustices (including persistent, near-universal noncompliance with rural minimum wage legislation and other agricultural labor code provisions) are undimmed by time, fueling recurrent peasant unrest.

The legacy of tenure-related grievances also figured in several uprisings during the American colonial era. It is, however, the *Hukbalahap* (Huk) rebellion of the mid-1940s and the present insurgency of the New People's Army that best illustrate the role of peasant grievances in shaping civil unrest in the Philippines.

The Huk Rebellion

The Huk organization had its origin in scattered grassroots movements in central Luzon in the 1930s. These movements were responding to deteriorating relations between landlords and tenants, as increasing population and declining availability of new land turned the "terms of trade" further against the tenants. Tensions were exacerbated during the Japanese occupation. Shortly after the war the *Hukbong Mapagpalay ng Bayan* (HMB, or People's Army of Liberation) turned to armed struggle to protect peasants from repression and pursue agrarian demands, which included increased tenant shares of farm output and collateral-free, low-interest loans. The Huk rebellion lasted from 1946 to 1954.

Alarm in the United States over the strength of the insurgent movement led to renewed attention to rural problems in the Philippines, culminating in the Hardie report of 1952. The report recommended that the Philippine government abolish the institution of tenancy and establish a rural economy based on owner-operated family-sized farm units. Unfortunately for the course of Philippine development, these proposals were largely rejected by the landed elite and their representatives in the Philippine Congress. Nor was support for the proposals forthcoming from the U.S. government, whose colonial policies had cemented political, as well as important personal, ties with those elites.

Improved performance by the Philippine military, coupled with modest land grants to some Huk surrenderees (through resettlement, primarily in Mindanao), initiation of community development programs, and extensive anti-Huk propaganda, led to effective defeat of the Huks by 1954. Still, the grievances underlying the rebellion persisted.

Moreover, with the end of the military conflict, what little interest the politico-economic elites had in reform largely evaporated. Indeed, the waxing and waning of interest in reform coincident to the fortunes of the insurgency of the moment is a recurrent theme of Philippine history, as it often has been elsewhere.

The Current Insurgency

Established in late 1968, the *Partido Komunista ng Pilipinas—Marxismo-Leninismo-Kaisipang Mao Zedong* (Communist Party of the Philippines—Marxist-Leninist–Mao Zedong Thought, or CPP) and its military wing, the *Bagong Hukbong Bayan* (New People's Army, or NPA), have blended and transformed nationalist impulses and agrarian grievances into a potent commitment to Marxist armed revolt. Unlike the Huks, whose activities were confined to central Luzon, the CPP/NPA is a nationwide organization. Estimates by the armed forces of the Philippines put the CPP/NPA armed forces at 25,200 as of December 1987. More than 12 percent (4,993) of the country's 40,761 *barangay* (villages) were considered "infiltrated"; that is, they were "areas where the insurgents stay for long periods of time . . . without fear of being discovered or attacked by government forces."[3]

The CPP/NPA lost considerable political ground because of its boycott of the February 1986 presidential elections. Recent atrocities have tarnished its reputation further. Moreover, it now confronts a very popular president. Yet the CPP/NPA remains a significant military and popular force.

Recent interviews, however, reveal a relatively sanguine attitude among a number of government officials, members of Congress, and business leaders. In turn, some view the pressure for land reform as having abated. Their optimism and conclusion seem at considerable odds with firsthand impressions of rural life. Whatever the momentary setbacks suffered by the insurgents, most of the underlying conditions against which their struggle is aimed and around which they have so successfully organized in the past remain fundamentally unaltered.

A History of Philippine Land Reform

Since the turn of the century there have been repeated, although ineffectual, initiatives to address land-tenure grievances in the Philippines. These land-reform programs have historically been limited to tenanted holdings devoted to grain crop production for domestic consumption. The political influence of the large sugar, coconut, and tobacco landowners has in the past assured the exemption of holdings devoted to export crops. The land-reform programs have also involved very generous retention limits (amounts affected landowners could retain successively declining from 300 hectares in 1955, to 75 hectares in 1963, 24 hectares in 1971, and 7 hectares in 1972).

The primary enactments regarding Philippine land reform were the Friar Lands Act of 1903 (Commonwealth Act 1120); the Rice Share Tenancy Act of 1933; Commonwealth Act 539 (1940); the Agricultural

Tenancy Act of 1954 (Republic Act 1199); the Land Reform Act of 1955 (Republic Act 1400); the Agricultural Land Reform Code of 1963 (Republic Act 3844); the Code of Agrarian Reform (Republic Act 6389, 1971); and Presidential Decree 27 (PD 27, 1972). The achievements, as of the end of 1985 (shortly before Marcos's ouster), under the three principal reform programs are detailed in Table 1.3.

Table 1.3   Summary of Accomplishments Under Philippine Land Reform Programs as of December 31, 1985

Program	Program Scope		Cumulative Progress	
	Beneficiaries	Area (ha)	Beneficiaries	Area (ha)
Presidential Decree 27 (1972)				
Operation Land Transfer	587,775[a]	822,000[a]		
EPs[b] generated			137,931	183,592
EPs distributed			17,116	11,197
Payment verified			179,285	286,922
Payment approved			134,371	258,638
Direct payments[c]			27,269	34,750
Republic Act 3844 (1963; as amended)				
Operation Leasehold	527,667	562,230	533,808	566,444
Commonwealth Act 539 (1940; as amended)				
Landed Estates program				
CLT[d]	56,302	88,143	33,503	54,986
Deed of Sale	43,130	62,965	12,270	19,611
Resettlement	78,450	565,079	16,998	94,977

Source: Department of Agrarian Reform, Accomplishments Report CY-1986.

[a] As of December 31, 1988. The original program goals were 520,000 beneficiaries and 1,000,000 hectares. The 1986 DAR Accomplishment Report cites goals of 427,623 beneficiaries and 716,520 hectares.

[b] Emancipation patents (equivalent to final title).

[c] These are beneficiaries who chose to make amortization payments directly to the ex-landlord rather than through any government agency.

[d] Certificate of land transfer (preliminary documentation of land rights).

Operation Land Transfer

Although Operation Land Transfer dates from the 1963 Agricultural Land Reform Code (RA 3844), it was only with the adoption of Presidential Decree 27 in 1972 that the program was to have national effect. Pursuant to PD 27, rice and corn tenants whose landlords held more than seven hectares were permitted to purchase the parcels they tilled. Valuation was set at two and one-half times the value of average annual production, with the beneficiary repaying the land costs to the government over fifteen years at 6 percent interest.

Shortly after the enactment of PD 27, the Department of Agrarian Reform (DAR) estimated the number of rice and corn tenants at 914,000. Other observers believed actual tenancy to be as much as 50 percent higher. That the program initially embraced little more than one-half of the government-estimated number of such tenant families reflected the program's seven-hectare retention limit. The successful postwar land reforms of Japan, South Korea, and Taiwan all featured much lower retention limits. The Japanese reform allowed *no* retention of tenanted land owned by landlords not resident in the village, and resident landlords were permitted only *one* hectare of tenanted land. The South Korean reform allowed *no* retention of tenanted land regardless of landlord residency. Taiwan, under conditions of scrupulous administration of land registries and the disallowance of land transfers in the year preceding adoption of the reform, permitted landlord retention of *three* hectares in the case of average land.

Apart from rice and corn tenants excluded from land redistribution by the high retention limit, PD 27 excludes tenants on lands devoted to crops other than rice and corn, as well as all landless laborers. Yet, even judged against the modest program goals of Operation Land Transfer, Marcos-era performance was dismal (although admittedly better than that for earlier reforms, as discussed below). By year-end 1985, emancipation patents (EPs) had been generated for less than one-quarter (23.4 percent) of the (presently) targeted beneficiaries. Under the most pessimistic reading of program accomplishments, only 3 percent of the beneficiaries now targeted had actually received emancipation patents in the first fourteen years of implementation of Operation Land Transfer.

The compensation figures are not easily reconciled with the data on emancipation patents. The area in holdings for which payment by the Land Bank of the Philippines had been approved was much greater than the area covered by the emancipation patents (258,638 versus 183,592 hectares). At the same time, the number of beneficiaries associated with that 258,638 hectares seems low. No explanation of these discrepancies is offered in DAR reports. The issue cannot be resolved here, but the figures suggest that an additional 75,000 hectares, not yet titled, may have been acquired under the program.

Recent administrative changes (permitting earlier and easier distribution of emancipation patents), coupled with renewed commitment to completing the program, have resulted in substantial progress since 1986. In the past three years emancipation patents covering 203,072 hectares have been distributed to an additional 157,743 beneficiaries. Cumulatively, emancipation patents have been distributed to 174,859 beneficiaries (29.8 percent of the program goal), transferring 214,269 hectares (26.1 percent of the program target). Progress on land acquisition, by contrast, continues to be slow:

inclusive of progress in 1986–1987, compensation payments have been approved for a total of 291,943 hectares, an increase of only 33,305 hectares in the first two years of the Aquino administration.

Operation Leasehold
Operation Leasehold (which dates from the 1963 law, with revisions in 1971) was designed to convert share tenancies to fixed-rent leaseholds. A rent ceiling was set at 25 percent of the average normal harvest for the three years preceding establishment of the leasehold, after deducting various production costs. On paper, the program had exceeded program goals by 1985. Even so, it reached an additional 17,576 beneficiaries with 10,014 hectares in 1986–1987. However, an informal survey by the author and the observations of other researchers suggest that the provisions of this program are often ignored. Sharecropping continues to be practiced, and rent levels, whether determined on a share or leasehold basis, often exceed the rent ceiling. Tenancy regulation, particularly in a developing country setting, is a largely futile endeavor, fraught with administrative pitfalls and opportunities for evasion.

Landed Estates Program
The Landed Estates program had its inception in Commonwealth Act 539 (1940). Its aim was government acquisition of large private estates for redistribution to the tenant cultivators. As of 1955, individually owned estates of 300 hectares or more and corporate-owned estates of 600 hectares or more were, upon petition by a majority (later reduced to one-third) of the tenants, subject to expropriation. In 1963 the program scope was expanded to include holdings of more than seventy-five hectares, regardless of mode of ownership. Under the 1963 reform code, the program focused on tenant-operated rice and corn estates, exempting "lands under labor administration" (that is, land cultivated by hired labor) such as sugarcane and coconut plantations, orchards, and commercialized farms.

As of 1985, the program had delivered certificates of land transfer (CLTs; a preliminary documentation of land rights) to only 33,500 beneficiaries, covering some 55,000 hectares. Nearly half of the program's limited achievements occurred under the Rural Progress Administration in the period 1940–1950. In 1986–1987 another 962 hectares were transferred to 1,718 beneficiaries. In explaining the failure to issue deeds of sale to nearly two-thirds of those who had received a preliminary certificate, DAR points to beneficiary difficulties in meeting amortization repayment obligations.

Resettlement Programs

Finally, some 95,000 hectares of public land have been the subject of government resettlement programs. Most of the program achievements date back to the years following the Huk rebellion, notably 1950–1954. Dwindling public land resources and the high financial and social costs of resettlement argue against DAR committing any substantial part of its resources to further resettlement efforts.

Cumulative Land Reform Achievements

Previous to the Aquino administration, less than 315,000 hectares[4] of private land had been acquired under Philippine land reform, or only 4 percent of the 7.8 million cultivated hectares. Associated with this land were just over 168,000 beneficiary families,[5] a figure equal to roughly 5–6 percent of those presently landless. With the Aquino government's expedited distribution of emancipation patents under Operation Land Transfer, the number of beneficiaries receiving formal title has increased substantially. Still, during 50-odd years of Philippine land reform, no more than 350,000 hectares of private land, less than 5 percent of the country's cultivated area, have been acquired for distribution so far to some 210,000 families,[6] representing less than 8 percent of those presently landless.

Reform in the Aquino Era:
Campaign Promises and Early Inactivity

In the month before the February 7, 1986, "snap" presidential election, in a campaign otherwise short on substance, Corazon Aquino made agrarian reform a cornerstone of her rural social and economic program. In her first major policy address, delivered before the Manila business community, she promised to undertake "genuine" land reform, phrasing that echoed the demands of the more militant peasant organizations. (In a later speech, she tempered her commitment to one of "viable" land reform.)

Yet during the campaign the specifics of such a reform received scant consideration in the Aquino inner circle, nor were they much debated in public. Aquino's pledge to "*explore* how the twin goals of maximum productivity and dispersal of ownership and benefits can be exemplified for the rest of the nation" (emphasis added) on her family's 6,000 hectare sugar estate, Hacienda Luisita, was characteristic of her public statements. Even this pledge was accompanied by remarks suggesting ambivalence concerning the extension of reform to crops other than rice and corn or to farms operated under arrangements other than tenancy.

Following the February "Revolution" relatively little was said or done about land reform until the convening of the Constitutional Commission in early June 1986. President Aquino had reiterated her pro–land-reform stance in early April and appointed Heherson Alvarez as the new minister of agrarian reform later that month. Whether symbolic of the divisions within her advisory group or of ambivalence to the reform issue, Alvarez was the last appointee to the new Aquino cabinet. The only substantive proposal at the time was a draft executive order for extending the reform program to lands foreclosed by government banking and financial institutions. The measure was tabled. (So, too, was a proposed order, drafted in August, extending reform coverage to idle and abandoned private agricultural lands.)

Explanations for Aquino's inactivity on the land issue during the early period of her presidency are varied. Some observers point to the reluctant nature of her candidacy/presidency and her predisposition for laissez-faire governance. The more militant left cites her class background and that of her principal advisers as explanation. (Meanwhile the CPP/NPA, having boycotted the February election, had effectively dealt itself out of a role in influencing government policy.)

Observers more sympathetic to President Aquino explain her inaction on land reform in terms of other, and in their view more pressing, issues. She had to address the imperatives of consolidating her presidency, drafting a new constitution and restoring democratic institutional forms, dealing with the debt situation and the ill-gotten wealth of Marcos and his cronies, releasing political detainees, and working toward negotiations with the CPP/NPA and several regional autonomy movements. Finally, her political survival became increasingly problematic in the face of rightist threats from within her military, leading to substantial concessions to the military and the avoidance of any measure, including land reform, viewed as potentially destabilizing (insofar as they threatened her middle-class support).

The Politics of Reform in the Philippines

It is appropriate here to briefly examine the various political forces for and against agrarian reform. At the outset it should be noted that the perceived political urgency of reform was such that very few went on record as being *against* agrarian reform; for the most part, resistance was couched instead in terms of support for the concept of reform but opposition to program specifics.

Corazon Aquino's campaign organization was a diverse coalition, combining a family-dominated personal organization, traditional opposition parties such as the United Nationalist Democratic

Organization (UNIDO) and the Philippine Democratic party (PDP), and the Catholic church. Contact was also established with the dissident "Reform the Armed Forces Movement" within the military.

Aquino's first cabinet featured conservative reformists, liberal democrats, and the military. The former, and dominant, group endorsed a generally conservative approach to issues of social reform. This group was politicized by the 1983 assassination of Benigno Aquino, Jr., and the economic crisis occasioned by Marcos's misrule. The liberal democrats had long favored a nationalistic economic policy and basic social reforms. The military members were belated participants in the anti-Marcos struggle, concerned primarily with military prerogatives and a military approach to the NPA insurgency. The disparate viewpoints represented in the Aquino cabinet promised a prolonged and fractious debate over issues as politically charged as land reform.

Also demanding a role in policy formulation were the Catholic church and myriad sectoral and cause-oriented groups. The former had slowly evolved into a powerful opposition force in the years following the 1972 imposition of martial law, playing an instrumental role in the events of February 1986. The church hierarchy and church-affiliated organizations, such as the Institute on Church and Social Issues and the Bishops-Businessmen's Conference for Human Development, played an active, pro-reform role in the debate on land reform.

Most democratic grassroots organizational activities were curtailed for much of the martial law era (1972–1981). However, sectoral and cause-oriented groups began to proliferate in the later Marcos years to defend member interests and, in many cases, to pursue a broad agenda of social and political reform. In the absence of large, ideologically oriented political parties, these groups (and the church) have served as the principal vehicles for democratic articulation of the interests and demands of the poor, although these groups remain politically weak. Prominent among such groups are the *Kilusang Magbubukid ng Pilipinas* (Peasant Movement of the Philippines, or KMP), a militant peasant organization claiming some 750,000 members, and the Congress for a People's Agrarian Reform (CPAR), a unique confederation of twelve peasant organizations with a claimed collective membership of some 1.5 million peasants and fisherfolk (inclusive of KMP) and fourteen nongovernmental organizations. These groups and others prepared draft legislation and worked to educate and lobby members of both the executive branch and Congress concerning the desirability of agrarian reform.

Arrayed against them were crop-specific planters' organizations, the Council of Agricultural Producers of the Philippines, and militant groups such as the Movement for an Independent Negros, a sugar planters' organization that threatened armed resistance, even secession, in the event of land reform. Throughout the deliberations, large landowners successfully phrased their concerns and objections in terms calculated to establish common cause with small landowners, particularly on the crucial retention limit issue.

Landowners should not be mistaken for a monolithic interest bloc, however. The policy thrust of the new reform law suggests that congressional deliberations were strongly influenced by domestic corporate and commercial farmers, at the expense of traditional rentiers and, to a lesser extent, multinational corporations.

Note that another part of the political equation, particularly regarding implementation, consists of the many local private armies, some controlled by Marcos loyalists, others by local, ostensibly pro-Aquino, landed elites. Such groups have, in settings such as El Salvador, seriously impeded reform efforts through intimidation and assassination of farmer-beneficiaries, peasant organizers, and government land-reform officials.

These private armies are prohibited by the 1986 constitution, but little effort has been made to disband them. Indeed, after the breakdown in negotiations with the NPA, Aquino adopted a policy of "total war" and offered conditional praise of vigilante groups. This policy shift reflects both frustration with the NPA response to the negotiations and the growing autonomy of the military in waging the counterinsurgency campaign. However, her praise was taken by some as carte blanche approval of abusive vigilante groups and private armies, as well it might be in the absence of effective enforcement of government guidelines on the operation of anti-communist civilian groups. (As of June 1988, there had not been a single successful prosecution of a member of a vigilante group. Further, as of March 1989, there had not been a single human-rights case even brought against a member of the armed forces—this despite widespread reports of abuses by both groups.)

For its part, the insurgent NPA has also engaged in significant human-rights abuses, including the massacre of a group of anti-communist religious cultists, several regional purges of its own ranks, and assassinations of police, military personnel, and civilians under the guise of "revolutionary justice."

Particularly important in terms of the politics of agrarian reform is the NPA's enactment of its own, increasingly publicized, land-reform program. This reform program typically involves well-enforced rent reductions coupled with reductions in money-lending interest rates, but there are instances in which landowners have been driven off their property and the laborers given individual or communal usufruct rights.

In cases of land redistribution, beneficiaries are required to pay 5–10 percent of their net annual income to the NPA. Military estimates put the area so distributed at more than 31,000 hectares as of December 1988. Personal observations suggest that insurgent activity has also indirectly facilitated abandonment of other properties (often coincident with the downturn in sugar and coconut prices several years ago), leaving the permanent labor force in a position to negotiate with the banks or DAR for acquisition of the land. In the battle for "hearts and minds," the NPA reform is becoming a counterpoint against which many peasants will measure the government's agrarian reform program.

Land Reform and the Constitution

Of those appointed to the Constitutional Commission, only Jaime Tadeo of the KMP could be characterized as a bona fide representative of the tenant and farmworker sector. Nonetheless, with the backing of liberal democrats and church figures, the new constitution (adopted by the commission on October 15, 1986, and overwhelmingly ratified by national plebescite on February 2, 1987) contained unprecedented provisions on land reform, albeit with important qualifications:

> Art. II Sec. 21. The State shall promote comprehensive rural development and agrarian reform.

> Art. XIII Sec. 4. The State shall, by law, undertake an agrarian reform program founded on the right of farmers and regular farmworkers, who are landless, to own directly or collectively the lands they till or, in the case of other farmworkers, to receive a just share of the fruits thereof. To this end the State shall encourage and undertake the just distribution of all agricultural lands, subject to such priorities and reasonable retention limits as the Congress may prescribe, taking into account ecological, developmental, or equity considerations, and subject to the payment of just compensation.

> Art. XIII Sec. 5. The State shall recognize the right of farmers, farmworkers, and landowners, as well as cooperatives, and other independent farmers' organizations to participate in the planning, organization, and management of the program, and shall provide support to agriculture through appropriate technology and research, and adequate financial, production, marketing, and other support services.

Significantly, the latter two provisions appear in the article entitled "Social Justice and Human Rights," signaling the primacy of social justice concerns as the impetus for agrarian reform. The deliberations of the Constitutional Commission make clear its intention that farmers (tenants) and regular farmworkers have the right to own land and that the government guarantee that right. Moreover, this right encompassed *all* agricultural land without regard to crop. Landless agriculturalists were to have a preferential right to the land they were then cultivating, save where the particular parcel was, for example, within the retention area permitted the owner. In such cases the commissioners expected that alternative land would be made available to the farmer-beneficiary. Provision was made for freedom of choice of ownership mode, be it individual, cooperative, or collective, with the decision left to the beneficiaries.

The constitution thus enshrined many of the peasant demands concerning agrarian reform. However, on the issues of "just compensation" and retention limits, among others, strenuous objections were heard from militant and moderate peasant organizations alike.

In reaffirming the landowners' right to just compensation the commission rejected notions of selective or progressive compensation whereby payment would take account of past landowner behavior (compliance with labor legislation, and so on) or would be a declining proportion of land value with increasing farm size. Previous legislation had tied compensation to productive capacity (PD 27), or to annual legal rent capitalized at 6 percent per year (RA 3844). Little reference was made to these definitions during commission deliberations. Just compensation was interpreted by some commissioners as fair market value. In the end, no categorical agreement was reached on the meaning of just compensation, a view confirmed by the Philippine Supreme Court in a recent decision.

At the same time, although the Constitutional Commission appeared to reject militant peasant groups' calls for free land distribution in favor of a principle of "affordable cost" (whereby beneficiaries would pay what they were able and the government would bear the monetary difference), it did not adopt specific language concerning beneficiary repayment.

The provision on retention limits and, more generally, the scope of authority left to Congress, caused further consternation among peasant organizations. Most were distressed to find even the notion of retention limits accorded constitutional recognition. As to the particulars, efforts within the commission to limit the right of retention to owner-cultivators were defeated.

Once the Constitutional Commission had completed its deliberations, attention shifted to President Aquino and the possibility that she would preempt congressional action by issuing an agrarian reform decree pursuant to the executive powers she retained pending the convening of the new Congress. Executive Order 229 was issued on July 22, 1987, but it left the determination of the key elements of the reform program to Congress. The story of the evolution of EO 229 and the subsequent legislative enactment (Republic Act 6657, the Comprehensive Agrarian Reform Law) is perhaps most easily told by subject area. Before turning to specifics, however, a brief description of the chronology of events is appropriate.

Cabinet and Congressional Deliberations on Land Reform

When repeated demonstrations in the July–October 1986 period failed to arouse any apparent government action on agrarian reform, the KMP and several other peasant organizations initiated a series of land occupations. (The KMP invasions encompassed some 70,000 hectares as of mid-1989.) The KMP launched a new series of demonstrations in front of the Department of Agrarian Reform in mid-January 1987. These rallies culminated in a January 22 march on Malacañang (the presidential palace), which ended in tragedy as some thirteen participants were killed and more than ninety others were wounded when police and military forces opened fire on the demonstrators as they approached the Mendiola Bridge.

This bloodshed galvanized the establishment of a special Cabinet Action Committee (CAC) on January 28, 1987, which first convened on February 4, 1987. The creation of the CAC marked new, meaningful government consideration of agrarian reform. For the next six months this committee deliberated, drafting and redrafting a proposed decree in concert with an Inter-Agency Task Force on Agrarian Reform (consisting of representatives of concerned ministries and the academic and research community). With each ensuing draft, the scope of the reform was narrowed. Importantly, there was no permanent secretary of the Department of Agrarian Reform during most of these deliberations, Alvarez having resigned in March to run for the Senate. DAR was thus unable to provide forceful leadership within the CAC. (Alvarez's replacement, Philip Juico, was not named until EO 229 was announced in July.)

Even as the CAC conferred, those with private access to President Aquino were making their case for revisions in the land-reform agenda. In early June, Jaime Ongpin, Secretary of the Department of Finance, and Deogracias Vistan, President of the Land Bank of the Philippines, made known their opposition to several key features of the program then under consideration by the CAC, preparing their own draft decree. Trade and Industry Secretary José Concepcion cautioned against a seven-hectare retention limit as discouraging foreign and domestic investment in aquaculture. Justice Secretary Sedfrey Ordonez argued the constitution precluded the Executive from setting retention limits or determining just compensation by decree.

The June–July 1987 period also witnessed an extraordinary private and public campaign by anti-reform landowners. Most conspicuous was an anti-reform pledge, signed in blood by Negros sugar planters, accompanied by threats of armed resistance and secession in the event of land reform.

In the end, the decree issued by Aquino (EO No. 229) was not the product of the CAC, but of a select group of presidential advisers. The result was an amalgam of the CAC draft, the Vistan/Ongpin draft, and position papers submitted by various outside groups. Excluded cabinet members were told to acquiesce or resign.

Executive Order 229 was issued five days before the scheduled opening of the new Congress. The new decree left the crucial determinations of implementation priorities and retention limits to the landowner-dominated Congress. Compensation was to be based on the owner's declaration of current fair market value (subject to controls to be subsequently adopted by the Presidential Agrarian Reform Council, or PARC). Corporate landowners could meet their reform obligations by giving workers the right to purchase stock commensurate with the relative value of the land assets. Finally, the decree permanently disqualified as beneficiaries any "persons, associations, or entities who prematurely enter the land to avail themselves of the rights and benefits" provided by the law. As the decree deferred to Congress on the most important and controversial issues, its promulgation, it would seem, was intended not so much to preempt congressional action as to give the appearance of President Aquino personally fulfilling her agrarian reform pledge.

Thereafter, the legislative process substantially mirrored that of the cabinet deliberations; that is, progressive (even radical) draft reform provisions were successively watered down. The more progressive bills were those introduced by six members of the nationalist bloc, by Bonifacio Gillego, then chairman of the Agrarian Reform Committee of the House of Representatives, and by Senator Agapito "Butz" Aquino, brother of the president's late husband. The landowner bloc in the House, led by Romeo Guanzon of Negros Occidental, attempted to introduce its own bill. When this effort was defeated on procedural grounds their focus shifted to amending the committee bill. Such was their success in amending the House bill that Congressman Gillego and thirteen other original co-sponsors eventually withdrew their sponsorship of that bill.

On the Senate side, Senator Heherson Alvarez, chairman of the Senate Agrarian Reform Committee, introduced several bills. They served principally to flesh out EO 229. The Senate bill, having lower retention limits, was marginally more progressive than the House bill, although each had important flaws.

House-Senate conferees then engaged in several weeks of often heated debate. In the end, the House conferees largely prevailed on such crucial issues as retention limits. On June 10, 1988, President Aquino signed into law Republic Act 6657, the Comprehensive Agrarian Reform Law. In fact, the law, as it is likely to be implemented, holds relatively little promise of effectuating comprehensive agrarian reform. (Still, disgruntled landowners challenged the constitutionality of the law, only to be rebuffed by the Philippine Supreme Court in a recent decision upholding the law.)

The Scope of the New Agrarian Reform Law

Table 1.4 illustrates the systematic reduction in program scope that characterized the deliberative process in the cabinet.

Table 1.4   **Scope of Philippine Land Reform Proposals (Area in Hectares)**

	1/23/87	3/13/87	4/27/87	12/1/87
Program A:	557,000	557,000	557,000	727,800
Program B:	939,000	939,000	600,000	560,000
Program C:	3,852,000	2,138,500	1,280,000	1,280,000
Haciendas under labor administration	*2,333,000*	*1,516,450*	*1,199,000*	*1,199,000*
Tenanted croplands other than rice and corn	*957,000*	*622,050*	*81,000*	*81,000*
Tenanted rice and corn lands within the retention limit	*562,000*	*0*	*0*	*0*
Totals:	5,348,000	3,634,500	2,437,000	2,567,800

Sources: Inter-Agency Task Force on Agrarian Reform, *Accelerated Land Reform Program*, drafts (Quezon City: January 23, 1987; March 13, 1987; March 27, 1987); DAR Planning and Project Management Office, *Policies, Priority Concerns and External Assistance Needs* (Quezon City: December 1, 1987).

The January 23, 1987, *Accelerated Land Reform Program* report of the government's Inter-Agency Task Force (prepared before the Mendiola massacre and hastily released after it) established a four-part program of implementation:

- Program A would complete the distribution of tenanted rice and corn land on holdings above seven hectares during 1987–1989.

It would provide for administrative reforms geared to expediting the land valuation and compensation processes.

- Program B would implement reform on expropriated, foreclosed, and idle and abandoned lands, as well as on lands made available through "voluntary offers" (again during 1987–1989).
- Program C would, in the years 1989–1992, extend land redistribution to haciendas under labor administration (subject to a twenty-four-hectare retention limit), to tenanted holdings devoted to crops other than rice and corn (ultimately subject to a seven-hectare retention limit), and to tenanted rice and corn holdings below seven hectares (with a zero retention limit for such holdings).
- Program D (not included in Table 1.4) would implement land reform on public lands suitable for agriculture during the period 1987–1992.

Most notable in this initial draft is the relative scale of the various programs affecting private holdings: Program C was projected to involve fully two and one-half times as much farmland as Programs A and B combined. Together the three programs were expected to affect over 5.3 million hectares, or 55 percent, of all land in farms.

Additionally, Program D was slated to encompass some 1.35 million hectares. In practice it is likely to primarily involve regularizing the status of *existing* squatters on public lands. Expansion beyond that will be constrained by limited land availability, environmental protection concerns, and the high cost of resettlement projects on marginal lands.

By March 1987, the scope of the reform, specifically Program C, had been significantly curtailed. With the April 1987 draft came further reductions, primarily in Program C but embracing Program B as well. The overall program was by then reduced to 2.4 million hectares, or only 25 percent of farm area. This, of course, was the theoretical scope of the program. All previous Philippine experience suggests that the area actually subject to reform would be substantially less than the target. (For comparison, the land reforms of Japan, South Korea, and Taiwan actually redistributed 41, 30, and 33 percent of all cultivated land, respectively.)

By June 1987 Secretaries Vistan and Ongpin were arguing for deferral of Program C pending development of crop-specific retention limits. They argued that implementation of Programs A, B, and D would fully occupy Philippine administrative capacity; would fulfill President Aquino's promise to deliver a meaningful, comprehensive reform program; and would minimize landowner resistance.

In December 1987, DAR appeared to increase the scope of Program A. This reflected only the changed view of the Marcos-era accomplishments. Earlier estimates assumed the area still to be reformed was that not covered by previously *generated* emancipation patents, whereas the new estimates reflect the larger area not covered by previously *distributed* emancipation patents.

Unfortunately, official estimates of the program scope for the Comprehensive Agrarian Reform Law as enacted in June 1988 are not yet available. Again, one approach for promptly generating such information would be to tailor the field tests and implementation of the 1990 agricultural and population censuses so as to provide a rapid national sample survey.

Two foreign reform specialists[7] put the scope of RA 6657, as it is likely to be implemented, as follows: 200,000–300,000 hectares under Program A; another 200,000–300,000 hectares under Program B; and less than 100,000 hectares under Program C. Because the legal authority for Programs A and B predates RA 6657, the new law will, in their judgment, involve the incremental distribution of less than 100,000 hectares, barely 1 percent of cultivated farmland, to fewer than 100,000 families, or 3 percent of the presently landless.

Implementation Priorities
The new law provides for a protracted, three-phase reform process, with implementation to be completed in not more than ten years (although exemptions for commercial estates will push back completion for another five years or so, assuming such estates are reformed in practice). The successful land reforms of Japan, South Korea, and Taiwan were all carried out in much shorter time frames, in no instance involving more than four years of implementation.

Provision is made for the PARC to declare certain provinces or regions "priority land reform areas" in which case implementation may be expedited. To date, some twenty provinces have been classified as priority areas, although the practical effect of this is not readily apparent.

Ten-Year Exemption of Commercial Farms
Section 11 of the new law defers application of the reform for a period of ten years in the case of commercial farms. Such farms include those devoted to "commercial livestock, poultry and swine raising, and aquaculture, . . . fruit farms, orchards, vegetable and cut-flower farms, and cacao, coffee and rubber plantations." In the case of new farms,

the deferment period runs from the first year of commercial production and operation, extending the deferment another three to five years for newly planted crops such as coffee.

Moreover, the legislative language is ambiguous, leaving open the possibility that lands might be converted to commercial crops *after* the effective date of the reform. The prohibition in Section 73(e) of the "sale, transfer, conveyance or *change in the nature* of lands . . . after the effectivity of this Act" (emphasis added) can be read as governing such conversions, although this may require judicial clarification.

Stock Distribution on Corporate Farms
Section 31 of RA 6657 permits corporate landowners to satisfy their reform obligations by giving their farmworkers the "right to purchase such proportion of the capital stock of the corporation that the agricultural land, actually devoted to agricultural activities, bears in relation to the company's total assets." The provision creates obvious incentives to either undervalue the land assets or overvalue the nonland assets in order to dilute the value of the workers' shares. The workers are guaranteed only one seat on the corporate board of directors.

This provision appears to be a prima facie violation of the constitutionally mandated right of landless farmers and regular farmworkers to "*own* directly or collectively the lands they till" (emphasis added). However, creation of separate corporate entities, with one corporation having ownership of *all land* assets, coupled with distribution of *all stock* of that corporation to the worker-beneficiaries, should meet the constitutional requirement. (This question was not addressed by the Philippine Supreme Court in its recent decision.)

The president's family plantation, Hacienda Luisita, has been the most prominent subject of stock distribution in lieu of land transfer. Of Hacienda Luisita's 6,000 plus hectares, 4,915.75 hectares are deemed to be agricultural for purposes of the reform. This land is valued at P196.63 million (US$9.36 million at P21=US$1) or P40,000 (US$1,900) per hectare. The nonland assets are valued at P393.92 million (US$18.76 million), or two-thirds of the total value of corporate assets.

The worker-beneficiaries are to receive, at no apparent cost, their one-third minority stock shares in thirty equal annual installments, a further dilution of their benefits that seems without basis in the law. Even ignoring noneconomic benefits, analysis suggests they would be no worse off, indeed may be substantially better off, if they were to purchase the land assets of Hacienda Luisita under the terms of the reform law rather than accept the proposed "no cost" stock distribution.

Continuation of Lease and Management Contracts
Section 72 of the new law provides that reform beneficiaries take their land subject to existing lease, management, grower, or service contracts. There is, in theory, the possibility of such prior contracts effectively preempting all profits derived from the land, leaving the reform beneficiary with nothing but a title document for the duration (theoretically unlimited) of such contracts.

Anticipatory Transfers
Even more troubling than the lease and management contracts, in terms of their impact on the reform program, is the recognition accorded transfers of land up to the effective date of the law. It appears that transfers to relatives, friends, and straw men, in anticipation of the reform law, have been massive. Such subdivision of ownership, if recognized, could drastically reduce the amount of land owned in excess of the relevant retention limit. Section 6 of RA 6657 provides that transfers executed prior to the effective date of the law will be valid if registered within three months of that date; this provision raises the additional problem of possible post-law execution of fraudulently predated land transfers. Section 73(e), by contrast, recognizes only those transfers duly registered or the subject of the issuance of a tax declaration as of the effective date of the law. No resolution of the apparent conflict between these provisions has been forthcoming.

Landowner Retention Limits
Reviewing the protracted, phased implementation of retention limits (with a final retention limit of twenty-four hectares for Program C) contemplated in the March 13, 1987, CAC draft, a World Bank land-reform mission[8] concluded:

> Potentially most damaging to the ultimate goals of the land reform are both the step-wise introduction and the high levels of the retention limits on private lands. The proposal to phase in the retention limits in three successive steps . . . would encourage evasion, leave out a high proportion of tenants and landless [laborers], and add to the administrative burden . . . . *The Government should decide on the ultimate retention limit and enact it from the start . . . the Mission recommends that the Government consider adopting a uniform land ceiling of 7 ha for all Programs and implementing Programs A, B, and C simultaneously.* [emphasis added]

Legislative proposals concerning retention limits were, as might be expected, quite varied. The most radical provisions set the general retention area at two hectares, whereas several drafts established a zero retention limit for absentee landlords. As passed out of the House, the retention limit was set at seven hectares with an additional three hectares permitted each legal heir. Landowners who had received title under homestead or free patent were entitled to retain up to twenty-four hectares. On the Senate side, a five-hectare limit was eventually set, with owners who had already been the subject of reform under PD 27 entitled to retain seven hectares.

The compromise struck in the Conference Committee and embodied in RA 6657 is a *maximum* retention area of five hectares. An additional three hectares could be awarded to each child of the landowner provided the child was at least fifteen years old (as of what date is not stated) and was actually tilling the land or directly managing it.

A universal five-hectare retention limit alone would exempt 75.6 percent of total farm area from the reform. If on average one to two heirs per landowning family also receive the maximum retention rights, the effective retention limit will be eight to eleven hectares. Under this scenario farms with some two-thirds to three-quarters of all land will be completely exempt from the reform. Of those farms that remain subject to the reform, only the excess above eight to eleven hectares would be available to the reform. When such retention areas are netted out, even without evasive landowner behavior only 13 to 16 percent of the land in farms will be available for redistribution under the combination of preexisting and new legislation, and much of this may not be subject to reform for a decade or more.

The law leaves open the possibility that the Presidential Agrarian Reform Council could set a retention limit lower than five hectares. Similarly, the retention limit for children is couched in terms allowing for PARC action setting a lower limit. As a practical matter, however, there is no evidence that the PARC, as currently configured, will establish lower limits for either the owners' retention areas or those of their children.

Land Valuation
Again, the more radical provisions were introduced in the House, with one bill providing for outright confiscation of property and free distribution to farmer-beneficiaries. The original Gillego bill, adopting language proposed by the Congress for a People's Agrarian Reform, established a scheme of selective and progressive compensation, whereby compensation as a percentage of market value (determined from the owner's tax declaration, subject to some controls) declined with increasing farm size, as did the cash portion of that compensation. Owners of holdings greater than fifty hectares were to receive *no* compensation. The landowner bloc argued instead for valuation based

on the owner's declaration of fair market value, with payment entirely in cash.

As reported out, the House bill would have DAR and the owner determine the land value. The various Senate bills generally set valuation at the owner's tax declared value, subject to PARC controls.

The law, as adopted, values tenanted rice and corn lands above seven hectares at two and one-half times the value of average crop production (the valuation formula of PD 27), and introduces an array of valuation variables for all other lands. Among such variables are the cost of acquisition of the land, the current value of like properties, the sworn valuation by the owner, tax declarations, and the assessment made by government assessors. Social and economic benefits contributed by the farmers, farmworkers, and the government are also to be considered.

The complexity of the valuation process lends itself to abuse and protracted administrative and judicial proceedings. Equity and administrative efficiency have been far better served in other Asian land reforms through the use of a multiple of average annual productivity in calculating land values. The recent Philippine Supreme Court decision appears to validate the constitutionality of such an approach. Instead DAR compounded the legislative flaws by adopting valuation regulations that effectively set the total land value at 133 percent of market value.

A major scandal involving overvaluations of land marked the first anniversary of the new reform law. In the most notable instance lands voluntarily offered for sale to the government were valued at twenty times the price paid three months earlier. The DAR had already approved the transaction for payment when the fraudulent valuation was discovered by officials of the Land Bank of the Philippines. The fallout from this episode included the resignation of Secretary of Agrarian Reform Philip Juico, the naming of Miriam Defensor-Santiago—best known for her antigraft campaign while commissioner of immigration and deportation—as the new secretary, and a considerable, and desirable, shake-up in DAR personnel. The result, however, was a near paralysis of the program for several months, a situation exacerbated by congressional refusal to confirm Defensor-Santiago's appointment.

(In the aftermath of the coup attempt of early December 1989, Aquino substantially revamped her cabinet, including naming Congressman Florencio B. Abad as the new secretary of DAR. A member of the nationalist bloc that introduced the most radical reform bill in the House, Abad could be expected to be very sympathetic to the reform cause. However, landowner resistance in Congress and ineffectual support from President Aquino doomed Abad's nomination. The turmoil bodes ill for the reform process.)

Meanwhile, recent press accounts suggest that DAR is considering a valuation formula tied to the income produced by the property, with the aim of both simplifying and rationalizing valuation.

Landowner Compensation

The new law provides cash payments as an inverse function of farm size: 25 percent cash for lands in excess of fifty hectares, 30 percent cash for lands of twenty-four to fifty hectares, and 35 percent cash for lands below twenty-four hectares. In all cases the balance was to be paid in government bonds maturing in equal annual installments over a ten-year period. Generous provisions were made for transferability and negotiability of these bonds. In upholding these provisions, the Philippine Supreme Court distinguished the taking of property under the agrarian reform program from the traditional exercise of the government power of eminent domain, deeming it "revolutionary" expropriation and thus exempt from the standard of payment entirely in cash.

Beneficiary Repayment

The World Bank mission recommended a one-time, nominal payment of P600 (US$29) per beneficiary. The mission concluded there was little prospect of an immediate improvement in the disposable family income of reform beneficiaries if beneficiaries were required to repay land costs over thirty years at 6 percent interest. Elimination of further amortization obligations was urged in order to effect an instant and significant increase in beneficiary income.

The most radical House bill provided for free land distribution, echoing the demand of the KMP peasant organization. Eventually the House adopted a seventeen-year amortization schedule with zero interest, coupled with a two-year deferment of initial repayment. Payments were not to exceed 10 percent of the net value of current production. Further, all previous land rentals and uncompensated labor (defined as the difference between actual wages and the government-mandated minimum wage, including other benefits provided by law) were to be deducted from the resale price of land to the beneficiary.

The Senate opted for a thirty-year repayment period at 6 percent interest. Payments in the first three years were to be reduced, and the first five payments were in no event to exceed 5 percent of the value of annual gross production. Thereafter adjustments were to be made in the event amortization obligations exceeded 10 percent of annual gross production, where the failure of production was not the fault of the beneficiary.

The Senate provisions were adopted *in toto* in RA 6657. Nonpayment of an aggregate of three annual installments will be grounds for foreclosure by the Land Bank of the Philippines. Peasant groups have objected to the repayment provisions, arguing that the high cost of inputs, most notably chemical fertilizers, render amortizations equivalent to 10 percent of gross production value onerous, if not unaffordable. Although these claims seem overstated—the amortization payments appear to be lower than typical rent payments—they do underscore concerns that the reform will effect only a modest immediate redistribution of income.

Penalties for Noncompliance

Section 74 of the new law provides for imprisonment for one month to three years or a fine of P1,000–15,000 (roughly US$50–715) in the event of willful or knowing violation of the terms of the act. Imprisonment is not, in this context, a credible penalty, and will not serve as an effective deterrent. The maximum monetary penalty is roughly equivalent to the value of one-half hectare of average farmland. Inasmuch as this fine is set without regard to the number of hectares affected by landowner misconduct, it too will have little deterrent effect, particularly in the case of larger landholders. Higher, but credible, penalties are important to successful reform.

Complementary Measures in Support of Land Reform

From the earliest drafts, provision was made for complementary services such as liberalized credit, marketing, extension, infrastructure, and research. As enacted, RA 6657 mandates the provision of beneficiary support services (as well as support services for affected landowners). The law further requires the setting aside of at least 25 percent of all agrarian reform appropriations for support services. It leaves all details of such support services to the determination of the PARC, however.

Program Costs

Although cost estimates for the reform program have fluctuated, most place the cost over the first five years at P60–70 billion (US$2.9–3.3 billion) and the life of program costs at P160–170 billion (US$7.6–8.1 billion). In each case, land transfer costs were to be the largest single component of the budget.

Government estimates suggest that roughly one-half of the land reform financing will have to come from foreign sources. Although the language is open to other interpretations, the law appears to limit the use of foreign resources to financing production credits, infrastructure, and other support services. If this provision, thus interpreted, is enforced, and if foreign donors are willing to provide the necessary funds, foreign donors will effectively be financing the *entirety* of all program costs *not* related to land transfers.

In any event, the multilateral donors, as well as most bilateral donors, appear predisposed to limit their funding to activities other than land transfer. A $50 million U.S. appropriation was available for land transfer costs, but the U.S. Agency for International Development (USAID) opted to commit it to general budgetary support for the land reform *exclusive* of compensation. Disbursement of funds was, however, conditional on progress in land surveying and generating and distributing titles. The Japanese have expressed willingness to similarly tie the release of cash transfers, but have not done so yet. The inconsistency of donor signals, arguing for nonconfiscatory land reform, yet refusing to directly finance compensation, is not lost on the Philippine government nor those hostile to reform. The fungibility of government resources, however, should permit donors to underwrite other portions of the government budget and thereby free up domestic resources for payment of compensation.

Peasant Reaction

Militant and nonmilitant peasant organizations alike have denounced the new law as setting retention limits that are too high, effectively exempting commercial farms while allowing corporate farms to transfer stock in lieu of land, and establishing beneficiary repayment obligations that are unaffordable. As previously noted, several peasant organizations have responded by initiating land invasions.

The Congress for a People's Agrarian Reform, meanwhile, has, pursuant to provisions in the constitution (which were to be, but have not yet been, formalized in legislation), begun a nationwide signature campaign for a national referendum on its alternative, the People's Agrarian Reform Code (PARCode). This reform proposal sets a single five-hectare retention limit, eliminates the deferment for commercial estates, establishes a program of selected and progressive compensation, and mirrors the beneficiary repayment provisions of the final House reform bill. Some 500,000 of the estimated 2.5–3.0 million signatures needed have now been gathered.

The campaign's greatest achievement may lie in its role as a vehicle for education and democratic mobilization of the peasantry. Democratic grassroots organizational activities are still in their infancy, a legacy of the years of martial law. At the same time a substantial violent Left has opted out of the ongoing political process. In consequence, the leaders of CPAR acknowledge their continuing political weakness, holding little hope that they will be able over the near-to-medium term to successfully pressure the Philippine Congress into adopting progressive amendments to the reform.

Conclusion and Recommendations

The Aquino government's new Comprehensive Agrarian Reform Law promises far more than it is likely to deliver. Unless its shortcomings are redressed through administrative action—and this seems quite unlikely—inequitable land tenure will continue to plague Philippine development and threaten its political institutions, stifling agricultural yields while fueling the rural grievances that are so much a part of the current insurgency.

Correcting the flaws of the new law will require strong administrative action on numerous fronts. The present, decade-long implementation schedule invites landowner evasion of the law as written, and further, debilitating legislative amendments. Exemption of commercial farms from application of the law for ten years or more only exacerbates these problems. Taking advantage of provisions already in the law, DAR should declare provinces or regions with extensive landlessness "priority areas" and rapidly accelerate program implementation in those areas. The target should be substantial completion of the reform process within five years.

Corporate farms are effectively insulated against redistribution of their land, with corporate stock distribution permitted in lieu thereof. This provision appears to be in violation of the constitutional right of farmers and farmworkers to own the land they are tilling. To comply with the constitution, DAR should insist that any such distribution entail the spin-off of a corporate entity having full ownership of the land assets, with *all* stock in that corporation distributed to the farmworker-beneficiaries.

The contradictory provisions of the new law afford little protection against anticipatory and fraudulent land transfers. Beyond strict scrutiny of recent land transfers, DAR must be prepared to vary the retention limit below five hectares to counter such transfers and assure that adequate land is available for redistribution. Similar adjustments will be necessary in the event anticipatory lease and management contracts tie up the profits from the land otherwise subject to reform.

Even apart from the question of land transfers, landowner retention rights severely constrain the reform's potential impact. The maximum retention areas are set well above those of the successful Asian land reforms and will exempt some seven-eighths or more of the land in farms. If this reform is to have appreciable impact in terms of area transferred and families benefited, the Presidential Agrarian Reform Council must set retention limits well below five hectares, at least for better quality land. The limits should be variable, with the aim of acquiring at least the 2,138,500 hectares of privately owned Program C land identified in the Cabinet Action Committee draft of March 13, 1987. This target, coupled with the other elements of the reform, would have the Philippine reform approaching the successful Asian reforms in terms of the percentage of cultivated land redistributed.

The complex provisions regarding land valuation seem to invite landowner abuse, a finding amply corroborated by recent scandals. Moreover, the valuation provisions could embroil the program in protracted administrative and judicial proceedings. A consistent and simplified valuation procedure is thus essential to rapid implementation of the program. The value of crops produced, appropriately capitalized, commends itself from the standpoint of both equity and administrative simplicity. It appears to be within DAR's discretionary powers to adopt such a standard, perhaps supplemented by previous landowner valuations for tax purposes.

One simple check on excessive valuations is to treat the valuation of the president's family plantation as establishing a ceiling on Philippine land values. (Recall that Hacienda Luisita's lands—which are well-irrigated, level, and fertile—are valued at P40,000 (US$1,900) per hectare. DAR working figures for the reform program have, by contrast, assumed *average* land values of P37,000–45,000 per hectare.)

In the event of landowner efforts to sabotage the reform program the provisions for legal sanctions are at present either weak or not credible. In extreme cases, imprisonment should be sought. In cases involving fines, offenses should, where appropriate, be treated as separate and multiple, with fines levied for *each* offense. These penalties might be set on a per-hectare basis, or compensation might be forfeited for land that is the subject of illegal landowner behavior. Forceful leadership from President Aquino; education and mobilization of beneficiaries concerning their rights; and early, highly publicized punishment of illegal landowner behavior can help create a climate of respect for the law.

The provisions of the new law and prevailing political configurations do not bode well for genuine agrarian reform. However, some of the scope and significance of the reform is yet uncertain, to be determined by administrative decisions of the Aquino government. In this context, financial support from the donor community must be conditional if it is to be responsible. The best mechanism for assuring that resources in support of the reform process further actual implementation of the reform is the use of reimbursement financing or "progress payments." Inasmuch as the Aquino government has cited the agrarian reform as the "centerpiece" of its development program in discussions of the new Multilateral Assistance Initiative, foreign donors should stand ready to provide generous general budgetary support for the reform and direct support for compensation, both conditional upon verifiable progress in taking land and redistributing it to beneficiary families. Further, due concern for human rights and the initial promise of the "People Power Revolution" argues for conditionality of all assistance on improvements in the human rights situation in the Philippines. In the absence of progress on both the reform and human-rights fronts, donor resources will be largely wasted in an environment of acute landlessness, agricultural stagnation, and ongoing civil unrest.

Notes

1. Keijiro Otsuka and Yujiro Hayami, "Theories of Share Tenancy: A Critical Survey," *Economic Development and Cultural Change* 37, no. 1 (October 1988): 31–68; Roy L. Prosterman and Jeffrey M. Riedinger, *Land Reform and Democratic Development* (Baltimore: Johns Hopkins University Press, 1987), pp. 35–71; Ronald J. Herring, *Land to the Tiller: The Political Economy of Agrarian Reform in South Asia* (New Haven, Conn.: Yale University Press, 1983), pp. 239–267.

2. Reynaldo Ileto, *Pasyon and Revolution: Popular Movements in the Philippines 1840–1910* (Quezon City: Ateneo de Manila University Press, 1979).

3. *Winning the War Against the Insurgency: Issues and Answers* 1, no. 5 (Manila: Office of the Press Secretary, April 1989), p. 6.

4. This figure reflects the area approved for payment of compensation under Operation Land Transfer (258,638 hectares) and the area covered by certificates of land transfer under the Landed Estates program (54,986 hectares).

5. This is the number of families associated with land approved for payment of compensation under Operation Land Transfer (134,371) plus those families who have received certificates of land transfer under the Landed Estates program (33,503).

6. Calculated as the number of families to which emancipation patents have been distributed under Operation Land Transfer (174,859) plus those families to which certificates of land transfer have been issued under the Landed Estates program (35,221).

7. Roy L. Prosterman and Timothy Hanstad, "Whether Failure is Inevitable Under the New Philippine Land-Reform Law," memorandum, University of Washington School of Law, November 3, 1988.

8. World Bank, *Agrarian Reform Issues in the Philippines: An Assessment*

of the Proposal for an Accelerated Land Reform Program (Washington, D.C.: World Bank, May 12, 1987), pp. vi–vii.

Selected Bibliography

Accelerated Land Reform Program, drafts. Quezon City: Inter-Agency Task Force on Agrarian Reform, January 23, 1987; March 13, 1987; March 27, 1987.

Chapman, William. *Inside the Philippine Revolution*. New York: W.W. Norton, 1987.

Hayami, Yujiro, Ma. Agnes R. Quisumbing, and Lourdes S. Adriano. *In Search of a New Land Reform Paradigm: A Perspective from the Philippines*. Quezon City: Ateneo de Manila University Press, (forthcoming).

Herring, Ronald J. *Land to the Tiller: The Political Economy of Agrarian Reform in South Asia*. New Haven, Conn.: Yale University Press, 1983.

Ileto, Reynaldo. *Pasyon and Revolution: Popular Movements in the Philippines 1840–1910*. Quezon City: Ateneo de Manila University Press, 1979.

Kerkvliet, Benedict J. *The Huk Rebellion: A Study of Peasant Revolt in the Philippines*. Berkeley: University of California Press, 1977.

1980 Census of Agriculture. Manila: National Census and Statistics Office, September 1985.

Otsuka, Keijiro, and Yujiro Hayami. "Theories of Share Tenancy: A Critical Survey." *Economic Development and Cultural Change* 37, no. 1 (October 1988): 31–68.

Prosterman, Roy L., and Timothy Hanstad. "Whether Failure is Inevitable Under the New Philippine Land-Reform Law." Memorandum, University of Washington School of Law, November 3, 1988.

Prosterman, Roy L., and Jeffrey M. Riedinger. *Land Reform and Democratic Development*. Baltimore, Md.: Johns Hopkins University Press, 1987.

Putzel, James. "Prospects for Agrarian Reform Under the Aquino Government." In Mamerto Canlas, Mariano Miranda, Jr., and James Putzel (eds.), *Land, Poverty and Politics in the Philippines*. Quezon City: Claretian, 1988.

Vigilantes in the Philippines: A Threat to Democratic Rule. New York: Lawyers Committee for Human Rights, 1988.

World Bank. *Agrarian Reform Issues in the Philippines: An Assessment of the Proposal for an Accelerated Land Reform Program*. Washington, D.C.: World Bank, May 12, 1987.

Wurfel, David. "The Development of Post-War Philippine Land Reform: Political and Sociological Explanations." In Antonio J. Ledesma, Perla Q. Makil, and Virginia A. Miralao (eds.), *Second View from the Paddy*. Quezon City: Institute of Philippine Culture, 1983.

chapter two

Explaining Anomalies in Agrarian Reform: Lessons from South India

Ronald J. Herring

Summary

Land reforms in the South Indian state of Kerala have demonstrated the potential for fundamental alterations of agrarian society in the direction of greater equity through democratic and constitutional means. Contrary to the general pattern of stasis and broken promises on land reform in the subcontinental region, legislation implemented in the 1970s effectively vested land in tenants and abolished landlordism as an institution. Landlordism in the state had historically operated as an especially oppressive and exploitative system, depriving lower orders of rural society of political rights, dignity, and basic human needs. These reforms could be legislated and implemented because of the extraordinary mobilization of a coalition of the rural poor and reformist urban groups under the auspices of the local Communist party, which had abandoned the insurrectionary path and functioned electorally much as a social democratic party in the European sense. The length, intensity, and staying power of that mobilization stands out as anomalous for India.

Despite their liberating effects on subordinate classes in rural areas, the reforms by no means solved the agrarian crisis in economic terms. Land has passed in general to cultivators who are more involved in agriculture than were the old landlords. Yet these agriculturalists have shown some tendency to use their new wealth to upgrade their social status and consumption at the expense of new on-farm investment. One reason for their less than expected (in the economic theory of land reform) performance is the class conflicts exacerbated by the land reforms. A newly confident and politically aware agricultural proletariat, which benefited far less from reform than the tenants, has pressed claims to higher wages and other benefits, which farmers believe squeeze profits too severely. The state government has picked up some of the burden of fulfilling demands of the laborers in the form of

*welfare policy, but serious problems remain in generating agricultural
dynamism.*

*A number of lessons are suggested by the Kerala experience. First, a
mobilized coalition of the rural poor behind a reformist political party
can overturn systems of rural oppression and exploitation within a
democratic and liberal framework. Second, it is difficult to see how
improvements in human dignity and human rights in the context of
extreme rural inequality could be achieved without land reforms; the
status of out-caste and landless laborers in other parts of the
subcontinent (and in many other parts of the poor world) illustrates the
alternative. Third, land reforms must be seen not through the lens of a
solution mystique, but rather as a necessary component of any program
to address the needs of the rural poor under conditions of land scarcity,
demographic pressures, political inequality, and oppression, which still
characterize many parts of the world.*

Critical Questions in the Analysis of Agrarian Reform

Planning documents in India have repeatedly stressed the failure of
land reforms other than the partially effective abolition of
intermediaries (generically lumped together as "zamindars") in the
1950s. That failure has been called officially "the greatest hiatus
between promise and performance" of a state constitutionally and
programatically committed to reduction of inequalities and amelioration
of poverty. The reasons for national failure are not puzzling, and
indeed reflect a general pattern in poor countries: the absence of
effective mobilization of underclasses in rural areas; the lack of linkages
to committed political parties with serious redistributive programs; the
structural and electoral power of landholders and their propertied allies;
and the multiple connections between bureaucracy and society at the
local level, which thwart implementation of whatever reformist
measures are thrown up by populist politicians. It is in this context that
the serious and successful land reforms of Kerala state in southwestern
India require analysis.[1]

One should ask of the Kerala reforms what one should ask of land
reforms in general. The central issues are as follows:

1. What are the counter-inertial dynamics? Inertial dynamics here
means simply that any social system forms routines and institutions that
tend to reproduce existing distributions of power and privilege, placing
limits on the extent of redistribution possible under normal conditions.
There is no assumption here of a perfectly coherent Parsonian world,
nor is change unusual. Rather, the claim is that the most basic structures

of society are supported by a formidable array of ideological and institutional props that resist fundamental change. In agrarian societies, institutions surrounding land control are the most fundamental of these structures.

The real puzzle of land reforms is therefore not that so many fail, but that some succeed in overturning systems that have operated for generations, buttressed by cultural expression, multidimensional dominance of individuals at the bottom of society, and embedded administrative and legal routines ultimately guaranteed by the coercive power of the state. How is the inertia of reproduction of the basic outlines of such structures broken? India presents a special puzzle, for common mechanisms of pressure for reform from outside the system (e.g., the U.S. occupation of postwar Japan or the conquest of Taiwan by nationalist forces who had just lost a peasant war on the issue of agrarian reform on the mainland) have been absent. If anything, external pressures (from Delhi) have worked against, not for, agrarian reform in the state of Kerala.

2. Who benefits? Not only is agrarian class structure more complex than is often realized, but there is the possibility that the state and nonagrarian political forces will be the principal beneficiaries of changes in agrarian structure. That the very powerful lose does not necessarily mean that the most powerless win. In typical situations, it is virtually impossible for the entire bottom of society to be established as economically secure with the fruits of land reforms. How the limited boons are to be distributed raises crucial moral and political questions and must be central to analysis. Analysis of the distribution of benefits must then address the policy logic of specific reforms, tactical compromises in political process, and distortions in implementation that alter overt legislative intent. To answer these questions, analysis must proceed to the ground level, where real social change occurs.

3. What are the economic effects of reform? Virtually all land reforms are justified as a means of inducing agricultural dynamism. One of the major shifts in development economics has been the recognition that agriculture cannot be neglected (or bled dry) in the vague hope that peasants eventually will disappear into the ranks of industrial workers. Not only has the importance of agriculture to economic growth been reestablished, but the (often rhetorical) shifts in development thinking in the 1970s to concern with basic human needs and the "poorest of the poor" have challenged analysts to focus on the sector in which absolute poverty and the worst manifestations of underdevelopment are concentrated.

Increasing difficulties in international payments since the mid-1970s have also focused attention on the import-substitution and export possibilities inherent in the agricultural sector. And whether or not the academic fad of dependency has abated, real people in poor countries recognize the perils of dependence on food imports (just as in U.S. politics, dependence on foreign oil still carries some weight). Definitive answers to the economic-impact question are difficult to come by, as the economic theory is murky and too many variables besides tenurial structure and size distribution of holdings (price policy, producer margins, input availability, infrastructure, and so on) affect agricultural performance. Nevertheless, we must make some attempt to sort out shifts in economic dynamics that are engendered by land reforms, precisely because of the centrality of economic arguments in the political case for and against land reform.

Anomalies

Kerala is unusual in so many ways that Indologists prefer not to deal with it. Keralites are fond of saying that what they are thinking today, India will be thinking next year. By Indian standards, Kerala is a small state, yet it contains a population of 28 million, about three times that of Sweden.[2] Population density is among the world's highest, at 654 per square kilometer (1981). State per capita income is below the Indian mean, and yet Kerala ranks highest in India on scores such as the Physical Quality of Life Index, which measures (albeit imperfectly) performance on basic human needs and normally varies directly and strongly with income. Its infant mortality rate, life expectancy, and literacy rate are by far the best in the nation and rank with the very best in the poor world. The birth rate in Kerala in 1986 was 22.4 per 1000 population, compared to an all-India figure of 32.4, and the death rate was 6.7, compared to India's 11.1. The population growth rate has been considerably below the national average. Life expectancy has been between ten and fifteen years above the national average. The infant mortality rate was 27 per 1,000 live births in 1986, compared to a national average of 96, and, significantly, was only 28 in rural areas (compared to the national rural figure of 105). By most measures of basic human needs satisfaction at the bottom of society, Kerala is anomalous in national and international terms given its very low level of income.

The politics of Kerala are likewise anomalous; the first freely elected Communist government in India, indeed in the world, was formed in Kerala in 1957. Communists have been major contenders for power continuously, and currently constitute the state government. Although Communist in name, the party in practice participates vigorously in the democratic process, has decided against nationalization of land, and occupies a political niche typical of social democratic parties in other parts of the world. Kerala's agrarian organizations have historically been the most developed in India, and its recent land reforms have been the most radical.

Clearly the strength of agrarian mobilization, Communist electoral success, and effectiveness of land reform are integrally connected. For social theorists, one important conclusion on the origins of this leftist mobilization is the structural configuration that spawned agrarian radicalism and discontent. Such a structure is crucial, but must be placed in the context of extra-agrarian social dynamics and political strategies of the leading contenders for power.[3] This chapter will look at the mobilization of an effective social force for reform because of the absolutely crucial nature of political dynamics in opening legislative possibilities for reform, energizing the reform process as obstacles appeared, and effecting implementation on the ground.

Leftists coming to power at the state level through electoral means in a nation of decidedly centrist tendencies (rhetoric notwithstanding) pose an important puzzle, and make land reform an expected consequence. But having Communists in power is no guarantee that redistribution will reach the bottom of the agrarian structure. As will be developed later, there are important issues of tactics and strategy that intervene between electoral success for the left and agrarian policy on the ground. One of the most important current puzzles in India is raised by differences in strategy between Communists in Kerala and those in West Bengal, both of which have achieved considerable electoral success. The Kerala Communists have run recognized risks of eroding their support base through granting property rights to tenants (who not surprisingly then worry about further redistribution and are pulled to the political right, or Congress party). The party in West Bengal has decided against abolishing landlordism and granting land to the tenants, relying instead on limited distribution of surplus land, credit reforms, public works, and security of tenure and limitation of rents for sharecroppers. Because the Left has been the engine of agrarian reform in India, the differences between the two parties raise important questions about the viability of opposing political strategies for incorporating land reform into an agenda for social revolution under parliamentary auspices.

Structure and Agrarian Radicalism in Kerala

Agrarian radicalism has a long history in Kerala, particularly in Malabar (the northern third of contemporary Kerala), which was called by one colonial official "the most rack-rented place on the face of the earth."

Changes in legal structure introduced by the British in the early nineteenth century put extraordinary pressure on the middle strata of tenants who had been accustomed to stable rents and security of tenure. With colonial support for claims of landlords to absolute property rights, market forces in the existing demographic situation permitted new demands for renewal fees and higher rents, as well as waves of evictions, enforced by courts and police. Resulting agrarian violence took on communal overtones; the "Mappilla [indigenous Muslim] outrages," which broke out with increasing intensity in the nineteenth century, were couched in terms of Muslim assertion of rights against a European state and Hindu landlords. The first discussion of land reform was generated within the colonial administration in recognition of the tenurial base of peasant violence. Fear of rural instability preceded concerns for production and social equity in discussions of land reform, which were to continue intermittently for a century. The Mappilla revolt of 1920–1921 was the culmination of these disturbances and was among the most significant uprisings in colonial India.

Uprisings in Malabar illustrate two important points about the origins of mobilization of agrarian underclasses for redress. First, in line with social theory about the causes of agrarian protest, an agrarian structure characterized by high levels of tenancy, extreme inequalities in land ownership, and the resulting miserable terms of exchange between landed and landless generated the potential for agrarian radicalism. But, of equal importance, the Mappilla revolts illustrate how overlays of social oppression may accompany economic exploitation. The self-definition of Muslims as Muslims provided the symbols and forms of organization without which mobilization is extremely difficult. Similar issues of ethnic identification and mobilization were later to play important roles in the growth of a radical and redistributive coalition centered around the Communists. What marks the Kerala Communist leadership as exceptional was its responses to inchoate radicalism and reformism emerging in society in terms of that society, unhampered by theoretical baggage imported from Europe. Biographies and autobiographies of leftist leaders indicate clearly a process of learning from indigenous praxis, with few preconceived notions of revolutionary models. By the 1950s, revolution had receded to a rhetorical flourish superimposed on electoral politics rooted in the agrarian poor, working class, and radical intelligentsia.

Larger societal structure proved as important as the narrow agrarian structure in generating a leftist coalition. Kerala was integrated into international trading networks at a very early date. Indeed, the Roman Empire worried about its terms of trade with the region. Trade wars among Arab forces and European companies extended commercial penetration in the fifteenth and sixteenth centuries. The extensive connection to the international trading system (coir, rubber, cardamom, pepper, ginger, and so on) was especially apparent in the depression of the 1930s, which produced severe dislocations and furthered leftist mobilization in Kerala. From 1931 onward, the number of landless or virtually landless agricultural laborers increased dramatically both in absolute terms and as a percentage of agriculturalists.

This early and penetrating commercialization was coupled with a settlement pattern that differentiates Kerala from much of India; rather than discrete villages of the modal sort, Kerala presents a continuous gradient of urban to peri-urban to rural communities. The agrarian poor often had one foot in economic activities associated with trade, simple agro-industrial processing (coir is archetypal), and small-scale industrial activities. The familiar leftist exhortation to form a "worker-peasant alliance" was achieved in part by the very structure of settlement patterns, physical ecology, economic activity, and occupations.

This historical configuration goes a long way toward explaining the preconditions for agrarian reform. If one were to look at the data on important structural variables across India, coupled with social theory on the origins of agrarian radicalism, Kerala, and Malabar in particular, would stand out as likely candidates for leftist mobilization. Kerala, in conjuction with having the most valuable land, historically has had the highest rates of tenancy, landlessness, sub-subsistence holdings, and rural unemployment in the subcontinent. The ratio of people to land is three times the Indian average. There are, of course, good theoretical reasons that these variables should appear together. Communist electoral strength is highly correlated with measures of agrarian distress in Kerala. Likewise, the broader economy was uniquely suited to alliance of movements of industrial workers and agrarian radicals. But the real puzzle is why these structural predispositions were translated in Kerala into effective pressure for agrarian reform, whereas similar pressures elsewhere spawned only abject dependency and quiescence. A large part of the answer to this puzzle lies in the linkage of agrarian issues to broader social ferment and demands for national independence from the 1920s onward by a leftist group uniquely willing to learn from practice and remarkably dedicated to their constituency.

Politics in the Broader Society: Coalition Formation

The agrarian configuration of Kerala in the second decade of the twentieth century clearly provided a structural niche for both radical agrarianism and linkage of agrarian issues to working class agitations.

But in the absence of political response, the agrarian structure might well have produced no more than periodic local outbreaks of suicidal rage and eventual knuckling under to the superior resources of the state and landlords, as exemplified in Kerala by the Mappilla uprisings. Two factors worked for the formation of an integrated and effective political response—one local and one societal—although the two are intertwined.

Locally, landlordism was a coherent and multidimensional social system of oppression and inequality. The hierarchy of land control and privilege roughly paralleled the hierarchy of social status and deprivation. Caste distinctions were so extreme and severely sanctioned in Kerala that the great reformer Vivekananda called Kerala "the madhouse of India." Untouchability extended to "unapproachability," with explicit rules for physical separation of "polluted" castes. The penalties for abrogation of caste separation (e.g., failing to move far enough or quickly enough off the road for the approach of a Brahmin) included death. Untouchables were denied the right to cover certain parts of their bodies and forced to make a continuous sound to warn of their approach. Sexual exploitation of poor women was widespread. Agrestic slavery was practiced, despite formal abolition by colonial authorities, and a form of serfdom akin to slavery was common. Even today, many laborers say that within their lifetime, before the land reforms, they effectively occupied the niche of slave (*adima*).

Lower orders were excluded not only from land ownership, but also from public discourse, participation, and dignity. Moral outrage at this systematic degradation was crucial in sustaining tactical and substantive radicalism. Moreover, the system of landlordism was buttressed and compromised by association with the colonial state, which was becoming the object of challenge by nationalist forces from the 1920s until independence in 1947. An early organizer of the Left in Kerala, and twice Communist Chief Minister of the State, E. M. S. Namboodiripad reflected on the early Congress movement as follows: "Not only was the peasantry the most numerous section of the Indian people, but it was in the villages that imperialism had its most reliable ally—the feudal landlords. The police *thana* [station] functioning in close collaboration with the big landlords was the center of imperialism's oppressive machinery."

Concretely, any challenge to one leg of the social system of oppression and exclusion inevitably spilled over into challenges to the system as a whole; such challenges are the stuff of revolutionary politics.

The extraordinary social rigidity and extreme inequality represented by local landlordism were not restricted to the villages. By the late nineteenth century, Kerala was clearly a society experiencing multiple challenges to the social, political, and economic oligopoly. British land policy and the quickening pace of commercialization disrupted traditional social relations. The dramatic evolution to market society—what Karl Polanyi called "the great transformation"—generated unprecedented mobility and challenged existing legitimations of status hierarchies. Colonial law and norms simultaneously provided mechanisms for challenges. By way of example, one oppressed caste group demanded with encouragement from missionaries the right for their women to cover their breasts, leading to upper class/caste violence in recognition that significations of social inferiority were central to maintenance of social control. Newly aggressive participants in the commercial economy, such as Christians, disrupted the traditional monopoly of land control. Downward mobility of previously dominant castes such as the Nairs led to both internal caste reform and radicalization of younger scions of ruined families. Caste reform movements among such "untouchable" groups as Iravas focused on access to new avenues for mobility such as government, schools, and jobs. Responses to social turmoil introduced by colonial domination and expanding market forces produced not only sporadic protest and organization, but also took the form of both caste reform and rejection of caste with a new (and socially radical) rationalist outlook.[4]

Added to the generalized social ferment was the introduction of the independence movement as a political force. The Left activists who eventually founded the Communist party in Kerala were recruited into active politics by idealists organizing against colonial rule, inspired by Mahatma Gandhi. Agrarian issues figured prominently in the origins of splits between Left and Right in the umbrella Indian National Congress, beginning in the 1920s. The split was both tactical and ideological. Significantly, one of the leaders of the Left faction in Congress was E. M. S. Namboodiripad, who began his reformist and increasingly radical political role in the movement to reform his own caste of Brahmins. The Right faction was socially tied to traditionally dominant groups in Kerala society and adopted a Gandhian view of both tactics and substantive ideology. Tactically, violence, or any form of divisive class confrontation, was unacceptable. Substantively, the Right promoted Gandhian notions of trusteeship in which moral suasion was to substitute for redistribution by changing the values of elites in the direction of paternalistic concern for the poor.

The early Congress in Kerala fused the issues of social reform, of which caste disabilities formed the most important component, and demands for self-rule and social justice. An indigenous radicalized intelligentsia was central to this process. Organizationally, despite the ambivalence of the Gandhians, encouragement was given to the growing formation of local groups of workers, peasants, women, and students. Reflecting on his own experience, Namboodiripad noted: "It is the combination in one person of the office bearer of the Village Congress Committee, the leader of the Teachers' Union, and the organizer of the Kisan Sangham [peasant association] that made the anti-imperialist movement strike deep roots in the countryside."

To illustrate the fusion of issues and the dispute over tactics in the umbrella Congress, we may note that earliest agitations were for temple entry for "untouchables," in which Gandhi, in a familiar pattern, called off agitations, which threatened to evoke confrontation. Young radicals in the Congress rejected not only Gandhian ideals of moral suasion to redress exploitation, but also the tactical constraints placed on their activities by Gandhian ideology. Leftist tactics, organizational strength, and ideology were in an important sense forged in the battle for control of the independence movement.

By the 1930s, the Left within the Congress had grown much stronger than the Right, primarily because of its championing of local organizations and militant attacks on social injustice. The result was formation of a powerful separate organization within the Congress: the Congress Socialist Party. The Socialists controlled the organizational structure of the Congress and by 1940 felt strong enough to declare themselves a local unit of the Communist Party of India (CPI). They had captured the core of the mass political energy unleashed by the Congress, most importantly its carefully nurtured organizational units at the local level. The peasant association established local branches and organized through such tactics as forming village defense committees, physically opposing evictions, creating study groups and reading rooms, and sponsoring popular dramas with such telling titles as "Arrears of Rent" and "Drinking of Blood."

After a brief experimentation with insurrectionary tactics in the immediate postindependence period, the CPI settled into electoral politics with a platform that basically held that the extraordinary reformist promises of the national Congress party could be implemented only by the Communists, as Congress was too committed to power brokers of the old society to move toward the new. In this they proved prophetic. The first Communist electoral victory in 1957 demonstrated not only the popular belief that the CPI stood for the oppressed majority, but also the astuteness of the party in exploiting Congress failures to govern effectively or to deliver on the promises of independence.

Unlike the situation in many parts of India, there existed in Kerala soon after independence a clear alternative to a floundering Congress, well organized and connected to the people in virtually every village and neighborhood in the state. The dismissal of the state's Communist ministry by Nehru in 1959 simply confirmed the popular belief that the Congress was the enemy of redistribution, as the government's land reform modeled on official Congress guidelines was thus rendered infructuous. The following elections showed the CPI with a million more votes than in 1957 and furthered both polarization and leftist mobilization in the countryside, which eventually culminated in the land reforms of the 1970s.

The brief sketch above is not meant to summarize the history of Kerala, but to make several points about the origins of agrarian mobilization, which enabled the reforms to be discussed below to occur. A structural niche and history of agrarian radicalism had been established prior to organized leftist politics by colonial land policy and colonial failures to respond to agrarian distress. The disruptions of extensive commercialization unleashed social forces of various kinds, cumulatively destabilizing the status quo. A Left faction within the independence movement rejected Gandhian politics, which dominated India in the period, and won sufficient social support to split from the Congress and establish a viable leftist alternative. The structure of extortionate landlordism provided a mechanism for mobilizing the agrarian poor: the massive quantity of rent collected by a rentier class with no economic functions. Finally, early Congress failures to govern in the state after independence created a specifically political niche for an alternative party to make a credible appeal to voters. The first Communist ministry demonstrated concretely that they alone would press for an overturn of the agrarian system and that the Congress was the implacable foe of policies embedded in their own legitimating promises. It was this history that produced the land reforms that finally effected the abolition of absentee landlordism in the 1970s.

Implementation on the Ground

Coming into effect on January 1, 1970, the Kerala reforms abolished the landlord-tenant system completely, along with the institution of ground rent. In theory, all cultivators were to be owners and there could be no ownership without cultivation. These provisions constituted the claim to establishing "land to the tiller" so often proclaimed as a goal nationally. In addition, the lowest ceiling in the region was established on nontenanted land, at five standard acres (or roughly 2.4–3 hectares) per adult, with a ceiling of 20 ordinary acres (about 8 hectares) for a very large family. The ceiling itself netted very little land for redistribution (about 65,000 hectares, or less than 3 percent of operated area), as landowners had seen it coming for decades and had subdivided holdings within extended families or sold surplus land (a not insignificant redistributive by-product of land reform, although one limited to farmers with surplus cash).

The ceiling obviously would have been far more effective had the first Communist ministry been allowed to implement its 1959 land reform, but dismissal by Delhi thwarted implementation and gave owners more than another decade to rearrange their holdings. The core of the reform was thus the abolition of tenancy, vesting land in the cultivators, affecting about 43 percent of the nonplantation land in the state. Tenants constituted about 43 percent of the families with interests in land, or about 1.3 million families.

At the time of the ceiling legislation, it was understood that few families could be established as farmers by redistributing the surplus. Availability of land per person engaged in agriculture stood at 0.42 hectares, by far the lowest in India. Because little land could be expected for distribution, landless laborers were not centrally included as beneficiaries of the land reforms per se. An exception was the special provision for house and garden sites for a special category of attached laborers known as *kudikidappukars* (about 12 percent of the families with interests in land on the eve of the reforms). These sites were tiny, usually less than 0.04 hectares, and were granted to only a minority of agricultural workers (271,080 of about 2.2 million). Nevertheless, the plots have proved nutritionally and economically important; kitchen gardens and commercial crops (such as coconuts, pepper, and turmeric) have added to the important security benefits of land ownership. Second, more land has been distributed to landless families from state properties (184,615 hectares as of 1988) than from the ceiling provisions. Surplus land from the ceiling (independent of *kudikidappu* plots) was distributed in small parcels averaging 0.26 hectares and typically was of low productivity. Some laborers also benefited from the tenancy provisions because the categories of laborer and tenant overlapped considerably on the ground; because the majority of all tenants cultivated less than 0.4 hectares, the major source of income for many tenants was agricultural labor.

Implementation of the ceiling provisions and house-garden plots for attached laborers was a struggle, marked by massive demonstrations, direct action by the landless, administrative bottlenecks, and continuous legislative tinkering to alleviate obstacles. There was some violence, but certainly no more than is the norm in elections in other states in India. An important dynamic in insuring eventual implementation was electoral competition between the two major Communist parties (which had split in 1964 along Left-Right lines). With the right Communists (CPI) leading a coalition government during the 1970s, the left Communists (CPI-M) were the major opposition. Competition between the two parties was a major factor in energizing implementation. It was the left Communists who mobilized the mass energy of the tenantry and landless laborers to pressure the bureaucracy and government at every step along the way. Officials in the land revenue administration were quite candid about the effect: without mass pressure and exposures of fraud and bureaucratic misbehavior, implementation might well have moved in the sluggish and corrupt manner typical of reforms in the region.

Institutional innovations resulting from organized pressure on the ground and in the capital were necessary because of unanticipated lacunae in the legislation, which were exploited by superior lawyers of the landed. The courts proved a major obstacle, gutting key provisions of the law with determined consistency. Amendments and appeals took time; a great deal of land remained tied up in the courts even a decade after the effective date. Moreover, the situation on the ground is always messier than the neat language of law. Mass pressure resulted in legislation to form village committees to speed land-reform implementation, despite opposition from Delhi. These committees were not formed, however, due to complicated reasons of partisan politics and fear of violence. Yet channels for local participation existed before the reforms in the local units of the peasant association and landless laborer unions, and new ones were added in the form of *taluk*-level land boards through amendments to the law.

Mass pressure on the implementation process resulted from conditions that differentiate Kerala from much of the subcontinent and the poor world generally: widespread literacy, effective local organizations of the underclasses, and extensive politicization. Newspapers are extensively and intensively read; malpractices were widely exposed in the press, often resulting in demonstrations at the site for redress. Certainly there were lapses—everyone seems to have a favorite story about some fraud or the other—but the aggregate results are extremely impressive by the standards of land reforms and administration generally (compared, for example, to the U.S. Internal Revenue Service, to use a homey example). Careful analysis of the ceiling implementation indicates that the small yield is almost exactly what one would expect on the basis of prereform data on the size distribution of holdings. None of this could have been achieved without militancy of class-based organizations with firsthand knowledge of local situations and physical presence on the ground.

In contrast to the difficulties in implementing the ceiling and hut-garden site provisions, tenancy was abolished with comparative ease.

On the effective date of the reform, January 1, 1970 (which resulted in a derisive term for former tenants as "1-1-70s"), the landlords' titles became null and void. Tenants no longer had to pay rent, and had little incentive for the case to be settled formally, because settlement and conferring of title meant the beginning of compensation payments. Eviction was obviously difficult in the highly politicized atmosphere; local units of the peasant association and party were generally available to at least mitigate attempts at coercion. Arrears of rent, which were considerable, were scaled down dramatically by law; any tenant with less than two hectares was liable for no more than one year's rent, regardless of the size of his debt. Landlords, on the other hand, had strong incentives to comply with the reform in order to begin receiving compensation. Some cut deals with tenants, fearing that government compensation would never come. The effectiveness of the tenancy legislation was thus a function of the local political situation, which usually favored tenants, as well as the rigor of the law.

Tenancy provisions did not make any distinctions among size categories, but rather assumed that all tenants were equally deserving of rehabilitation. On equity grounds, one could argue for a lower ceiling limit for large tenants (who in practice were subject to the same retention ceiling as landowners). Some tenants were relatively large operators by Kerala standards. Official data do not permit disaggregation by size of holding (as "cases" are the operative accounting units, and many tenancies consisted of plots rented from different landowners, each of which is a case legally). Nevertheless, calculations from a representative sample survey of the whole state suggest considerable concentration of benefits in the larger size categories of tenants; holders of more than two hectares received about 64 percent of the redistributed tenanted land. It was this class of "large" tenants that aroused some anger among laborers who received no land at all. In international terms, a two-hectare holder hardly seems privileged; in rural Kerala, more than two-thirds of all holdings are smaller than this threshold, and the figure is much higher in the nonplantation sector.

To assess the effects of these reforms on the ground, I conducted studies in 1979–1980, 1983, and (briefly) 1989 in two villages in Palghat district, where the alteration of agrarian structure had been especially dramatic. In my randomly selected samples, there were no instances of what one could call a rentier relationship. All cultivators (in the legal sense of farmers who paid for inputs for production) were indeed owners and there were no rental payments, although there were instances outside my samples of what one might term frictional tenancy—short-term arrangements among farmers to rationalize cultivation. But even cases of frictional tenancy were extremely rare. Everyone recognized the force of the law; when owners were asked about being tempted to rent land out, they cited the law and then a Malayalam proverb to the effect that it is best not to allow someone to sleep on your veranda because he may claim occupancy in court the next day. About two-thirds of the farmers in these samples were previous tenants who had gained land through the reforms. All had experienced dramatic improvements in income and, more importantly, in economic security and opportunity.

The effects of the separate program of ceiling implementation in these villages were mixed. Owners indeed lost land above the ceiling, but the redistribution of land exhibited a familiar pattern: beneficiaries received tiny, sub-subsistence parcels, often of land that was unproductive and difficult to improve without capital (which they lacked). There is a difficult normative and political question of rationing here. With a given amount of surplus land, does one try to spread it as widely as possible on equity grounds, or provide subsistence holdings to a much smaller number? The answer of politicians seeking patronage networks is clear: maximize beneficiaries. Yet it is possible that this is indeed the fairest solution because even tiny plots give workers some sense of dignity and security and provide some opportunity. Moreover, most recipients were of the most depressed social groups and thus were most in need of security and the minimal status of minimal landownership. The problem of limited spread of benefits lay less in implementation (as is typically the case in the region) than in legislative compromises and, of course, in demographics; Kerala has by far the highest person-to-land ratio in India.

A far more vigorous effort to offer credit and extension services to beneficiaries of surplus land would have improved the equity and productivity effects of reform. One plausible explanation for the lack of effective pressure to produce these results locally is the bitterness felt by the vast majority of laborers who received no land at all; their local organizations would be the logical conduit for demands for better treatment of beneficiaries, but there was some backlash resentment felt against the fortunate few. I was told repeatedly (with some bitterness) that only untouchables benefited from surplus land distribution; although this was not strictly true, priority was given to the most depressed social groups in redistribution. It is also true that the political channels for expression of lower-class needs have been far more attuned to welfare policy than to production. Moreover, Kerala faces extraordinary fiscal constraints; it is already the most heavily taxed state in India and incurs anomalously high costs for social welfare expenditures.

To the extent that the reforms failed to establish an even more just society, the fault lies more in political compromises in conceptualization and legislation than in implementation. The decision to exempt plantation crops from the ceiling on grounds of economies of scale, although consistent with directives from Delhi, severely limited the impact of the ceiling. The major plantation crops are tea, coffee, and rubber, covering 448,095 hectares, or 20.3 percent of net cultivated area (in 1987). The definition of plantation in the legislation concerns not organization of production, but simply crops grown.

It is not clear what more could have been done with the ceiling in a federal system that significantly constrains state-level powers, but this compromise precluded the possibility of testing the limits of the national political system. Besides the perceived constraint from Delhi, there was an internal consideration in exempting plantations. In Marxist logic, the first priority in Kerala's concrete historical situation was eradication of the vestiges of feudalism in the form of functionless rentiers. Capitalists were not the target, and indeed the objective of reform was in part to inject capitalist dynamism into agriculture. I spoke in 1989 with the chief minister who presided over implementation and an economist appointed by him to investigate the issue; the government's position was that economic logic argued against carving up the plantations, and, more politically telling, that unions on the plantations were opposed to dividing the land for individual plots, favoring nationalization instead. Like most people in Kerala, plantation workers would understandably rather be government servants than farmers.

More important than the exclusion of plantation crops from redistribution was the decision on how to define beneficiaries on tenanted land. The decision to define tillers as those who undertook the "risk of cultivation" (operationally defined by advancing cash costs of production) rather than those who actually sowed, plowed, and harvested excluded the field laborers from the major redistribution (beyond the important provisions for house and garden sites for a section of the agrarian proletariat). This conceptualization of exactly who were the tillers is curious, because it clearly opened the possibility for a split in the agrarian Left between the rural working class and tenants who hired labor. It also reflects a decidedly non-Marxian view of the real contributions to production, privileging extension of capital (accepting the "risk of cultivation") over the criterion of provision of labor. This curious conceptualization had clear political-tactical roots, as tenants were the core of the local leadership cadres, but it contributed to the fracturing of leftist unity after the land reforms. An alternative formulation favoring workers over tenants would also have strained the credibility of a party that had promised land to the tenants for decades. Nevertheless, agrarian politics after the reforms have been complicated for the Left by a new rupture in an effective class coalition.

The conflict between labor and farmers is more severe in Kerala than in India generally; even very small holdings tend to hire in a great deal of labor. In paddy production, about 92 percent of farm labor is hired; the variation across size groups is small: 91 percent in holdings less than four-tenths of a hectare, 97 percent in those more than two hectares. Similar, but less extreme, patterns hold in other major crops. The romanticized self-sufficient family farm is not much in evidence. Holdings are concentrated at the bottom end, increasingly so over time, with subdivisions from inheritance. The top end of the distribution is dominated by plantation crops. Holdings of less than one hectare constituted 91.5 percent of all holdings in the 1985–1986 agricultural census results, but covered only 46.1 percent of the land. Holdings larger than ten hectares (mostly in plantation crops exempt from the ceiling) constituted 1.7 percent of holdings, but 9.6 percent of the land area. Agriculturalists whose primary source of income is field labor are two-thirds of the agricultural work force; many of these families are technically not landless, but fall at the extreme bottom of the holding distribution: 9.4 percent of the holdings are less than two-tenths of a hectare. Given this postreform structure, it was perhaps inevitable that the next stage of agrarian conflict would be land versus labor.

Winners and Losers: New Class Conflicts

All too often, land reforms are presented with a solution mystique: the resolution of agrarian crisis. In fact, reforms are part of a process. Reforms in Kerala resolved one class contradiction—that between landlords and tenants—but aggravated another—that between newly landed cultivators and field laborers. In the long mobilization of the rural poor along leftist lines, the slogan "death to landlordism" was joined by "cultivators and agricultural laborers are one." The clear message was that tenants would get the land, but would share their gains with the laborers, who are not only the largest class in the state, but also were the shock troops in the costly struggle to abolish landlordism. Laborers recognized that breaking the power of the landlords was crucial for their political and social liberation. But they also understood the leftist program as a promise of material benefits as well.

On the ground, I found that laborers were quite bitter about both the political and economic outcomes of the reforms. Most laborers felt that they had not gained from the reforms in any way. They also felt that some tenants, especially the larger ones, had deserted the party after getting what they wanted. The best formulation was "as soon as they got the *pattaya* [deed], they put on the *khadi* [handspun cloth symbolic of the Congress party]." When asked whether the tenants at least invested in production with their windfall wealth, as theory suggests, and thus indirectly shared their gains through provision of more employment, laborers responded with a long list of examples of conspicuous consumption by former tenants: enrollment of children in private schools, tiled roofs, synthetic shirts, wristwatches, and the like. A local quasi pun ran: "the *kudiyaans* [tenants] have become *kudiyans* [drunkards]." The summary comment about what the tenants did with the surplus was "they ate it."[5] This perception is not entirely accurate, as tenants in my samples were somewhat more likely to have made investments on the land than were farmers who did not gain new rights in land, but the gist of their comments remains valid: a fairly accurate predictor of whether or not one was approaching a newly landed tenant's household was whether or not obvious new consumption was visible—new tiles on the roof, a motorcycle, and the like.

The response of field workers to this state of affairs was a series of quite militant strikes in the early 1970s. The conflict highlighted the sense in which former tenants were seen as Marshallian maximizers, cutting labor costs and resisting wage increases whenever possible. The laborers had a clear alternative view of the moral economy of paddy production: the wage should be high enough to provide a decent standard of living given the average number of days of employment. They needed, by their calculations, either double the wage or twice the number of days of work (which averaged under 100 days per year in my sample, and somewhat more for the state as a whole).

Labor militancy prompted new agrarian legislation, a truly remarkable piece of law entitled the Kerala Agricultural Workers Act (KAWA) of 1974. The KAWA mandated a workday reduced from twelve or more hours to eight hours (less for plowing), tea and lunch breaks, a minimum wage, permanent reconciliation machinery, a Provident Fund to which farmers had to contribute, and, most significantly, permanency of employment for attached laborers. The CPI-M, having recognized the tactical error of supporting worker militancy, which alienated farmers from the Left, supported the KAWA as providing security for workers and an institutional framework for localized corporatism as an alternative to class struggle. Representatives of the state, farmers, and laborer unions were joined in local committees to resolve disputes before they reached the level of class conflict and violence, which had characterized the immediate postreform years.

Farmers were infuriated by the KAWA. New "peasant associations" grew up to press the farmers' demand that subsidies of input costs and raising of producer prices should compensate for the losses entailed in higher wages and a shorter work day. Hired labor constitutes about half the cost of production locally and is a critical determinant of farm profit. Challenges to the KAWA on the ground and in the courts produced violent confrontations. More than prices and profits were at stake—the permanency provisions of the act effectively removed control of the labor process from cultivators. They could no longer threaten anyone with dismissal, and rulings of the Industrial Relations Committee over time specified constraints on bringing in laborers from cheaper labor pools in the neighboring state, using family labor at harvest, selling land, and deciding the number of workers to be used for specific operations. Wages were not only sticky downward, despite the wide fluctuations in paddy prices, but legally stuck; prevailing wages legally became the minimum wage in a ratchet effect that frightened farmers.

If we think of land not as a physical patch of soil, but as a socially constituted "bundle of rights," the Kerala reforms have gone beyond the tenancy reforms of West Bengal and most other parts of India in transferring the entire bundle we call ownership to tenants at the expense of landlords. The landlords were clear losers; many lost hundreds of hectares and were reduced to destitution. (Compensation, paid by tenants through the government, was fixed at a level of sixteen times one-half the contract rent but has been slow in coming and eroded by inflation. The government has had difficulties recovering costs of compensation from tenants and has now formally assumed the burden from general revenues.) Locally, people speak of Brahmin women reduced to prostitution (a particularly poignant theme of long standing). Precisely because a large section of the landlord class were pure rentiers, the blow to income and wealth was extreme. Of course many others were quite diversified; one landlord in my sample astonished me by mentioning that his son was a doctor in Chicago.

But beyond that significant transfer to tenants, sections of the bundle of rights have been further transferred to the laborers, but only enough to irritate farmers and not enough to ensure a locally defined decent standard of living. This process has gone so far that a solatium is now widely recognized as due the permanent laborers when land is sold, the amount being a function of years of service, value of the land, and relative bargaining power of the parties. Despite these significant gains, continued implementation of the KAWA remains dependent on the militancy of local organizations and the priority placed on enforcement by the government; there are significant variations not only across districts, but also across villages, reflecting the historically uneven development of organization.

Further redistribution of the bundle of rights is uncertain. Many laborers and owners believed that "just as the tenants got the land from the landlords, the laborers will eventually get the land from the tenants, for they are the real tillers of the soil." Electoral politics and coalition strategies suggest otherwise. The fragmentation of the leftist alliance in rural areas was initiated by the land reforms; subsequent struggles over control of the labor process and distribution of the surplus have deepened that fracture. There is a division here between local and state-level politics. In Kerala, laborers outnumber cultivators by more than two to one, whereas in India generally cultivators outnumber agricultural workers by about 60 percent. Thus, at the local level organized laborers can exercise significant power. Yet, at the state level agricultural laborers in Kerala make up only 28 percent of all workers, precisely because the secondary and tertiary sectors in Kerala are proportionately so much larger than in India generally, due to the long and intensive commercialization of the economy of the state.

The Communists try to maintain a fragile agrarian unity by damping class conflicts and pressing instead sectoral claims in a neocorporatist manner—enlarging the pie by making demands on the center in Delhi for price supports, input subsidies, and investment. That has long been the strategy of conservative parties. Their problem is that Kerala has an extensive and relatively effective program for food subsidies. In a society of very poor and politicized people, higher producer prices (which encourage investment and make the farmer section of the coalition happy) mean either increased malnutrition or, more likely in Kerala, higher costs for public food programs. Yet Kerala is already the most heavily taxed state in India, and its fiscal dependence on Delhi limits options. The only unique political claim the Communists can now make is that they are more sincere than others in their commitment to the poor and that they are less corrupt in implementing strategies other parties claim to support. These seem to be the primary grounds for their continued electoral success, but it is a precarious hold on the electorate.

What Has Been Accomplished?

Critics of the Communist reforms, both in the villages and in the intelligentsia, claim that nothing very revolutionary has been accomplished. Local people sometimes say that the old *jenmis* (landlords) have been replaced by new *jenmis* who are more arrogant and tightfisted than the old. Socially, this latter critique is a familiar objection to a newly rich stratum putting on airs. But the social and economic transformations were profound. The Brahmins of Palghat district have been transformed from "gods on earth" to petitioners before the assembly for relief as a "depressed class."

The derogatory use of the term *jenmi* for the former tenants is a conceptual distortion rooted in historical amnesia. The new *jenmis* are nothing more nor less than petty capitalist farmers maximizing profits. Their power vis-à-vis labor is the power of capital, not of abject dependence, diadic authority, and social oppression. The obvious parasitism of the rentiers (some of whom stated flatly to me that they did not even know exactly which fields they had owned) is not matched by the newly landed proprietors, who know agriculture and organize production. Their perceived arrogance is not complemented by control of the police and social dominance. Simultaneously, their organization of production is calculating and lacks the aura of paternalism of the old landlords. Their greatest vulnerability in ideological terms is that laborers do not recognize their contribution to production; when I asked laborers what percentage of output could be attributed to the farmers, most felt little, and many said none: "they are only standing on the *varambu* [bund, embankment] with an umbrella." Positions on social justice in the Communist party are not so radical; the party seeks a kinder and gentler capitalism, not a distribution system based on the labor theory of value.

With some historical perspective, the land reforms represent a profound transformation of social structure, albeit one that is no more nor less than an agrarian bourgeois revolution. The Communists have been the mechanism for abolition of a social system with distinct residues of what may appropriately be called feudalism. Laborers remain largely dependent on others for access to the means of production, but agrestic slavery, serfdom, acute social humiliation, and oppression have been obliterated or dramatically reduced by social processes of which the land reforms were a central part. As one large-scale farmer said: "We used to beat them for being late to work; now they beat us for complaining when they are late."

The same organizational development that permitted the abolition of landlordism as a social system now protects the most basic interests of Kerala's largest and most depressed class. Compared to the rest of India, these are remarkable gains, although they fall short of abolishing poverty and associated malnutrition and ill health. Where else in the subcontinent do field laborers have legally mandated permanency of employment and assured old-age pensions (inadequate by the standards of rich nations though these may be)? The extraordinary record on basic indicators of human needs in the state, referred to previously, is not the direct result of land reform, but, like land reform, reflects the sense in which Kerala's unusual degree of social mobilization and political activism sets it apart from the experience of underdevelopment characteristic of the region and of most societies with low incomes.

Among the many critiques that one could make of the reforms, two address limits that had the greatest impact on redistribution. The exemption of certain crops—whatever their organization of production or efficiency—from the ceiling has already been discussed. Second, given the scarcity of land and employment in Kerala, a more just rationing process would have limited beneficiaries to working farmers. Too much land is held by families that have other primary sources of income: government service, professions, trade. Cultivation on these lands is organized by the owner, but often in a perfunctory supervisory manner; the land is held for security and possible appreciation rather than for maximizing production. There is no way to make an aggregate estimate of the area involved, but it is considerable. It should not be difficult locally to differentiate working farmers from those whose involvement is secondary or tertiary. Daniel Thorner once suggested that a fair and simple test was to look at the hands of the owner.[6]

Beyond the question of beneficiaries, a serious critique of the reforms is that redistribution took precedence over production. The KAWA and accompanying tensions have produced something of a stalemated class conflict, with neither antagonist possessing sufficient power to resolve the situation on their own terms. Farmers are reluctant to invest because of lower profit margins, have taken marginal land out of production because of wage increases, and sometimes leave land fallow to "teach the workers a lesson." Strikes and lockouts have increasingly disrupted production. In 1965–1966, there were 50 registered agrarian workers' unions outside the plantation sector, and 37 registered disputes; by 1976–1977, there were 205 unions and 4,279 disputes. Paddy land under production has declined from an index of 100 in 1969–1970 to 78.7 in 1986–1987. Rubber, exempted from the land-reform provisions, has increased in area over the same period from index 100 to 296.4. The index of productivity for all crops over this period has increased by only 7 percent, despite extensive use of new varieties and modern inputs.

From the point of view of the welfare of the most depressed class, the decline in paddy area and production is the most significant of these indicators of agricultural stagnation, for it is in the paddy sector that the agricultural laborers are concentrated. Almost 91 percent of the laborers in my samples reported declining employment opportunities (primarily because of mechanization, changes to less labor-intensive crops such as coconut, labor disputes, and higher wages). For the state as a whole, rural unemployment is now 24.7 percent; underemployment, 14.6 percent. Available days of employment for agricultural laborers declined by 26 percent for males and 30 percent for females between 1963/1964 and 1983/1984. The workings of the market defeat the laborers' strategy of raising wages to compensate for inadequate days of employment, as farmers retain the strategic power to reduce the total wage bill. This stalemated class conflict contributes to both hardships for labor and low rates of growth in output, the former mediated by the state's assumption of some welfare functions previously attributed to landowners (in ideology, less so in practice).

Ironically, the "feudal" pattern of labor control prevalent before the reforms was uniquely suited to hydraulic agriculture, although the pattern of management and investment was not conducive to dynamism. Workers were on call twenty-four hours a day, and would frequently work through the night with torches to save a harvest or redirect excess water that threatened crops. Now, as farmers say (and many laborers agree), "they are only interested in the clock." Control of labor is a serious problem in any economic system; irrigated agriculture employing advanced varieties exhibits the dilemmas in acute form. The stagnation in the paddy sector throughout Kerala, with serious effects on already severe underemployment, is not entirely due to these conflicts (as there remain familiar problems in credit, producer margins, water control, and environmental degradation), but is certainly exacerbated by them. Politically, there is no going back, and the only obvious resolution would be further redistribution to the field laborers, unifying labor and management in family units.

A more politically plausible resolution of ubiquitous land hunger and insufficient employment would be a re-examination of the issue of plantation crops and the rationale for designating that land as a separate sector subject to a different logic of distribution. There is nothing in comparative experience that suggests inevitable inefficiency in small-holder production of tea, coffee, and rubber given sufficient organization of support services and processing facilities. The task would be monumental, and it is not clear that the state's administrative capacity is commensurate with the task. To make a significant impact, large numbers of the poor would have to relocate their families to take up unfamiliar forms of cultivation. Moreover, it remains unclear what position Delhi would take on the threat to foreign exchange earnings entailed in general permission for the states to infringe on plantations.

There is a certain irony in the role of a Communist party in the transformations sketched above. In Marxian theory, abolition of "feudal" relations should "unleash the productive forces" of nascent capitalism. Yet the social process of abolishing landlordism raised new demands for distribution, which divert the state's share of the social surplus away from investment. To take but one example, maintaining the farmers as part of the leftist coalition has meant that the government backed away from the legal requirement that farmers pay into the Provident Fund for laborers; the state picked up the fiscal burden by default. In general, the party has yet to find an accumulationist strategy but remains committed to extensive distribution to alleviate destitution. Capital is hobbled in its social function of driving accumulation by the regulatory and redistributionist commitment to the poor, and yet the state is incapable of assuming that role. As in Communist practice on a world scale, the critical question concerns the role of the market in a social formation that seeks to differentiate itself from market capitalism. To date, the remaining legitimacy of the party in Kerala is based on its redefinition of itself as a social democratic force committed to presiding over a regulated and constrained capitalism. Although no longer revolutionary, that role has certain electoral appeal so long as stagnation does not overwhelm the economy.

This final comment on accumulation does not imply that solutions are easy to come by. Were Kerala a nation-state (which would not be unreasonable in terms of international norms of population and territory), a broader range of options would appear. As it is, the federal structure of political power has allowed Delhi to undermine and block leftist governments in Kerala rather than facilitating their experimentation with solutions to difficult dilemmas.[7] But more than political structure is involved. Kerala is part of a national economy; efforts to rehabilitate the landless, for example, run the risk of inducing capital flight to neighboring states where the minimum wage is one-half that of Kerala and indifferently enforced. Attracting capital to a state where labor is so well organized, protected, and expensive is difficult when labor-intensive rural industries are presently moving operations to neighboring states. Rural unemployment, historically the highest in India, is increasing. The lesson is that although agrarian crisis must be addressed first on the ground, and not relegated to expectations of disappearance of peasant society, resolution of that crisis cannot finally be divorced from broader economic and political forces beyond the reach of peasant associations and their political allies.

Implications

The broad complex of distributive and redistributive measures undertaken in Kerala have effectively abolished a system of absentee landlordism characterized by extreme exploitation and oppression. In the process of breaking the back of landlordism through mobilization of the rural poor, the conditions for genuine participatory democracy and protection of human rights at the local level have been firmly established. Redistribution has not solved the agrarian crisis of underemployment and poverty, but one section of the agrarian underclass has experienced significant gains. Even the laborers who bitterly noted how little they benefited from the reforms had no doubts that the social changes of the last two decades had transformed their lives. The common formulation was "the fear is gone." Paternalism is gone as well, but contrary to the romanticized view of landlords and too many social scientists, paternalism in practice was not effective in guaranteeing human rights, subsistence needs, or dignity.

A necessary condition for these changes was a long and intensive leftist mobilization. The changes were accomplished within the framework of a liberal constitution and through democratic means. These features of social activism and political structure are by no means ubiquitous, particularly in those parts of the world most in need of agrarian reform. There are implications here for the international position of the nation most associated with pressure for land reform globally. If U.S. foreign policy is serious about democracy, human rights, and social justice, it must drop a long-standing attachment to the cold war interpretation of leftist movements in terms of a Manichean geopolitical worldview. Prospects for that enlightenment seem brighter now than at any previous period in my lifetime. In the great uncertainty of development policy, the one certainty is that lack of independent access to the means of production in poor agrarian societies is associated with most of the affronts to human dignity that development is supposed to remove. Land reforms are neither easy nor costless—nor are they a panacea. But it is difficult to find a more direct route to creating some security and opportunity for those whose labor makes it possible for the rest of us to eat.

Notes

1. These points are elaborated in comparative perspective in Ronald J. Herring, *Land to the Tiller: The Political Economy of Agrarian Reform in South Asia* (New Haven, Conn.: Yale University Press, 1983; also published in Delhi by Oxford University Press, 1983). That account treats the historical record and broader developmental context only in passing. For a detailed historical account of the Kerala experience, see P. Radhakrishnan, *Peasant Struggles, Land Reforms, and Social Change: Malabar 1836–1982* (London: Sage, 1989). On development policy more generally in Kerala, see United Nations, Department of Economic and Social Affairs, *Poverty, Unemployment and Development Policy: A Case Study of Selected Issues with Reference to Kerala*

(New York: United Nations, 1975).

2. Data in this chapter are taken primarily from reports of the government of Kerala: *Statistics for Planning, 1988; Selected Indicators of Development, 1989; Economic Review, 1988; Cost of Cultivation of Important Crops, 1985–86; Agricultural Census, 1985–86;* and *Report on the Survey of Unemployment in Kerala, 1987.*

3. The following account can only skim the surface of these issues; for more extensive treatment, see Ronald J. Herring, "Stealing Congress Thunder: The Rise to Power of a Communist Movement in South India," in Kay Lawson and Peter Merkl (eds.), *When Parties Fail* (Princeton, N.J.: Princeton University Press, 1988). On Communist politics in the state generally, and in comparative perspective, see T. J. Nossiter, *Marxist State Governments in India* (London: Pinter, 1988).

4. An excellent elaboration of these points, stressing the disequilibrating effects of the spread of capitalist relations, may be found in K. P. Kannan, *Of Rural Proletarian Struggles* (New Delhi: Oxford University Press, 1988), chapters 1–3. The quotations from E. M. S. Namboodiripad in this section are from his *Kerala: Past, Present and Future* (Calcutta: National Book Agency, 1968), pp. 156, 183. Similar perspectives are voiced in the memoirs of the great peasant leader, A. K. Gopalan, *In the Cause of the People: Reminiscences* (Bombay: Orient Longman, 1973).

5. For details of the village-level work, see Ronald J. Herring, "Dilemmas of Agrarian Communism," *Third World Quarterly* 11, no. 1 (January 1989): 89–115. For further data on distributive consequences, see Ronald J. Herring, "Abolition of Landlordism in Kerala: A Redistribution of Privilege," *Economic and Political Weekly* 15, no. 26 (June 1980): A-59–A-69. For more information on conditions of agricultural laborers, see Government of Kerala, Department of Economics and Statistics, *Report of the Survey on Socio-Economic Conditions of Agricultural and Other Rural Laborers in Kerala* (Trivandrum: Government Press, 1985). Comparative statements on strategy and extent of organization are taken from various issues of All-India Agricultural Workers Union, *Proceedings* of annual conferences.

6. Daniel Thorner, *The Agrarian Prospect in India* (New Delhi: Allied Publishers, 1976; first published in 1956).

7. The most comprehensive account is T. V. Sathyamurthy, *India Since Independence: Studies in the Development of the Power of the State, Volume I, Centre-State Relations: The Case of Kerala* (Delhi: Ajanta, 1985). Also see T. J. Nossiter, *Communism in Kerala* (Berkeley: University of California Press, 1981).

Selected Bibliography

Dhanagare, D. N. *Peasant Movements in India: 1920–1950.* Bombay: Oxford University Press, 1983.

Hart, Henry C., and Ronald J. Herring. "Political Conditions of Land Reform: Kerala and Maharashtra," in Robert E. Frykenberg, *Land Tenure and Peasant in South Asia.* Delhi: Orient Longman, 1977.

Herring, Ronald J. *Land to the Tiller: The Political Economy of Land Reform in*

South Asia. New Haven, Conn.: Yale University Press, 1983.

Herring, Ronald J. "Dilemmas of Agrarian Communism." *Third World Quarterly* 11, no. 1 (January 1989): 89–115.

Kannan, K. P. *Of Rural Proletarian Struggles.* Delhi: Oxford University Press, 1988.

Krishnaji, N. "Agrarian Relations and the Left Movement in Kerala." *Economic and Political Weekly* 13, no. 6–7 (February 1979).

Mencher, Joan P. "Lessons and Non-Lessons of Kerala: Agricultural Laborers and Poverty." *Economic and Political Weekly* 14, no. 9 (June 1979).

Oommen, T. K. *Social Transformation in Rural India.* New Delhi: Vikas, 1984.

Panikkar, K. N. *Against Lord and State: Religion and Peasant Uprisings in Malabar, 1836–1921.* Delhi: Oxford University Press, 1989.

Polanyi, Karl. *The Great Transformation.* New York: Farrer and Rinehart, 1944.

Radhakrishnan, P. *Peasant Struggles, Land Reforms and Social Change: Malabar 1836–1982.* London: Sage, 1989.

Rouyer, A. R. "Political Capacity and the Decline of Fertility in India." *American Political Science Review* 81, no. 2 (June 1987).

Thorner, Daniel. *The Agrarian Prospect in India.* New Delhi: Allied Publishers, 1976. (First published in 1956.)

United Nations, Department of Economic and Social Affairs. *Poverty, Unemployment and Development Policy: A Case Study of Selected Issues with Reference to Kerala.* New York: United Nations, 1975.

chapter three

Bangladesh: A Strategy for Agrarian Reform

F. Tomasson Jannuzi
James T. Peach

Summary

We suggest that the primary impediment to economic progress in Bangladesh is the traditional system of relationships of people to the land. This traditional system of relationships is characterized by a hierarchy of interests in land that not only confirms the distribution of land as a factor of production, but also defines peoples' status and relative power within that hierarchy. We note that the traditional land system of Bangladesh is one in which a dominant minority of landholders have secure rights to land whereas the majority in rural areas have either tenuous rights to land or no land at all. Those having secure rights to land seldom perform labor on it or make investments in its improvement. Instead, they have assigned labor and investment functions to actual tillers, who can be evicted by the superior landholder at will. Within the framework of this system, with ownership and control of land traditionally separated from labor and investment, neither the owner nor the tiller of the soil has a strong incentive to increase productivity.

We outline the historical evolution of the land system of Bangladesh, and assess the most recent attempt, by means of the Land Reforms Ordinance of 1984, to effect change in that system. We conclude that the Ordinance of 1984 is an ineffective means of establishing a land system that would be conducive to sustained economic progress in Bangladesh.

We argue for a particular kind of land reform in Bangladesh: one having the limited objective of conferring secure rights in land to one category of actual tillers—those currently classified as sharecroppers or bargadars. Such a reform would also aim at taking away rights to land from landholders in Bangladesh who do not reside on their land and who do not invest personally in the agricultural production process or perform labor on the land. Finally, we suggest a means by which such an agrarian reform could be implemented—a means we believe to be worthy of the support of external aid agencies.

It is difficult to overstate the poverty of Bangladesh. The average Bangladeshi lives on an annual income of about US$150, and life for most Bangladeshis has been reduced literally to a struggle for subsistence. Surveys of nutrition and caloric intake indicate that the average citizen of Bangladesh simply does not get enough to eat.[1] Yields per acre of Bangladesh's most important crop (rice) remain among the lowest in Asia two decades after the start of technology-driven (Green Revolution) strategies of rural development by which it was hoped that agricultural abundance would be ensured in Bangladesh, as well as in other low-income agrarian societies. And, notwithstanding low yields per acre, even in the late 1980s nearly two-thirds of total employment and half of gross domestic product in Bangladesh are derived from the agricultural sector. By any reasonable measure, it is difficult to argue that Bangladesh has benefited significantly from either the Green Revolution or the export-led industrialization strategies that have reshaped the economies of the newly industrializing countries (NICs) of East Asia, such as South Korea, Hong Kong, Singapore, and Taiwan.

Bangladesh's escape from poverty is made more difficult by rapid population growth, which reinforces predictions of economic stagnation so easily projected within the context of neo-Malthusian arithmetic. Already, in the late 1980s, Bangladesh has 110 million people in a land area about the same size as Wisconsin. Bangladesh's 14.2 million hectares contain just 8.9 million hectares of arable land—about 0.08 hectares per person. Projections by the World Bank and government of Bangladesh suggest that by the year 2000 there will be more than 140 million people in Bangladesh, a figure that would reduce arable land per person to about 0.06 hectares.[2] Based on the simple arithmetic of worsening man-land ratios, it would be easy to conclude that Bangladesh will never be capable of achieving self-sufficiency in food production or exhibit signs of economic progress. But neo-Malthusian scenarios are not inevitable in Bangladesh nor elsewhere.

The technical knowledge needed to increase food (and nonfood) production significantly in Bangladesh already exists. Stated differently, widespread poverty in Bangladesh is not primarily due to a population that has grown too large, a scarcity of natural resources, or the constraints of an unalterable production possibilities frontier. The primary impediment to economic progress in Bangladesh is the traditional system of relationships of people to the land. This traditional system is a hierarchy of interests in land[3]—a hierarchy of interests that not only confirms the distribution of land as a factor of production, but also defines peoples' status and relative power within that hierarchy. This system is one within which those who have secure rights in land (the rough equivalence of ownership in the West) seldom perform labor on it or make investments in its improvement.[4] Instead, they have commonly assigned labor and investment functions to actual tillers (for example, sharecroppers or bargadars) who, because they lack secure rights in land, are bound to be subservient to those who do enjoy such rights. In this complex system, with ownership and control of land separated from labor and investment, neither the landholder, who has secure rights in land, nor the tiller of the soil has a strong incentive to increase agricultural productivity. Within such a system, the primary concern for those who enjoy secure rights in land is to maintain and enlarge on those rights. Maintenance of the existing hierarchy of rights, together with the power and authority confirmed by those rights, becomes at least as critical a part of the political economy of the countryside as concern for what and how much is produced on the available land. Within this system, secure rights in land have always been concentrated in a few hands, and the landless and near-landless have formed a large and growing proportion of the rural population. Finally, within this system and deeply rooted in the history and culture of the region, change in existing conditions is always resisted by those who derive their power from control of land and is, therefore, difficult to promote by those who advocate change—especially change in the distribution of rights to land that would confer authority or power on those who traditionally have been powerless.

In the remainder of this chapter, we will describe and analyze the historical development of the agrarian structure of Bangladesh, various attempts to implement reforms in that structure, our own assessment of what is needed in Bangladesh, and the prospects for meaningful reform. In this process, we draw heavily on our fieldwork in Bangladesh during the late 1970s.[5] And, because of that experience, we write with appreciation of the difficulties that would attend any attempt to alter long-established institutions that define not only rights in land but also the system of human relationships that is at the core of the political economy of the country.

The Historical Development of the Agrarian Structure of Bangladesh

Bangladesh, which literally means land of the Bengalis, contains some of the most fertile deltaic land in the world. Historically, this area was the breadbasket of the Indian subcontinent and, until about fifty years ago, was a net exporter of rice. Yet, as indicated earlier, productivity per acre in contemporary Bangladesh is low by international standards, and Bangladesh has been a net importer of rice (and wheat) since before independence was achieved in 1971.

Many observers have attributed Bangladesh's lack of food-grain self-sufficiency to factors such as population growth, the failure to adopt appropriately modern agricultural technology, government interference with agricultural prices, inadequate financial institutions, or insufficient investment in irrigation facilities. All of the conditions on this list have two things in common. First, at least in principle, they are conditions capable of being addressed by technological means—means, moreover, that already exist. Second, it is commonly assumed that these conditions can be addressed by means that do not require a fundamental restructuring of rights to land. However, even a brief review of the historical evolution of the agrarian structure of Bangladesh provides powerful evidence that Bangladesh's rural development problems cannot be resolved simply by means that are technological, except when those means are complemented by agrarian reforms that alter long-established institutions affecting peoples' access to and rights in land.

In the eighteenth century the British took control of the area that is now Bangladesh. They encountered a confusing hierarchical system of rights in land under which the Western concept of private property in land was not applicable. What existed was a hierarchy of interests in land. Within this hierarchical system of rights in land, ultimate rights in land were vested in the state or ruling authority. Below the state there were gradations of superior and inferior rights of occupancy, as distinct from ownership. Thus, at the base of the agrarian hierarchy, the cultivating peasantry enjoyed what might appropriately be considered today "security of tenure" (i.e., a permanent right of occupancy of lands being tilled by them) rather than ownership of the land in their possession.

This security of tenure, or permanent occupancy right, was in fact conditional on the payment of a share of rents in the form of land revenue to zamindars who had been granted the power by Mogul authorities to act as their agents in the countryside. The zamindars therefore were overlords who acted as intermediaries between the actual tillers and the ruling authority or state. Not even zamindars had the privilege of Western-style ownership of land. No less than the cultivating peasantry, their rights were conditional and qualified, and subordinate to those of the state or super-landlord. However, their rights as intermediaries in the collection of land revenue for those who ruled gave them de facto control over vast estates and the people who inhabited them.

The British did not understand the system that was operative within the region into which they had intervened. In particular, they assumed that the zamindars were in fact landowners not unlike their presumed counterparts in Britain. This erroneous assumption that revenue collectors were in fact landowners as much tied to the land as cultivating peasants led to decisions whose effects condition the political economy of Bangladesh to the present day. Thus, when the British implemented the Permanent Settlement of 1793, which applied to much of East India including contemporary Bangladesh, the actual cultivators in the area were mistakenly classified as "tenants" of the zamindars, rather than as tillers having secure rights to land in their cultivating possession. Within the context of the Permanent Settlement, the zamindars were now free to set their own terms of tenancy with their tenants. The zamindars' only obligation to higher authority was to transfer to government a rental share (designated as land revenue) fixed in perpetuity by the Permanent Settlement. The amount the tenant had to pay the zamindar was not fixed—a provision of the settlement that opened the door to legal and illegal exactions associated rightly in time with the "rack-renting" of the cultivating peasantry by the zamindars. The Permanent Settlement also gave the zamindars the legal authority to transfer their rights to others and to divide their lands without the permission of the British East India Company, and later the state.

The British eventually recognized the fact that local practice prior to the Permanent Settlement did not confer absolute property rights on anyone. As earlier noted, the traditional system was one emphasizing only a hierarchy of interests in land or rights to land. Accordingly, in the aftermath of the Permanent Settlement, the British periodically attempted to restore certain rights to cultivating peasants, now classified legally as tenants of the zamindars, and to restrict the rights of the zamindars. Such efforts were less than successful. In 1859, for example, the British granted permanent occupancy rights to cultivators who had tilled the same land for a period of twelve years or more. Enforcement of this and other attempts to improve the lot of the cultivators was weak, and the power of the zamindars continued to increase.

The major British attempt to reform this system was the Bengal Tenancy Act of 1885, which, as amended periodically, remained legally operative until 1950. The most important feature of the Act of 1885 was that it gave de jure recognition to the rights in land of some, if not all, tillers of the soil. The act thereby restricted, in principle if not in practice, the authority and prerogatives of the zamindars. Further, the 1885 act established the basis for all subsequent legislation designed to affect rights in land in the region. Indeed, the system of rights in land in contemporary Bangladesh was largely shaped by this legislation.

The 1885 act established a system in which the state (at that time, the provincial government of Bengal) held the most significant land rights—rights equivalent to those of a "super landlord." Below the state in the hierarchy of rights were those with the authority to act on behalf of the state as revenue-collecting agents. Beneath these revenue collectors were various categories of tenants who were rent payers with specified conditional rights in land. For example, tenants who were legally classified as "occupancy raiyats" were persons who had acquired from a rent-collecting intermediary or zamindar a right to hold land for the purpose of cultivating it themselves or with the labor of family members, hired servants, sharecroppers, or wage laborers. Such occupancy raiyats had permanent, but conditional, rights in land. They could be evicted from the land by revenue-collecting zamindars for a failure to pay rent due or for other reasons, real or imagined, as determined by the zamindars.

Far below the rent-paying raiyats were additional categories of actual tillers (classified as sharecroppers and wage-laborers) who had either extremely limited or no rights to the lands they tilled. Thus, for example, within the terms of the act, a sharecropper had no permanent right to lands tilled by him, but could acquire such rights if he were somehow permitted to till the same land for twelve consecutive years and could prove this in a court of law.

Meanwhile, nothing in the Act of 1885 provided the legal means by which a wage-laborer could hope to acquire a permanent right to lands tilled by him. In essence, the 1885 act, even as it sought to clarify the status of some in the agrarian hierarchy whose rights to land had been uncertain or tenuous, reconfirmed the superior rights of a landholding elite whose primary function was to collect revenue for the state. The act helped to institutionalize a system in which there was a fundamental dichotomy between rent receivers who were not directly involved in tilling the soil and various categories of actual cultivators. This dichotomy persists in the agrarian structure to the present day in Bangladesh and is a primary obstacle to increasing agricultural productivity in the region.

The next major legislation concerning rights to land in Bangladesh was the East Bengal State Acquisition and Tenancy Act of 1950, which repealed the Bengal Tenancy Act of 1885. In fact, although the 1950 act has often been referred to as landmark legislation, it did not alter significantly the historical land system. A basic purpose of the 1950 act was to abolish the right of rent receivers to act as agents of the state in the collection of land revenue. This purpose was accomplished. Under the new law, the state would collect land revenue directly, without the assistance of traditional intermediaries. However, zamindars and other rent-collecting intermediaries were not abolished, as has often been suggested. These rent-collecting intermediaries, now classified by the 1950 act as maliks (landholding tenants of the state), retained permanent occupancy rights to the bulk of their landholdings together with the right to have others cultivate those holdings. Moreover, the 1950 act did virtually nothing to encourage the new maliks to become active participants in the agricultural production process. As before, they remained for the most part divorced from either investment or labor on lands over which they continued to exercise their right of permanent occupancy.

Nor did the act confer significant new rights to sharecroppers or agricultural laborers. Indeed, the 1950 act eliminated provisions of the 1885 act that enabled sharecroppers and others, in principle if not in practice, to obtain permanent occupancy rights to land that they had tilled for a specified number of years. In fact, the share of produce paid to a landholder (malik) enjoying a right of permanent occupancy by a sharecropper was not even considered rent under the new act. With the share no longer regarded as rent, the share contract under the new law was not regarded as a contract. Thus, with the 1950 act, the sharecroppers lost whatever minimum protection against abuse could have been claimed previously from the courts within the provisions of the 1885 act.

The 1950 act remained the basic land legislation in Bangladesh even after independence from Pakistan in 1971. The government did, however, modify some provisions of the 1950 legislation in 1972 and again in 1976. This was in the context of attempts to set ceilings on the size of landholdings. In particular, landholdings of twenty-five standard bighas (3.4 hectares) or less were exempt from payment of land revenue, and the ceiling on the maximum size of landholdings was reduced from 375 standard bighas (about 50 hectares) to 100 standard bighas (13.5 hectares). Further, landholders were given the right to reacquire lands sold in distress following the 1974 floods.

None of these postindependence changes altered the basic land system in any fundamental way. In contemporary Bangladesh, those who have secure rights to land (generally classified as maliks within existing law) remain dominant in the countryside. Land is concentrated in their hands. (Adequate time series data describing whether or not the concentration of landholdings has increased over time simply do not exist.) The 1978 Land Occupancy Survey (see Table 3.1) indicated that 11.6 percent of rural households (those with farms of more than four acres) "owned" approximately 56.3 percent of all land and the top 25.4

percent of households (those with farms of more than two acres) "owned" almost 78.9 percent of all land.[6] The 1978 survey did not include an attempt to identify urban absentee landholders having ownership-like rights to land, and in all likelihood provides an underestimate of the concentration of landholdings. Moreover, notwithstanding laws enacted to place ceilings on the size of landholdings, little land has been redistributed; landholders have exercised every means, including fictitious transfers of land, to thwart attempts to limit the size of holdings by means of ceilings legislation.

These conditions set the stage for The Land Reforms Ordinance of 1984. The provisions of this ordinance will be discussed in some detail below. Before doing so, however, we shall (1) review tenancy arrangements as these apply to Bangladesh, (2) make some observations about the landless and near-landless in Bangladesh, and (3) set forth a common argument against land reform in Bangladesh.

Table 3.1   Size Distribution of Total Owned Land[a] in Rural Bangladesh

Number of Acres[b]	Number of Households	Percent of Total	Area (Acres)	Percent of Total
Zero	1,767,334	14.69		
0.01-1.00	5,375,887	44.68	1,733,223	8.33
1.01-2.00	1,830,170	15.21	2,660,128	12.78
2.01-3.00	1,045,072	8.69	2,556,850	12.28
3.01-4.00	621,105	5.16	2,141,713	10.29
4.01-5.00	370,799	3.08	1,651,046	7.93
5.01-6.00	253,414	2.11	1,375,463	6.61
6.01-7.00	173,661	1.44	1,123,908	5.40
7.01-8.00	110,825	0.92	827,971	3.98
8.01-9.00	94,944	0.79	803,505	3.86
9.00-10.00	66,979	0.56	636,690	3.06
10.01-15.00	181,256	1.51	2,166,100	10.42
Over 15.00	95,790	1.16	3,137,282	15.07
Totals	12,031,272	100.00	20,813,879	100.00

Source: F. Tomasson Jannuzi, James T. Peach, and A.K.M. Ghulam Rabbani, "Summary Report of 1978 Land Occupancy Survey of Rural Bangladesh," Dhaka, Bangladesh Bureau of Statistics, 1978.

[a]Total owned land is the sum of all land for which "ownership" is claimed by any member of a household. Thus, total owned land includes homestead land, cultivable land, and any land not currently in use.

[b]The usual land unit measurement in this chapter is the hectare. The data presented above were gathered in terms of local units of measurement such as the bigha and converted to acres. Given the categories listed above in acres, conversion to hectares seems to make little sense.

Tenancy Arrangements

There is a vast theoretical and empirical literature on the effects of tenancy on agricultural output.[7] The tenancy literature contains powerful arguments regarding the relative efficiency of tenant farming versus owner cultivation. The classic argument, perhaps best summarized in Alfred Marshall's famous *Principles of Economics* text,[8] suggests that tenancy arrangements are inherently inefficient compared to owner cultivation of the same or similar land. This argument is based fundamentally on the idea that a tenant has less of an incentive to invest in the land than does an owner-cultivator because the tenant will receive only a portion of the returns from investment. The argument applies to long-term investments such as fences, irrigation facilities, and the like as well as to short-term investments in agricultural inputs such as seed, fertilizer, and labor.

Labor market conditions play a key role in determining whether or not share-tenancy is harmful to agricultural productivity. In areas in which labor is in short supply, tenancy arrangements can be relatively benign. In the U.S. Midwest and in the Jordan Valley, tenants frequently have the upper hand in terms of bargaining power. The resulting tenancy arrangements have not been shown to be harmful to agricultural productivity. In Bangladesh, however, labor is abundant relative to the amount of land; and tenancy arrangements, not surprisingly, reflect the fact that landowners can in general dictate the terms of tenancy. In the case of Bangladesh, therefore, it is not reasonable to assume, as is done in much of the theoretical literature, that landowners and tenants are equal partners who are freely and willingly engaging in a market exchange.

Understanding tenancy arrangements in Bangladesh is made difficult because landholders who have secure ownership-like rights in land (for example, maliks) are classified legally as "tenants" of the state, whereas sharecroppers who till lands in accordance with specific tenancy arrangements are not classified legally as tenants. In addition, an actual cultivator of land may simultaneously till some land over which he exercises an ownership-like right of permanent occupancy, till some land that he has taken in on a tenancy basis as a sharecropper, and give out some of his land held under conditions of permanent occupancy to others on a tenancy basis. In addition, this same cultivator may work for portions of a growing season as a wage-laborer on someone else's landholding or work in a nonagricultural job. The frequently used term "owner-cum-tenant" does not adequately describe such a situation.

The most common form of tenancy arrangement in Bangladesh is share tenancy with the tenant paying for virtually all inputs and sharing 50 percent of the output with the landowner.[9] In some regions of Bangladesh, however, tenancy arrangements include a cash payment in addition to the 50 percent share of output, whereas in other areas (Barisal and Patuakhali, for example) share payments generally exceed

50 percent. Rental arrangements on a cash-only basis are also reported. There is also considerable regional variation in the proportion of land under tenancy.

Traditionally, tenancy arrangements are almost exclusively oral agreements; tenants do not generally have security of tenure; and most tenancy arrangements are for relatively short periods of time.[10] The short duration and tenuousness of share tenancy arrangements, as well as the arrangement with the tenant paying for virtually all inputs and receiving only 50 percent of the output, operate in Bangladesh as an obvious disincentive for sharecroppers to invest in long-term improvements in the land that would enhance its productivity.

The Functionally Landless

In an agrarian society the ownership of land (or at least the right to occupy and cultivate it on a long-term secure basis) is for most of the population an essential element of economic well-being.[11] Those who own land generally have higher incomes than those who do not. Landowners are better fed, better educated, live in better housing, and live healthier and longer lives. They have easier access to credit and are likely to have more power and prestige than the landless (defined to include not only those, such as sharecroppers, who have tenuous rights in land, but also those, such as wage-laborers, who have no rights in land at all). The landless are generally at the bottom of the income distribution. Moreover, the landless are also unlikely to be the direct beneficiaries of development programs designed to increase agricultural productivity. Given their economic vulnerability and powerlessness, it is tempting to make the landless the primary focus of rural development programs, including land reforms that, if implemented, would ensure that they become recipients of land. Yet, given the existing population of Bangladesh, current rates of population growth, and the amount of arable land in the country, it is not feasible to base meaningful agrarian reform on the principle that all who want or need land can have it.

There is no generally accepted definition of a landless individual or a landless household. In previous fieldwork, we have used three definitions. A totally landless household (landless-1) is a rural household that claims to have no permanent right (in other words, no ownership-like right) to any land whatsoever. A different category (landless-2) was assigned to a household that claims ownership of no land other than household land (in other words, the small plot of land on which a modest, mud and thatch family homestead stands). Finally, a functionally landless household is one that claims ownership of less than 0.2 hectares of land excluding household land. We prefer the latter definition because, even in a nation of small and fragmented holdings, such a small holding is unlikely to be a viable economic unit. Such functionally landless households in rural Bangladesh comprise at least 50 percent of all rural households, and the proportion of functionally landless households is increasing.

The Argument Against Redistributive Land Reform in the Context of the Current and Projected Population of Bangladesh

High population density and high population growth rates in combination with a fixed supply of land form the basis of most arguments against land reform in Bangladesh.[12] The argument is obvious: There is simply not enough land that could be made available, whatever the schema for redistribution, to provide landholdings for a significant portion of the population. Additionally, a meaningful, redistributive land reform would disrupt current agricultural production. Superficially, these are compelling arguments—useful in deflating the views of proponents of land reform who focus only on the provision of viable landholdings to all of the functionally landless households of Bangladesh. However, such arguments seldom make adequate distinctions among different conceptions of land reform and agrarian reform. In fact, even if the case for a comprehensive, redistributive land reform is weakened in the context of contemporary Bangladesh, given the current man-to-land ratio, there are solid arguments that can be made for another kind of land reform that could be subsumed within a strategy for agrarian reform. We shall return to this theme in the final section of this chapter.

As noted above, Bangladesh's development prospects, with or without land reform, are constrained by rapid population growth. Bangladesh is the eighth most populous nation in the world, as well as one of the world's most densely populated nations. Using 1981 census data, the population density in Bangladesh was 4,155 persons per square kilometer. Using a 1989 Government of Bangladesh estimate of 109.5 million persons, population density is 5,155 per square kilometer. In order to place such figures in perspective, if one assumed that the 5.1 billion people of the world were all residents of the continental United States, the population density of the continental United States would be 4,373 per square kilometer.

It is not only the size of Bangladesh's population, relative to available land, that constitutes an obstacle to economic progress. The age and sex distribution of the population of Bangladesh (Table 3.2 and Figure 3.1) exhibits the bottom-heavy pattern of a nation that has not yet reached the later stages of the demographic transition. According to the 1981 census, 47.7 percent of the population is fourteen years of age or younger. The number of women of child-bearing age will have increased from 16 million in 1974 to nearly 26 million in 1990.[13] Thus,

Table 3.2   **The Age and Sex Distribution of the Population of Bangladesh, 1981 (in Thousands of Persons)**

Age	Male	Female	Total
0–4	7,449	7,344	14,793
5–9	7,183	6,975	14,158
10–14	6,226	5,425	11,650
15–19	4,129	4,018	8,147
20–24	3,224	3,535	6,779
25–29	3,241	3,179	6,240
30–34	2,492	2,471	4,963
35–39	2,538	2,081	4,439
40–44	1,920	1,774	3,694
45–49	1,585	1,277	2,862
50–54	1,417	1,273	2,690
55–59	924	697	1,621
60–64	1,046	903	1,949
65–69	535	380	915
70–74	535	414	949
75 and older	635	456	1,091
Total	44,919	42,201	87,120

Source: Bangladesh Bureau of Statistics, *Statistical Yearbook of Bangladesh: 1984–1985* (Dhaka: Government of Bangladesh, 1986), Table 2.13, p. 77. The data presented here are from the "enumerated census count." The census data were adjusted (upward) as a result of the 1981 postenumeration survey. The adjusted total population is 89,912 thousand.

even with significant reductions in fertility rates, the natural increase will be substantial over the next generation or two. Demographers refer to this effect of the age and sex distribution as demographic momentum.

Government of Bangladesh projections suggest a population in the year 2000 of between 131 and 142 million.[14] Both ends of this range of projections assume a significant decline in crude birth rates. Given an early 1980s population growth rate exceeding 3 percent per year, the higher figure is probably more reliable. And, although the rate of urbanization in Bangladesh has increased, there can be no doubt that Bangladesh remains, and will remain well into the next century, a predominantly agrarian society.

Recent Attempts at Land Reform in Bangladesh

The most recent attempt in Bangladesh to transform the traditional system of rights in land by means of land reform was in 1984 when a new ordinance (The Land Reforms Ordinance of 1984) was

Figure 3.1   Population Pyramid of Bangladesh, 1981

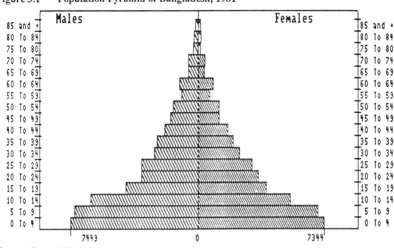

Source: Data of Table 3.2.

promulgated by Chief Martial Law Administrator (now President) Muhammed Hussain Ershad. This is a fascinating document, designed, in principle, to establish conditions in rural Bangladesh that would ensure increases in agricultural production and establish the basis for better relations between those who enjoy secure rights in land (mainly classified as maliks) and others (notably sharecroppers or bargadars) near the base of the agrarian hierarchy whose rights in land have not previously been accorded de jure status.

Unfortunately, the provisions of the 1984 ordinance, even if enforced, are not fully supportive of these explicit goals of increasing agricultural production and fostering better relations between landholders and sharecroppers. On the contrary, the ordinance contains a grab bag of provisions that are not adequately linked to one another or the overriding goals. Moreover, although changing the structure of power in rural Bangladesh was not an explicit goal of the ordinance, major sections of the act threaten changes in the status and rights of those who have long dominated the hierarchy of power in rural Bangladesh, as well as of those who have been virtually powerless within that hierarchy. Although the implementation of such changes might be beneficial to the greater community, the threat of change is unsettling (even to the presumed beneficiaries of change) and is hardly conducive to the immediate fostering of better relations between groups on whom the change is to be imposed. Nor does the threat of change necessarily foster an environment conducive to increases in agricultural production. In any event, a review of the main features of the 1984 land-reform legislation will confirm that the ordinance was written in such a way as to make many of its principal provisions either unenforceable or meaningless.

Setting a Ceiling on the Size of Landholdings

The 1984 ordinance bows in the direction of redistributive land reform. That is to say, it contains provisions designed to set a limit on the size of family holdings in Bangladesh. It reduces the maximum size of such holdings from one hundred standard bighas (about 13.5 hectares) to sixty standard bighas (about 8.1 hectares). And, the ordinance denies a family the right to acquire land in excess of sixty bighas by any means (including legal transfer, inheritance, and gift). It specifies, in addition, that any land acquired in excess of that limitation will be vested in the state for subsequent redistribution among landless households.

Ceilings legislation of one type or another has been in effect in Bangladesh for many years without being implemented in a fashion designed to ensure any meaningful redistribution of rights in land. Ceilings on the size of holdings have been systematically circumvented by landholders. A common way to avoid the ceiling has been to transfer and register land in excess of the ceiling in the name of another person, perhaps a distant relative or a family friend. Such bogus transfers of land sometimes confer rights in land to persons who have no idea that they have been so used. On occasion, the practice has been carried to absurd lengths—land held above designated ceilings has been registered, for example, in the names even of bullocks or other farm animals. While the 1984 ordinance declared such fictitious or benami transfers of land to be illegal and unenforceable in any court or official administrative proceeding, the practice of benami transfers is so longstanding in Bangladesh that it would now be exceedingly difficult to establish legitimate land records on the basis of which ceilings could then be enforced.

Notwithstanding the difficulty of implementing any ceilings on the size of landholdings, the 1984 ordinance outlined the terms and conditions that would govern the process by which land above the ceilings could be taken from landholders and redistributed. The principle was enunciated that landholders would receive compensation for any land taken from them for purposes of redistribution. The ordinance stipulated that payments of compensation to landholders for land in excess of the sixty bigha ceiling would be limited to 20 percent of the market value for up to fifty bighas of land. Beyond fifty bighas of excess land the compensation was not to exceed 10 percent of the market value of the land. Land acquired by the state through the operation of the ceilings legislation would be distributed among the landless. How much land might become available for redistribution if the ceilings could be implemented has been variously estimated. Peter Bertocci, for example, using ownership data given in Bangladesh's agricultural censuses, has suggested that only 185,000 hectares —about 2 percent of total arable land in Bangladesh—might be made available.[15] However, such numbers, whether they reflect high or low estimates of land that theoretically might become available, are unreliable. As noted above, landholders have systematically disguised the size of their holdings for many years. This limits the prospect of determining precisely how much land might become available given the implementation of ceilings legislation.

Homestead land (any land used as a homestead, including land occupied by out-buildings, storage sheds, and the like) was given special consideration in the 1984 ordinance. In particular, homestead land was exempted from "all legal processes, including seizure, distress, attachment or sale by any officer, court or any other authority." In short, the law apparently prohibits the eviction of a rural resident from his homestead for any reason. Although this is an admirable provision of the law, and, if enforced, could have political significance in rural Bangladesh, security of tenure on homestead land is a much less significant reform goal than providing security of tenure for the actual tillers of agricultural land, if the goal of agrarian reforms is to provide new incentives to cultivators and thereby provide a basis for increases in productivity as well as enhanced status and dignity to beneficiaries.

Terms of Tenancy
The 1984 ordinance also sought to change the terms under which land may be sharecropped in Bangladesh. The new law required that there be a written contract covering the terms of cultivation by which land is "taken in" by a tiller or "given out" by a landholder on a sharecropping agreement. It specifies how the agreement is to be executed and provides a standard form for such agreements. The new law declared that a sharecropping (barga) contract would be valid for a period of five years from the date the contract was properly executed. The ordinance stipulated how shares of the produce from the land would be divided between the landholder and the sharecropper.

The new law provided specific conditions under which a landholder could terminate the sharecropping agreement. These conditions were so broad in scope as to nullify largely any real enhancement of a bargadar's security of tenure (even within the terms of a written agreement covering a five-year contractual period) on lands taken in by him. This should be apparent from the seven stipulated conditions, enumerated below, by which a bargadar can be evicted from the land in his temporary possession:

1. The bargadar fails to cultivate the barga land
2. The bargadar fails to produce a crop on the land "equal to the average output of such crop in any land similar to the barga land in the locality"
3. The bargadar uses the land taken in for purposes other than agriculture
4. The bargadar has "contravened" any provisions of the ordinance or the rules stipulated within the ordinance
5. The bargadar "has surrendered or voluntarily abandoned his right of cultivation"
6. The person giving land out for purposes of sharecropping confirms that his land is not being "personally cultivated" by the bargadar
7. The person who has given out land for sharecropping simply decides to take back the land "for personal cultivation"[16]

Finally, the law gave qualified rights (to retain lands taken in for purposes of sharecropping) to the family of a bargadar who dies within the contractual period of an agreement with a landholder.

With regard to the provisions of the ordinance concerning the terms of share tenancy, it would be a step forward in Bangladesh if written contracts were in fact substituted for oral arrangements between landholders and sharecroppers. With only a verbal contract, the sharecropper (and, for that matter, the landowner) has little recourse under law in the event of a dispute concerning the terms or execution of a sharecropping agreement. However, even within the framework of the new ordinance, the relative positions of the landholder and the sharecropper in the rural hierarchy make it likely that disputes will be resolved in a fashion favoring the superior landholder.

Moreover, as already noted above, the security of tenure of the bargadar, as conferred by the ordinance for a five-year period, is highly qualified. After all, the landholder can, in effect, legally terminate the contract because he "requires the barga land bona fide for personal cultivation." What is more, the definition of "personal cultivation" applicable under the new law is one that permits the landholder not only to cultivate the land he takes back himself, but also with the labor of any family member, servant, or hired worker. Further, the law does not specify how long the landholder must then engage in the "personal cultivation" of the land he has taken back. It would appear that a landholder could, for example, evict a sharecropper, till the land himself or with family members, servants, or hired labor for a single growing season (or perhaps less), and then enter into a new share agreement with a more pliant sharecropper. In short, the provisions of the 1984 ordinance give negligible security of tenure to the bargadar—even if the ordinance were faithfully executed as written. The bargadar is vulnerable to eviction under terms and conditions stipulated in the law itself that give him little recourse, even if one could ignore conditions derived from the existing hierarchy of interests in land in Bangladesh and the power relationships that govern de facto interactions between "superiors" and "inferiors" in that society. As to the latter, even though there is a clause in the ordinance that establishes the rules by which an evicted bargadar might get back the land from which he has been evicted, the procedure places a heavy burden on the bargadar. He must apply in writing to the prescribed authority in the hope that that authority will take the land from the landholder and restore it to the bargadar. And, even if the bargadar's application leads to a result favorable to him, the bargadar's renewed right of possession would extend only for the duration of the existing contract—a period certain to be less than five years. Given the unlikelihood of a bargadar's successfully seeking redress, together with his vulnerability to those above him in the agrarian hierarchy, can one expect bargadars, commonly, to seek redress when evicted from lands that had been in their temporary possession?

A closely related provision in the 1984 ordinance permits sharecroppers to purchase land from a landholder. Under this provision of the law, a landholder must provide the sharecropper notice in writing of his intent to sell the land and allow the sharecropper fifteen days in which to respond with an offer of his own to buy the land. However, this rule does not apply when the landholder seeks to sell the land in question to "a co-sharer or to his parent, wife, son, daughter or son's son or to any other member of his family."[17] Furthermore, if the bargadar cannot, for whatever reason, meet the price required by the landholder for the land, the landholder "may sell the land to any person he deems fit," provided that the landholder does not sell to such person at a price lower than that offered to the sharecropper. The fact that the ordinance makes plain that the landholder cannot sell the land at a lower price than that offered by the bargadar, as noted above, in no way ensures that such a transaction between unequals will be an honorable one, devoid of subterfuge. Moreover, if a landholder does act dishonorably and sells the land to someone other than the bargadar, and at a price lower than that offered by the bargadar, the only penalty for the landholder is a fine of only 2,000 taka (about US$50). Also, there is no clear indication in the law that multiple offenses of this sort can receive multiple fines.

Other terms of a share tenancy contract besides its duration are important. Within the framework of the 1984 ordinance, the sharecropper is to receive one-third of the produce of the land; the landholder is to receive one-third of the produce as rent, and the remaining third is to be divided between landholder and sharecropper on the basis of the proportion of nonlabor inputs provided by each party to the contract. Conceptually, this arrangement is a significant improvement over the traditional fifty-fifty split of the crop regardless of who provided the nonlabor inputs, which was most often the sharecropper. If this provision of the law could be enforced, it would clearly provide an additional incentive for the sharecropper to increase production. However, the share contract can be broken easily by the landholder. For example, should there be a dispute concerning the produce share due the landholder, the landholder may refuse to give the sharecropper a written receipt confirming the amount of the share. In such circumstances, the burden falls on the sharecropper to petition the "prescribed authority" to step in and resolve the dispute. To do so takes courage and an obvious willingness to jeopardize future barga contracts with members of the local landholding elites. In rural Bangladesh, there can be little doubt who holds the upper hand in the event of such a dispute. Even if one assumes that the sharecropper is courageous to a degree bordering on foolhardiness, he must also be prepared to pay such fees and bribes as may be necessary to encourage an early resolution of the dispute.

In addition to specifying the terms of share tenancy, the new law also placed a ceiling on the amount of land that can be sharecropped. Under the new law, no bargadar can cultivate more than fifteen standard bighas (2.02 hectares) of land. This ceiling was made applicable both to lands taken in on a share tenancy basis and to any other land in the bargadar's cultivating possession (including land, if any, held by him in permanent occupancy). The ceilings provisions for bargadars stipulated that the produce on land in excess of the ceiling would be subject to confiscation without compensation by the state.

The Land Reforms Ordinance of 1984 was promulgated with a view to maximizing production and ensuring a better relationship between landholders (having permanent occupancy rights over land in their possession) and sharecroppers. Enhancing the legal status and rights of sharecroppers was not an explicit purpose of the ordinance. Nevertheless, the 1984 ordinance accords de jure status and rights—although extremely qualified by their terms—to this category of actual tillers who, in the modern history of the region, have not enjoyed such status and rights. However, as earlier emphasized, it is almost impossible to enforce provisions of the ordinance that would confer new status and rights to sharecroppers, given the existing distribution of power, legal and de facto, in rural Bangladesh.

With regard to the explicit goal of taking steps (within the framework of the ordinance) aimed at maximizing production, there is little in the ordinance, excepting changes proposed in the traditional division of crops between landholders and sharecroppers, that would ensure fulfillment of that goal. There are no provisions in the ordinance, for example, to ensure that sharecroppers will have access to nonusurious sources of credit, and, as seen above, there is little or no practical improvement in security of tenure.

With regard to the explicit goal of ensuring a better relationship between landholders and bargadars, it is questionable whether the ordinance will yield positive results. Indeed, the clear prospect is for the converse to happen. What the ordinance does is to threaten change in the landholders' erstwhile absolute authority over those tilling segments of landholders' lands as sharecroppers. By giving the sharecroppers some status under law, the ordinance in fact gives impetus to a process already under way in Bangladesh by which the land of landholders (i.e., maliks who have a permanent occupancy right to their land that is roughly equivalent to ownership) will henceforth be tilled increasingly by tillers classified as "servants" and "wage-laborers" (categories of actual tillers whose interests in land continue to be unrecognized under law). That is to say, astute landholders, even if they continue to enter into share-tenancy agreements, will find it advantageous to avoid even the possibility of conflict with bargadars concerning rights in land by ceasing, in effect, to define their tillers as bargadars. By proclaiming that their actual tillers are their servants or wage laborers, whether this accords with the actual situation or not, landholders not only can circumvent provisions of the 1984 ordinance that apply to bargadars, but also can ensure that the institution of sharecropping within the framework of recognized barga contracts will in due course cease to exist. Under such circumstances, it could be said with irony that the new ordinance may well ensure a better relationship between landholders and sharecroppers, mainly by speeding up the process by which "visible" sharecroppers having recognized rights cease to exist.

Elements of a Meaningful Agrarian Reform in Bangladesh

We believe that change in the traditional agrarian structure of Bangladesh is the sine qua non for sustained increases in agricultural production in the region within a social and economic framework that encourages broad participation in economic progress. We believe that this is so, notwithstanding the record of failure to effect such change in the region in the nineteenth and twentieth centuries, and notwithstanding the fact, noted above, that the prospect of change may sometimes be threatening both to those who enjoy secure rights in land and those who do not.

It is not surprising that the need to change the historical system of relationships of man to the land in Bangladesh has been ignored by many in the past and continues to be ignored by policymakers today. "Their position is reinforced by the tendency of some scholars to focus on constraints to agricultural innovation that abstract from the agrarian structure."[18] This position is often rationalized with the assumption that, once the incentive of overpopulation is present, a peasant's access to inputs at the right price is the primary determinant of his subsequent behavior. Such a position fails to take into account that a peasant cultivator functions within an environment that conditions his behavior and sets limits on his capacity to innovate—limits that are linked to his place in the agrarian hierarchy of the society in question. This applies with particular force in Bangladesh—where institutional constraints imbedded in the traditional agrarian structure are more severe than we have encountered in any other society. In this context, agrarian reform is the best means at the disposal of policymakers by which those constraints can be removed.

What we mean by agrarian reform in the context of contemporary Bangladesh is critical. Our definition of agrarian reform is not synonymous with "land reform," if "land reform" were defined as a panacea by which existing land resources would be redistributed in Bangladesh to provide landholdings to all possible claimants of rights to land. Our overriding concern is for an agrarian reform that would focus on changing the tradition in Bangladesh by which landholders' control of land is divorced from their direct involvement in agricultural operations. This means taking steps to establish conditions in the countryside to ensure that secure rights in land are conferred only on persons who are prepared to perform manual labor on the land and to assume the costs and risks of agricultural operations. The most meaningful agrarian reform therefore would be one wherein the principle was established that landholders enjoying secure rights in land would (1) reside on their lands, (2) invest personally in the agricultural production process, and (3) perform manual labor (themselves and their families) on their lands. This would mean denying all rights in land to landholders who customarily give out land on a share-tenancy basis to others. This would mean conferring effective permanent occupancy rights on the actual tillers of the soil.

The mechanism for determining whether a landholder should be permitted to retain portions of his land or be required to transfer his permanent rights to others would be village committees backed on the spot by the judicial and military apparatus of the state. By this process, landlords and peasants, persons with secure rights in land as well as tenuous rights to land, would alike have to convince a committee in their own village that it is they who (1) customarily reside on the land in question or in an area contiguous with it, (2) invest personally in the agricultural production process, and (3) perform manual labor themselves on the land.

The major advantage in entrusting village committees with the primary responsibility for making decisions concerning the redistribution of land is that such committees would know, better than any outsider, who controls and who tills what land in each village. Such committees could bypass time-consuming pre-reform activities such as the cadastral surveys that have been institutionalized in South Asia in accordance with the provisions of antiquated manuals of procedure that are part of the British colonial legacy in the region. To be effective instruments of reform, the village committees would have to be so constituted that persons representing those having tenuous rights in land would predominate over persons representing those who presently enjoy superior, permanent rights to land.

There is a parallel with the experience of agrarian reform in Japan in our recommendation that village committees be established in contemporary Bangladesh to ensure implementation of the proposed reform program. In the successful reform in Japan, local land commissions (the rough equivalent of our proposed village committees) were established and were designed to favor the interests of tenants. Toward this end, the local commissions in Japan were comprised of five tenants, three landlords, and two owner-cultivators. The relative proportions for each group were set by the state, and elections were carried out at the village level. The governing assumption was that the villagers themselves would know better than outsiders who owned and tilled the land in their own communities. Moreover, it was rightly assumed that the local commissions would eliminate the need to establish a complex and easily circumvented administrative apparatus. The subsequent speedy nature of agrarian reform in Japan was a derivative of this bold plan to trust to village-level committees the primary responsibility for making the difficult decisions on redistribution of more than 30 million plots of land. The guiding principle was that villagers would be invested with power and responsibility previously appropriated by the landlords. In fact, the Japanese villagers demonstrated the ability to take the necessary action to transform the traditional land system.

In Bangladesh, no less than in post–World War II Japan (notwithstanding the obvious differences in the conditions applicable then and now in both countries), it is the villagers themselves who know best the details concerning who tills whose lands for whose benefit. In our view, entrusting the primary responsibility for implementing agrarian reform to village committees in Bangladesh offers the most appropriate means of ensuring expeditious implementation of the proposed reform.

If the proposed agrarian reform could be enforced, it would provide the minimum basis in Bangladesh for transforming the traditional agrarian structure by increasing the number of peasant cultivators who would be able to adopt new technology in agriculture and who would derive direct benefits from their innovative behavior.

It must be emphasized that, although the reform would provide the basis for more broadly based participation in economic progress, it would not in itself be sufficient to ensure economic progress in rural Bangladesh. In this context, no agrarian reform can be fully effective to ensure increases in productivity unless it is complemented by a full range of ancillary programs, which, for example, would ensure cultivators institutional sources of credit, timely access to modern inputs, and the advice of agricultural extension workers.

Agrarian reforms do not occur simply because they are enacted into law. Agrarian reforms do not happen because they appear to be justified as a rational means of providing the basis for broader participation in agricultural innovation, increases in agricultural productivity, improved distribution of income, social justice, or long-run political stability. Agrarian reforms do not happen in any country because they appear to outsiders to be necessary. Such reforms are initiated and implemented generally when there are local constituencies advocating reform and when those who govern have the will to invest in the future well-being of a whole people, rather than of only a privileged few. Such reforms occur when those who govern also have the capacity to employ, when necessary, coercive means to neutralize the inevitable opposition of traditional landholders to reform measures of any kind.

The historical record of other reform initiatives, as partially outlined in this chapter, suggests that the agrarian reform we have proposed would not be likely to be implemented within the existing political economy of Bangladesh. The political will of the government of Bangladesh to initiate such a far-reaching transformation of the agrarian structure of Bangladesh would need to be bolstered significantly before such a reform could be effectively implemented. However, the government's recognition of the advisability of such a reform could be encouraged and supported if external aid institutions would endorse the need for it and give impetus to it by means of supporting services and investments in the process.

Notes

1. There is a lively debate concerning the average caloric intake in Bangladesh. Given high levels of grain imports, this topic is highly controversial in a policy context. For a different perspective, see E. Boyd Wennergren and Morris D. Whitaker, "Foodgrain Self-sufficiency in Bangladesh: A Reappraisal and Policy Implications," *Journal of Developing Areas* 21 (October 1986): 1–14.

2. The projections are from The World Bank, *World Development Report 1988* (New York: Oxford University Press, 1988), Table 27, p. 274; and Bangladesh Bureau of Statistics, *Statistical Yearbook of Bangladesh: 1984–1985* (Dhaka: Government of Bangladesh, 1986), Table 2.70, p. 141. The World Bank projection is 145 million persons in the year 2000; the government of Bangladesh projections range from 131.7 million to 142.1 million in the year 2000.

3. Previously described as such in F. Tomasson Jannuzi and James T. Peach, *The Agrarian Structure of Bangladesh: An Impediment to Development* (Boulder, Colo.: Westview Press, 1980).

4. While it is common to refer to landholders in Bangladesh who enjoy permanent occupancy rights to land as "owners" of land, as on occasion in this chapter, it is important to note that the historical land system of Bangladesh is one within which landholders' rights to land have invariably been qualified and subordinated to those of the state or ruling authority. No landholder in Bangladesh, even when he is referred to casually as a landowner, has the exclusive right "to occupy, enjoy and dispose of land which, in practice, is the hallmark of Western private ownership" (Daniel Thorner, *The Agrarian Prospect in India* [Delhi: University Press, 1956], p.7).

5. In particular, parts of the discussion are based on our previously published works. See F. Tomasson Jannuzi and James T. Peach, "Report on the Hierarchy of Interests in Land in Bangladesh," report prepared for the U.S. Agency for International Development, Dhaka, Bangladesh (Austin: University of Texas, 1977); "Bangladesh: A Profile of the Countryside," report prepared for the U.S. Agency for International Development (Austin: University of Texas, 1978); and *The Agrarian Structure of Bangladesh*. See also F. Tomasson Jannuzi, James T. Peach, and A. K. M. Ghulam Rabbani, "Summary Report of the 1977 Land Occupancy Survey of Rural Bangladesh" and "Summary Report of the 1978 Land Occupancy Survey of Rural Bangladesh," both mimeos (Dhaka: Bangladesh Bureau of Statistics).

6. In this context, "owned" means land over which the holders enjoy a permanent occupancy right that is likely to be upheld in a court of law.

7. For a more extended discussion of this topic, see Jannuzi and Peach, *The Agrarian Structure of Bangladesh,* Appendix F, pp. 121–130.

8. See Alfred Marshall, *Principles of Economics,* 8th ed. (London,

MacMillan, 1920).

9. Jannuzi and Peach, *The Agrarian Structure of Bangladesh*.

10. In a 1978 survey, for example, more than three-fourths of tenants indicated that they had been tenants on the same land for three years or less. See Jannuzi, Peach, and Rabbani, "Summary Report of the 1978 Land Occupancy Survey of Bangladesh."

11. In particular, see Jannuzi and Peach, *The Agrarian Structure of Bangladesh*, upon which much of this discussion of landlessness is based. For a different perspective, see Mead Cain, "Landlessness in India and Bangladesh: A Critical Review of National Data Sources," *Economic Development and Cultural Change* 32 (October 1983): 149–167.

12. For a recent summary of this perspective see E. Boyd Wennergren, "Land Redistribution as a Developmental Strategy in Bangladesh," *Land Economics* 62 (February 1986): 74–82.

13. U.S. Bureau of the Census, *Country Demographic Profiles: Bangladesh* (Washington, D.C: U.S. Government Printing Office, 1982).

14. Bangladesh Bureau of Statistics, *Statistical Yearbook of Bangladesh: 1984–1985*.

15. See Peter Bertocci, "Bangladesh in 1984: A Year of Protracted Turmoil," *Asian Survey* 25 (February 1985): 155–168.

16. *The Land Reforms Ordinance 1984* (Dhaka: Government of Bangladesh, 1984), chapter V, section 9.

17. Ibid., chapter V, section 11 (e).

18. Jannuzi and Peach, *The Agrarian Structure of Bangladesh*, p. 47.

Selected Bibliography

Bangladesh Bureau of Statistics. *Statistical Yearbook of Bangladesh: 1984–1985*. Dhaka: Government of Bangladesh, 1986.

Bertocci, Peter. "Bangladesh in 1984: A Year of Protracted Turmoil." *Asian Survey* 25 (February 1985): 155–168.

Cain, Mead. "Landlessness in India and Bangladesh: A Critical Review of National Data Sources." *Economic Development and Cultural Change* 32 (October 1983): 149–167.

Jannuzi, F. Tomasson, and James T. Peach. *The Agrarian Structure of Bangladesh: An Impediment to Development*. Boulder, Colo.: Westview Press, 1980.

———. "Bangladesh: A Profile of the Countryside." Report prepared for the U.S. Agency for International Development. Austin: University of Texas, 1978.

———. "Report on the Hierarchy of Interests in Land in Bangladesh." Report prepared for the U.S. Agency for International Development, Dhaka, Bangladesh. Austin: University of Texas, 1977.

Jannuzi, F. Tomasson, James T. Peach, and A. K. M. Ghulam Rabbani. "Summary Report of the 1978 Land Occupancy Survey of Rural Bangladesh." Mimeo. Dhaka: Bangladesh Bureau of Statistics, 1978.

———. "Summary Report of the 1977 Land Occupancy Survey of Rural

Bangladesh." Mimeo. Dhaka: Bangladesh Bureau of Statistics, 1977.

The Land Reforms Ordinance 1984. Dhaka: Government of Bangladesh, 1984.

Marshall, Alfred. *Principles of Economics*, 8th ed. London: Macmillan, 1921.

Thorner, Daniel. *The Agrarian Prospect in India.* Delhi: University Press, 1957.

U.S. Bureau of the Census. *Country Demographic Profiles: Bangladesh.* Washington, D.C: U.S. Government Printing Office, 1982.

Wennergren, E. Boyd. "Land Redistribution as a Developmental Strategy in Bangladesh." *Land Economics* 62 (February 1986): 74–82.

Wennergren, E. Boyd, and Morris D. Whitaker. "Foodgrain Self-sufficiency in Bangladesh: A Reappraisal and Policy Implications." *Journal of Developing Areas* 21 (October 1986): 1–14.

World Bank. *World Development Report 1988.* New York: Oxford University Press, 1988.

chapter four

China: A Fieldwork-based Appraisal of the Household Responsibility System

Roy L. Prosterman
Timothy M. Hanstad

Summary

Fieldwork carried out in five provinces and one province-level municipality in China in 1987 and 1988 gives results consistent with national-level statistics on the positive effects of the household responsibility system in agriculture. After a quarter century of very slow growth under various forms of collectivization, production by individual households on the almost universally decollectivized farmland after 1980 surged dramatically. Households interviewed were substantially more productive than before decollectivization, even while spending far less time to produce the crops. They ate far better, new brick houses and new household amenities such as televisions were widespread, and there was tremendous growth in both agricultural and non-agricultural sidelines. However, after the initial surge of production growth from 1980 to 1984, grain production has stagnated. Although farmers made initial improvements in their annual farming practices (such as more careful timing of agricultural operations, better seeds, more assiduous weeding, and improved water management), they have lacked the assurance of long-term security of possession of the land that would lead them to make the long-term capital investments (such as irrigation wells, land leveling, terracing, drainage, or soil improvement) that are essential for further gains in grain production. The farmers interviewed made clear that only the acquisition of individual ownership (privatization) of the land would lead them to make such long-term investments, and that neither longer-term "use" contracts, nor increased prices, nor other alternatives would provide a basis for such investments. Long-standing legal rules in most of Eastern Europe as well as important aspects of the present Chinese legal system indicate that privatization of agricultural land is consistent with communism. At the same time, experience in a number of other Asian land-reform settings shows that privatization can be carried out in such a way as to maximize benefits to both farmers and the state, and, by including prohibitions on tenancy and excessive land accumulation, to avert any potential negative consequences.

What difference has the household responsibility system made to the farmers who constitute 70 percent of China's total population? Yang Weibo, a farmer interviewed in Sichuan Province, grinned broadly when asked if life has been better since the Chinese government instituted its policy of decollectivization and adopted the household responsibility system in agriculture. "Much better," was his reply as his neighbors grinned and nodded in agreement. "I hope the party will continue their present policy for a long time." Mr. Yang has good reason to smile. Since 1981, when the collective farm on which he worked was broken up and his family of five was allocated just under 6 mu (0.4 hectares; 1 ha=15 mu) to farm on their own, their situation has improved dramatically.

Yang Weibo, like nearly all the peasant farmers in his village in Sichuan Province, grows two main crops: rice in the summer and wheat in the winter. (More than 75 percent of China's arable land is planted in grain.) Before 1981 he farmed the surrounding land collectively with about thirty other households and was compensated according to the amount of time he spent working in the fields. The collective, with each worker contributing about 300 days of labor per year, produced paddy rice yields equivalent to 6,000 kg per hectare and wheat yields of 4,125 kg per hectare. A few years after the breakup of the collective, the Yang family was getting 9,000 kg of paddy rice per hectare and 6,000 kg of wheat per hectare on their small "contract" plot, although the yield figures have leveled off since 1985. The enhanced efficiency of their labor is just as impressive as the increased production. With the increased incentive of their individualized rights, they are spending sixty days per year on their crops, only one-fifth of the time that was needed on the collective. They have used some of their increased free time to expand sideline production of hogs, chickens, and ducks, and in addition Mr. Yang is now working about 100 days per year in a local factory. Their cash income has more than quadrupled.

The Yangs built a new brick house in 1985 and they, like most of their neighbors, have purchased a television set, electric fan, and tape player—consumer goods that only a few years ago were considered luxury items. The Yang family's nutritional intake has also greatly improved from the days on the collective farm. Ample rice has replaced thin rice porridge as standard fare. Meat appears on the Yang table several times per week instead of several times per year, and vegetables have become commonplace.

The Yangs' experience is illustrative of perhaps the most stunning agricultural turnabout of the twentieth century, which has quietly taken place in China since the beginning of the 1980s. Since the commencement of this decade, China has almost totally decollectivized its agriculture, creating a nation of small, family farmers. The number of people directly affected is staggering. Of China's 1.1 billion people, 750 million are engaged in farming—a group comprising one out of every three agriculturalists on the planet. The countrywide decollectivization has improved the standard of living for nearly all of them.

The increased productivity of the Yang family is not an isolated experience. From 1980, the last year preceding the widespread adoption of the household responsibility system, to 1984, there was a 30–35 percent increase countrywide in grain yields (defined to include

Table 4.1   Growth of Various Productivity and Income Indicators in China, 1978–1987

Year	Index of Rural Total Product (constant prices) 1978=100 (1)	Index of Gross Output Value of Agriculture[a] (calculated in constant prices) 1978=100 (2)	Index of Gross Output Value of Crop Farming (constant prices) 1978=100 (3)	Grain Productivity[b] (kgs/ hectare) (4)	Average Per-Capita Net Income of Rural Household[d] (constant Rmb) (5)
1978	100.0	100.0	100.0	2528	133.57
1979	N/A	107.6	107.2	N/A	N/A
1980	108.6	109.1	106.6	2738	151.64
1981	N/A	116.2	112.9	2828	N/A
1982	N/A	129.3	124.5	3124	N/A
1983	143.2	139.3	134.8	3396	N/A
1984	167.9	156.4	148.2	3716 (3608)[c]	N/A
1985	194.3	161.8	145.3	3583	248.27
1986	215.9	167.3	146.6	3624	246.80
1987	244.9	177.1	154.4	3715	244.74

Sources: (1) William T. Liu, Ed., *China Statistical Abstract 1988* (New York: Praeger, 1989), Table 3.2; and *Rural Economic and Social Statistics of China* (Research Center for Rural Development of the State Council of the People's Republic of China), p. 11. (2) *China Statistical Abstract 1988*, Table 3.4, p. 27. (3) *China Statistical Abstract 1988*, Table 3.4, p. 27. (4) *Rural Economic and Social Statistics of China* (for 1978–1983); and *FAO Production Yearbook 1987* (United Nations Food and Agriculture Organization, 1987), vol. 41, Tables 15, 25, and 37 (for 1984–1987). (5) *China Statistical Abstract 1988*, Table 8.14, p. 107.

[a] Figures at comparable prices. "Agriculture" here includes crop farming, animal husbandry, fishing, and other household sideline activities.

[b] Data include all cereals, tubers (converted 5-to-1 to grain equivalent), and soybeans.

[c] 1984 figure for grain productivity in the *Rural Economic and Social Statistics of China*.

[d] Inflation adjusted using an inflation adjuster based on *China Statistical Abstract 1988*, Tables 3.3 and 3.4.

rice, corn, wheat, other cereals, soybeans, and tubers—converted 5-to-1 to grain equivalent). However, whereas the gross output of agriculture has continued to grow since 1984, albeit at a slower rate, grain yields and total crop output have leveled off in recent years and the government has been searching for new methods to continue the productivity improvements.

The dramatic progress in various productivity and income indicators is shown in Table 4.1. As this indicates, China's gross agricultural output value increased in constant, inflation-adjusted terms by 48 percent from 1980 to 1985, and the rural total product rose by nearly 80 percent in constant terms during the same time period. The increased productivity and the additional economic activities have translated into rapidly rising incomes for most peasants. The average per capita income of peasant households jumped 64 percent, in inflation-adjusted terms, in the five years after the decollectivization policy was adopted by the Chinese government.

History of Changes in the Chinese Countryside

1950 Land Reform
The 1980 land reform was not the first postwar restructuring of the Chinese countryside, but the latest in a series of alterations. Mao Tse-tung relied on peasant grievances against the landlord to recruit the rank-and-file of his revolutionary army, just as revolutionary armies had done earlier in Mexico and Russia. Following the Communist victory in 1949, a land-reform law based on a system of peasant landownership was published in June 1950. The general principles of the land reform were stated in Article 1 of the law: "The land ownership system of feudal exploitation by the landlord class shall be abolished and the system of peasant land ownership shall be introduced in order to set free the rural productive forces, develop agricultural production and thus pave the way for New China's industrialization."[1]

The law, which applied nationwide, confiscated landholdings of landlords and rich peasants and distributed them free of charge in individual parcels to peasants, giving them full ownership of the parcels. As intended, by the time this first round of land reform was completed in 1952, an impression was created among the peasants that the Communist government was to thank for their new land acquisitions. The land reform consolidated the Communist party's power in the countryside, effectively destroying any possibility that the Nationalist government would regain power.

Before the land reform, less than 10 percent of the rural population owned more than 70 percent of the total arable land, and the rent charged to tenant farmers was typically about 50 percent of the total output. In the rice-growing region as a whole, which contained three-fifths of the entire agricultural population, between 62 and 73 percent of regular cultivators were either tenant farmers or part tenants–part owners, and a small additional percentage of agricultural families (one regional figure was 8 percent) were hired agricultural laborers.[2] The land-reform program distributed 46.7 million hectares of land to about 300 million peasants, thus covering about one-half of the total arable land and more than 60 percent of the total rural population.

For the beneficiaries, ownership of the land they tilled provided a great incentive to improve farm management and practices and to make longer-term capital investments in the land. As a result, grain production increased from 111.2 million metric tons (mmt) in 1949 to 188.4 mmt in 1956, a 70 percent increase in just seven years.[3]

Collectivization

Although the government viewed the distribution of private farms as necessary to consolidate power among the large rural population, its eventual goal was to replace the peasant economy with collective agriculture. Two major policy changes of the 1950s were initiated to help speed along this transformation. First, in 1953, the central government introduced the system of "uniform purchase and uniform sales" of grain, combining compulsory procurement and food rationing. Although the state agencies were given monopoly power in grain marketing, peasants were still allowed to sell their own grain in local private markets. Second, behind the driving force of Mao Tse-tung, the collectivization process was introduced and accelerated.

In 1955, the government adopted the First Five Year Plan, which envisioned collectivization as a developmental policy capable of raising farm productivity without state investment. According to the First Five Year Plan, the collectivization process would be voluntary and gradual, progressing through the following transitional steps: seasonal mutual-aid teams, year-round mutual aid teams, elementary agricultural cooperatives, and collectives or advanced agricultural cooperatives. The plan outlined a fifteen-year timetable for the collectivization process, in which the great majority of the Chinese farmers would be organized into collectives by 1970. However, Mao, believing that collectivization was a basic solution to China's agricultural problems, accelerated the timetable.

More than one-half of the farm households had been organized into mutual-aid teams by 1955. The mutual-aid team was simply a formalization of the Chinese farmers' traditional practice of pooling labor or exchanging equipment and draft animals, especially during peak seasons. It typically involved ten families who arranged compensation among themselves, but included no changes in actual ownership.

The shift from the mutual-aid teams to the elementary agricultural cooperatives took place in 1955–1956. The average elementary cooperative contained thirty to forty households who pooled their land under the unified management of cooperative authorities. The peasant households, however, still retained ownership of the land, which was regarded as a capital contribution to the elementary cooperative. Although the great majority of the land was farmed collectively, each household was allowed to retain for its own use a small private plot of land, which was not to exceed 5 percent of the average individual landholding.

The cooperative members were compensated in the following manner. After the harvest, the cooperative managers first met the cooperative's tax and state procurement quota obligations. After paying production costs, contributing to a common welfare fund, and setting aside for investment, the managers distributed the residue to the cooperative members. The residue was allocated in the form of dividends to the land shares and other capital contributions, and as remuneration for work performed by members.

Beginning in 1956, the socialist transformation of agriculture was further accelerated as the elementary cooperatives were converted into collectives. The collectives differed from the elementary cooperatives in terms of size, system of ownership, and the method of distributing income. The collectives, formed by merging a number of elementary cooperatives, contained up to 300 households. Unlike the elementary cooperatives in which individual members retained ownership of land, title was held by the collective in this stage. Ownership of all draft animals and large farm equipment was also transferred to the collective. The remaining exception was the small private plots, which individual households were allowed to keep as owners.

Income in the form of dividends to land shares was abolished as a result of the changed ownership system. So income, after deducting taxes, quota, production costs, and reserve and welfare funds, was distributed to members solely on the basis of work done, using a "work point" system. Work points were assigned to a farmer according to the length of time required for a job and the difficulty of the work done. At the end of a fiscal year, after all deductions were made from a collective's income, the surplus was divided by the sum of work points accumulated by all members. Each individual's income was then calculated by multiplying their total work points by the value of one work point.

The procession from cooperatives to collectives led not only to a decrease in farmer incentives, but to a host of other problems. Communist Party member Teng Tzu-hui, a critic of Mao's agricultural policy, summarized the shortcomings of the collective farms in a speech to the People's Congress in June 1956. He pointed to wasteful and luxury spending, chaotic management and accounting, domineering attitudes of managers toward members, and the problem of disincentives as some of the defects of the collectives. The difficulty in managing the larger collectives became so formidable that many collectives in 1956–1957 attempted to simplify their administration by adopting egalitarian distribution of income among members, which only intensified the collectives' disincentive effects. Incentive problems were further exacerbated with the abolition of all private grain marketing in 1957.

Despite the problems, the socialist transformation of agriculture proceeded beyond the stage of large collectives to that of giant communes. In the summer of 1958, Mao toured the country, promoting the new movement toward giant communes. The transition to communes was part of the state policy of the "Great Leap Forward," in which economic policies were modeled on the Soviet pattern, characterized by centrally planned industrialization with highest priority given to heavy industry and large-scale factories. Agriculture was to play a supporting role as a source of raw materials and market for industry (besides the role of food supplier). Mao believed that the move toward giant communes was the only way to increase agricultural production in order to properly support accelerated industrialization. By the end of that year, about 680,000 agricultural collectives merged into 26,578 rural people's communes. About 90 percent of the rural population (approximately 550 million people) became commune members within half a year. In 1958, the average commune included 20,000 people (about 4,500 households) and 4,000 hectares of arable land. The communes were not only agricultural production units, but most took over social, educational, and military functions from the local government and began running banks, factories, stores, nurseries, schools, and militia units. All activities of the commune members were centrally regulated by the commune leaders. Under the commune system, agricultural tasks were done by large groups of people, so that individual fields were no longer tended by peasants who knew them. Commune members typically worked twelve hours a day, except during harvest time when the workday was even longer.

From the point of view of ownership, the fundamental characteristic of the commune, which distinguished it from the previous organization, was the abolition of the last vestiges of private property.

The commune took sole ownership of all property, including the private plots (which were absorbed into the commonly worked land), private dwellings, livestock, and certain consumer durables. The only means of personal earnings for the commune members was by participating in production activities governed by the collective authorities on the collective's land and with the collective's equipment and inputs.

The system of income distribution also underwent significant changes. The system of part-supply and part-wage, following the principle of "to each according to his need," replaced the earlier system of wage payments on the basis of work points. On the commune, all members were provided common meals in the commune mess hall free of charge. The commune also provided other goods and services that the households had previously furnished for themselves, including clothing, housing, weddings, haircuts, and so on. After deducting quotas, taxes, reserve and welfare funds, and the costs associated with the meals, goods, and services furnished by the collective, the surplus remaining was distributed as wages to the members. Only 20–50 percent of compensation was in this wage form, roughly differentiated according to the grade of labor, whereas 50–80 percent of compensation consisted of subsistence supplies in order to fulfill the communist principle of "to each according to his need."

The disastrous effects of the new system on incentives exceeded even the difficulties of efficiently administering the extended communes. All labor on the commune was paid monthly from the pittance of surplus, and based on a wage rate established by the commune. Because the communes were so large, farmers could see little connection between their work and their wages. Consequently, production incentives declined even further. During the harvest of 1958, the unmotivated peasants did such a poor job of reaping and threshing that the government initiated a campaign to recover grain left in the fields and on the threshing grounds. The peasants' lack of incentive also led to widespread weed calamities that plagued China in 1960. According to news reports from six provinces, the areas affected by the weed calamities ranged from 10 to 82 percent of the cultivated area. In many areas the weeds overgrew crop plants and became so high that men could hardly enter the field to weed. Although the government described the problem as a "natural calamity," weed calamities had never before been a problem for China's agriculture, because motivated peasants had previously removed weeds throughout the growing season.

The Great Leap Forward's effect on agriculture was disastrous. Foodgrain production declined substantially for three years in a row starting in 1959, leading to perhaps the planet's worst famine of the twentieth century. China suffered 20–30 million incremental deaths during these years of shortage as the daily per capita availability of food energy decreased from more than 2,100 calories in the mid-1950s to only 1,500 calories. Although natural disasters are customarily cited as contributing to the famine, their impact should not be overstated. Government statistics show that the amount of farmland termed "disaster-affected" in the years 1959–1961 was similar to that in both 1956–1957 and 1962–1963. The principal reason for the sharp decline in agricultural production in 1959–1961 was the organization and functioning of the giant communes.

The peasants' loss of incentive and passivity following the creation of the communes was a key factor contributing to the foodgrain crisis in 1959–1961. The state for the first time became the sole owner of practically all the agricultural resources of the country, and the peasants were turned into landless laborers. As they lost their rights in the share of the crop they produced, it mattered little to them whether they produced more or less. The new system of distribution based on "to each according to his need" also had a serious disincentive effect on the peasantry. Each peasant on the giant communes received virtually the same amount of food and other compensation, so most dawdled over work.

Adjustment in the 1960s
The serious mistakes and grave consequences of the Great Leap Forward policies were eventually recognized, and the government began making adjustments in 1961. Private plots were formally reinstated, now on the basis of usership rather than ownership, and some rural free markets reopened. The original work-point system was reintroduced, and throughout the first half of the 1960s communes were allowed to experiment with piece rates and work grades to link assignment of work points with effort. As administrative units, some exceedingly large communes were broken up into smaller ones, and within each commune a decentralization process was initiated.

The history of the socialist transformation in China made the decentralization task rather simple. The giant communes had been formed by merging collectives, which in turn were created by combining elementary cooperatives. In most communes, the same three tiers were maintained, but given new names. The former collectives closely coincided with what were now called production brigades. A number of production teams, which were comparable to the earlier elementary cooperatives, were under each brigade. In some cases the production teams broke into even smaller units similar to those of the former mutual-aid teams. The decentralization process simply reactivated all the lower layers of the commune.

The policies of the Great Leap Forward recognized the three levels—the commune, the brigade, and the production team—but had appointed the commune as the basic accounting and administrative unit. In the period of adjustment following the Great Leap Forward, first the brigade and then the production team assumed the role as the independent accounting unit responsible for its own losses and gains.

Within each basic administrative unit income continued to be distributed in proportion to work points earned, but there was movement away from the earlier extreme egalitarianism and the strong emphasis on the principle of "to each according to his need" as the criterion of distribution. Some piece-rate compensation was introduced and the method of assigning work points was changed to at least somewhat reflect an individual's contribution to production.

Individual households were allowed to engage in some private sideline activities, such as the raising of poultry, pigs, and fish. However, these private activities were severely circumscribed by the requirement imposed upon each member to engage in a certain number of days of collective work.

The ownership system in the communes also underwent a series of changes that paralleled those in the administrative system. During the Great Leap Forward, properties in a commune were classified into three groups according to their nature and functions and were to be owned, respectively, by the commune, brigades, and teams. Among the subsequent adjustments was designating first the brigade and then the production team as the basic unit to own most of the common properties.

Actual changes in control of land in some areas went beyond what the central government sanctioned. The size limitation on private plots was ignored in some localities, and communal land was sometimes reallocated to individual households under the guise of plots for breeding animals or for specialized forms of cultivation. Some communes introduced the responsibility land system under which a specific plot, with an attached quota, was assigned to each household. After the quota was submitted to the team for collective distribution, the household was allowed to keep the excess.

In late 1962 this responsibility land system was proposed to the Central Committee as an official agricultural model, but the proposal was defeated with the strong opposition of Mao Tse-tung, who reaffirmed the production teams, not individual households, as the basic units of administration and ownership. Despite this central government policy, the responsibility system was practiced in a few localities.

In sum, the agricultural organization in the years of recovery following the Great Leap Forward was a heterogeneous mixture including characteristics of both the original communes and individual farming. The restoration of incentives inherent in the private plots, decentralized administration and ownership at the production-team level, and more open rural markets caused agricultural output to rebound from the disastrous years of 1959–1961, although it was not until 1971 that China restored per capita grain production to its 1958 level.

The onset of the Cultural Revolution, beginning in 1966, was accompanied by a resurgence of radical doctrine, but despite propaganda broadsides against material incentives and capitalist practices, the government did not repeat the grave mistakes of the Great Leap Forward. The production team remained the basic accounting unit in about 90 percent of the brigades, although distribution of a part of collective income according to need irrespective of work points earned was increasingly emphasized.

Private plots, sideline activities, and private commerce at village markets came under attack as capitalistic practices during this period. In some areas private plots were reduced or even eliminated. The majority of households, however, retained the usership of small, individual private plots, which together amounted to 6.4 percent of arable land in 1975.

Introduction of the Household Responsibility System
Shortly after Mao's death in 1976, the leadership of the dominant group during the Cultural Revolution was overthrown and arrested. However, there was little change in the government's rural policy until 1978, when a group of moderate leaders who were strongly opposed to many of Mao's agricultural development policies gained power. This group supported a basic reversal in the old commune system that would relate compensation more directly to work; reverse the trend toward greater administrative centralization; and promote private plots, sidelines, and free markets.

These reform-minded leaders recognized that earlier rural policies were at the root of agriculture's poor long-term performance. Because the great majority of China's arable land is planted in grain, grain production is often used as a yardstick for measuring agricultural performance. The long-term growth of grain output (defined as cereals plus tubers and soybeans) had barely kept up with population growth during the socialist transformation of agriculture. Indeed, 1978 grain production per capita was less than 6 percent greater than that of 1956, and 1977 per capita grain production had actually been lower than 1956. The slow growth of grain output and declining marketing rates led China to become increasingly dependent on imported foodstuffs during this period. By 1978, about 40 percent of China's urban population was entirely dependent on imported cereals.

The failures of agricultural performance extended beyond cereals to include other major crops. The absolute level of soybean production had fallen 25 percent from mid-1950s levels. Total cotton output in 1977 remained stagnant at the 1965 level, while per capita production fell 25 percent.[4]

The sluggish growth in the farm sector was accompanied by even slower growth in peasant income. Income from collective sources increased only 0.5 percent per year between 1965 and 1977. Income from household sideline activities decreased over the same years as increasing constraints were placed on private marketing activities and private plots were reduced. By 1977–1978, rural real income per capita was, at best, only slightly above the 1956–1957 level.

Even the government's goal of egalitarianism had not been achieved. Although there had been a substantial reduction in income inequality within rural localities, the large differences between rural and urban incomes that prevailed before 1949 were not reduced (the ratio between the living standards of urban and rural workers had basically remained about 2 to 1). In addition, income differences between rural localities or from region to region had not narrowed, but continued to widen.

In the Third Plenary Session of the Eleventh Central Committee of the Communist Party of China (CPC), held in December 1978, the Chinese leaders recommended sweeping changes in rural policies. Elements of these changes included expansion of free markets, a rise in government procurement prices, diversification of the rural economy, and product specialization and crop selection in accordance with rural comparative advantage. However, the most radical and important of the eventual reforms, the adoption of the household responsibility system, was not among the early policy changes. It was still considered by many to be a reversal of the socialist principle of collective farming and was actually prohibited in a document issued in September 1979 by the Fourth Plenary Session of the Eleventh Central Committee of the CPC. The official position was that the production team was to remain the basic unit of production, income distribution, and accounting.

In late 1978, despite the position of the central government, several production teams in Anhui Province, located in areas that were frequently victimized by flood and drought, began trying the system of contracting land and output quotas to individual households. These early adoptions of the household responsibility system were initially done secretly, and later with the blessing of local officials. A year later these teams produced yields far larger than those of other teams in the same localities. The central authorities, upon seeing the increased productivity effect, approved the adoption of the household responsibility system but required that it be restricted to poor agricultural regions. This restriction, however, was not closely followed as both rich and poor agricultural regions accepted the new household responsibility system. The system was already spreading rapidly when official recognition of its universal acceptability was given in late 1981. By the middle of 1983 the household responsibility system had been adopted by 93 percent of the production teams in China.

Characteristics and Impact
of the Household Responsibility System

The basic characteristics of the household responsibility system as it now exists in agriculture are succinctly described by Thomas Wiens of the World Bank:

> A wide variety of contractual forms have been tried, and in agriculture one system has become nearly universal: *bao gan dao hu* (BGDH). Loosely translated, this means "contracting all actions to the household." In BGDH, management of collectively owned land was contracted to households, usually in proportion to household size or labor force. Other collective assets were divided up, sold, or contracted to individuals or groups willing to manage them. The household was obligated to pay taxes, make contributions to collective welfare funds, provide its share of state procurement requirements, and contribute labor to maintain or construct public infrastructure. All remaining output could be retained by the household.[5]

From 1978, the year of initial reforms, to 1980, the last year before the household responsibility system became widespread, through 1987, agricultural output, rural total product, grain productivity, and the per capita net income of peasant households have all risen strikingly, as shown in Table 4.1. These increases have occurred despite a sharp decrease in the level of state investment in agriculture since 1978.

Indeed, in the longer term, total grain production (including cereals, tubers, and soybeans) increased from 111.2 million metric tons (mmt) in 1949 to 180.2 mmt in 1955, the initial period of individual farming under the original land reform; after 1955 and through 1980, the period covering various forms of collectivized farming, grain production increased to 320.6 mmt; then, in the second period of individual farming under the household responsibility system, through 1984, grain production increased to 407.3 mmt.[6] Thus, over some twenty-five years of collectivized farming, nationwide grain production had increased by 140 mmt, an average increase of 5.6 mmt per year. By contrast, the increase during 1949–1955, the initial six-year period of individual farming, was 69 mmt, an average increase of 11.5 mmt per year, and the increase from 1980 to 1984, during the first four years under the household responsibility system, was over 86 mmt, an average increase of more than 21 mmt per year. In percentage terms, the average compound increase in grain production was 8.37 percent per year during 1949–1955, plummeted to 2.33 percent per year (not much above population increase) during 1955–1980, and then rebounded to 6.18 percent per year during 1980–1984 in the first four years under the responsibility system.

Although numerous factors contributed to the increasing rural productivity in the early 1980s, the switch to the household responsibility system was the primary and overriding factor. Justin Yifu Lin, an economist at Beijing University, conducted a study aimed to measure directly and isolate the impact of the change to household tenure from the impact of the initial agricultural reforms of the late 1970s (rise in government procurement prices, expansion of the free markets, and product specialization in accordance with comparative advantage). Although these earlier reform measures were introduced in 1978, their impact was believed to have spillover effects through the 1980s. The evidence from Lin's study indicates that almost all of the productivity growth that occurred in the early 1980s was the result of the household responsibility system.[7]

However, as Table 4.1 indicates, and as has been widely recognized, there has been a leveling off of grain productivity gains and total crop output since 1984.[8] The reason for this plateauing, and the possible means by which strong grain productivity and total crop output gains could be resumed, appear instructive not only for China but for other countries as well, and will be a principal focus for much of the rest of this chapter. At the same time, we should note that the present picture is hardly a bleak one, as some have suggested. The plateauing of grain production has come at levels that represent both per-hectare productivity and per-capita calorie availability that are high in relation to Third World norms. Moreover, the figures for gross output value of agriculture in Table 4.1, which include (apart from the crop farming component itself) components for animal husbandry, fishing, and other activities, reflect continued growth in the noncrop sector, albeit slower growth since 1984.

Fieldwork Findings

In addition to our review of the literature, we carried out field trips to China in 1987 and 1988, during which we spoke with officials and academics about the household responsibility system in agriculture and completed eighty-one extensive, unstructured interviews with farm households in five provinces and one province-level municipality (Sichuan, Jiangsu, Anhui, Hainan, Hebei, and Beijing Municipality). Usually, members of at least two households were present and expressed their views during each interview session, so our findings reflect the experiences and concerns of roughly twice that number of Chinese farmers.

The farmers we spoke with reflected the following typical situations: Their holdings are small, usually around 0.4 hectares. But on these small holdings, and supplemented by agricultural sidelines such as hog-raising and sometimes by nonagricultural employment, the households are able to produce (or trade for) enough food to give them an adequate and reasonably varied diet, plus a sufficient surplus to acquire a range of goods and services. Overall, every family we interviewed except for one believed themselves to be substantially better off than they were before the household responsibility system was introduced.

Land Tenure

The families' position on the land has some owner-like characteristics—similar to the earlier possession of private plots, which most families still regard as a minor, delineated, part of their holding—but is perceived in important ways to fall short of the characteristics we would normally associate with ownership. Perception and local practice are important in attempting to define the relationship of the peasants to the land because there presently appears to be a somewhat variable and uncertain regulation of the peasants' rights and obligations. In terms of what can be regarded as formal, legal regulation there are only a few general pronouncements that have been made at the central government level (and only sometimes repeated locally) and the contents of written responsibility contracts, which only some households (in varying forms) possess. These written contracts may reflect certain standards that have been sent from the central government down through the administrative hierarchy to the townships (former communes), villages (former brigades), and chosen leaders of the erstwhile production teams.

For example, a typical usership contract in a 10 x 15 cm red booklet, which was brought out by an interviewed farmer, contained the following on the first page:

Based on Doc. #1 1984 this certificate is issued in order to obtain stability of usership. Contract period is from 1985 to 1989. [Note: some contracts stated 15-year usership periods, but others like this one did not. The contract period here was pre-printed, suggesting fairly widespread use in the locale, and, indeed, we were told this form was used county-wide.] For fruit trees, forests, and wild lands the contract period can be longer. All the land is owned collectively. Farmers have only usership, not ownership. Land cannot be sold or leased. No farmers can build houses or tombs on contracted land. Land can be transferred, but only without compensation. During contract period, if contracted land is used by state or collective, it will be dealt with according to current policies [unstated]. Public facilities on contracted land (road, canals, etc.) should be protected by the farmer and cannot be destroyed. During period of contract, usership of contracting farmer cannot be violated by state or collective—usership is guaranteed. Contracting farmer must pay fees according to requirements of the contract. [Note: In this case the contract document did not contain a statement of the household's quotas, taxes, and fees as well, but others often did—Au.]

The second page contained names of county, township, village, and household; number of people in the household; and official seals of the township and village. The third page contained entries for the various kinds of land that might be covered—in this case, 5.3 mu (0.35 ha) of "wet land" and no "dry land." There were also spaces to enter any "forest land," "bamboo gardens," and "water area," but none were contracted here, with an indication that the contract period for any of these lands would have been fifteen years.

The following pages contained spaces to enter the size and location of each separate parcel covered by the contract (typically there were several parcels, sometimes 1 mu or less). Parcels were described in relation to the local monuments (west of Li's house, east of Wang's tomb), and boundaries shown as running by lands of these or other named persons, although without an explicit, "surveyor's" starting point. The water source is also shown for each parcel.

The next pages contain spaces to enter any land or water transferred: date, name of land, classification of land, size of parcel. We were told that any separate parcel could be transferred.

Some comments may be offered on the foregoing:

• There have been widely varying degrees of communication to the farmers—either via a contract or by other means—about a 15-year usership period, which is what the central government has stated to be the governing standard for security of possession under the responsibility system in agriculture. But even if such a period is stated in the contract, and even if the farmer *knows* it is in the contract (which, ironically, we found was frequently not the case), the more salient point is that the farmers generally give little credence to such a promise of tenure security, given that the collective is still owner of the land and that the cadre can take it back. "Stability of usership," to use the opening words of the contract, is not considered reliable by the farmers.

• The quoted contract appears internally inconsistent as to the rights of the state or collective to resume control of part or all of the land, although what it may mean is that the state or collective can take land back for a public purpose such as a road or forest preserve (or factory?), but not simply to grant agricultural usership to another farmer. Either according to the rules or not, such resumptions of control do occur, at least frequently enough so that virtually every farmer has heard of such cases, and several of those we interviewed had either experienced it directly or had it hanging over their heads. All farmers considered it to be a potential threat. If land is taken, the vague reference to "current policies" indicated how little legal assurance is afforded the farmer in obtaining compensation—either for the disturbance of his usership or for improvements he may have made in the land. It appears that only nominal compensation, if any, is given. In some cases, a small amount of unallocated brigade land may be available for reallocation to a farmer whose land is taken. In other cases small amounts of land may be reallocated to him from contracted lands of others in the production team. In either case, the farmer will not keep the continuing benefit of long-term improvements (e.g., trees planted, irrigation improvements) if he has made them on the taken land, and in the latter case the direct experience of insecurity will be spread to neighboring families.

• It seems to be the general perception that uncompensated transfer to another person during the farmer's life is permitted, and that whatever usership rights a farmer has will pass to the other members of his household upon his death, but there are occasional cases of compensated transfer. Since the duration of usership rights is uncertain, such transfers do not appear to be in the nature of a "sale" of multiyear usership rights for a single lump-sum payment, but rather amount to a year-to-year "lease" of these rights while they continue.

• Either the contract document or a separate document contains the farmer's obligations to provide a quota of grain (and sometimes other products) to the state at a fixed low price, or sometimes without payment. Although the quota has theoretically been subject to voluntary negotiation and agreement between local authorities and each farmer since 1985, it is clear that in practice it remains a firm quota, allocated by the local cadre in accordance with what they have been told to acquire and deliver in their area. In addition, farmers have express, although typically small, obligations to make payments for taxes and various local dues at the township (commune) level. In many cases the quota and other obligations do change during the contractual usership period, and thus may have some similarity to an annual land rent, fixed in advance, which is changed every year or two in accordance with changing production and other conditions. Unlike the rent charged by a private landlord, however, the quota is responsive in substantial part to national exigencies determined by the state that may not be closely related to the particular farmer's production; and, fortunately, the effective level of these charges, which are typically equivalent to around 10–25 percent of a farmer's gross annual crop production, is much lower than the private rent levels one would expect to see in comparable conditions of population pressure on land and in circumstances of open bidding for land. For example, we would expect the latter to be in the range of 40–60 percent of gross crop production.

• The actual allocation of individual parcels seems generally to have been done by lot at the production team level, after the necessary number of separate parcels were calculated and delineated. Local-level administration by land-reform beneficiaries performed this process of identification and allocation of more than half-a-billion discrete parcels to roughly 150 million farm households, mostly during a period of only two years. The Chinese experience underlines once again how rapidly the allocation side of land reform—giving tenant farmers land they already cultivate or giving portions of plantation land or other parcels to landless laborers—can be carried out by a regime that has genuine political will and is ready to utilize localized, beneficiary-dominated administration. (We might, in this connection, contrast the successes of local-level, beneficiary-dominated administration in the 1946–1948 Japanese and 1970–1973 South Vietnamese land reforms, with the extreme slowdowns created in part by the lack of such administration in the Philippines from 1972 to date, and in El Salvador from 1980 to date.)

• One other matter that is not covered by any contract we encountered, and that seems subject to widely variable treatment, is the question of whether usership of all the land covered in the contract is viewed as being allocated to the household as a unit, or whether separate parcels (or possibly a proportionate undivided interest in each parcel) are viewed as being allocated to different family members. Assuming that usership rights are viewed as inheritable, this question is most likely to arise if a daughter leaves the household to marry a man living in another production team or village. In some townships, it appears that the daughter is viewed as having a separate interest, which she is now abandoning. The proportion of the land farmed by the household that is her land therefore reverts to the production team for reallocation, perhaps based on the addition of members to other households (such as a new daughter-in-law marrying into a household, or a child born, at least if the birth is within the limits of the family-planning policy). In other townships, however, usership rights are apparently viewed as belonging to the household as a whole, and there is no reversion or reallocation except in the event of an entire household ceasing to farm the land. Obviously, a rule requiring involuntary reversion further impairs security of possession.

How owner-like are the usership rights of the Chinese farmer? The household has a nominally multiyear but ambiguous security of possession. It has quota and other obligations, which are somewhat rent-like but are fortunately far lower than a market rent would be. It makes its own production and marketing decisions but often subject to outside suasion and with an eye to the quota it must provide to the state (although it *can* grow something else, and buy the quota grain on the free market). Aside from quota and similar obligations, the household can sell on the free market, but in practice transaction costs (finding a middleman, or transporting and marketing by oneself in small lots) are sufficiently high so that most product surpluses are sold to the state at a constructed "near market" price. The farm household will probably get at least some, although inadequate, compensation for improvements made if the land is taken; and the rights probably survive death and can be transferred, during lifetime, at least gratuitously.

Altogether, the Chinese farmer has a bundle of rights and powers that are somewhat owner-like. But, they are, for example, far less owner-like than those of the permanent, registered low-rent "tenants" under the 1950s Egyptian land reform, or those of the long-term protected "tenants" created under the laws of several Western European countries. Indeed, the principal dimension in which the Chinese farmer under the responsibility system falls short of being truly owner-like is that of long-term assured security of tenure, with consequences that we examine below.

Agricultural, Economic, and Social Situation

What was the agricultural, economic, and social situation of the farm households we interviewed—households that have had the relationship to their basic productive resource that we have just described?

Productivity of rice, wheat, rapeseed, and other basic crops was up substantially since the introduction of the responsibility system, consistent with the national-level data. When we asked more detailed recall questions, it likewise appeared that most increases had occurred in the initial years, and that productivity had since plateaued, again consistent with the national data. There also had been some, although seemingly not great, diversification into new crops.

Importantly, there had been very little in the way of capital or long-term improvements to the land by those interviewed, even though, in almost every case, they were aware of long-term improvements that would increase their productivity. Most of these potential long-term improvements were "divisible"; that is, they could be made on each single, small parcel. For those improvements that are not always divisible, such as water wells, farmers stated that cooperation with neighbors who farmed adjacent parcels would certainly be possible if all farms had long-term security on the land. But farmers had not invested money or labor in tubewells, drainage, terracing, or land leveling, or planted new tree crops taking years to mature. Even working of organic fertilizer from penned animals into the soil—an investment of labor in soil improvement perceived to give returns over a period of years—was often done preferentially or exclusively on the small portion of the land long held as a private plot.

The initial increases in yields had instead resulted from improvements in agricultural practices of the kind whose returns are all or nearly all realized in the same season, such as timing of agricultural operations more carefully, applying more fertilizer or applying it more carefully, using better seeds, improving water management, and more assiduous weeding. These changes have been made because the individual household now receives the benefits, and receives them immediately. By contrast, capital or long-term improvements that could improve current yields above their mid-1980s plateau have not been made, it appears, because farmers do not feel adequately assured that they will remain on their present land long enough to recover their investment and reap a profit. (This difference between immediate and long-term investment by farmers, its importance for productivity, and its inextricable relation to the farmer's perceived security of tenure is a fundamental fact of rural life in country after country. The theoretical economic literature often has a curious blind spot in regard to this fact.)

Besides the increases in crop production, most families have also experienced substantial increases in income from agricultural sidelines, including production of hogs, chickens, ducks, geese, water buffalo, and fish. Many families also have new incomes from nonagricultural sidelines—either a new job for a family member in a village or township enterprise, or a private household activity like tile-making, house construction, or local transport.

Despite the increase in crop production, it was striking that farmers now spend far less time in the fields, freeing up time for the sideline activities as well as for leisure. Farmers consistently responded that the working members of the household had spent from 250 to 320 days a year on the fields of the collective, in what might be described as a kind of "competitive featherbedding" in which little was actually accomplished. By contrast, the same households presently spend 60 to 90 days a year on the same fields, now individually partitioned and allocated, and produce substantially more per square meter. Household surveys conducted by China's Ministry of Agriculture confirm a dramatic reduction in the labor-days for the cultivation of major crops since the onset of the household responsibility system. The enormous labor inefficiency of the Chinese collective—and probably of other collective systems—is difficult to grasp fully until one has talked to farmer after farmer, all repeating the same account. One effect of decollectivization has been to free up as much as 100 billion person-days a year for other productive activities and leisure.

The physical and economic consequences of increased productivity were manifest. Rice consumption was now ample, meat consumption among these households roughly quadrupled, and cash incomes usually more than quadrupled. New brick houses were being built everywhere, generating extensive private-sector construction work, and consumer goods such as black-and-white television sets and electric fans—and, increasingly, tape decks and washing machines—were becoming common household fixtures. Such consumer outlays become even more likely when the peasants are unwilling to make long-term investments in the land, and recognize that the interest on bank savings is not sufficient to keep up with inflation.

Contrary to what has been suggested by at least one writer, medical care for the households we interviewed was perceived to be at least equal to, and perhaps better than, that under the collective. Small fees were now required, but medical personnel were consequently more responsive, and there were somewhat more options in care. Likewise, education was perceived on the whole to be better than before, although now fees, sometimes substantial in size, were required. We did not encounter a single case in which a child was now kept home from school to perform agricultural tasks—indeed, with the reduced time requirements on the land, this would make little sense—but such cases were sometimes known under the collectives because of the household's drive for work points.

Ultimately, the social and political consequences of decollectivization may be at least as significant as the economic effects. The 1960s image of robot-like, gray-clad figures shuffling off to the communal dining hall has been replaced with voluble, colorfully clad and increasingly independent-minded farmers. In the wake of the crushing of the pro-democracy movement in June of 1989, it is obvious that the process of democratization in China still has far to go, but it is not coincidental that in Poland, a communist society that has ventured far down the path of democratization, agriculture has long been dominated by independent-minded family farmers rather than regimented collectives. Empowerment at the grass roots occurs whenever a state loosens its tight reins of control over farmers. Economic freedoms lead to more independent-minded farmers, whose calls for political freedom cannot be forestalled forever.

Steps Toward Further Increases in Productivity

What then, to return to our basic question, is needed to move to still higher levels of crop productivity, and to achieve all the benefits for the farmers and for Chinese society that will go with such increased productivity? With virtually all the practicable annual improvements in farming practices now in place, this is essentially to ask: What is needed to cause the farmer to invest in long-term improvements? In our 1988 round of interviews, we explored this question carefully, and found a single answer emerged: ownership.

We asked questions encompassing other alternatives. Would higher prices lead the farmers to make long-term investments in the land? The farmers' answer, for entirely logical reasons, is no. Even with substantially higher prices for agricultural products, capital investments in the land will require a number of years of returns to justify the farmer's outlay, whether that outlay is in cash or family labor or a combination of the two. The principal point is not how high the prices are this year, but whether the farmer is assured of being on the land enough years to produce a long enough series of improved crops out of his investment to recover that investment and ultimately make a profit. Irrigation or drainage works cannot be paid for out of the higher prices for one or two years' crops, and fruit trees bought and planted today may not even begin to yield for four or five years. Long-term security of possession, not price, is the primary issue. Moreover, any price increases for the basic food crops, which are the subject of the heavily subsidized monthly ration the government provides to nonfarmers, must either be paid for by the cash-strapped government, or lead to a corresponding increase in the ration price paid by the urban consumers, a matter of great political difficulty.

What, then, of extending the use rights, but without granting full ownership to the farmers? Again the farmers' answer is no. Even when the farmer has been clearly told that he has fifteen-year usership rights, he does not presently make long-term investments. Is the period, then, too short? Would changing it to twenty-five, fifty, or even ninety-nine years make any difference? The problem, it turns out, does not reside nearly so much in the difference between a substantial period and a very substantial period, as it does in the *credibility* of either. As long as the collective still *owns* the land, and the cadre consequently have power to take it back or violate the use rights given, the farmers will not make long-term investments, whether the avowed period of their "rights" is fifteen years or ninety-nine years. There have been enough examples of the cadre snatching land away—whether legally but as an essentially uncompensated exercise of their rights to take land for a public purpose, or extra-legally—to make everyone's future rights uncertain. Indeed, just the simple knowledge that the cadre *have* that power, even if unexercised, may be sufficient, whatever the nominal period of the usership rights.

Conceivably, if tight constraints on takings by local officials were adopted by the central government and effectively overseen, and actions by the cadres against possession in fact sharply declined, then this in conjunction with a highly publicized grant of express fifty-year usership rights to all individual farmers might lead to a gradual dissipation of the farmers' insecurity and a growth of the willingness to invest. Could the farmers, in other words, be made to feel at least as secure about all their use rights to land as they do about the foundation plot on which their home stands? Possibly. This could be reinforced by an end to all local rules that allow land to revert and be redistributed if daughters marry or other changes occur in household size. But this, at best, would be a process that would take many years to realize, and it would prove very difficult to hold the cadre tightly in check during all this time because the collective entity would still be the formal "owner" of the land. There is little prospect, we believe, that such changes, even if enforceable on a nationwide basis, would lead to immediate and substantial increases in farmers' long-term investment.

Other kinds of "tinkering" with the present usership system would have little additional effect on long-term investment. Giving the farmer the power to mortgage the land in return for a bank loan, for example, might permit investment in small tractors or other equipment that the farmer could own and keep, separate from the land, but it would have little impact on the farmer's willingness to make long-term investments in the land itself, which he would lose if the land were taken. Furthermore, the principal problem is not in inducing the farmer to make long-term investments with government funds that are loaned to him by a bank, but in getting the farmer to use his own savings and his own household labor in making significant improvements on the land. A new, strenuously enforced rule requiring that the farmer receive the full value of all improvements made if the land were subsequently taken might possibly help. But—apart from the difficulties of enforcement and valuation,[9] especially with regard to the value of the farmer's own time and labor in planning and carrying out any improvement—it would again be years before most farmers were sufficiently convinced that such a rule was being enforced against the cadre and the collective with its ultimate "ownership."

Another form of tinkering would give the farmer the power to sell his usership rights to the land. But what *is* it that the farmer is selling? A buyer would have the same uncertainties as to long-term possession, and he is no more likely to pay full value for improvements made—in the confident expectation that he will possess the land long enough to recover his investment and realize a profit on it—than the present possessor is to make those improvements in the first place. In fact, what is apparently sold today where such compensated transfers are allowed, is a year-by-year usership right in return for a year-by-year payment; in effect, a yearly land lease, with no added incentive to make long-term investments on either side—indeed probably with a further reduction of such incentives. Some of these tinkering approaches are being tried in an experiment in Meitan County of Guizhou Province, including an end to reversion and redistribution based on changing household size and allowing sale of usership rights.

When all of the other alternatives are explored and rejected, what remains is full ownership for the farmer, or "privatization," as it is generally called in China. In interview after interview, the farmers indicated that this would supply the missing motivation to make long-term investments on the land. Moreover, such transfer of ownership of at least a significant part of agricultural land will bring other major benefits as well. Not only would it increase productivity, it would probably help solve serious inflationary problems that result largely from high rates of consumption and low rates of investment. Farmers currently use their profits to buy consumer goods, in part because they are unwilling to invest in capital improvements on the land.

Granting full ownership would also raise much-needed revenue for the state. By charging the farmers even a modest amount per mu, depending on land quality, in exchange for legal title, the government could raise very large sums. The farmers we interviewed were more than willing to pay 100–200 Rmb (US$27–54) per mu, amounts that would quickly result in tens of billions of Rmb of added revenue for the government. A portion of the incremental revenue could be placed in a special account and used to augment public investment in agriculture, which, in addition to private agricultural investment, has been severely lacking. State investment in agriculture had never been lower than 10 percent of the total investment in capital construction until the 1980s. In the early 1960s the figure stood at about 18 percent, but between 1981 and 1985 the percentage averaged only 5 percent, and slumped to 3 percent in 1986 and 1987.

Also, as further discussed below, it would be quite simple to include restrictions in such a grant of ownership similar to those successfully used in other major Asian land-reform programs. Such restrictions would leave in place only the positive consequences of ownership transfer and forestall possible negative consequences. Thus, there could be a prohibition on any renting out of the owned land to prevent any landlord-tenant relationships from arising, and a restriction requiring that any sale or transfer be to other small farmers so that intensive farming was practiced and larger accumulations of land could not occur.

The transfer of land ownership to farmers need not be regarded as violating any ideological imperative of the communist system. First, there has been an expanding conception of what personal property may be privately owned in China. Formal recognition of private ownership now includes not only everyday items for household use, private bank accounts, and privately owned stock in certain state enterprises, but farmers' houses (but not the land on which they stand). Notably, it also includes items that can be considered direct "means of production"—vehicles, farm equipment, tools, and machines of small businesses, even trees for personal use around farm dwellings, can all be individually owned.

Second, many, if not most, other communist societies permit private ownership of farmland, or are seriously thinking about permitting it. In the Soviet Union, selling ownership of land to farmers, beyond simply leasing it to them, has been suggested before a televised session of the new Congress of People's Deputies as a solution to both agricultural and budgetary problems. Indeed, the Lithuanian Republic has recently passed a law that appears to allow for the ownership of farmland at least at the household level, although they might prefer to characterize this as a sort of micro-cooperative. And most of the communist societies of Eastern Europe recognize the legality of private ownership of farmland. In both Poland and Yugoslavia, most farmland is still privately owned; in Romania, about 15 percent of farmland is privately owned; in both Hungary and Czechoslovakia, although only small percentages of farmland are held in private ownership, the legal possibility of private ownership of farmland is still recognized. It might also be noted that the recognition of private ownership of farmland in these five Eastern European countries is not a recent phenomenon, but represents long-standing legal rules of these communist societies.

Finally, there is precedent in China for private ownership of farmland. The 1950 Agrarian Reform Law of the People's Republic of

China, passed after the communist victory in 1949, established a system of peasant landownership. It was not until later in the 1950s that China started down the road of collectivization.

Recommendations for "Privatization"

If China were to privatize farmland (perhaps calling it something like "universal asset endowment," or referring to it as creation of "micro-co-ops" with ownership at the household level, if such formulations would further ease ideological problems), it would be perfectly possible to move initially on only certain categories of land, and make no decision on the rest. Private-plot land, constituting perhaps 6 percent of the 100 million hectares of cultivated land, would be a logical candidate for transfer of full ownership. By itself, however, it would be too small a quantity of land to make a significant overall difference for investment and production. Self-consumption land would be a second logical candidate, constituting about 20 million hectares, or a further 20 percent of cultivated land. Conceptually, these are parcels or portions of parcels whose production is entirely for the farmer's own consumption, whereas the remaining, quota land is that on which the grain to be supplied to the government is produced. In practice the land is treated equally, and the quota grain in fact comes from the combined harvest of the self-consumption and quota lands, but the distinction offers a theoretical basis on which additional land for immediate privatization—enough land to make a significant difference in investment and production—could be identified. Waste land (or "wild land") would be a third logical candidate for privatization. This category comprises roughly 20 million hectares of land that is presently uncultivated but considered cultivable. The government plans to bring waste land under production in the hands of individual farmers over future years. Clearly, this is land on which substantial investment will be needed, and on which the difference between granting merely usership and granting ownership is likely to make an even more significant difference for future productivity than on presently cultivated lands. Altogether these three categories of land—private-plot, self-consumption, and waste land—total around 46 million hectares; with waste land brought into production, these lands would comprise about 38 percent of all land then under cultivation.

Whether in an initial program of privatization that focused on these three categories of land, or in a full-scale program that might be carried out in the future, a number of sub-issues would arise. We address here what some of these sub-issues might be and how they might be dealt with.

1. *Title Document; Publicity*

To the extent privatization occurs and ownership is granted to the farmers, everything possible must be done to give full significance to the change. For example, it is important to have a title document, given to the farmers, which would be in a large, impressive, official-looking format, rather than distributing something in the format of the small red booklet that farmers sometimes receive in connection with their present land-use rights or quota obligations. Any such privatization process should also be accompanied by an extensive public-information campaign.

The description of the land being privatized should be included in the title document. The description should initially be in the simplified form that is presently used in the booklets that are given out to describe farmers' land-use rights (typically, these indicate who holds the land on the north, south, east, and west of each parcel and the approximate area for each parcel). Later, this initial description of the land being privatized can be supplemented with a document based on aerial photography technology, which shows a picture of the parcel or parcels in relation to adjacent lands and may contain added descriptive information that has been generated by simple computer processing of the picture (such as exact area, or length of the boundary lines). If aerial photography was carried out for all cultivated lands, the resulting information could also be used to provide a more exact description of farmers' responsibility lands as well as their privatized lands.

2. *Farmer's Choice*

To give maximum reality to the act of privatization, the farmer should be given the opportunity to choose between receiving full ownership of certain parcels of land (for example, his self-consumption and private-plot lands) or keeping the present arrangement for his use of those parcels. This choice should be embodied in a standard form of document that each farmer should initially sign, indicating whether he chooses privatization or the continuation of the use arrangement for those lands. This document should also indicate both the standard price per mu that farmers will be required to pay if they choose to privatize a portion of their land and the basic payment schedule. For example, if the price is to be paid over four years, the document might explain that 25 percent of the price is to be paid each year.

If, in a particular township, self-consumption (or, as occasionally occurs, even private-plot) lands are not in fact separately identified, a simple formula might be used. For example, a farmer might be allowed to choose (or perhaps have chosen for him by the production-team leader or other local leader) parcels or portions of parcels totaling 20 percent of all the land he farms as the self-consumption land to be privatized. He might also choose, where necessary, a parcel or portion of a parcel equal to 6 percent of all the land he farms as the private-plot land to be privatized.

3. Payment

Payment for land will give maximum reality to the act of privatization, and affords an occasion both for adding to government budgetary resources and reducing inflationary pressures arising from farmers' expenditures for consumer goods. Different prices could be set for multiple-cropped and single-cropped land. Or, farmers might, for example, typically be required to pay 200 Rmb per mu (US$800/ha) of wetland and 100 Rmb per mu (US$400/ha) of dryland for land that is being privatized. These prices are quite reasonable, both in relation to market values of land in other Asian less-developed-country settings with comparable population pressure and, even more important, in relation to prices for land in Asian land-reform settings where a substantial—although still less than full-market-value—price was being set. In the latter, land values have tended to be set at around 2.5 times the gross value of annual crop production, whereas the prices suggested here are less than 1.0 (unity) times that value.

For purposes of illustration, if initially 90 million mu (6 million hectares) of private-plot land are privatized, together with 300 million mu (20 million hectares) of self-consumption land, and if 30 percent of this land is sold for 200 Rmb per mu, 60 percent for 100 Rmb, and 10 percent for 50 Rmb, the total land price will be 48.75 billion Rmb, apart from the possibility of charging interest. If an additional 300 million mu (20 million hectares) of waste land are privatized, at an average price of 50 Rmb per mu, this will be a further 15 billion Rmb. (The total equals US$17 billion at 1989 exchange rates.) Part of the resources received as land payment should, in turn, be devoted by the state to the maintenance and improvement of irrigation and other rural infrastructure at the village, township, county, and higher levels. Such overall maintenance and improvement activities would complement and be complemented by the on-farm investments that the new owners will themselves make in such areas as land leveling, drainage, and terracing.

The payments should be spread over several years. The amounts could be adjusted downward for counties that are in particular ecological, cultural, or low-productivity zones, and also for those farmers with very small holdings, as well as for special cases of hardship. Those households that hold so little land that they already have grain ration allowances, for example, might be charged only half as much or charged nothing for whatever land they receive.

At the same time that a farmer receives his title document, he should receive a document that contains his payment schedule. The payment document should indicate the price per mu for each type of land, how much the farmer is required to pay for each parcel he is receiving, and what amount he is to pay each year. The date for making payment (which should be sometime after the main harvest) should also be indicated. The state would also need to decide the extent to which it wishes to receive payment in cash or in grain, and require the obligation to be stated, at the local level, in a corresponding form. To whatever extent payment is to be made in grain, it would be desirable to value grain at above quota, near-market prices. In addition, the state would need to decide whether interest will be charged on portions of the land price that are not to be paid until future years.

The payment document should also indicate that farmers have the right to make payment ahead of schedule if they wish. The state should decide whether it will allow a small discount as an incentive for advance payment. For example, a payment of 100 Rmb due in 1992 might be satisfied by 90 Rmb paid in advance in 1991, or 80 Rmb paid in advance in 1990.

4. Powers of the New Owner

The farmer who receives land under privatization should have the power to pass the land to heirs upon his death as well as the power during his life to sell (or give) full ownership of the land to another person. He should also have the power to mortgage the land to a public-sector financial institution or as security for any lawful loan.

There should probably be certain limitations on the powers of the owner, however, as there have been in other major Asian land-reform programs. The farmer should not be able to sell (or give) the land to another person until the farmer himself has paid the land price to the government. In addition, it is important that the person *to whom* he sells: (1) should be an agricultural cultivator, who presently cultivates his own land or cultivates with a parent, (2) must continue to use the newly acquired land for agricultural purposes (that is, like the original owner, he cannot build a house or factory on the land), and (3) must not be a person who has ownership or use rights *altogether* to a greater total amount of land than some set ceiling, after including the land that is the subject of the sale or gift. Concerning the latter point, which, as in other successful Asian land reforms, is intended to prevent undue accumulations of land, the ceiling might be set by the state according to region and kind of land—such as single-cropped or multiple-cropped land—and might range, for example, from 15 to 45 mu (1 to 3 hectares) per household under most circumstances.

Also, although the new owner should have the power to sell or give full ownership to another, he should *not* have the power to rent or lease out the land, whether for a crop season, a year, or a period of years. Any attempted renting or leasing out should be void and unenforceable, as well as subject to penalties under law, which are discussed below. This will ensure that whoever is actually cultivating the land has the motivation to make improvements that accompanies full ownership. This does not, of course, foreclose the possibility that, after five or ten years, when most land has been improved by its owner, some leasing out to small-scale cultivators might then be permitted.

A question arises as to whether inheritance, sale, or gift can be of a portion of the land only—that is, whether the privatized land can be subdivided or not. The farmers' perception of their powers with respect to inheritance of land over which they have current use rights appears to be that it *can* be subdivided, and we are inclined to think that this present rule is the better one for privatized land also. The limitation of family size in the countryside through the family-planning program should place practical limits on the amount of subdivision that will occur; and, in any event, a certain number of people will have to be supported by a certain amount of land, regardless of rules as to subdivision. But the state, if it chooses, could place limits on the power to convey less than the whole amount of privatized land.

If the privatized land is mortgaged, a separate set of rules should probably deal with possible foreclosure and acquisition of the land by the lending institution in the case of persistent and unexcused failure to pay the loan by the borrower. After any such foreclosure, the land must then be sold by the lending institution to another small-scale cultivator or child of a small-scale cultivator, again subject to limits as to the maximum amount of land any farmer can hold.

5. Duties of the New Owner

The new owner should be required to pay the price for the privatized land in a timely fashion consistent with the agreed repayment schedule, and to continue to pay any taxes on the privatized land (also to pay any quota, although if the initial program involved private-plot land, self-consumption land, and waste land, there presumably would be no existing quotas assessed). In addition to the initial land payments, as productivity increased the state should be able to assess a continuing property-ownership tax on this land at a level that would help support ongoing governmental activities in the maintenance and improvement of rural infrastructure, and for other rural development purposes.

Moreover, for any sale of the land during, say, the first ten years, the government may want to assess a significant transaction tax—perhaps on a sliding scale adjusted downward as time progresses—against the price received.

The new owner must not rent or lease out the privatized land, nor have ownership or use rights on a total quantity of land exceeding the set ceiling amount. He also must ensure that the land continues to be used for agricultural purposes.

These duties should all continue to apply to a person who receives the privatized land from the original owner through inheritance, purchase, or gift (except, presumably, for the payment of the land price in the case of sale or gift, as we suggest this should already have been fully paid as a precondition for any effective sale or gift of the land).

6. Penalties

Failure by the owner to carry out any of his duties should lead to appropriate penalties, specified in advance by law. These should normally begin, we suggest, with a specific written warning demanding performance, delivered by the administrative authorities to the farmer. In the case of an uncorrected violation of the owner's duties, a mandated sale of the land by the farmer to another small cultivator or child of a small cultivator should be required within a stated time period, such as six months. In the case of failure of the farmer to sell within that time, or a still uncorrected violation of the duty by the buyer, a mandatory reacquisition of the land by the state and its resale to another small cultivator or child of a small cultivator should be required. Again, any sale should be subject to maximum limits on holding size applicable to the farmer acquiring the land.

7. Government Acquisition of Privatized Land for Public Purpose

Government acquisitions of privatized land should be limited to essential public purposes, and authority to exercise this power should be limited to officials of the central government or provincial officials acting only with advance central government approval. County, township, and village officials should *not* be permitted to exercise this power with respect to privatized land.

Whenever a parcel of privatized land is taken by the government from the owner for a public purpose such as an essential road, or for any other public use warranting the government's exercise of its eminent domain power, it is vitally important that full recompense be given to the former owner. In most cases, primary compensation should probably take the form of allowing the farmer to become full owner of an equivalent parcel of land selected out of his remaining, responsibility land (or selected out of some other nonprivately owned land, if possible, when *all* of his land—privatized as well as responsibility land—has been taken for a public purpose). The farmer will then, however, have lost some of the land over which he has rights of usership, and should be paid cash compensation for the loss. In addition, when privatized land is taken for a public purpose, it is essential that the farmer should receive the full value, in cash, of any improvements he has already made on that privatized land.

8. Monitoring
While any privatization of lands is being carried out, it is important that there should be a continuing round of random-sample surveys (as well as less rigorous "rapid rural appraisals") carried out with beneficiary farmers in order to discover any problems in the program or in its implementation and correct those problems immediately.

Conclusion

Although the household responsibility system was effective in freeing up incentives in the Chinese countryside and led to substantial gains in agricultural productivity, the potential for further increase remains. The largest remaining stumbling block is the insecurity of tenure that Chinese farmers have on their individual parcels of publicly owned land, which has been a disincentive for any long-term improvements to the land. Privatization of farmland will be the most effective solution to these remaining agricultural productivity problems. With full legal ownership of the land they till, along with full communication and enforcement of the accompanying ownership rights and duties, Chinese farmers can be expected to make the increased long-term investments in farmland needed to achieve additional significant increases in agricultural production.

Notes

1. The Agrarian Reform Law of the People's Republic of China, promulgated by the Central People's Government on June 30, 1950.

2. Roy L. Prosterman and Jeffrey M. Riedinger, *Land Reform and Democratic Development* (Baltimore, Md.: Johns Hopkins University Press, 1987), p. 19.

3. C. Carter and F. Zhong, *China's Grain Production and Trade* (Boulder, Colo.: Westview Press 1988), p. 5.

4. D. G. Johnson, "Economic Reforms in the People's Republic of China," *Economic Development and Cultural Change* 36, no. 3 (April 1988): S229; N. Lardy, "Prospects and Some Policy Problems of Agricultural Development in

China," *American Journal of Agricultural Economics* 68, no. 2 (May 1986): 451.

5. Thomas Wiens, "Issues in the Structural Reform of Chinese Agriculture," *Journal of Comparative Economics* 11 (September 1987): 373.

6. Carter and Zhong, *China's Grain Production and Trade*, p. 5.

7. Justin Yifu Lin, "The Household Responsibility System in China's Rural Reform," unpublished paper prepared for the Twentieth International Conference of Agricultural Economists, 1988, p. 7. Our fieldwork findings were consistent with the findings of Lin's study. When we asked peasants to identify the reasons for their increased productivity, the household responsibility system was always cited as the primary factor.

8. For unmilled rice alone, productivity per hectare in 1980 was 4.13 metric tons and in 1984 was 5.37 metric tons, an increase of 30 percent. The figures since 1984, in metric tons per hectare, have been 5.26 (1985), 5.33 (1986), 5.41 (1987), 5.30 (1988, preliminary), and 5.43 (1989, projected).

9. Assigning a proper value to a particular parcel, with or without improvements, is difficult if no private land market exists. If farmers are given the power to sell their full rights to a parcel of land (whether those rights are ownerships or usership rights), a market will emerge for those rights, and the price paid in the case of a taking for a public purpose, such as a road, should then be made to approximately reflect this market price.

Selected Bibliography

Agrarian Reform Law of the People's Republic of China, The, promulgated by the Central People's Government, P.R.C. June 30, 1950.

Ashton, B., K. Hill, A. Piazza, and R. Zeitz. "Famine in China, 1958–61." *Population and Development Review* 10, no. 4 (1984): 613–645.

Bandyopadhyaya, K. *Agricultural Development in China and India.* New Delhi: Wiley Eastern, 1976.

Carter, C., and F. Zhong. *China's Grain Production and Trade.* Boulder, Colo.: Westview Press, 1988.

Chao, K. *Agricultural Production in Communist China 1949–1965.* Madison: University of Wisconsin Press, 1970.

Jan, G. P. "The Responsibility System and its Economic Impact on Rural China." *Asian Profile* 14, no. 5 (1986): 391–408.

Johnson, D. G. "Economic Reforms in the People's Republic of China." *Economic Development and Cultural Change* 36, no. 3 supplement (1988): S225–S245.

Khan, A., and E. Lee. *Agrarian Policies and Institutions in China After Mao.* Bangkok: International Labour Organization, 1983.

Lardy, N. R. "Agricultural Reforms in China." *Journal of International Affairs* 39, no. 2 (1986): 91–104.

———. "Prospects and Some Policy Problems of Agricultural Development in China." *American Journal of Agricultural Economics* 68, no. 2 (1986): 451–457.

Lin, J. Y. "The Household Responsibility System in China's Agricultural Reform: A Theoretical and Empirical Study." *Economic Development and Cultural*

Change 36, no. 3 supplement (1988): S199–S224.

————. "The Household Responsibility System in China's Rural Reform." Paper presented at the XX International Conference of Agricultural Economists, Buenos Aires, August 1988.

Liu, William T., ed. *China Statistical Abstract* 1988. New York: Praeger, 1989.

Peng, Xizhe. "Demographic Consequences of the Great Leap Forward in China's Provinces." *Population and Development Review* 13, no. 4 (1987): 639–670.

Prosterman, Roy L., and Jeffrey M. Riedinger. *Land Reform and Democratic Development.* Baltimore, Md.: Johns Hopkins University Press, 1987.

The Research Center for Rural Development of the State Council of the People's Republic of China. *Rural Economic and Social Statistics of China.*

United Nations, Food and Agriculture Organization. *FAO Production Yearbook 1987*, vol. 41, 1987.

Wiens, T. "Issues in the Structural Reform of Chinese Agriculture." *Journal of Comparative Economics* 11 (1987): 372-385.

part two

Latin America

chapter five

Land Reform in Central America

Rupert W. Scofield

Summary

A wave of violence and political upheaval has engulfed Central America during the past ten years. At the heart of this unrest is gross inequity in the distribution of wealth in most of the Central American societies, and fundamental injustice in the political system whereby new aspirants are permitted to acquire a toehold in the region's potentially robust economy and bountiful natural resources. As agrarian societies, much of the wealth in these countries has been associated, directly or indirectly, with ownership of the land, which in all cases except Costa Rica and Belize has been historically extremely concentrated in a small ruling elite. Over the past decade, two countries, El Salvador and Nicaragua, made real efforts to redress the inequities in their land-tenure structures via sweeping expropriatory and redistributive measures. Guatemala, in the 1950s, undertook a major land-reform effort that was later largely overturned. Honduras and Costa Rica have pursued less radical (and less significant) measures on a steady but much slower basis.

The focus of this chapter is to summarize the recent history of land-reform efforts in five countries of Central America—El Salvador, Nicaragua, Guatemala, Honduras, and Costa Rica—and to explore the larger question of how land-tenure problems may affect the future configuration of economic and political power in the region.

El Salvador

In terms of land area, El Salvador is the smallest country in Central America. Like its neighbors to the north and south, Guatemala and

Nicaragua, El Salvador's topography consists of a Pacific coastal plain rising into volcanic, rugged highlands. This topography creates a variety of climatic zones that can accommodate diverse agriculture, including coffee, sugarcane, cotton, citrus fruits, and basic grains. In 1987, El Salvador achieved the second highest coffee and sugarcane production in the region—141,000 metric tons and 3.1 million tons, respectively. A record maize crop of 572,000 metric tons was achieved in 1987. Livestock is another important activity in the agricultural sector, although grazing land is restricted to only 610,000 hectares by the pressure to use all available arable land for cropping.

El Salvador's population of approximately 5 million ranks it second in the region after Guatemala. Slightly more than one-third (37.8 percent) of the population derives its livelihood from agriculture. In 1971, El Salvador had the highest population pressure on the land in Central America: 5.5 persons per hectare of cropland. Since 1985, the population has been growing at the rate of 1.9 percent per year, excluding migration. In a trend found in other countries in the region, the infant mortality rate has dropped from 87 per 1,000 live births in 1975 to 57 per thousand in 1989. Between 1980 and 1988, the gross domestic product (GDP) declined by 5.7 percent, and on a per capita basis by 15.2 percent. As measured by this latter statistic, El Salvador's performance ranked it third among other Central American countries, behind Costa Rica and Honduras, but ahead of Guatemala and Nicaragua. Per capita GDP in all countries in the region was negative over this period.

History of the Land-Tenure Situation
El Salvador's precolonial land-tenure structure was similar to that of its northern neighbor, Guatemala. The original inhabitants held land in common, although actual farming was on the basis of individual parcels with extensive exchange of labor. As in Guatemala, this system was gradually dismantled by the conquistadores and their progeny, dying a final death in 1879 when a coffee ordinance catalyzed a type of enclosure movement wherein large landowners were encouraged to usurp land legally and supplant the Indians' basic grains with the increasingly popular and lucrative "brown gold." The gross inequities propagated under this system have been credited in part with stimulating the Communist-led peasant uprising of 1932, which, after exhausting its brief course, culminated in the slaughter by the army of thousands of campesinos. In the same year, a concerned government established the first land-reform agency, which, over the next forty-seven years, distributed a total of 61,650 hectares of farmland to some 15,000 peasant farmers, who today comprise what is commonly

referred to as the "traditional reformed sector."

As might be surmised, such token measures failed to address in any meaningful way the criminally inequitable land distribution situation, in which, by the late 1960s, six families owned more land than 133,000 small farm families, and over half of the rural population was without any access to land whatsoever. By 1971, the situation had worsened to the point that the landless population had grown to an estimated 250,000 families, or 70 percent of the population making its living from agriculture. In this group, tenants (including sharecroppers) and hired agricultural laborers could be found in more or less equal proportions. With few exceptions, the attitude of the landholding class was one of extreme indifference to the deplorable living conditions of the landless, whose diet and working and living conditions were often far inferior to those of the landlords' livestock. If anything, the landlord class perceived an economic advantage to themselves in the growing pool of cheap labor.

In the 1970s, the general discontent among the rural poor and the disenfranchised urban population, which had witnessed the callous theft of the presidency from Napoleón Duarte in the stolen elections of 1972, found expression through a number of guerrilla factions. These guerrillas were dedicated to the violent reversal of the tradition of military dictatorships, which, in collusion with the oligarchy, had been systematically looting the wealth of the nation during the postwar era. The overthrow of Somoza in Nicaragua in the summer of 1979 was like the firing of a starter pistol for similar insurrections in El Salvador and Guatemala. On October 15, 1979, heretofore invisible "reform-minded" officers of the Salvadoran armed forces staged a preemptive coup to topple President (General) Romero, cutting short by several weeks his planned departure to join his Miami bank accounts. Less than three months later, the first junta disintegrated, ripped asunder by accusations and countercharges of bad faith between its ideologically diverse factions, which ran the spectrum from right-wing conservatives to borderline guerrillas. The minister of agriculture at this time was Enrique Alvarez Córdoba, a landlord with a social conscience who had undertaken a mini–land reform on his own Pacific Coast farm. Later to be assassinated in the company of several *Frente Democratico Revolucionario* (FDR) members, Alvarez managed to oversee the drawing up of an emergency land-reform decree, rendered stillborn by the second, Christian Democrat–led junta, which came to power in January 1980. One of the first junta's last actions before its collapse was to prepare the ground for the eventual promulgation of a land–reform decree by freezing land sales and rental contracts.

The human story behind the making of the Salvadoran land reform of 1980 is unique in the history of U.S. diplomacy in the region. Had it not been for an extraordinary friendship between Michael P. Hammer, a labor advisor with the AFL-CIO's Latin American Institute, and Rodolfo Viera, the cunning leader of the country's largest campesino union, the *Unión Comunal Salvadoreña* (UCS), the reform, in all likelihood, would have never succeeded, and the second junta probably would have shared the fate of the first one, throwing the country into open civil war.

By all logic, Viera, a fiery-tempered, utterly fearless campesino born into abject poverty on a large Pacific Coast plantation, should have been one of the first defectors to the guerrillas. Largely owing to his trust in Hammer, who had given him his first trade unionist training back in the 1960s, Viera accepted the position in the *Instituto Salvadoreño de Transformación Agrícola* (ISTA) vacated by Alvarez, and entered into a social pact with Duarte's Christian Democrats, who promised, among other things, a genuine land reform. The conditions under which these agreements and the eventual Basic Agrarian Reform Law were transacted belong more to the realm of a high adventure epic than reality. Viera survived no less than five assassination attempts in the first three months of 1980, once by jumping his bullet-riddled jeep over railroad tracks to avoid an ambush. But the greatest pressure of all came from the murderous decimation being suffered by the UCS rank and file at the hands of Roberto D'Abuisson's infamous *Escuadrones de la Muerte*, for whom anyone seated to the Left of Adolf Hitler was a card-carrying Communist.[1] At one point, after an entire UCS cooperative had been wiped out, Hammer had to physically restrain Viera from leaving a land-reform decree drafting session and handing in his resignation. Less than a year later, Hammer, Viera, and a young lawyer, Mark Pearlman, were machine-gunned to death by two army corporals as they sat having dinner at the Sheraton Hotel. The two corporals have since been pardoned under an absurd interpretation of a political amnesty decree. The intellectual authors of the murder, close personal friends of Roberto D'Abuisson, have never been brought to trial.

Perhaps the most distinctive feature of the El Salvador land-reform program is the speed with which it was conceived and executed. Indeed, the bulk of the post facto criticism leveled at the decree starts with the notion that the Salvadoran and foreign advisors authoring the decree operated in isolation, and with incomplete or false information regarding the proposed beneficiaries and expropriatees of the process.

Few would contest that the two land-reform decrees—154 (Phase I), which expropriated all farms in excess of 500 hectares, and 207 (Phase III), the so-called "Land to the Tiller Law," which transferred sharecropped lands to their "direct cultivators"—were conceived under less than ideal circumstances, in terms of availability of information and time constraints. However, the allegation that the campesinos were not adequately consulted is false. Rodolfo Viera, as secretary general of the UCS and president of ISTA, was intimately involved in the process, and reported regularly on the tedious progress made in perfecting the language of the decree, often pirating out copies of drafts for review by his board of directors and the foreign advisors who worked with the AFL-CIO. In this regard, the role of the foreign advisors, in particular Roy Prosterman, in the process has also been the subject of great controversy. In fact, one finds in the substance and tenor of the attacks an interesting balance, with partisans of the Right denouncing the measures as having been too radical, and critics on the Left arguing that they did not go far enough. (Ironically, the right-wing ARENA party in power today sings the praises of Decree 207, albeit as a means of discrediting the Phase I co-ops; more will be said on this later.) Certainly, those close to Prosterman at that time recognize that his principal contribution to both 154 and 207 was in closing the multiple loopholes blasted in the legislation by panicked landlords in the Christian Democratic provisional government. Each of these landlords tried to tailor the decree in such a way as to exempt their family's farms. Prosterman also allayed the trepidations of the junta, who, most of all, feared that the decrees would be impossible to implement under the conditions prevailing in the rural areas at the time. One exception to Prosterman's generally beneficiary-biased approach was his insistence on a compensatory, rather than confiscatory, model. On this point he was at odds, initially, with Viera, who wanted to know why the wealthy landlord class, the majority of whom had already abandoned the country, needed to extract any more wealth from the country's depleted coffers. Eventually, however, Viera conciliated. Unfortunately, this capitulation did nothing to placate the ex-landlords or slow the progress of the bullets through Viera's body.

Nine years later, a campesino (now an owner of the Finca "Las Carretas" in the department of Santa Ana) would recall how he arrived at the gates of his patrón's plantation on the morning of March 6, 1980, to find a platoon of soldiers at the gates. A young corporal tried to turn him back, when the commander, recognizing him as one of the permanent workers on the farm, allowed him to enter. After walking six kilometers down the road to the hacienda at the heart of the 500-hectare farm, the campesino came upon a curious scene: another group of soldiers, standing in the midst of the other hundred or so workers on the finca, informing them that from this day forward, they were the new owners.

By the end of April 1980, the land-tenure situation in El Salvador, at least on paper, had been altered dramatically. Phase I had affected the 469 largest and wealthiest farms in the country, with a total land area of 219,000 hectares, or 15 percent of the total farmland in El Salvador; Phase II added another 100,000 hectares from some 2,000 farms between 100 and 500 hectares, much of it prime coffee land; and, finally, Phase III potentially affected an area roughly similar to Phase I, with the difference that this was largely marginal land, rented out as a source of income by small- and medium-size landowners.

In all, some 67,000 agricultural laborers (31,000 under Phase I; 36,000 under Phase II) and 118,000 tenants, renters, and sharecroppers were to have received land under the program, or approximately 60 percent of the 300,000 landless rural families who existed in El Salvador as of 1980, and 43 percent of the total rural population.

Table 5.1 illustrates the gap between the promise and the reality of the Salvadoran land reform. In actuality, only 18 percent of the rural population was affected, versus the 43 percent envisaged to have benefited. Thus, to date, the reform has benefited approximately 80,000

Table 5.1 Land and Families Affected by Salvadoran Land Reform

	1980 Decrees (planned)	Implemented (1989)
Phase I		
Land (ha)	219,000	263,295
Families	31,000	29,545
Phase II		
Land (ha)	100,000	5,000 [a]
Families	36,000	1,170
Phase III		
Land (ha)	200,000	71,000
Families	118,000	49,000
Totals		
Land (ha)	519,000	339,295
Families	185,000	79,715

[a] The beneficiaries from Phase II are in fact campesinos who received land through a voluntary sale program, intended as a substitute for Phase II.

campesino families, or 27 percent of the 300,000 then landless families. In the intervening years since the reform, however, further population growth may have generated another 50,000 landless families within the rural population, thus still leaving the degree of landlessness in El Salvador at an unacceptably high level. For this reason, even the right-wing ARENA government recognizes the need for continued land distribution to avoid a reoccurrence of the social crisis of 1979.

The above statement does not imply, of course, that the measures taken to date were fruitless; on the contrary, had they not been undertaken it is inconceivable that the country would have survived in anything like its present form. Indeed, there are some who argue that the country should have been plunged into chaos, and that a victorious leftist government would have undertaken a more meaningful, sweeping reform, akin to that of Nicaragua. For better or worse, this will remain, for the moment, of academic interest only.

A more relevant concern is how to continue the reform process. In fact, there seems to be a general consensus in El Salvador at present that the only feasible way of reviving the economy is to reactivate the great number of idle farms in the country, and that, because it is virtually impossible for large- or medium-size farmers to work in certain areas of the country (due to harassment by the Farabundo Martí National Liberation Front, or FMLN), these lands must be somehow transferred or sold to the rural poor, who are more immune to sabotage from the Left.

In a recent interview with the author, the current president of FINATA (the provisional Land Bank) indicated that this institution had received as many as 1,500 voluntary offers of land sales from medium-size landowners. As of April 1989, when the change of administration took place, there were 769 properties offered for sale with a total of 57,055 hectares, and a total asking price of approximately US$100 million. If the current FINATA president's figures are accurate, then there are probably close to 100,000 hectares potentially available for purchase and redistribution.

Unfortunately, the same politicoeconomic situation that gave rise to this unprecedented opportunity also left the national treasury without the means of capitalizing upon it. Furthermore, although the U.S. legal barriers to the Agency for International Development (USAID) underwriting land purchase have been removed since the reform was enacted (with the amendment of Section 620(g) of the Foreign Assistance Act in 1985), the current USAID budget allocates a meager US$4 million to the Land Bank's capital, with no further contributions envisaged in the FY 1990–1994 Country Development Strategy Statement. In the conclusion to this chapter, some creative financing alternatives will be explored as a solution to this resource constraint.

Performance of the Reformed Sector: Success or Failure?
Although pushing ahead with further redistributions is of primary concern, it is certainly not the only "hot" issue on the Salvadoran land-reform agenda these days. Of equal interest is the current policy regarding the fate of the Phase I cooperatives and beneficiaries, a

significant percentage of which are thus far failing economically, at least in the traditional financial sense of being able to pay their debts and produce distributable surpluses for their members. In this regard, to what extent the Phase I co-ops have succeeded or failed to live up to their economic and social promise, and why they have or have not, is a key issue, for the future policy of the new administration will be predicated upon it.

Beginning with the least contentious issue, most observers of the process agree that, at the minimum, the reform achieved its immediate political objective of defusing the social crisis of 1979 and buying time for the Christian Democratic junta to enact the needed structural reforms of the judicial, financial, and electoral systems, which have resulted in the limited pacification of the country. The most often cited evidence of the reform's fever-breaking effect on the near-anarchic situation prevailing in 1979 was the fact that in January 1980 the FDR was able to put 100,000 demonstrators into the streets of San Salvador, but three months later, after the enactment of the reform decrees, attendance at the guerrillas' May Day rally dropped to less than 2,000. Even the hopelessly atavistic tabloid *El Diario de Hoy* concedes today that in terms of dealing the insurgents a strategic reversal, the reforms achieved their objective.

Unfortunately, the ratings given the economic performance of the reform enjoy no such consensus. The exception here is Phase III, which all parties to the debate seem to agree has been at least a limited economic success. ARENA, USAID, and the Christian Democratic Party (PDC) alike have been inspired by the heroic manner in which the Finateros (a term used to describe the Phase III beneficiaries)—despite their having received vastly inferior quality land, and less of it (an average of one to two hectares versus nine hectares for Phase I), as well as a mere 10 percent of the credit and technical assistance lavished on the reformed sector—have wrung from their parcels a net annual income over 300 percent higher per hectare than that of the Phase I beneficiaries. Furthermore, the Phase III beneficiaries have had far higher debt repayment performance, both on short-term loans and the long-term agrarian debt.

On the other hand, the Phase I beneficiaries are viewed with the utmost scorn by all except their main patrons, the PDC. In addition to accusations of sloth and inefficiency, the Phase I co-ops are accused of having become a new campesino elite, selfishly holding onto their disproportionately large holdings, even when they cannot manage to farm these themselves, renting out the surplus land at usurious rates, and denying admittance to new, land-starved campesinos. The overpowering deficiencies of the Phase I sector, economic and moral alike, are attributed by ARENA and USAID to ideological causes—the pernicious effects of the collective or "communitarian" model promoted by the PDC.

In fact, according to a 1986 study by the Ministry of Agriculture's land-reform planning and evaluation unit (PERA), Phase I beneficiaries already farm some 11,485 hectares in more than 25,000 individual plots, in addition to the land farmed collectively, suggesting that the farmers themselves may have already made initial decisions as to which lands are more suitable for collective cultivation and which are more appropriate for family subsistence plots. More recent data suggest that this trend has continued toward de facto parcelization on the Phase I co-ops.

Returning to the central point: What is the factual basis for this near-universal indictment of the Phase I co-ops? An examination of other data, not cited above in the comparison of the first and third phase of the reform (prepared for the government by USAID), casts at least reasonable doubt on the supposition that Phase I of the land reform has been a colossal economic disaster. For one thing, if one analyzes the comparative yields for certain crops (maize, sorghum, sugar, coffee, cotton), with the exception of cotton and coffee, the "damage" wrought by the reforms—even if this were somehow distinguishable from the impact of the war—is not apparent. Country-wide sugar yields per hectare declined marginally by 3 percent (whereas reform sector yields exceeded the national average), maize and sorghum yields have increased slightly, and total meat production has declined by 4.8 percent. The total value of agricultural exports between 1981 and 1986, after declining by as much as 26.5 percent in 1984, has recovered to within decimal points of its 1981 level. In terms of basic grain yields, Phase I markedly and consistently outperforms Phase III: in the 1983/1984 season, maize yields per hectare average 2,377 kilograms on the Phase I farms versus only 1,632 kilograms on the Phrase III farms. Even for those crops that have suffered the greatest decreases in production—coffee (–32 percent) and cotton (–90 percent)—reform sector yields exceed the national average.

Perhaps a more interesting statistic, which ARENA and USAID choose to perceive in negative terms, is that after nine years 27 percent of the Phase I co-ops are "autogestionarias," or administratively self-sufficient. In most cases, the fact that a co-op has been granted this status also means that it is able to pay its debts and is returning an annual profit to its members. A more benign critic, taking into consideration the incredibly difficult environment in which the reform was undertaken, might view such an accomplishment as at least as heroic as the achievements of the Phase III beneficiaries. As one attempts to analyze why some Phase I co-ops are succeeding, others are struggling, and still others floundering, an interesting pattern emerges. The most relevant determinant of success appears to be not mode of organization (collective versus mixed versus individual), but rather whether the co-op has a viable cash crop such as coffee, and its location—that is, whether it is in a conflictive zone or a relatively peaceful part of the country where normal commerce can be carried out. Another critical success factor is the quality and honesty of the management.

Given this situation, one begins to question the motives of ARENA and USAID (particularly the latter) in depicting Phase I as an economic disaster. Suspicion deepens when one analyzes the ARENA/USAID prescription for rectifying this situation: the parcelization of the failing Phase I co-ops. The argument runs something like this: The natural inclination for the Salvadoran campesino is to own his own land, as in the Phase III system. When he is forced to work collectively, he produces less. Therefore, the Phase I sector should be made to work more like Phase III; that is, the campesinos should be issued individual titles and "freed" from collective ownership.

Similar arguments are heard in the area of beneficiary rights, which has also been the focus of recent debate. Here, the question is when, if ever, the beneficiaries should be permitted to sell the land, and, if so, to whom. The position of radical free marketers is that there should be no restrictions; that to limit the salability of any commodity is to reduce the potential pool of buyers, and therefore lower its value—a disadvantage to the seller. Obviously, such an argument makes no allowance for the realities of the power structure in rural El Salvador, which, if permitted to seek its own level, would quickly produce a situation similar if not identical to that prevailing in 1979. The government's official position is that land sales should be permitted (without saying when), but that sales should take place only among campesinos.

In hearing ARENA's officials make their case, both in favor of parcelization and beneficiary rights, one is struck by their surprising concern for the situation of the campesinos, whom they have historically viewed as merely a source of cheap labor. A key point, which is also receiving much attention in El Salvador at the moment, is what the Phase I beneficiaries themselves want in terms of land tenure. Here again, there is an interesting dichotomy, and it divides, in general, along lines similar to the crop mix and geographical disparities. In general, if a co-op is performing well, the beneficiaries tend to want to stay with the mixed system: collective ownership and work in the cash crop sector and individual exploitation of the food crops. (Another important point is that 100 percent of the co-ops *already* operate on the mixed system; all permit the members to farm their own family plots.) On the other hand, if a co-op is not working well, and the cash crop sector is nonexistent or subject to constant sabotage, then the members favor parcelization. All parties to the debate also agree that parcelization is the *only* viable option for the thirty-three abandoned properties in the eastern, central, and paracentral regions.

Here again, the question of motive arises. Do economic reactivation and the national welfare completely explain ARENA's abiding interest in parcelizing the Phase I co-ops? Or is it the knowledge that, without the group structure to rely upon and defend them, the small, individual campesinos will be easy prey for the former landlords who, although perhaps not interested in recovering ownership of the land (but this cannot be ruled out in every case), are definitely interested in reestablishing some kind of commercial relationship with their former workers and farms in the lucrative areas of marketing and processing. Certainly the campesino unions, who comprise the chief resistance to the ARENA strategy at present, suspect that this is the true motive behind the government's intended policy.

The PDC Betrayal: What Went Wrong?

With the PDC electoral victory in the spring of 1984, which brought Napoleón Duarte in as president and left a PDC majority in the Congress, the stage should have been set for a broad consolidation of the reform process. For the first time, everything was in place: political will in the government and ample financial support from USAID. Most important (and to the astonishment of many), Duarte had made good on his preelection promises to share power with the campesino organizations, giving them important participation in the key land-reform-related agencies: ISTA, FINATA, the Ministry of Agriculture, and the Agricultural Development Bank.

To fully appreciate the dimensions of the opportunity squandered, one need only to rapidly appraise the situation today. In many respects, it is remarkably similar to the situation prevailing in 1983, a year in which ARENA gained control of ISTA, and the right-wing alliance (or anti-PDC alliance, at least) dealt the reform a number of serious legal reverses, principal among these being the evisceration of Phase II.[2] Today, ARENA is in full control of not only the executive and legislative branches, but the judicial as well. And, judging from some of the early court rulings, such as declaring as "unconstitutional" the Committee of Campesino Organization (COC), a body which provided beneficiary participation and oversight of the reformed sector, and from the fact that more than thirty previously expropriated (and some titled and paid off) Phase I and III farms are threatened by appeals of the expropriation, the land reform, legally, is in for a rough ride. Another action taken by the ARENA courts since taking power was the derogation of the final shreds of Decree 895 (Phase II), which essentially returns El Salvador back to 1979 in the sense that there are no legal limits on the size of landholdings.

What went wrong? First, the campesino unions had no sooner established themselves in power than old rivalries—some dating from the 1960s when the UCS first fractured into its different splinter groups—began to reassert themselves. Soon, the bureaucracies of ISTA and FINATA became converted into headquarters for plotting raids on the membership of other unions' cooperatives and base groups. In the end, a disgusted Duarte cleaned house, replacing most of the campesinos with technocrats.

The other poison unleashed during the Duarte administration, slower to take effect but ultimately even more deadly, was corruption. The final reckoning is still being toted up, but it is clear that the PDC shamelessly looted both the government and the land reform, and that this corruption began at the top and eventually filtered down to the lowest level functionaries. Worse, in the case of land reform, the PDC technicians, who were supposed to train boards of directors of the co-ops in sound administration and management, instead coached them in creative ways to loot and rob their fellow members.

By 1989, disgusted with the violated promise of the PDC, the Salvadoran people handed them a resounding defeat, preferring instead the party of repression and death squads to the one of social reforms and corruption. At the same time, ARENA had utilized the out-of-power years wisely, building a shell of respectability and moderation about the deadly core of its spiritual leadership, and cultivating its ideological kindred spirits in the embassy. By the time ARENA swept into power in the spring of 1989, the strongest advocates for the argument that ARENA and D'Abuisson were "born again democrats" could be found in the U.S. Embassy.

The Future: What Lies Ahead

At this writing, the Salvadoran land reform is at great risk of legal and administrative reversal. Worse, its traditional defenders—the U.S. Embassy, the campesino organizations, the liberal wing of the army, and the Christian Democrats—have been largely neutralized, the first through clever public relations work on the part of ARENA, and the latter through the disunity and confusion spawned by the center's humiliating defeat in the elections of spring 1989. Most disturbing, land-reform policy within the government has been delegated as the exclusive province of Roberto D'Abuisson, in his capacity as head of the Department of Evaluation of the Land Reform of the Congress.

Sadly, any technical recommendations, however sound, will stand little chance of implementation until the political equilibrium is restored in El Salvador. For this to occur, the traditional supporters of the reforms must rediscover their common ground, regroup, and launch a counterattack before it is too late. Perhaps the very shamelessness of the ARENA offensive in dismantling the reform would prod the reform's historic defenders back into action.

Some Recommendations

1. Some argue that moderate elements exist within ARENA, which, if supported, could prevail over the agenda of the D'Abuisson faction. This hypothesis is worth testing, although thus far the Cristiani faction has emerged the weak loser in every confrontation. Nevertheless, the tension between the campesino organizations, on the one hand, and the ARENA-controlled agencies of ISTA and FINATA on the other, should be defused through a reinstitution of the COC or similar structure, which provides a forum for the airing of each new policy initiative.[3]

2. A coercion-free process should be established through which the beneficiaries can democratically decide how they will own their land in the future. One way of ensuring open and full debate at the co-op level would be to organize a forum in each co-op, to which representatives of ARENA and the campesino organizations are invited to present their points of view in a debate-type format. At the option of the co-ops, the campesino organizations could be invited to be present at the voting as observers.

3. Prior to the passage of any national legislation on parcelization, the legal minds, national and foreign, who have traditionally been involved in the reform process should fully analyze the present and future impacts—legally, economically, and politically—of a decision to parcelize. The campesino organizations should draft their own proposal on this issue and not wait to react to the ARENA decree, which, it may be virtually assured, will not be to their liking. USAID should remain neutral in this debate rather than adopt positions that reflect its own ideological preferences.[4]

4. The "front end" of the reforms, or the distribution of additional lands to a significant percentage of the 250,000 plus still-landless families in El Salvador, must continue. Under the existing regime, involuntary expropriation as a policy tool has been eliminated; in its place, some punitive fiscal measure should be enacted to discourage

the holding of idle land. This measure should fall with equal weight upon current landlords and beneficiaries of the land reform (Phase I) alike.

At the same time, the Land Bank, flooded with offers of sale, has only token government and USAID resources to draw upon. Also, what resources the government does have appear earmarked for "topping up" of previous compensation to ex-landlords, and not for purchase of new farms.

Clearly, an alternative is needed. One possibility, of course, is for USAID to alter its priorities and channel more resources to the Land Bank. (Indeed, a sense-of-Congress resolution adopted with the 1989 foreign aid appropriation points in this direction.) Another possibility is the financing of land sales through owner-financed mortgages. These could operate as follows:

a. A seller is put together with potential buyers via the Land Bank.
b. The seller and buyer negotiate a price, with the Land Bank serving as mediator. The Land Bank has a special fund to do a technical study, at the buyer's request, of the productive potential of the farm and the potential cash flow available for note amortization.
c. When a deal is struck, the Land Bank immediately advances to the seller 10 percent of the sale price in cash, and gets the signatures of the buyer(s) on a five-year note for the same amount. Alternatively, if the buyer(s) has the resources, he may provide the 10 percent directly.
d. The buyer(s) also executes a twenty-year note with the seller for the balance (90 percent).

The effect is the same as a bond-financed sale, with the exception that the seller and buyer directly negotiate the sale price, and the seller may collect directly from the buyer. Other features that could make the deal more palatable would be: (i) to make the interest income to the seller tax-exempt for five years; (ii) to have the government (and, secondarily, USAID) guarantee the notes in case of default to the extent of 75 percent.

5. The technical assistance component of the reform should be depoliticized by allowing the co-ops to choose the desired source, whether it be ISTA, FINATA, a private firm, or the technical department of one of the campesino organizations. This would serve to expedite the privatization of the reform sector. Similarly, steps should be taken to ensure that credit is allocated according to technical, versus political, criteria.

6. The so-called rights of the beneficiaries should be the subject of an in-depth study by the same legal minds mentioned in (3). At this delicate stage, however, ensuring that the beneficiaries remain in possession of the land is a far higher priority than guaranteeing their right to sell or transfer their land, as seems to be the abiding concern of USAID and ARENA. Here again, it would be to the advantage of the beneficiaries, through their campesino organizations, to seize the initiative in developing the first drafts of this legislation.

Nicaragua

In terms of land area, Nicaragua is the largest country in Central America, with a total area of 131,000 square kilometers (13.1 million hectares), of which an estimated 5.8 million hectares are in farmland—roughly 20 percent in cropland and 80 percent in pasture.[5] Geographically, Nicaragua holds a central position on the isthmus, bordered on the north by El Salvador and Honduras, and on the south by Costa Rica. The topography consists of a broad Pacific coastal plain, a central mountainous region, and a tropical rain forest/jungle area on the Atlantic Coast. Nicaragua's population of 3.6 million ranks it as the second smallest in Central America, after Costa Rica, although its population growth rate of 3.4 percent per annum is currently the highest in the region. The rural population is estimated at 1.38 million.

Nicaragua's economy is principally agricultural, the most important crops being cotton, coffee, sugarcane, and basic grains. Livestock is a traditional mainstay of the economy; in 1987/1988 this sector contributed 29,946 metric tons of meat, of which 7,260 metric tons were exported.

The economy of Nicaragua has been the hardest hit of any country of Central America; since 1979, real wages have dropped by 90 percent, agricultural production has declined by 25 percent and agro-exports by 40 percent, and the national herd has shrunk from 2.7 million to 1.6 million head. In 1988, Nicaragua broke the world record for inflation, surpassing Bolivia, with an official annual rate of 32,000 percent.

History of the Land-Tenure Situation

The popular image of Nicaragua in the prerevolutionary period, promoted in great part by the Sandinista government, is of a medieval fiefdom ruled by a series of family dictators, the Somozas, who owned and/or controlled 100 percent of the country's productive assets. Although it is true that the Somoza family's grip on the economy was considerable, in fact its influence was felt only in the larger agricultural and industrial enterprise sectors, which by themselves accounted for less than 50 percent of the total GDP. In the agricultural sector, the Somoza family owned approximately 20 percent of the total farmland, most of this in large units of 350 hectares or greater. Small and medium producers in the agricultural sector are now recognized as making a substantial contribution to total agricultural production, accounting for nearly 70 percent of basic grains production and nearly 40 percent of agro-exports in 1983.

Given its extensive land area, prerevolutionary Nicaragua suffered nothing like the population-on-land pressure of Guatemala or El Salvador. Still, the land-tenure situation before the revolution was extremely inequitable, with 36 percent of the total farmland (over 2.1 million hectares) controlled by fewer than 3,000 families (2 percent of the population) in farms of 350 hectares or larger, and with 75,000 families, or 43 percent of the rural population, landless. There was also, however, a substantial medium-size landholder population composed of some 30,000 families with farms in the 35- to 350-hectare range controlling 46 percent of the land, and a small farmer class of 65,000 families owning plots of fewer than 35 hectares (see Table 5.2).

Prior to the revolution of 1979 there were no significant land-reform measures carried out by the government, save for some token colonization programs. Beginning immediately after the revolution, however, the Sandinista government adopted sweeping confiscatory measures, most of these affecting the lands owned by Somoza. Decrees 31, 38, and 329, adopted in 1979, confiscated a total of 21 percent of the agricultural land, including 30 percent of the farms of more than 350 hectares (and all of the Somoza holdings), much of it the best agricultural land in the country. The vast majority of this was converted into state farms, the so-called "Public Property Areas" (PPA).

By most accounts, the situation of the workers on the state farms was not measurably improved from the time of Somoza; in fact, for some it was worse. Often the state farm managers discontinued the previous owner's practice of allowing the workers to farm subsistence plots on a seasonal basis (with no passage of permanent ownership rights).

Perhaps as a result of the campesinos' dissatisfaction and nascent feelings of deception,[6] in 1981 the reform took a new turn. The Agrarian Reform Law of July 1981, Decree 782, redistributed to its "direct cultivators" all land currently under rental, sharecropping, or tenant-farming arrangements, and also established a 350-hectare maximum ownership limit for the Pacific Coast and a 700-hectare limit for the Atlantic Coast. A total of 373,859 hectares was expropriated under this act, 24 percent of which was previously abandoned, 63 percent of which was owned but idle, and the remainder (13 percent)

Table 5.2   Changes in Nicaraguan Land Tenure Since the Revolution (1978–1987)

Year	1978				1982				1987			
Type of Holding	Farm Families	% Families	Hectares	% Has.	Farm Families	% Families	Hectares	% Has.	Farm Families	% Families	Hectares	% Has.
A. Estimated Landless (excl. state farm workers)	75,000	43			25,000	13			52,000	23		
B. Private												
1. > 350 has.	2,920	2	2,088,000	36	1,135	1	812,000	14	778	0	556,800	10
2. 35 to 350 has.	31,531	18	2,668,000	46	29,475	15	2,475,300	43	18,163	8	1,525,772	26
3. < 35 has.	65,700	38	1,044,000	18	28,900	15	464,000	8	0	0	0	0
Subtotal Private	100,151	57	5,800,000	100	59,510	30	3,751,300	65	18,941	8	2,082,572	36
C. Reform (Individual) Small Farmers < 33 has.	0	0	0	0	0	0	0	0	46,096	20	1,331,428	23
D. Reform Co-ops												
1. Credit & Service	0	0	0	0	46,000	24	522,000	9	45,900	20	553,000	10
2. Production (CAS)	0	0	0	0	5,000	3	116,000	2	29,300	13	664,000	11
Subtotal Co-ops	0	0	0	0	51,000	26	638,000	11	75,200	33	1,217,000	21
E. State Farms (PPA)	0	0	0	0	60,000	31	1,345,500	23	37,140	16	819,000	14
F. Abandoned Farms	0	0	0	0	0	0	65,200	1	0	0	350,000	6
Totals	175,151	100	5,800,000	100	195,510	100	5,800,000	100	229,377	100	5,800,000	100

Notes: The source of all figures on land area and families in reform sector is MIDINRA (Government). The source of the figures for private sector holdings, and numbers of families from 1978 is MIDINRA. After 1978, the figures for private sector families and land area, and number of landless families, were estimated by the author according to the following assumptions:

The total number of rural families grew at a rate commensurate with population growth; i.e., 2.8% 1978–82; 3.3% 1982–1987.

All families not accounted for in the reform sector or private sector (as estimated) are considered landless.

The figures for private sector land area for 1982 are based on MIDINRA figures.

The figures for private sector families for 1982 and 1987 are estimated by dividing the total land area by the average holding per family in the previous year.

It is assumed that in 1982 the majority of the category D.1 membership came "at the expense of" category B.3.

It is assumed that in 1987 the majority of the families in category C came "at the expense of" categories B.3 and, when exhausted, the balance from B.2.

rented or sharecropped. Much of this land went into the formation of some 700 production cooperatives known as *Cooperativas Agrícolas Sandinistas* (CAS). The members of these in large part were near-landless small farmers or laborers, but were also urban revolutionary veterans receiving rewards for services rendered. At the same time, another type of cooperative, the *Cooperativa de Credito y Servicios* (CCS) was formed. The CCS was primarily a means of organizing already landed small farmers for political purposes and for channeling credit. In the CCS, if land was distributed, it was worked and owned individually under a de jure internal allocation arrangement.

Despite these measures, the basic emphasis of the reform on state farms did not change, and the state sector expanded its share from 21 percent to 23 percent of the total farmland by the end of 1982, whereas actual land distributions—both on a collective and service cooperative basis—had benefited only 8,045 families. The resistance of the Sandinistas to individual distributions, aside from its ideological basis, interestingly enough, was grounded in the same trepidations that had afflicted the Somozas: a fear that their source of agricultural labor would dry up and put the export sector in jeopardy. A further characteristic of the new rulers of Nicaragua that mirrored the old was the Sandinistas' basic skepticism regarding the productive potential of the small- and medium-size farmer, whom they perceived as interested exclusively in his own subsistence and not as a producer of marketable surpluses or export crops. This view was changed, at least among the less ideological, by the work of economist Eduardo Baumeister, who debunked these myths.

As Table 5.2 indicates, between 1982 and 1987 other fundamental changes in the reform occurred. One of these was the transfer of some 500,000 hectares out of the PPA and into the Production Cooperative Sector. This was in response to two factors: (1) increasing pressure from the landless laborers for their own land, and (2) the increasingly evident failure of the state farms as economic units. Another development, also due to popular pressure, was a more concerted effort at both distribution and titling of lands on an individual basis. As can be seen in Table 5.2, some 46,000 campesinos received land and/or titles (i.e., formal confirmation of existing land rights) in this period, involving 23 percent of the country's total farmland.

At present, the land-tenure situation is radically different from that of the prerevolutionary era. Most significant, the number of landless families has declined from 43 percent to an estimated 23 percent of the rural population.[7] Presently, large private farms (more than 350 hectares) occupy only 10 percent of total farmland versus 36 percent in 1978.

At the same time, from the intended beneficiaries' perspective, the process cannot be said to have been completed, although, officially speaking, the "reform sector" presently covers 58 percent of all farmland and 69 percent of rural families. In fact, the amount of land distributed is less than 40 percent, and the number of families, even in the reform sector, without land of their own (state farm laborers) is still a significant 16 percent of the rural population. As real wages deteriorate, owning one's own land versus earning paper money becomes increasingly attractive. Furthermore, a good number of the 11 percent of the rural families on the production cooperatives (if one can assume that the Nicaraguan campesino is basically similar to his other Central American counterparts) probably would prefer at least some individual ownership.[8]

Before turning to an assessment of reform in terms of its economic, social, and political impact, it is of interest to remark upon the legal evolution of the Nicaraguan agrarian reform. In this regard, the progress of the reform can be distinguished by three distinct stages: (1) the confiscation of all abandoned lands and land of more than 350 hectares, regardless of use; (2) the expropriation of some farms between 75 and 350 hectares, depending on whether these were rented, sharecropped, or had idle land; and (3) the most recent stage, characterized by an end to expropriations, and as an alternative, a trend toward land purchases or conversion of PPA lands to co-ops or individual holdings. A further trend has been the increased attention to the land-tenure security needs of the individual and independent farmers through land titling on an individual basis. A further interesting development is a stated policy on the part of the government of respect for the beneficiaries' rights, even on the collectives, to choose their own form of working the land.

In explaining this trend toward individualization of the reform, one cannot discount, of course, the impact of the insurgency. For one, much of the individual distribution and titling has taken place in the north, in areas under partial Contra control. For another, the government's own reports on the progress of the reform admit that a primary force behind this liberalization of the reform is the need to do something concrete for the independent farmers, and thus lessen the appeal of the opposition.

Economic, Social, and Political Impacts of the Reform
As in the case of El Salvador, it is exceedingly difficult to isolate any changes that have occurred in the Nicaraguan economy and attribute these directly to the land reform, when the impact of the war on the economy has been so pervasive. Clearly, however, the case of

Nicaragua strengthens the hand of those who would argue that land distribution by itself cannot work economic miracles: there must be a favorable policy environment as well. In this regard, the agricultural policy of the Sandinistas can most kindly be described as one of continuous experimentation. In the early stages, like most young Communist regimes, the government felt honor bound to relearn the lessons of the failed Soviet and Chinese state farms and collectives. Then, when it became obvious that to feed the nation they would have to rely on the still productive private sector (as well as provide increasing incentives to the cooperative sector), they began to use the nationalized banking system to channel negative-interest-rate loans for both investment and production purposes to all borrowers, regardless of size. At the same time, on the pricing side, the government set controlled prices at levels well below what producers could obtain through the black markets and through smuggling. The result was a double loss for the government: banks were decapitalized and the production was sold in Honduras and Costa Rica, creating chronic shortages.

Problems of the Agrarian Reform

State Farm Sector (PPA). Possibly the greatest disappointment of the reform, from the campesinos' point of view, has been the government's decision to retain most of the best lands in the form of state farms, as opposed to distributing these to the farmers. The campesinos are not alone in their disenchantment; although production and cost figures of the PPA are a closely guarded secret, it is commonly suspected that this sector has generated enormous losses. Some of the recognized shortcomings of this sector will come as no surprise to those familiar with the problems of the state industrial and agricultural sector in the Soviet bloc countries:

1. obsession with fulfillment of production quotas without attention to cost
2. selling prices fixed at uneconomic levels
3. bureaucratic delays in receipt of sales revenues from state marketing boards, resulting in late loan repayments and exaggerated interest costs
4. poor administration and financial control
5. overstaffing and inflated personnel costs

As part of the liberalization process, the government has stated that all operating subsidies to state enterprises will be suspended, and hereafter these enterprises must operate solely with revenues generated. It will be interesting to see how many can survive under these new conditions, and the social impact of having to charge market rates for their outputs after years of subsidizing their consumers.

Cooperative Sector. The economic performance of the cooperative sector is likewise difficult to assess, due to the nearly total absence of comprehensible financial records on the cooperatives. However, judging from the relatively high desertion rate of the production co-ops,[9] it would appear that many campesinos view them as incapable of meeting their minimum subsistence needs. As in El Salvador, the production cooperatives as units often require technical and capital assistance of a magnitude beyond the capability of the near-bankrupt government. The conscious policy, in the early years of the revolution, of pouring resources upon a select group of production co-ops in the hopes of finding a successful model ("few but good") left the majority impoverished. Furthermore, of those that did receive massive assistance, many are buried in debt. And although hyperinflation has done an effective job in returning some to solvency, those who received equipment or infrastructure loans since the indexing policy was instituted show little promise of paying these off, nor does the government display much inclination toward enforcing their collection.

The clear preference of the government for the collective model, which on the whole requires a much higher quality of administration and management, over other forms of organization of labor and land tenure has generated a host of other problems, all thrown in stark relief against the deteriorating macroeconomic situation. One direct consequence of the economic crisis has been an exodus of the best qualified technicians, and a huge deficit in the public sector, which has translated into dismissal of employees and the reduction of the wages of those who remain to sub-subsistence levels. As a consequence, most of the cooperatives have become, by force majeure, self-administering. The Ministry of Agriculture and Agrarian Reform's (MIDINRA) annual reports summarize the problems of the cooperative sector at present as follows:

1. a high desertion rate, as a consequence of several factors, including (a) aversion of the farmers to the collective form of exploitation; (b) resistance to the forced conscription policy, which targets many CAS for obtaining military recruits; and (c) the lower-than-subsistence levels of production on some of the

co-ops as a consequence of poor soils, bad administration, lack of resources, or a combination of these

2. emphasis on political organization versus production objectives on the part of the ministry
3. chronic shortages of technical assistance, credit, and, to a lesser extent, inputs
4. deteriorating on-farm infrastructure for storage and processing, and the lack of foreign exchange to repair or replace it

The Future

The great tragedy of the Nicaraguan land reform is that, as the shrinking cadres of the defenders of the Sandinistas tirelessly point out, the intentions behind it appear to have been largely honorable. Beyond these intentions, save for the glaring blind spot of the state farms, there has been a genuine and concerted effort to train and prepare the campesinos for a role other than that of simple producers and feeders of the rest of the society. On the best run of the CAS, this is still evident in campesinos who have received training abroad in technical subjects, which in most developing countries would be limited to secondary school graduates or higher. And, of course, there is the overall indoctrination in the perceived role of the farmers within the larger society, which a cynical free marketer might find quaintly utopian, but which has clearly raised the consciousness of many campesinos beyond worrying about their own immediate situation.

The question is, then, how the positive aspects of this unique experience may be preserved, particularly considering the likelihood that the Sandinistas will be defeated in the coming election, or, even if not, that the trend toward privatization in the agricultural sector will continue. The following are some recommendations.

1. Transfer the PPA to the Farmers. If the opposition is indeed victorious at the polls in February of 1990, and they are permitted by the army to govern, one can expect an immediate move to privatize the PPA. One does not know, at this stage, what debts may have been incurred by the Chamorro campaign, but it is not inconceivable that such a policy, if left to its own devices, could result in these lands being transferred to those with the immediate means and skills to exploit them; that is, the oligarchy-in-exile. The present government, then, should take preemptive steps to transfer ownership of these lands to the present laborers, under whatever form of ownership and organization they democratically elect, be it individual, collective, cooperative, or mixed.

2. Continue the Trend Toward Liberalization. As agonizing as austerity measures are for the urban sector, the government should continue the processes of liberalization of the agricultural sector and the larger economy as the only feasible means of resuscitating investment and production.

3. Give Land to Former Soldiers. As part of the peace process, both former EPS (*Ejercito Popular Sandinista*, the national army) and Contras should be given land in exchange for turning in their weapons. According to government reports, there are close to 300,000 hectares of land presently under Contra control plus another 350,000 hectares in idle lands in abandoned co-ops and bankrupt state farms, which could be distributed under a program of this kind. Needless to say, such a policy, by reducing the bloated military payroll, would have a salubrious effect on the deficit.

4. Offer Assistance to the Cooperative Sector. If the elections normalize the situation, and donors resume the flow of aid, then a concerted effort should be made to resurrect the service cooperative sector via the organization of regional cooperative service centers, which, on a cost-plus-profit basis, would provide essential technical assistance, inputs, credit, and marketing services. A plan of this type already exists within the Ministry of Agrarian Reform, referring to the creation of a national network of *Centros Campesinos.*

Guatemala

In terms of natural resources, Guatemala is the wealthiest country in Central America. Its 4.2 million hectares[10] in farms include some of the best soils in the world, and its varied topography, featuring a volcano-rimmed central highland bordered by a jungle to the north and a fertile coastal plain to the south, can support nearly every crop known to civilization. On the coast, tropical fruits such as bananas, papaya, and melons are cultivated; in the middle highlands or *altiplano*, between 500 and 1,500 meters high, export crops such as coffee and cardamon are grown; and above 2,000 meters, crops more typical of northern countries, such as wheat and apples, can prosper. Historically, Guatemala has been the region's largest livestock and agricultural producer. In 1988, Guatemala produced nearly 1.4 million metric tons of maize, almost two and a half times that of the nearest competitor in the region (El Salvador); 162,000 metric tons of coffee (slightly more than El Salvador or Costa Rica); and 7 million metric tons of sugarcane, more than double the production of its neighbor, El Salvador. Meat production has remained consistently above 135,000 metric tons per year, a level nearly double that of Nicaragua, El Salvador, and Honduras. In terms of yields, however, Guatemala is generally behind Costa Rica and El Salvador in maize and sugar, suggesting a more extensive (versus intensive) production pattern.

Guatemala also has the highest population in Central America (8.7 million in 1988) and the third highest growth rate (2.9 percent per year). Some 4.56 million persons, or 52 percent of the population, make their living from agriculture. The distribution of land among these 850,000 families is extremely skewed: in 1979, farms of more than 450 hectares, representing 1 percent of all farms, controlled over one-third of the farmland. At the same time, farms of less than 1.4 hectares, representing slightly over half of all farms, controlled only 4.1 percent of the land. The total number of landless households in 1980 was estimated at 400,000. Extrapolating from the annual growth rate of 2.9 percent, the low end of the estimate may have grown to as high as 375,000 families today. Precise estimates are difficult, however, when one takes into account the possible effects of the violence of the early 1980s, which resulted in the deaths and dislocation of thousands of highland families.

In any case, given the lack of significant redistributive measures over the past three decades in Guatemala, one is probably safe in assuming that the core proportion of landless prevailing in 1980 has remained unchanged, and that today roughly one-quarter of the total population and 43 percent of the agricultural population is landless.

Such alarming statistics would lead one to expect that in Guatemala every available hectare of land is cultivated or dedicated to intensive pasturization. In fact, however, one is astonished to learn that over 1.4 million hectares, the vast majority of it in farms of more than 450 hectares, is lying idle or is underutilized grazing land. Furthermore, because these farms comprise more than one-third of all farmland in Guatemala, this statistic suggests that the majority of the land in these larger farms is lying idle or underutilized. The explanation for this phenomenon is found in the history of the land-tenure system.

Evolution of the Present-Day Land-Tenure Situation
When the conquistadores arrived in Guatemala in the fifteenth century, the major centers of Mayan culture (such as Tikal) had already collapsed, and the Indians were living in scattered villages throughout the western highlands, living mainly from agriculture. Ownership of the land was communal, although the forms of exploitation were probably individual. The Spanish invaders promptly "modernized" this system into a feudal arrangement of *repartimiento y encomienda*, closely resembling that of the continent from whence they had come. This

system, which involved the division of lands and the people living on them into fiefdoms under the control of individual conquistadores, was legalized in 1513 by royal decree from the mother country (Spain), and remained essentially intact when independence was won in 1821. In 1825, the first agrarian law was passed, which began the transfer of public domain lands to the private sector, a trend that has continued unabated until the present time. The transformation of Guatemalan agriculture from a subsistence mode to a commercially oriented operation effectively began with the introduction of coffee in 1840. From the beginning, the perception of the ruling class was that in order to activate the rural economy, fair-skinned European entrepreneurs had to be imported to organize the labor of the supposedly more indolent indigenous class. Although the first efforts at promoting European immigration failed, despite generous offers of public-domain lands, eventually a number of Germans accepted the challenge. Between 1896 and 1921, 1.6 million hectares were transferred to private hands. Coffee cultivation was greatly expanded, and the Indians, who were still interested mainly in subsistence farming of basic grains, were driven off the best lands onto the steep shoulders of the valleys. Many of those who had lost their lands were now conveniently available as seasonal workers to the coffee farmers, under a *colono* arrangement, whereby the Indians were allowed to "rent" back part of their own land in return for participating at nominal cash wages in the harvest.

In 1924, the United Fruit Company came upon the scene, receiving slightly less than 200,000 hectares as a concession from the government in return for constructing a trans-Guatemalan railroad. These lands were planted mainly in bananas, and were later to be the subject of a series of transfers (private to public and back to private) as the first efforts at land reform were attempted.

The first legislation to recognize the need for stimulating more productive use of land was the *Ley de Impuesto sobre Riales y Latifundios* of 1936, which established a tax of between 2 percent and 4 percent of declared value on idle lands in farms of more than 500 hectares. Like most legislation inimical to the interests of the large landholding class, this law was cheerfully ignored. The only other legislative action that showed hints of the coming storm was the *Ley de Arrendamiento Forzoso* of 1949, which recognized the need to provide some tenure security for the growing renting class. Apparently, even at this early stage in the postwar period, the problem had grown to such dimensions that it was beginning to attract the attention of the more socially conscious members of Guatemalan society.

In 1952, under the administration of President Jacobo Arbenz, the first and only significant land-reform measures were undertaken, in the form of Decree 900, which had as its stated objectives the elimination of the feudal system and the distribution of land to the landless. The situation may have justified more radical measures, but Decree 900 was in fact a rather mild law. No farms smaller than 90 hectares were to be taken, and even farms larger than that could escape expropriation if they were in export crops. The owners were to be compensated, based on the value of the land declared for tax purposes in 1952. The beneficiaries were to be *mozos* (renters), *colonos*, and landless agricultural laborers.

In the space of seventeen months, 1,002 farms were expropriated, affecting 603,615 hectares. Another 280,000 hectares in existing state farms (formed on public lands, not through expropriation of private holdings) were also distributed to some 30,000 landless laborers working on them at the time. In all, 883,615 hectares were affected, benefiting, according to different estimates, 80,000–100,000 campesinos, or nearly 40 percent of the landless population at the time. As in the case of the Salvadoran Land Reform of 1980, the scope and speed with which the reform was carried out seems to have taken the landlords by surprise. Eventually, however, the forces of reaction coalesced, in this case around Colonel Castillo Armas, who, with support from the U.S. Central Intelligence Agency, overthrew Arbenz in June 1954.

More rapidly than the reform had been executed, it was undone. Decree 900 was rescinded, and, over the next several months, 550,000 hectares of the distributed land, including all the state farm land, was returned to its previous owners (the balance appears to have remained with the beneficiaries). The fact that there is no recorded opposition to this reversal, neither pacific nor violent, is indicative of one of the weaknesses of a top-down-type land-reform program, in which the role of the peasantry is reduced to that of serving as passive beneficiaries versus active participants in the formulation and execution of the program.

In place of Decree 900, Decree 559, which established a Department of Colonization and Agricultural Development, was passed. Over the next twenty-five years, this department carried out token land-reform efforts via settlement of some 30,000 landless families on undeveloped public lands. Approximately 70,000 hectares of the total land redistributed pertained to the old United Fruit lands, which had been switching back and forth between the public and private sectors. In fact, this period was also characterized by significant concessionary sales of the public lands in large tracts to military officers and members of the elite—a kind of land reform for the rich.

In 1970, USAID undertook a worldwide study of the situation of the small farmer. In Guatemala, the study took the government to task for the deplorable land-tenure situation, characterized, among other things, by the existence of some 1.77 million hectares of idle land in the private sector in the face of massive landlessness. The study rejected the colonization alternative as an inappropriate, vastly more expensive option versus that of expropriation with compensation.

The policy of the Guatemalan government, and that of USAID, did not change. Colonization programs have remained the centerpiece of the present token efforts at resolving the land-tenure problem, which each year grows more severe. The statistics, developed in a 1982 study commissioned by USAID, speak for themselves. In the period between 1955 and 1982, the government distributed 664,525 hectares[11] of land to approximately 50,000 families (including 30,000 beneficiaries of colonization programs)—219,090 hectares less than was distributed in seventeen months under Arbenz (before its reversal) to between 80,000 and 100,000 families. At the same time, the ranks of the landless have swollen to as many as 375,000 families.

Options for the Future
Despite the fact that the current agrarian reform law, Decree 1551 as amended, recognizes the right of the government to expropriate idle lands, the process for affecting these is so full of legal loopholes and administrative obstacles as to render it, in the words of the USAID study, "inadequate for carrying out the stated or ostensible purpose of the law." To those interested in a direct approach to the problem of landlessness in Guatemala, a reasonable strategy might begin with a revamping of both the decree and the implementing regulations. Clearly, however, a reading of the history of land reform in Guatemala to date certifies the impression that the political will for a direct assault on the problem of landlessness simply does not exist. The question is, then, with expropriation ruled out for the foreseeable future, what other options are there?

The authors of the 1982 USAID study, whose hands were essentially tied by a directive from the government that prevented them from even considering the expropriation alternative, wring feeble optimism from some recent progress in a land bank–type program run by the Penny Foundation. The approach employed is essentially one of simple purchase of farms by groups of landless campesinos, financed by long-term money provided by USAID. The advantages of this option are argued to be (1) that it is "voluntary" versus "coercive"; (2) as it involves previously developed lands, normally, it can be implemented at approximately 20 percent of the costs of colonization programs, which usually involve hacking a homestead out of the jungle; and (3) theoretically, it should be faster and easier to implement than colonization programs.

In fact, however, neither of the USAID-financed options has broken records, either for speed or coverage. The colonization option settled fewer than 2,000 families over a period of five years; the Penny Foundation land bank initiative has resulted in the settlement of only 1,700 formerly landless families on 6,257 hectares over five years.

The authors of the 1982 USAID study ran some projections and determined that, for a total investment of approximately US$200 million net present value (or roughly two years' military aid to El Salvador), enough land could be purchased over a seven-year period to settle 30,000 landless families annually, or, considering the present population growth rate of almost 3 percent per year, a net inroad into the problem of landlessness of approximately 20,000 families per year. Implied in these projections is the distribution of an average of 4 hectares per family, at a purchase cost of approximately US$300 per hectare, plus a "settlement" cost of approximately US$1,000 per family. Theoretically, a program of this type would then distribute a total of 840,000 hectares, and resolve the problems of approximately 50 percent of the landless population. The authors contend that an amount of land close to that is potentially for sale in Guatemala, given the proviso that sales be on a cash basis (to the seller). The reasons that such quantities of land could be placed on the market are similar to those in El Salvador: the political and economic situation makes farming of cash crops on a large scale exceedingly difficult.

The response of the landholding class in Guatemala to even such a private-sector, nonexpropriatory recommendation was a storm of criticism, resulting in the immediate removal of the minister of agriculture, who, ironically, had been instrumental in persuading USAID and the authors not even to consider the expropriation option in their report.

The Consequences of Inaction

If the Christian Democrat government of Vinicio Cerezo has social-reform aspirations similar to those of its partisan relations in El Salvador, they have yet to betray them. Perhaps they have simply judged (accurately, possibly) that the time is not right for such measures, and that under a Republican administration in the United States they would likely find themselves forced to underwrite the initiative themselves. In any case, the stage appears set for a fresh round of bloodshed and confrontation such as that experienced in the early 1980s, when the social inequities had grown to such proportions that a relatively small, externally supported guerrilla movement was able to capitalize on the social discontent and recruit tens of thousands of landless campesinos into insurrection. In the future, as the situation grows increasingly intolerable, no external spark may be required to detonate this social powder keg that is the landlessness problem. But for the moment, the situation remains relatively quiet, as the irresistible force of exploding population swells to confront the intransigent, unyielding oligarchy.

Options for U.S. Policymakers
Guatemala, more than any other Central American country, has shown skill in limiting the options of U.S. foreign policy to supporting those programs that have little or no impact on the severe social problems they face. The consequences of this strategy—both for them and for the United States—have been painfully evident these past ten years. Traditionally, the response of the U.S. State Department and USAID to this emasculating situation has been to argue both the long and short view: in the long run, we must maintain our presence and influence at all costs, and in the short run, token programs that benefit a handful of the poor (or at best kept the lid on the problem) are better than no programs at all.

At some point, as a citizen, one loses patience with this approach, particularly when the cost of cleaning up the mess—billions of dollars in military aid for El Salvador and hundreds of millions for the Contras—begins to bleed the public treasury. Also, there is always the underlying suspicion that if the United States ever called the oligarchy's bluff—as Carter did on several occasions just before being deselected—they might prove more conciliatory. At the same time, the level of present financial support is so small (owing to the meager and shrinking resources the United States allocates to foreign aid in general, and to Guatemala in particular), there seems precious little the United States can do on the incentive side to persuade the oligarchy that the enactment of these measures can, even in the short term, be to their advantage.

Still, the United States is not completely powerless, either in terms of the carrot or the stick. One potentially fruitful area is trade. Although the United States has frequently been loath to restrict the free flow of goods on the basis of what are generally perceived to be "internal" policy prerogatives, the sanctions would not need to operate as such, but rather as "reverse preferences," in which Costa Rican, Honduran, or Salvadoran exports receive higher quotas than countries such as Guatemala, whose policies were determined to constitute a threat to the security of the region.[12] Furthermore, there are precedents: consider the effect of the U.S. boycott of Nicaragua, which, through its adverse impact on the economy, pressured the Sandinistas both into channeling more resources and undertaking policy changes that benefited the small, independent farmer sector, even when this was at odds with their ideological preference (see Nicaragua section of this chapter).

Another possibility is employing a multilateral versus bilateral approach to the problem. Although coordination among donors (even at the project level, let alone the diplomatic) is notoriously difficult, there is a clear advantage to the United States in not trying to "go it alone" when urging governments to undertake difficult but necessary social reforms. Clearly, a number of European nations are interested in doing business in Guatemala for its coffee and for its tremendous tourism potential, which was reaching its peak just as the violence of the early 1980s struck. If all those with an economic interest in Guatemala began to speak the same language vis-à-vis how land reform could lead to a more stable society, and the concomitant advantages of this for the foreign investment climate, the message might begin to get across. It would certainly be helpful if a nation other than the United States could take the lead on this effort.

At the same time, one should be realistic as to how productive any initiatives of this type can be at a time in which the outward symptoms of the social problems spawned by the disastrous land-tenure situation are in broad remission. Concerned policymakers and observers of the process might then spend their time more fruitfully in drawing up a contingency plan wherein idle farmland and likely beneficiary groups are identified and different scenarios—including quantities of land available, costs, and implementation strategies—are developed. One advantage of this type of advance planning would be that when the crisis comes the provisional government (whoever they might be) and USAID would have at their disposal a ready-made set of plans, rather than having to rely on eleventh-hour improvisation.

Other Central American Countries

Honduras and Costa Rica, perhaps because they have not suffered the political traumas of their neighbors, have attracted less attention in recent years from the news media and policymakers alike. Nevertheless, their respective land-tenure situations and the policies they have developed to deal with them provide, in some cases, instructive comparisons to those of Nicaragua, Guatemala, and El Salvador.

Honduras

Honduras, with large areas of undeveloped and even unpopulated rural lands (total land area approximately 11.2 million hectares, including 1.8 million hectares of presently cropped land as well as 2.5 million hectares of pasture), is similar to Nicaragua in that, until recently, it had not experienced the same types of land pressures as its immediate neighbors, El Salvador and Guatemala. Nevertheless, land was traditionally greatly concentrated, with 4 percent of the landowners controlling 56 percent of the farmland, and 58 percent of the farmers controlling less than 7 percent of all farmland. Various land-reform initiatives, the first of which took place in 1962 under the administration of Villeda Morales, have resulted in the adjudication of slightly more than 300,000 hectares, benefiting approximately 50,000 families, or some 10 percent of the rural population. These modest achievements confirm the Honduran agrarian reform's status as one of the least significant in the region—inferior, perhaps, even to the efforts of Guatemala and Costa Rica.

Another interesting feature of the Honduran agrarian reform is its near-exclusive emphasis on distribution of public and former banana company lands (only 16 percent were expropriated from individual owners). This "campesino as pioneer" approach, in which largely undeveloped lands are distributed, perhaps explains the high attrition rate characterizing the reform, in which as many as three-tenths of the original beneficiaries have since abandoned their lands. At the same time, studies have pointed to the existence of large tracts of idle pseudo-pasture land, which has eluded expropriation through the propagation of phantom herds of livestock.

Given the low man-to-land ratio in Honduras (2.8 persons per hectare of cropland, one of the lowest in the region), one might be tempted to conclude that more sweeping measures are not required; however, the data on landlessness argue otherwise. At present, there are an estimated quarter of a million landless farm households in Honduras.[13] Furthermore, there is a growing trend toward subdivision of smaller farms, creating a situation in which an increasing percentage of farms are not large enough to support a family. Statistics on the standard of living round out this depressing picture: some 90 percent of rural children under five years of age are considered malnourished, and Honduras has the highest infant mortality rate in the region.

What little has been accomplished in the Honduran agrarian reform can be attributed to a fairly militant campesino movement. The *Asociacion Nacional Campesina Hondurena* (ANACH) was first organized by the Banana Workers Federation in the 1960s as a pressure group, and has since managed to negotiate land for a large percentage of the present land-reform beneficiaries. The tactics employed in the early days were land invasions; to some extent, these are still practiced.

Each of the eight military and civilian governments have decried such aggressive measures as illegal, yet it is clear that without them the amount of land distributed would be considerably diminished. This is not to say that the governments have not been vocal supporters of the concept of land reform; in terms of promised areas of land to be distributed, were words equal to deeds, the Honduran reform would have adjudicated more than one million hectares.[14]

The Structure of the Reform

The Honduran land reform, like other "mature" social programs, has a built-in duality in the sense that its beneficiaries and administrators alike are concerned with two fundamental processes: (1) continued expansion of the reform to new beneficiaries, and (2) consolidation of the productive processes on existing lands. In the former process, as noted, the campesino organizations play a vital role as a counterweight to the powerful landholding class. At the same time, as has occurred with the land-reform movement in El Salvador, the older campesino movements have a split allegiance between the newer "land hungry" members and the older "founding fathers," who are now interested in the problems of production, marketing, and national-level agricultural policy rather than with invading cattle ranches. As such, it is not surprising that some of the more militant campesino organizations in Honduras are the more recently organized ones, where the "fire in the belly" burns stronger.

Regarding the consolidation process, one finds problems among the Honduran group farms similar to those on the collectives of El Salvador and Nicaragua, and, likewise, a similar small but growing number of farms that are making a success of it. The pattern is well established now. A group of farmers invades and, after a lengthy struggle, achieves legal ownership of the land. Initially there are internal problems, but eventually, the dissidents are weeded out and some reduced number of the original beneficiaries remain on the land and begin to develop it. At first, the bank will provide credit only for basic grains, which are a losing proposition in Central America, given the low prices, high production costs, and difficulties in competing with the more efficient neighbor to the north. Eventually, however, through the pressure of its campesino organization, the co-op negotiates a livestock loan and purchases a dairy herd, or, alternatively, plants a long-term crop like coffee. Government technical assistance is poor and unreliable, but the co-op comes to develop its own expertise, and, if it is fortunate enough to find a competent, honest business manager, either from outside or amongst its own ranks (their children have begun to grow up now and get educated), the beneficiaries begin to break out of the subsistence mode and into the commercial economy. Along the way there will probably be much refinancing or forgiveness of loans, but this can all be chalked up to the "social cost" of the reform.

The Future

Of all countries in the region, Honduras has the oldest and best organized campesino movement, and hence its prospects for continuing the process, albeit at a slow pace, appear good. At the same time, one questions which will occur first: the increased democratization of the country, with an attendant greater responsiveness and commitment to the resolution of its social problems, in particular landlessness, or, in the face of mounting frustration with the slow pace of the reform, a polarization similar to what has occurred in El Salvador and Guatemala. In this regard, the role of the United States has been ambiguous. On the one hand, the use of Honduras as a staging ground for the war in Nicaragua has distracted everyone from the growing social crisis in Honduras, and turned elements of a society always lukewarm toward the United States openly hostile. And, typically, USAID has chosen to focus its efforts on support of titling of existing lands rather than on the "front end" of the program. Always reluctant to antagonize the ruling class, USAID will probably push a voluntary solution along the lines of creation of a land bank rather than press the government to confront the remaining inequities in land tenure in a more direct manner via expropriation. Once again, as in the case of Guatemala, it appears that Honduras is in a kind of limbo, waiting for its problems to become so acute as to be forced to take more decisive action. The United States, likewise, has chosen to remain on the sidelines, in a reactive instead of an actively supportive mode.

Costa Rica

Until the advent of the Nicaraguan revolution, Costa Rica had the most equitable land distribution in the region, with 40 percent of the farms and 22 percent of the farmland in holdings between five and fifty hectares, 51 percent of the farmland in holdings of less than five hectares, and only 27 percent of the land in holdings of greater than 500 hectares. Slightly fewer than 100,000 families, or 20 percent of its population of 2.8 million, are landless. Over the past twenty years, the pace of land reform in Costa Rica could be described as "slow but steady" (with emphasis on the former), as contrasted to the more "radical surgery" type reforms of El Salvador, Nicaragua, and Guatemala (1952-1954). Since 1962, the government's Agrarian Development Institute (IDA) has purchased and resold 663,889 hectares of land to slightly less than 33,000 families. Many of these were prompted by real or threatened land invasions organized by a number of fairly militant campesino organizations. In keeping with their democratic tradition, the Costa Ricans have generally managed to resolve their land-tenure disputes without resorting to violence. Recently, however, in what could be construed as a hardening of the position of the conservatives, the Arias administration declared it will no longer negotiate with "invaders." Presumably, the quid pro quo for the campesino organizations relinquishing the invasion option is a more aggressive legal land-distribution program.

The option being pursued by both the government and donor community at present is the search for a viable "land-market" program. But in the absence of an insurgency to stimulate a flight from agriculture on the part of large landowners, the only real stimulus to land sales is on the price side and from expropriatory legislation, which, even in a democratic, socially conscious nation like Costa Rica, often lacks "teeth." Price incentives, of course, mean that the meager resources available for this activity domestically and from donors will be even less adequate. The prospect, then, is that land reform in Costa Rica will probably fall to a still slower pace in the coming decade.

This said, the case of Costa Rica is of interest, as it will serve to test the premise that noncoercive, market-oriented alternatives can make more than a token contribution to the problem of landlessness. If such a solution cannot work in Costa Rica, then there is little basis for supposing it could be successful in the more polarized societies of Honduras, Guatemala, or El Salvador, even with the stimulation of an insurgency in the latter two.

Conclusions

The Countries

The recent decade has seen Central America pass through a turbulent period—economically, politically, and socially—during which both violence and social reforms were tried as means of redressing long-standing social inequities. In the case of El Salvador, a rare interlude of political will, on the part of both the reform-minded Salvadoran military and the since-cashiered U.S. State Department officials, to take decisive action on behalf of the poor and landless resulted in a important land reform. Subsequent backsliding on the part of the Reagan administration and the increased power of the conservatives have blunted the momentum of the reform, however, with the result that more than 250,000 campesino families still remain landless. The future direction of El Salvador remains uncertain at present, with major legal questions as to the tenure status of the Phase I beneficiaries remaining to be worked out.

In Nicaragua, the land reform has greatly reduced the problem of landlessness; however, the disastrous economic situation, coupled with a stodgy adherence to collective forms of exploitation discredited virtually everywhere else in the world have combined to prevent the reform from realizing its productive potential. The major determinant of the future of the Nicaraguan land reform (as well as that of the country as a whole) will be the results of the coming election, which will either ratify Nicaragua's continued status as an outcast, and hence expedite its economic decline, or open the way to greater participation of all sectors in the political life of the country, and, equally important, end the economic blockade and restore foreign aid flows.

Guatemala, the only Central American country suffering through a major upheaval to emerge with the old inequities largely intact, is virtually guaranteed another major social upheaval in the decades to come. Honduras, having bought time by virtue of its land mass, will probably see in the next decade a sharpening of social inequities, economic decline, and mounting militancy among the ranks of the disenfranchised. It might, then, finally become obliged to expropriate for redistribution its underutilized livestock lands. Costa Rica, always the most promising country in the region in terms of its ability to confront and resolve social problems peacefully and democratically, has a plodding but continuing land-reform program, which may prove to be an interesting laboratory for testing whether the USAID-preferred land-market option can make a meaningful contribution to the land-tenure problem (so far it has not done so anywhere) or will prove to be just another palliative.

The Issues

1. A fundamental conclusion of this analysis, unfortunately, is that an objective assessment of the performance of recent land-reform initiatives in Central America, in terms of achievement of their economic, social, and political objectives, is impossible given the overriding impact of the political and economic upheaval affecting the region during this same period. With the exception perhaps of Costa Rica, land-reform measures have invariably taken place within the context of violent revolution, deep political polarization, or economic deterioration. As such, attribution of any impact on the implementing country's economy and socioeconomic situation to land-reform measures is a complicated and possibly fruitless exercise. This fact has not, however, been adequately recognized, either by the advocates or

opponents of these measures.

2. In a similar vein, one should recognize that land reforms are nothing less than major social changes and, as such, should not be subjected to the same kind of economic/financial evaluation as might be a hydroelectric project or the construction of an oil refinery. This is not to say that mistaken policies should be allowed to remain in place indefinitely or not be subjected to rigorous scrutiny and analysis; rather, adequate allowance should be made for the time required to develop the *human,* as well as the physical, infrastructure required to run a reform program.

3. The form of land tenure and organization at the farm level—collective, individual, or mixed—promises to be a difficult issue, which will remain alive and controversial into the foreseeable future. Governments as ideologically opposed as Nicaragua's and El Salvador's both pay lip service to "respecting the autonomy of the beneficiaries," and "free choice" in these areas, but in fact the state's apparatus seeks to push them in one direction or the other, often with consequences more disastrous than those perceived as stemming from the imagined evils of not subscribing to the government's own ideological thrust. In general, however, it is obvious that the collective form, either of ownership or organization, is a more difficult and complicated one to manage, both for the government and the beneficiaries. At the same time, the collective option, if not too dogmatically or coercively applied (i.e., allowing for family plots and compensation commensurate with effort), can yield social benefits that appear to government and beneficiaries alike to be worth the price of admission. Perhaps even more important than this aspect, in the case of countries like El Salvador (and to a lesser extent Honduras), where defense and/or further progress of the reform is a battle fought daily, the collective mode is prerequisite to forging the kind of campesino organizations that serve as the "rear guard" against the right wing's efforts to undermine the reforms.

4. At the risk of contradicting statement (2) above, it is possible to attribute certain intangible changes in countries that have experienced a major land reform (El Salvador and Nicaragua), and to note that, in a sense, these changes in attitude on the part of the previously isolated and ignorant campesinos constitute the firmest basis for any optimism regarding the economic and political future of the region. To summarize this point, even the most hardened oligarchs in these countries probably have come to realize that they can never again base the profitability of an agricultural enterprise on the exploitation of cheap and ignorant rural labor, and that in the future, they will be forced to deal with the campesinos—if not as equals, at least as a

group to be negotiated with, not dictated to. The implications of this, although dolorous to the bottom lines of the ruling class in the short term, are hopeful for the ultimate establishment of more democratic, stable, and just societies.

5. An inescapable conclusion of the recent progress of land reform in the region is that where significant progress has been made, other than as a result of actual revolution, it has been due not to sudden enlightenment on the part of governments or leaders, but rather in terrified response to the possible consequences of further inaction. The same could be said, of course, for U.S. policy in the region. By this standard, ironically, the greatest threat to further progress in redressing land-tenure inequities in the region is the much-touted "peace process." In this regard, one can only hope that, if peace does come, one result will not be for policymakers in the region and the United States to believe they can go back to sleep for another decade, in the illusion that, when they awake, the grave social ills of the region will have miraculously resolved themselves.

Notes

1. D'Abuisson, whose "Argentina School" counterinsurgency tactics won him the status of folk hero among the right wing in El Salvador, went on to pursue a political career, becoming at one point the candidate of the right wing Alianza Republicana Nacional (ARENA) party. Today, although holding the presumably respectable position of president of the Asamblea Nacional, he is still suspected by many of maintaining close links, if not de facto leadership, of the violent underground right.

2. Phase II's vivisection was gradual but eventually complete. The justification for not implementing Phase II when authorized (via Decree 154) was that it would hopelessly overburden the fragile junta administratively and financially (25 percent of the compensation was to be paid in cash). The junta already had its hands full attempting to implement Phases I and III. Toward the end of 1983, via Article 105 of the new constitution, the ARENA-controlled Assembly raised the legal holding limit from 100 hectares to 245 hectares, which effectively eliminated all but 21,000 hectares from risk of expropriation. In order to avoid expropriation (without compensation), the land in these farms above the reserve right was to have been sold by 1986. This did not occur, however, and the Assembly recently declared the remainder of Phase II null and void.

3. There is an apparent consensus, at least among the nominal leaders of the new administration, Cristiani and the minister of agriculture, to do this. Both the government and the campesino organizations have agreed that a new COC should be established with broader representation, including other campesino organizations besides ACOPAI, UCS, and FESACORA, who have traditionally been supporters of the PDC.

4. At present, the USAID Country Development Strategy Statement actually states as a goal "75 cooperatives divided and distributed as individual parcels by 1994." In another ill-advised measure, it has determined that the US$4 million it will make available as seed capital to the Land Bank cannot be utilized to purchase farms that will be worked collectively, regardless of whether it makes more sense to operate them as a unit (e.g., some coffee farms). Both these measures are paternalistic, and run counter to the administration's stated policy of respecting the autonomy of the beneficiaries to decide their own form of organization.

5. These are government figures; other estimates differ. The UN Food and Agriculture Organization (FAO) reports a total of 6.5 million hectares in farms. One possible source of the discrepancy is the severe decapitalization that has occurred, particularly in the livestock sector, which may have resulted in former pasture lands being reclaimed by jungle.

6. Carlos Fonseca, a revolutionary hero, had promised the campesinos "no land without farmers and no farmers without land."

7. Many sources believe the number of landless, which appears to have risen between 1982 and the present, is much lower. The author, however, was unable to account for this increase in rural families (due to population growth) in any other category, given available government statistics.

8. In fact, it is rumored that the primary use of profits distributed individually on production cooperatives is investment in private property, including farmland.

9. The annual desertion rate was once as high as 20 percent. Recently, however, the sector has stabilized, and the desertion rate is only 10 percent, by estimates of the Ministry of Agriculture and Agrarian Reform (MIDINRA).

10. Estimates differ. USAID reports 4.2 million hectares, of which 2.9 million are in crops and 1.3 million are in pasture. FAO reports 1.86 million hectares in cropland and 1.37 million in pasture, for a total of only 3.23 million. In this analysis, the USAID figures are used.

11. This figure does not include more than 100,000 hectares sold in tracts of more than 3,000 hectares each at concessional rates to the military and oligarchs.

12. In this regard, a creative definition of what constitutes a threat to U.S. security would need to be employed, i.e., policies (or lack thereof) that create such social inequity as to endanger a nation's, and the region's, stability.

13. Figure extrapolated from 1983 estimates, based on growth rate since that time (World Bank, Honduras, "An Inquiry into Rural Population, Small Farmers and Agrarian Reform, "Informe No. 3963-Ho, Washington, D.C., January 14, 1983).

14. The plans of the *Instituto Nacional Agraria* (INA) have called for at least three times more land to be distributed than actually has been. Dr. Ricardo Puerta, "Hacia Donde va la Reforma Agraria Hondurena?" *Panorama* (April–May 1984).

Selected Bibliography

Central American Historical Institute (CAHI). "The Nicaraguan Peasantry Gives New Direction to Agrarian Reform." *Envio* 4, no. 51 (September 1985).

Fagan, R. R., ed., "The Making of a Mixed Economy: Class Struggle and State Policy in the Nicaragua Transition." In *Transition and Development*, 1986, MRP.

Hough, Richard, et al. *Land and Labor in Guatemala*. 1983.

Kaimowitz, David. "Nicaraguan Debates on Agrarian Structure and Their Implications for Agricultural Policy and the Rural Poor." *Journal of Peasant Studies* (1985).

Ministry of Agriculture, El Salvador. "Analisis Comparativo de la Situacion Socioeconomica de los Beneficiarios del decreto 154 y decreto 207," 1988.

———. "Perfil de Beneficiarios de la Primera Etapa de la Reforma Agraria," 1986.

———. "Tercer Perfil de Beneficiarios del Decreto 207," 1988.

Prosterman, Roy L., and Jeffrey M. Riedinger. *Land Reform and Democratic Development*. Baltimore, Md.: Johns Hopkins University Press, 1987.

Puerta, Ricardo. "Hacia Donde va la Reforma Agraria Hondurena?" *Panorama* (April–May 1984).

Strasma, John. "Unfinished Business: Consolidating Land Reform in El Salvador." In *Searching for Agrarian Reform in Latin America*, William C. Thiesenhusen, ed., Boston: Unwin Hyman, 1989.

U.S. Agency for International Development. "Spring Review of Small Farmer Credit." 1970.

Wise, Michael L. "Agrarian Reform in El Salvador—Process and Progress". USAID Report, 1985.

World Bank, Honduras. "An Inquiry into Rural Population, Small Farmers and Agrarian Reform." Informe No. 3963-Ho, Washington, D.C., January 14, 1983.

chapter six

Agrarian Reform in Mexico: A Cautionary Tale

Merilee S. Grindle

Summary

Mexico is unlike a number of other countries reviewed in this book in that it has experienced a major agrarian reform. Equitable access to land, which had been an aspiration of the peasant-based armies of the Revolution of 1910, became a significant aspect of the Constitution of 1917. The agrarian reform, weakly pursued at first, was massively implemented in the 1930s under the leadership of President Lázaro Cárdenas. In subsequent years, land continued to be distributed, albeit much more slowly and in a much less supportive policy and program environment. Currently, approximately half of Mexico's farm area and 70 percent of its farm units are in the reformed sector.

Despite the extent of agrarian reform in Mexico, underproductivity, landlessness, and marginality characterize most of the country's rural people. These conditions can be traced to government policies that encouraged the emergence of large-scale commercial agricultural units and gave little or no support to reform beneficiaries. Population pressure and a poor agricultural resource base in many areas farmed by peasants exacerbate the difficulty of developing rural areas. The lesson of Mexico's experience is that in the absence of a supportive policy environment; in the absence of significant investment in credit, infrastructure, research, extension, Green Revolution technology, and human capital formation; and in the absence of a legitimate capacity of rural people to make sustained political and economic demands on the government, agrarian reform cannot resolve deep-seated problems of rural poverty, underproductivity, and inequity.

Peasants throughout Mexico have sought to remedy the conditions created by an incomplete agrarian reform by retreating into subsistence production, sharecropping, searching for wage labor and petty production activities locally, and engaging in frequent temporary labor migration. These strategies allow peasant households to get by, but

179

rarely to prosper. Several options are frequently discussed to create a
more dynamic rural economy in Mexico, but none offer quick fixes.
There are few opportunities available to rural inhabitants if they move
to the large cities; investments in agriculture can be promising but
probably will not resolve rural demand for employment and income; it
is unlikely that the agrarian reform will be either expanded or undone
significantly; and rural industrialization can create sources of
employment and income if appropriate investments are identified and
financed. The United States can assist Mexico in resolving its rural
development problems by addressing issues of trade and immigration
between the two countries and by undertaking measures to create a
healthier international economic environment that will allow Mexico to
address problems of debt, dependency, and development.

As he contemplates the 1990s, Don Agustín is concerned about his
family's future. Life in rural Hidalgo, which had once seemed so
promising, has left him, at the age of sixty-one, feeling broken and
disillusioned. In 1953, as he and twenty-two other claimants took
possession of the 257 hectares that composed the newly recognized
ejido[1] of Santa Rosa, he had been filled with hope and confidence
about the future. The grant of Santa Rosa was the culmination of an
effort begun in 1928 by Agustín's father and a group of other tenant
farmers who petitioned the government for the creation of an ejido out
of the land they farmed. For two and a half decades, this group made
repeated trips to the state capital and to Mexico City, bringing letters,
documents, and proposals to be considered by the governor, agrarian
reform officials, party bosses, delegates to Congress, whomever they
could interest in their cause. When he died in 1949, Agustín's father
had been given many promises, but no resolution had yet been made.
Then, as a favor to a claimant who had marshaled support for his
electoral campaign, a newly elected governor of Hidalgo initialed the
documents that the national level officials needed to proceed with the
grant. He followed this up with a personal request for attention to the
matter by the National Agrarian Commission and the president.[2]

Santa Rosa, carved out from a much larger landholding of a once-
prominent family in Hidalgo, was composed of uneven and
unimproved terrain. In fact, of its 257 hectares, only 124 were suitable
for farming. This amount was parceled out to the claimants and the rest
was reserved as communal land. Although the soil was poor and
farming would be dependent on the erratic rainfall of the region,
Agustín considered that his allotment of 5.3 hectares would enable him
and his wife, Ramona, to raise their family with dignity. He set about

planting the stony fields with corn, beans, and nopal, while Ramona worked equally hard raising eight children, caring for the house, and tending chickens and a few fruit trees. Some good years ensued, of course, but also many bad ones: when the rains did not come on time or came in torrents that washed away the fields, when no credit was available at the Ejidal Bank, when sickness and school fees depleted what little savings the family had, and when the government-set price for corn was so low that it did not even cover the costs of production.

Gradually, as their family grew, Agustín and Ramona began to search beyond the land for other ways to make ends meet. At age thirteen, their oldest daughter, Beatriz, was sent to Mexico City to work as a maid in the home of a wealthy family with a vacation house near the ejido. Each month, Beatriz sent half her meager earnings to her parents at Santa Rosa. In 1964, the oldest son, Pedro, qualified to become a bracero, or agricultural laborer, in a U.S.-Mexico temporary immigration program. The program ended that year, but Pedro's experience provided him with important contacts in the United States so that for six months each year after that, until 1972, he was able to work in Arizona and California as an undocumented laborer. Living in the fields, he worked along with the other migrants, and saved as much of his wages as possible to turn over to his father on his return to Santa Rosa each year. A second son, Hernán, was apprenticed to a metalworker in a nearby market town and, after several years, he began earning modest wages, most of which he gave to his mother when he returned home every Saturday afternoon.

Lilia, the second daughter, who had always wanted to be a teacher, left school when she was twelve because her parents needed her to join Beatriz in Mexico City and to work for wages in the same household. Eventually, through his contacts with a local political boss, Agustín managed to get Lilia a job as a cleaning woman in a government office building in Mexico City; although the wages were very low, union membership gave her confidence that she would not be fired. When Lilia married and moved to a squatter settlement in the capital in 1978, she stopped sending part of her wages to her mother. The two youngest sons, Cheo and Ramoncito, hired themselves out as agricultural laborers to richer peasants in the ejido and nearby communities. Ramoncito also worked from time to time in construction projects in a nearby town. With this, and helping out on their father's land, the boys managed to find work six to eight months of the year. Two girls, Luz María and Elena, helped their mother at home, embroidering traditional blouses and shawls for sale to tourists in Mexico City and baking sweets for sale in three local shops.

Unable to purchase sufficient fertilizer and improved seeds because of debts owed to the Ejidal Bank, Agustín began renting out two hectares of his land to sharecroppers, even though this was illegal under the Agrarian Code. Gradually, he stopped trying to grow corn to sell to the government's purchasing agency, CONASUPO, and grew only enough corn and beans for his family's subsistence. One year, when there was no rain and Ramona and three of the children required extensive medical attention, Agustín joined Pedro for his annual trek to the United States. Labor migration seemed the only way to pay the bills. Over the years, by pooling the incomes from such diverse sources, Agustín and Ramona managed to cover most household expenses for their family, a family that had grown to twenty-two members by 1990 as the children married and began to have children of their own.

But Agustín and Ramona know that the future is bleak for their family. The boys, grown now and with family responsibilities, are itching for independence from their father, but have limited prospects for acquiring access to farmable land in Santa Rosa or elsewhere. When Agustín dies, he will leave less than a hectare to each child, and although Beatriz, Hernán, and Lilia will undoubtedly sell their rights to the others, there is little chance for any of the rest to earn a living from the dry and eroded land. Growing even corn and beans on this marginal land is expensive because purchased inputs increasingly are required. Neither income nor employment opportunities can be expected on ejidos such as Santa Rosa. Moreover, lacking much education and important political patrons, there are only limited opportunities for stable jobs in urban areas. How will the rest of the family manage to survive in the future and care for their own families? Only increasing impoverishment can be expected, given what Agustín knows about the poor quality and small size of ejido plots, the lack of water, the poor roads, indebtedness to the bank, landlessness, and the increasing costs of living.

What happened to the bright dreams that Agustín and Ramona had for their future in 1953? Answers to this question lie in the history of Mexico's agrarian reform and the policies of the government that shaped that history. The problems that beset and worry Agustín are a legacy of the agrarian reform: years, even lifetimes, of petitioning the government for land; entitlements to land of low fertility; increasing inequality among ejidatarios as land is fragmented and reconcentrated; too many people for too little land; indebtedness to the rural credit bank; inadequate infrastructure of irrigation and roads; exploitive relationships with political party bosses; and lack of attention from the government. The remedies to these conditions sought by peasants throughout Mexico are similar to those of Agustín and his family: a retreat into subsistence, a search for wage labor and petty production activities locally, frequent involvement in temporary labor migration, and sharecropping the land. In the end, these strategies allow families to get by, but rarely let them prosper. All too often this is the fate of millions of Mexico's peasant households. A survey of the agrarian reform and the government policies that developed around it indicate how this fate was created.

Mexico's Agrarian Reform

Don Agustín and his family are beneficiaries of the agrarian reform that is enshrined in the Mexican Constitution of 1917, itself a consequence of the aspirations of the Revolution of 1910. Article 27 of the constitution legitimizes the right of the state to expropriate private property and establishes the legal and procedural framework for a massive redistribution of land through the communal ejido system and small private landholdings. Owners of land expropriated were to be compensated, and the constitution fixed no limit on the amount that could be redistributed or on the amount of time during which the reform could be carried out. The land could be distributed to corporate groups as ejidos, or to small private farmers.[3]

The Ejidos

The ejido is a communal landholding that can be granted by the state to an organized group of twenty or more claimants. These groups petition the state for legal status and title to the land. When and if the land is granted—through a procedural and legal process that can take years to accomplish—a committee of members is elected to administer the ejido. Ejidatarios (grantees) are assigned plots for themselves and their heirs by this committee and retain rights of usufruct to it as long as they fulfill certain obligations to the corporate membership. The most important obligation is that the land not be left idle for more than two consecutive years. Ejidatarios have the right to cultivate their land collectively or individually. To protect its integrity, ejido land cannot be sold, only relinquished to the ejido membership for reassignment. Until 1981, it was also illegal to rent ejido land. Under the law, subdivision and acquiring land from another ejidatario are both illegal; both are widely practiced, however, and the result has been both concentration and fragmentation of land, leading to considerable inequality among theoretically equal ejidatarios. In general, these conditions do not show up in agricultural census data because of their illegal or informal nature.

There are currently about 22,000 ejidos in Mexico, accounting for more than 2 million ejidatarios and their families and almost 50 percent of the farm area in the country. The central and southern portions of Mexico are. the areas most densely populated with ejidos. In many areas most intensively covered by ejido grants, conflicts over land rights and boundaries are endemic; there is little land left to distribute in such areas. Originally, grants to ejidos were to be large enough for each ejidatario to receive about ten hectares. Inheritance patterns have resulted in a considerable reduction of plot sizes, however. According to agricultural census data, a third of all ejido plots are smaller than two hectares and another third are between two and five hectares.[4] Most ejidatarios are poor. Based on the agricultural census of 1970, 52.3 percent of them can be classified as sub-subsistence farmers; that is, with insufficient land or resources to produce enough food for their families. A further 19 percent can be classified as subsistence farmers, and only 28.7 percent can be classified as able to produce a marketable surplus.

The ejido, modeled on a vision of a pre-Columbian tenure system, lies at the heart of Mexico's agrarian reform and has been a fundamental basis for remarkable political stability, despite the great inequities in the distribution of economic and political power that characterize the country. Ejidatarios receive not only land from the state, but also access to credit, agricultural inputs, social welfare services and facilities, markets, and infrastructure such as roads and irrigation. As protector and provider of goods and services to the ejido sector, largely through the dominant political party, the government has used its power to create a dependent clientele of the reform beneficiaries.

Private Farmers, Small and Large Scale
Small private landownership emerged haphazardly out of the agrarian reform. Former large landowners retained access to some of their land, at times a single large holding was divided up among many family members, at times the landowners sold off parcels to private individuals, and at times the government granted land titles to "colonists" as individual owners. Private ownership is most common in the north-central and northern parts of the country, where it predominated in the prerevolutionary period. About 50 percent of Mexico's farmland is owned privately and some 15 percent of it is in parcels of five hectares or less. Such parcels account for about 65 percent of private farm families. Many of these small farmers are poor. In fact, based on the 1970 agricultural census, 63.1 percent can be classified as sub-subsistence, and another 10.1 percent can be

considered subsistence farmers.

Farms of more than 100 hectares account for about a quarter of all farmlands, private and communal, but less than 1 percent of farm units. It is this group of farmers who have been among the most prosperous and who have benefited most from government policies since the 1940s. Especially prosperous have been those in the irrigation districts, some 100,000 farmers who are proprietors of modern commercial farms and who generally produce crops for export. Such well-endowed holdings and prosperous farmers are especially evident in the north and northwestern parts of Mexico. Farms in this region have developed primarily within large irrigation districts financed by the state and have received the bulk of the country's research and extension efforts. With the availability of irrigation has come preferred access to Green Revolution technology and subsidized credit with which to invest in it. These large commercial farms have benefited from highly subsidized energy prices, and as a result have become heavily mechanized. Transportation and marketing infrastructure have also received significant government support. Proximity to the large U.S. market, as well as controlled prices for many domestically consumed foodstuffs, have encouraged most of the agriculture in this region to specialize in export production. As large commercial farmers in the north and northwest increased in economic importance because of their capacity to generate foreign exchange, they also increased in political importance to the government.

The Uniqueness of Mexico

The agrarian reform in Mexico has resulted in land tenure relationships that are distinctly different from those of most other developing countries. Table 6.1 provides some insight into these differences. First, as is evident, the large majority of those who have access to land are reform beneficiaries. This stands in stark contrast to conditions in most developing countries, where agrarian reforms, if they have been legislated at all, generally affect only a small portion of farm households. Second, corporate or communal ownership characterizes a very significant portion of these beneficiaries through the ejido system. As indicated in Table 6.1, nearly 70 percent of farm households fall in the ejido and communal sector. Third, although not reported in Table 6.1, sharecropping and renting account officially for only about 50,000 farmers, although a very large amount of unofficial sharecropping and renting exists, especially on ejido lands. Most of Mexico's peasant farmers therefore have security of tenure, either as ejidatarios or as small private landowners.

Table 6.1   Distribution of Farms in Mexico by Type of Tenure

	Farm Units		Total Area of Farms	
	Number (thousands)	%	Hectares (thousands)	%
Ejidatarios	1,718.6		60,557.5	
Comuneros	129.0		9,194.7	
	1,847.6	69.1	69,752.2	49.9
Private Farmers	825.0	30.9	70,172.5	50.1

Source: P. Lamartine Yates, *Mexico's Agricultural Dilemma*, pp.154, 157.

In other ways, however, Mexico is not so different from other developing countries. Similar to them, for example, an increasing proportion—as much as 50 percent—of the rural population lacks access to the land. Similar also is the poverty and underproductivity of peasant agriculture. The poorest areas in Mexico are those regions in which ejidos are most numerous and where population pressures on the land are greatest. Moreover, although ejidos account for about 50 percent of the land, their productivity compares unfavorably with private farms. Ejidos produce only 65 percent of the per hectare value of crops produced by private farms. Landlessness, poverty, and underproductivity suggest that the agrarian reform in Mexico has not resolved fundamental problems of development in rural areas. To understand why this has occurred, it is important to review the history of the reform and the government policies that affected its development.

Revolution, Agrarian Reform, and Development Strategies

The first great social revolution of the twentieth century erupted in Mexico in 1910. Important to its course was a dispossessed peasantry whose goal was nothing less than the restitution of lands and livelihoods that had been wrested from it during fifty years of expanding agrarian capitalism.[5] Peasant armies, loosely organized under the leadership of local and regional chieftains such as Emiliano Zapata in central and southern Mexico and more diverse groups in the north, fought aggressively for land for individuals and whole communities. These armies and the communities they represented suffered greatly from the violence that lasted into the 1920s—some 1–2 million Mexicans died during the revolution, most of them from famine, disease, and dislocation rather than from the warfare itself. The largest toll was paid by those who were poor and rural. Such massive sacrifice and dislocation was not all in vain, however, for a decree in 1915 established the legitimacy of their claims and the Constitution of 1917 mandated a far-reaching agrarian reform. The revolution itself largely destroyed the power of the traditional landed elite, opening the way for a more equitable distribution of productive resources.

Many peasant villages that participated in the revolution seized the initiative legitimized by the new Constitution to claim the lands taken from them by large landowners. Many others began the lengthy legal and bureaucratic process of becoming officially incorporated as ejidos. In all cases, they returned to their villages to carry on with lives interrupted by injustice and violence, turning their backs on Mexico City and the political conflicts over control of the nation that continued throughout the 1920s. By returning to the land they fought for, however, the peasants gradually relinquished their ability to remain central and independent actors in the land reform and in the shaping of the country's development strategies.

In fact, most of the leaders who emerged victorious from the revolutionary conflicts were little concerned about the peasantry, envisioning instead a Mexico of large modern farms and factories, far removed from the small plots tended by peasant farmers. They wanted a strong state that would intervene actively to spur capitalist development and to maintain political stability and control in the country. After a further decade of internecine violence, the revolutionary leaders agreed to the formation of an inclusive national political party in 1928; intra-elite conflicts would subsequently be played out within the fold of the party and the "Revolutionary Family" that formed its core. The leaders of the 1920s and early 1930s actively supported a model of agricultural development that was to be based on large landholdings, capitalist principles of ownership, and the use of capital, labor, and land. Land reform during these years was pursued only reluctantly, and largely in response to activist peasant claims to regain control of ancestral lands. During this period, about 11 million hectares of land were distributed.

The agrarian reform did not become the basis for a massive attack on the structure of landholding in the country until after 1934, when President Lázaro Cárdenas radicalized the revolution, promoted the political organization of the peasantry, and began distributing land to peasants, particularly those organized as ejidos. Between 1935 and 1940, Cárdenas spearheaded the distribution of over 18 million hectares to 770,000 petitioners. This radical phase of the agrarian reform was notable not only for the extensiveness of the distribution of lands, but also for the support given by the government to the idea of a prosperous peasant sector based on the ejido tenure system. By 1940, when Cárdenas left office, half the cultivated area of the country was organized into ejidos and the sector accounted for 51 percent of the value of agricultural production. As another indicator of his impact, when Cárdenas assumed the presidency, 68 percent of the rural workforce was landless; when his term was completed, 36 percent was landless. In considerable contrast to later periods, much of the land distributed was of good quality and some of it benefited directly from irrigation works supported by the government.[6] Table 6.2 indicates the extensiveness of the redistributive initiative of the Cárdenas period compared to prior and subsequent administrations.

Table 6.2   Land Distribution in Mexico by Presidential Period

Period	Total Hectares	Arable Hectares	Arable Hectares per Beneficiary
Pre-Cárdenas (1915-1934)	11,244,817	1,610,561	1.7
Cárdenas (1934-1940)	18,360,344	4,297,294	5.7
Avila Camancho (1940-1946)	7,242,308	1,123,725	9.1
Alemán Valdés (1946-1952)	4,616,352	800,996	7.4
Ruiz Cortines (1952-1958)	6,182,017	1,035,665	4.6
López Mateos (1958-1964)	8,845,814	1,479,747	5.1
Díaz Ordaz (1964-1970)	24,729,499	2,101,534	5.6
Echeverría (1970-1976)	12,742,744	925,807	4.2

Source: CEPAL (Comisión Económica para América Latina), Economía campesina y agricultura empresarial, p. 221.

The Cárdenas period was also notable for its support of the collective farming of ejido lands and the channeling of government services, especially irrigation and credit, to the collective ejido sector. Health and education expenditures for rural areas increased notably. Along with this was the active support of political mobilization among the peasantry, as agrarian leagues were encouraged to emerge throughout the country and were then incorporated into regional and national organizations. This activity culminated in 1938 with the creation of the National Confederation of Peasants (CNC) and its inclusion as one of four corporate pillars (along with labor, military, and middle-class sectors) in the dominant political party, the Party of the Mexican Revolution (PRM), later to become the Party of the Institutionalized Revolution (PRI). Ejidos belonged to the CNC as corporate members. During this era, many local agrarian and party leaders effectively represented the interests of peasants directly to state and national leaders and were able to acquire access to credit and other benefits for their followers.

After the Cárdenas years, the pace of land distribution and the direction of government policy changed significantly. Under Cárdenas, there had been a genuine effort to build a rural social structure based on equitable rights to land, water, credit, and markets. After 1940, development in Mexico became identified with rapid industrialization, a state that supported the emergence of a strong entrepreneurial capitalist elite, and the promotion of rapid economic growth. According to development plans of the 1940s and 1950s, private and modern commercial agriculture was to play an important role in supporting the new, modern, industrial Mexico; the Cárdenas years came to be regarded by urban elites and policymakers as a period of dangerous radicalism; the collective activities of the period considered a threat to both private property and state hegemony.

The collective ejido, in particular, was singled out for disapprobation, and the cultivation of individual plots by ejidatarios was promoted. Fortunately, for statists and capitalists alike, the organization of the peasantry under Cárdenas made it relatively easy to turn rural organizations into captive support groups for the regime, whatever policies it chose to pursue. Because of their dependence on the state and the PRI for the distribution of government resources, organizational and ejido leaders quickly came to represent the goals of the government in Mexico City rather than the aspirations of their followers. Politically sensitive allocation of government resources and favors to reward loyal support and to punish the independent-minded did much to undermine the authenticity of peasant leadership in these years.

The pattern of distributing lands to quell isolated instances of rural conflict and to reward loyalty to the PRI became set in the 1950s and 1960s. The heroes of government development plans were the new capitalist farmers; they also became the principal beneficiaries of the government's investment in the agricultural sector. Beginning in the 1940s and 1950s, the gap between peasant agriculture and commercial agriculture emerged and grew wider. State financing for commercial agriculture—accounting for about 25 percent of farm families—accounted for 45 percent of credit for agriculture by the 1960s. For ejidatarios, credit often came tied to stipulations about types of crops that could be produced, types and quantities of inputs required, and marketing channels to be used. The government, which invested 75–85 percent of its allocations for agriculture in irrigation programs, largely centered in the north and the northwest, channeled assistance almost exclusively to the private large-holding sector.

As we have seen, the northern parts of the country, with the fewest minifundias and ejidos, also became the principal recipient of government-subsidized credit, research, extension, mechanization, marketing facilities, and distribution of inputs. Public investment in areas dominated by ejidos and poor peasant private farms was virtually nonexistent in this period. In addition, state-mandated prices for the crops most frequently grown by peasant producers, corn and beans, were held at low and stable levels to ensure cheap foodstuffs for the urban labor force (see Table 6.3). There were only two years between 1960 and 1982, for instance, in which the guaranteed price of maize was above what it had been in 1960 in constant peso terms. In 1982, the price was two-thirds of what it had been in 1960.

Table 6.3   Guaranteed Prices per Metric Ton for Basic Staples, 1960-1982 (1970 Pesos)

Year	Wheat	Beans	Maize
1960	1,290	2,119	1,130
1961	1,247	2,391	1,093
1962	1,211	2,321	1,061
1963	1,173	2,249	1,208
1964	1,111	2,129	1,144
1965	951	2,081	1,118
1966	915	2,002	1,076
1967	890	1,947	1,046
1968	869	1,900	1,021
1969	836	1,829	982
1970	800	1,750	940
1971	755	1,652	888
1972	711	1,556	836
1973	686	1,694	946
1974	834	3,851	963
1975	971	2,634	1,054
1976	812	2,319	1,085
1977	729	1,778	1,031
1978	792	1,904	884
1979	760	1,964	882
1980	699	2,362	876
1981	704	2,447	1,002
1982	552	1,581	706

Source: Merilee S. Grindle, *Searching for Rural Development: Labor Migration and Employment in Mexico*, p. 32

The results of this skewed allocation of government resources were marked. Thus it was that by 1970, 12 percent of all farm units incorporated 42 percent of its productive land, 48 percent of its irrigation and other government investment, 73 percent of its machinery, and 61 percent of its Green Revolution technology. This rich subsector of production, however, supplied only 20 percent of agricultural jobs. The implication of skewed resource allocations became apparent in the years after 1965, when the country began to fail in its ability to produce enough corn and beans to feed a burgeoning urban population. Annual imports of shortfalls began to occur and to account for significant costs in foreign exchange.

In the 1970s, under populist initiatives of President Luís Echeverría (1970–1976) and oil-financed initiatives of President José Lopez Portillo (1976–1982), greater attention was directed toward peasant agriculture, in large part because decisionmakers had come to see the underproductivity of the sector as a drag on further industrial development in the country. In particular, the increasing need to spend valuable foreign exchange on imports of corn and other staple crops emphasized the importance of a more prosperous peasant agriculture to policymakers. Recognizing that peasants produced the bulk of the staple foods in the country, they acknowledged that this sector needed greater public sector attention. Investments in rural development for peasant-based agricultural regions expanded notably in this period. This greater attention to domestic food crop producers was implemented without having to divert resources from the commercial agricultural sector because the government initially borrowed heavily to finance it and then used oil revenues to pursue a wide range of rural-focused initiatives.

Investment in integrated rural development initiatives was spurred under the Echeverría administration. Higher support prices for basic staples, subsidized credit, storage and marketing assistance, subsidized Green Revolution technology, and expansion of educational and health-care facilities were targeted for zones of rainfed, peasant agriculture. Between 1970 and 1975, agricultural investment increased from about 10 percent of total public sector investment to more than 15 percent. Because total public sector investment increased markedly in these same years, absolute amounts were dramatically above what they had been throughout the 1960s. Among the more well known of the rural development initiatives was PIDER (Program for Integrated Rural Development). Under this program, a series of microregions was to receive an integrated array of improvements for agriculture, physical infrastructure, health, sanitation, and education. By 1983, PIDER accounted for some $2 billion of investment by the government and international agencies.

The administration of Lopez Portillo, visibly alarmed by increased need to import food and its foreign exchange costs, also directed funds to the peasant agricultural sector. More than 17 percent of total public investment was directed to rural and agricultural development by the early 1980s. A program for rainfed districts focused on introducing technological improvements in peasant agricultural regions, and the Mexican Food System (SAM) introduced a wide array of subsidies—some $3 billion worth—in an effort to stimulate the production of staple food crops. Under initiatives such as PIDER, the rainfed districts program, and the SAM, rural infrastructure for production, health, and education expanded, and sources of credit, extension, and Green Revolution technology became more available to rural communities. By 1982, however, with the administration of Miguel de la Madrid, Mexico entered a period of extreme economic crisis; expenditures for agriculture and rural development dropped dramatically in absolute amounts in response to draconian austerity measures and also fell to about 8 percent of total public sector investment.

Despite investments of the 1970s and early 1980s, the general trend was one of increased landlessness because of population pressure on the land and the stagnation of production of staple crops because of the complexity and magnitude of resources required to stimulate greater production. The country continued to import basic staples and to spend large amounts of dollars to do so. Much of the failure to increase basic staple production can be blamed upon poor planning, inappropriately designed interventions, administrative weakness, confusion over pricing policy, and corruption. The already advantaged irrigation districts continued to receive the largest portion of government expenditures, and therefore increased spending in the sector probably benefited large- and medium-scale commercial farmers as much as it did peasants.

In addition to these factors, however, much more extensive investment in infrastructure, research and extension, small irrigation works, and human capital formation is needed in many rural regions before tiny plots of poorly endowed and often heavily eroded land can be made significantly more productive. Even then, some analysts have questioned if increased production can be expected from many farmers; they may still prefer to invest their time and effort in other income-generating activities rather than choosing to increase production on plots of land that are marginal at best. Moreover, as we will see later, increased production on peasant holdings may not resolve issues of poverty and landlessness that are increasingly evident in Mexico's rural areas.

Not only the high costs in foreign exchange of food imports, but also the threat of dependence on the "Colossus of the North" for food supplies, spurred considerable concern for peasant production during the 1970s and early 1980s. But only during a brief period in the 1970s and 1980s did land distribution play a significant role in government efforts to address the problems of peasant agriculture. In 1975 and 1976, President Echeverría attempted to mobilize the rural sector to expand the distribution of land in northern parts of the country. In late 1976, he expropriated 100,000 hectares of valuable land to turn over to some 9,000 peasant claimants. Conflict with commercial agricultural interests ensued and such was their capacity to wield economic power, primarily because of the foreign exchange commercial farmers generated from exports, that the succeeding government of José Lopez Portillo quickly announced that land distribution was no longer a feasible solution to the country's rural and agrarian problems. Most of the expropriated land was returned to the large commercial farmers. In the 1970s, the kind of rural instability that accompanied the agrarian reform of the 1930s was not acceptable to the government because of the increased importance of the modern commercial farm sector to the economy. Then, in the 1980s, under the impact of an economic crisis of massive proportions, the economic importance of the export-oriented northern farmers increased even more, and state investments in peasant agriculture and rural development infrastructure were cut back drastically as part of extensive austerity measures pursued by the government.

For most governments of the period after 1940, technological innovation, not structural transformation of tenure relationships, was the solution officially proposed to generate rural and agricultural advancement in Mexico. Moreover, private farmers and not ejidatarios were expected to accomplish this goal. These policies resulted in distinct patterns of production among distinct tenure groups. In comparison with private farmers, the ejido sector performed poorly. In the years between 1950 and 1970, ejidos produced on average half as much per unit of land as did private farmers. In the same period, ejidatarios appear to have produced only a quarter of the output per person as private farmers. Output value was much higher for private farmers, even those with under five hectares of land. Table 6.4 indicates that the value of crop output for ejidos reached only 393 pesos per acre in 1970, whereas large private farms produced 589 pesos of output value per acre, and even private farmers with less than five hectares produced significantly more. The poor natural resource base of many ejidos accounts for much of this poor performance, but so do government policies that discriminate against ejidos and basic crops. The heirs of the agrarian reform have in many ways become the orphans of the government's agricultural development strategies since the 1940s.

Table 6.4   Comparative Characteristics of Ejidal and Private Farms in Mexico, 1970

Type of farm	Irrigation as Percentage of Arable Land	Value of Crop Output per Arable Acre (pesos)	Value of Livestock Output per Animal Unit (pesos)
Private	24.4	—	721
Over 12.5 acres	—	589	—
Under 12.5 acres	—	514	—
Ejidal	15.1	393	284

Source: Yates 1981: 71, 134, 135.

This history of the agrarian reform in Mexico helps place the experience of Don Agustín and his family in a larger context of state-supported stimulation of export production; skewing of government investment and services toward zones of high agricultural potential; urban bias of pricing policies for domestically consumed commodities; and generalized lack of official investment in irrigation, Green Revolution technology, health, education, extension, and other services for peasant-based agriculture. Many of Mexico's peasants acquired access to the land, but in the absence of appropriate policies and support for the ejido and small-holder sectors, there was little potential to exploit the land effectively, in part because much of it was of inferior quality to begin with. The efforts of the 1930s to achieve greater equity through land redistribution and favorable investment and support policies were replaced in the years after 1940 by policies for agricultural modernization targeted for specific regions and specific types of farmers. The efforts of the Echeverría and López Portillo administrations were not sufficient to redress long-standing imbalances, in part because of the legacy of prior policies, but also because of the growth in the power of commercial agricultural interests that made it impossible to reallocate existing services to the ejidos and poor peasants more generally.

Mexico's Peasants and the Future of Rural Development

In response to these conditions, peasant farmers like Don Agustín have developed a series of strategies for getting by. Overall, getting by has come to mean diversifying sources of income to maximize the security of the family. Briefly, this means building a portfolio of income streams through handicraft production; labor migration; wage employment in agriculture, industry, and services; sharecropping; and, at times, retreat into subsistence production. By pooling income from diverse sources, peasant producers in Mexico have been able to persist despite the unfavorable conditions that affect them.

More than any other activity, temporary labor migration has come to be the means by which hundreds of thousands of rural Mexican households, whether they have access to land or not, manage to survive and even at times to increase their standard of living. As poverty and lack of opportunity have worsened, and as economic crises at national and international levels have affected local areas, temporary labor migration has increased. Some rural people go to Mexico City, some to other urban areas, and some to rural areas where harvesting or construction activities may exist. Increasingly, however, large numbers go to "the other side"—to the United States—where they find jobs in agriculture, industry, and services, and from which they remit earnings to their families remaining in rural areas in Mexico. In fact, income from seasonal or temporary migration forms a major portion of overall household income in hundreds of communities throughout the country.[7] In many of them, remittances sustain the population during much of each year. Massive temporary labor migration, usually involving young males but also women and older married men, points to the extent to which employment options are limited in rural communities. Its incidence also indicates that, increasingly, the location and security of employment opportunities are critical issues for Mexico's rural population, and have replaced land as a central focus of their needs.

Sometimes labor migration and other income-generating activities have enabled peasant families to escape from poverty by allowing them to invest in the education of children or to purchase productive resources such as a sewing machine, livestock, mechanical loom, truck, or tools for a particular trade. Rarely is such an escape made on the basis of access to land, however. Land is increasingly valued by peasant households, not as a directly productive asset, but as a bastion of minimal security for the family, to be turned to when all else fails. They hold onto it tenaciously, but look elsewhere for income and employment. As we have seen, land distribution in Mexico conforms to a bimodal pattern of large-scale, capital-intensive farms and a multitude of corporate and individual units that barely permit peasants to eke out subsistence. Little wonder they look beyond the land for other means of getting by, even when they have secure title to the land. Meanwhile, the rural population continues to grow in size, as does the incidence of poverty, landlessness, and malnutrition. In Mexico, then, security of tenure is not as much an issue as is the availability of land, and land may ultimately be less an issue than employment.

As will be argued shortly, a major renovation of the country's agrarian reform is unlikely. For Mexico, as well as for other countries, the creation of more viable rural communities is a matter of creating productive sources of employment, not just in agriculture, but in other sectors as well. For those concerned about the future of the country's rural areas and its peasant population, it is critical to begin to consider the opportunities that exist to fill the needs of villagers throughout the country, not just in the land, but in a wide range of other economic activities. In the following discussion, a series of questions about possible sources for rural economic growth are considered briefly.[8]

Should Mexico's peasants move to the cities to find more opportunities for work and income? Permanent migration to the cities, a solution to rural poverty that many peasants adopted in the 1940s, 1950s, and 1960s, is no longer a feasible option for those who have remained in rural areas. Mexico's industrial development, centered in its large cities, has long fallen short of the capacity to generate enough jobs for the population. In 1980, the economically active population of 23.9 million people was more than twice as large as it had been in 1960. Estimates for the year 2000 indicate that more than a million people will be joining the labor force annually. Mexico's major cities are already among the largest in the world, with some 15–18 million people residing in Mexico City alone. More than 60 percent of the country's population of almost 80 million people resides in urban areas, and its industrial sector is not creating jobs at anywhere near their rate of growth of population. Most migrants to the cities in the 1970s and 1980s have found employment only in the burgeoning informal sector. The urban population will continue to grow at more than 5 percent a year, but few new sources of employment are likely to be found.

Can significant numbers of jobs be created in the agricultural sector? Mexico has invested significant amounts of money in its agricultural sector. As we have seen, since the 1940s the vast majority of this investment has been targeted for zones of high productive potential, leaving the areas with high concentrations of ejidos and minifundia largely unattended. In the 1970s and early 1980s, however, even while the government continued to pump resources into commercial agricultural zones, it increased investment in rainfed zones through programs of integrated rural development and the national food system. Can increased investment in agriculture therefore resolve much of Mexico's rural development problem?

There are many areas in which investment in infrastructure—particularly in irrigation—and in research and extension, Green Revolution technology, and credit could enhance opportunities for agricultural production for peasants. As we have seen, peasants have traditionally had little access to improved technology, sufficient and flexible forms of credit, and good prices for the crops they produce. They should be receiving these benefits, as well as better access to physical and social infrastructure. It should be remembered, however, that the resource base for agriculture in much of Mexico's central plateau area is poor and affected by erratic rainfall, extensive erosion, and poorly endowed soils. Elsewhere, soils are often poor also, and there may be too much rain, not too little. Some improvements are possible in these regions, but agricultural growth potential in such areas is limited, even with extensive new investments. One study concluded that only 21.7 percent of all agricultural units in Mexico could benefit significantly from the introduction of better technology.[9] Improved prices for staple crops such as corn and beans would undoubtedly increase their production, but there are clear limits as to how much difference more realistic price structures can make with crops that tend to have low international prices. In any event, economists anticipate that employment opportunities in agriculture will decline, not increase, as the country develops. This does not mean that investment in peasant agriculture should cease, but it does raise the possibility that considerable amounts of money may have to be spent with relatively little payoff in terms of increased production and rural incomes. Increased investments in small-holder agriculture should certainly be made, but in many areas they should be assessed carefully in comparison with the economic returns that might be generated from alternative investment opportunities in the same region.

Can the ejido be changed to create new sources of employment? Another frequently advocated solution to Mexico's rural problems is to alter the structure of the ejido. Many critics have argued, for example, that the structure of the ejido—the group basis of landholding, the inability to sell or mortgage land, shared responsibility for the use of individual credit—is inappropriate because of the lack of incentives it provides for entrepreneurial talent and efficient production. As evidence, they cite production and investment statistics indicating the poor performance of the ejidos when compared to private farmers. Similarly, many have argued that the ejido should be opened up to markets for land, labor, and credit, allowing efficient producers to do well and inefficient ones to be bought out. A step in this direction was in fact taken in 1981 when it became legal to rent ejidal land and labor to private concerns. These critics have argued that it is the structure of the ejido that has limited Mexico's productive potential and stymied the possibilities for poor peasants to raise their income.

A counter to this criticism of the poor performance of the ejido is that its productive capacity is probably tied more to a poor agricultural resource base and lack of access to government services than it is to tenure relationships. According to some studies, ejidos that enjoy access to irrigation, technical assistance, and credit perform as well as private farms with these same endowments. One study, for example, argues that the critical factor differentiating farms in terms of value of output is not tenure type but access to irrigation.[10] When ejidatarios have access to irrigation, another study shows that they often invest as heavily in fertilizers as do private farmers.[11] These studies suggest that tenure type may not be the critical factor determining farmer investment and productivity.

Even more important in terms of undoing the structure of the ejido than the debate over its productivity, however, is the fact that the ejido is a highly important political institution with roots in the Revolution of 1910 and the agrarian reform of the 1930s. During the past fifty years, the political commitment of the peasant population to the government has been cemented largely through the distribution of ejido lands. In turn, rural political stability and loyalty have characterized the country for decades. Undoing the ejido could easily disrupt this situation, and leaders in Mexico City, however much they are swayed by arguments about efficiency, are unlikely to forget the *political* success of the agrarian reform.

Expanding the ejido through a renewed agrarian reform is another solution that has been advocated, especially as a way to bring greater equity to the countryside. This is an expensive proposition, for, as we have seen, land distribution cannot be expected to have a positive impact on household income and welfare, let alone on agricultural productivity, unless it is accompanied by extensive investments in infrastructure, credit, technological innovation, social welfare services, and other resources. Lack of access to such resources, in addition to price controls on basic products, have been important causes of poor agricultural performance among Mexico's ejidos. In the 1990s, under the continuing shadow of a grave economic crisis, it is likely that the government will have neither the administrative nor the financial resources to commit to expanding the agrarian reform, especially in the highly populated rainfed areas. And, whatever the administrative and financial resources, there is very little newly available land to expand onto, especially in areas in which high population densities exist.

The political and economic upheaval attendant upon a renewed distribution phase of the revolution should not be underestimated. Large landholdings are not traditional inefficient haciendas that can be taken over with little cost to the economy; they are instead modern commercial enterprises that generate significant amounts of foreign exchange and that have corresponding power to block redistributive initiatives. Within political circles there is not much support for "ejidoization" and it has not been viewed as an option by most recent Mexican presidents. In the 1930s, agrarian reform occurred within the context of committed political leadership, an organized and mobilized peasantry, and a weakened sector of large landowners. However, by the 1970s and 1980s, political leaders had become uninterested in agrarian reform, the peasantry had become largely co-opted and controlled by the dominant political party, and large landowners had become powerful politically and economically through the successful development of commercial agriculture. Land distribution is likely to be kept marginally alive as a palliative to local unrest and conflict, as it has been in the past, but it is unlikely to be selected as a mechanism to make major inroads into land and employment needs.

Can rural industries create sources of employment? Rural industrialization is another solution that is suggested as a way of addressing the problems of rural poverty and landlessness in Mexico. The creation of nonfarm employment opportunities does in fact offer opportunities for making rural areas more developed and self-sustaining, but investments need to be studied carefully. In areas where there is the potential for growing high-quality products, for instance, agroprocessing activities can provide at least seasonal employment opportunities. But investment in agroprocessing needs to be undertaken with caution because the industry is already large, complex, and sophisticated, and domestic and international consumer markets are relatively discriminating. Considerable capital; high quality-control standards; and expert planning, management, and marketing are probably requisite for entry into agroprocessing activities now and in the future.

Small-scale rural industries are also advocated as solutions to Mexico's rural conditions because they can produce additional sources of employment and income in local communities. Much of the development of rural enterprises would probably be located in small towns and market centers where infrastructure and marketing opportunities exist. Located here, they would encourage more balanced linkages between rural hinterlands and large urban areas. Rural households could benefit by having access to jobs that are within commuting distance. Similarly, a more vigorously pursued policy of industrial decentralization would also place more jobs within reach of Mexico's peasants who can no longer make a living from the land. Slowly, Mexico's border industry program, which has been responsible for the creation of large numbers of jobs in recent years, has been expanding into the interior of Mexico. Some potential for rural industrialization might be expected with this trend.

How can such activities be financed? For any of these strategies to work, however, sources of investment need to be identified. It should be clear by now that agricultural activities in much of the country's rainfed areas cannot be the "engine" for generating capital to invest in nonagricultural activities or in upstream or downstream industries related to agriculture. They simply do not produce a surplus for investing elsewhere. The principal rural investor of the past, the state, is unlikely to be channeling significant resources to the countryside for some time to come because of the nature of the economic crisis that became evident in the 1980s. Foreign investment may be a more likely source, but only if regional and local officials can learn to attract such investment and offer opportunities to investors. An additional source is the mobilization of the remittances that result from labor migration. With the extensiveness of labor migration out of rural communities, significant amounts of capital have in fact been flowing back. Much of this capital is spent on subsistence, of course, but efforts to mobilize the surplus from remittances, possibly through local development banks, community development corporations, or cooperatives with effective savings and loan programs, offer possibilities for generating capital for productive activities in agriculture and small-scale industrialization. Indeed, evidence is considerable that the purchase of an irrigation pump, a sewing machine, a tractor, industrial tools, a truck, livestock, or agricultural inputs can allow some rural inhabitants to expand their incomes and can create new sources of employment. Mechanisms for capturing rural savings potential need to be linked closely to mechanisms for identifying viable investment opportunities.

Local resources and opportunities, local interest and initiative, and local attitudes about potential and risk are central factors in determining the extent to which jobs can be created in rural areas to help alleviate the poverty and disillusion faced by millions of peasant households. In addition to local conditions, however, a national policy environment needs to be created that is more conducive to rural development. The traditional bias against agriculture in national policies regarding prices, trade, exchange rates, and inflation should not be replicated in the future. Sectoral policies biased against rural small-scale activities, such as those that set prices for basic staples, also need to be eschewed. Indeed, the economic crisis of the 1980s created an opportunity for introducing important changes in policies by adjusting the exchange rate, altering rural-urban terms of trade, and eliminating some subsidies for urban consumers. Decentralization of the highly centralized decisionmaking system in Mexico is another area where important changes could be made to stimulate greater rural development that is linked to employment and income generation.

What is the role for the United States? The United States has critical interests in helping Mexico resolve its rural development problems. There is approximately $5 billion in U.S. private investment in Mexico, and trade with that country amounts to about $25 billion a year. Over 65 percent of the value of Mexico's merchandise imports originates in the United States; the United States is the destination of approximately 64 percent of Mexico's merchandise exports. Mexico provides about 60 percent of the imports of winter fruits and vegetables to the United States and, among developing countries, Mexico provides the largest market for U.S. goods. Energy and technology transfers also figure prominently in the economic relationships between the two countries. Immigration and finance are other areas of mutual concern between them that have an effect on economic and political conditions on both sides of the border.[12]

Trade relations between the two countries can be improved to assist Mexico's ability to create sources of employment for its rural population. There is little in the way of a stable framework between the countries for discussing trade issues. Instead, case-by-case decisions about issues such as countervailing duties, unfair trade practices, and "dumping" have characterized the relationship. In particular, Mexico's exports of agricultural products have been subject to seemingly arbitrary regulations and judgments about quality, packaging, and dumping. The problems of resolving these issues and developing a more general commercial agreement between the countries are formidable, but the availability of markets in the United States is critical to Mexico's ability to deal with its development problems, among which those of rural areas loom large. Investment opportunities in Mexico, a larger market for U.S. goods, and a possible long-term solution to illegal immigration are benefits that can be derived from better trade relations between the countries.

Regarding illegal immigration from Mexico, this chapter has suggested that much of its cause lies in the poverty, inequity, and lack of employment opportunities in Mexico's rural areas. Restrictive U.S. immigration policies tend to exacerbate problems in both Mexico and the United States by presenting Mexico with an added burden of creating more employment just at the time it is suffering the worst economic crisis of the century and by imposing high regulation costs on the United States by driving the flow of immigration underground.

There is considerable evidence that the labor markets on both sides of the border, not legal strictures, strongly determine the flow of immigration. The economic crisis in Mexico has increased wage differentials and the incentive to migrate. The solution to high levels of illegal immigration lies not in the United States, but in the ability of Mexico to create employment opportunities for the rural poor who are most likely to migrate. Thus, the United States should search for ways to encourage and support the long-term development of Mexico's rural regions.

Concern about Mexico's capacity to develop should be particularly acute at the outset of the 1990s. Many of the short-term adjustment measures that the country has taken since 1982 have come at the cost of its ability to stimulate growth and investment over the longer term. Moreover, much of its longer-term capacity to grow is dependent on international factors over which it has little control—interest rates, international commodity prices, and opportunities for trade. And, indeed, more favorable conditions in terms of these factors depend to a considerable degree on U.S. domestic policies with regard to its public deficit, interest rates, inflation and recession, and trade policy. There is a role for the United States in assisting Mexico in building its capacity to respond to its rural problems, and this role consists not only of improved bilateral relationships between the two countries in terms of trade and immigration, but also in terms of efforts to build a more dynamic international economy that will assist a range of developing countries to deal with issues of debt, dependency, and development more effectively.

Conclusions

In countries such as Japan, Korea, and Taiwan, widespread agrarian reforms laid the basis for more dynamic and equitable economic development for the countries as a whole. The disturbing lesson of Mexico, where a massive agrarian reform also occurred, is that agrarian reform may not be an effective solution to poverty, underproductivity, or other ills of the countryside. In the absence of a supportive policy environment, in the absence of significant investment in the reformed sector, and in the absence of a legitimate capacity of rural people to make sustained political and economic demands on the government, poverty, underproductivity, and disillusionment are likely to result even from major land distribution programs.

Moreover, the Mexican case raises disturbing questions about opportunities for agriculture-led rural development in areas of rainfed agriculture where the resource base for agriculture is poor. It may well be that in many countries, like Mexico, much of the land has been overused as an economic and political resource. In the future, sources of employment beyond the land need to be created for rural people in Mexico. One way that policies can be changed in a more beneficial direction is for rural people to organize independently of government and begin to demand more insistently and persistently that the government pursue policies aimed at making poor rural communities into viable economic units. If this can occur, families such as that of Don Agustín and Ramona can prosper in the future.

Notes

1. An ejido is a communal form of landownership that is granted by the state to an organized group of claimants.

2. In 1958, The Department of Agrarian Affairs and Colonization was created. In 1974, this agency became the Ministry of Agrarian Reform.

3. A third category is very similar to the ejido tenure system. Corporate communities that owned land in common prior to liberal reforms of the 1850s were able to reclaim communal properties. "Comunidades," usually indigenous groups, are generally grouped with ejidos in agricultural statistics; many, in fact, are legally constituted as ejidos. Comunidades form a small portion of reform beneficiaries.

4. The figures reported in this chapter are based on official sources and have been taken from P. Lamartine Yates, *Mexico's Agricultural Dilemma* (Tucson: University of Arizona Press, 1981); Merilee S. Grindle, *State and Countryside: Development Policy and Agrarian Politics in Latin America* (Baltimore, Md.: The Johns Hopkins University Press, 1986); Merilee S. Grindle, *Searching for Rural Development: Labor Migration and Employment in Mexico* (Ithaca, N.Y.: Cornell University Press, 1988); Susan Walsh Sanderson, *Land Reform in Mexico: 1910–1980* (Orlando, Fla.: Academic Press, 1988); Steven E. Sanderson, *Agrarian Populism and the Mexican State* (Berkeley: University of California Press, 1981); and CEPAL (Comisión Económica para America Latina), *Economía campesina y agricultura empresarial* (Mexico: Siglo Veintiuno, 1983).

5. A particularly evocative book about this dispossessed peasantry and the goals for which it fought is John Womack, Jr., *Zapata and the Mexican Revolution* (New York: Vintage Books, 1968). Susan Sanderson, in *Land Reform in Mexico: 1910–1980*, estimates that on the eve of the revolution, about 50 percent of the rural population was composed of debt peons.

6. Approximately 23 percent of the land distributed under Cárdenas was arable; in later periods, only about 15 percent of the land distributed was arable (Yates, *Mexico's Agricultural Dilemma*, p. 153).

7. This statement is well documented in Grindle, *Searching for Rural Development*.

8. Most of the following has been adapted from Grindle, *Searching for Rural Development*.

9. CEPAL, *Economía campesina y agricultura empresarial*.

10. Kenneth Roberts, "The Impact of U.S. Technology on the Mexican Bajio: Seeds, Sorghum, and Socioeconomic Change," paper presented at Regional Aspects of U.S.-Mexican Integration, University of California, San Diego, Center for U.S.-Mexican Studies, May 21–22, 1984.

11. Yates, *Mexico's Agricultural Dilemma*.

12. For additional discussion of these and other issues, see Guy F. Erb and Cathryn Thorup, *U.S. Mexican Relations: The Issues Ahead* (Washington, D.C.: Overseas Development Council, 1984).

Selected Bibliography

Austin, James E., and Gustavo Esteva, eds., *Food Policy in Mexico: The Search for Self-Sufficiency*. Ithaca, N.Y.: Cornell University Press, 1987.

CEPAL (Comisión Económica para América Latina), *Economía campesina y agricultura empresarial*. Mexico: Siglo Veintiuno, 1983.

Erb, Guy F., and Cathryn Thorup, *U.S. Mexican Relations: The Issues Ahead*. Washington, D.C.: Overseas Development Council, 1984.

Grindle, Merilee S., *State and Countryside: Development Policy and Agrarian Politics in Latin America*. Baltimore, Md: The Johns Hopkins University Press, 1986.

————, *Searching for Rural Development: Labor Migration and Employment in Mexico*. Ithaca, N.Y.: Cornell University Press, 1988.

Johnston, Bruce F., Cassio Luiselli, Celso Cartas Contreras, and Roger D. Norton, eds., *U.S.-Mexico Relations: Agriculture and Rural Development*. Stanford, Ca.: Stanford University Press, 1987.

Sanderson, Steven E., *Agrarian Populism and the Mexican State*. Berkeley: University of California Press, 1981.

Sanderson, Susan Walsh, *Land Reform in Mexico: 1910-1980*. Orlando, Fla.: Academic Press, 1988.

Womack, John, Jr., *Zapata and the Mexican Revolution*. N.Y.: Vintage Books, 1968.

Yates, P. Lamartine, *Mexico's Agricultural Dilemma*. Tucson: University of Arizona Press, 1981.

chapter seven

Land Tenure and Land Reform in Brazil

Anthony L. Hall

Summary

This chapter analyzes the background, nature, and impacts of Brazil's land-reform program. It starts with an examination of the country's agrarian structure, which is characterized by growing indices of property concentration, landlessness, and rural violence arising from conflicts over access to land, as well as worsening environmental destruction. The roots of these phenomena are traced to historical factors as well as to more recent national agricultural policies and frontier settlement strategies in Amazonia. The agrarian reform of the post-1985 civilian government is then assessed, focusing on the gradual weakening of land-reform legislation under strong political pressure from landed interests, especially during the Constituent Assembly, and on the subsequently poor implementation record of the program during the Sarney presidency. This is followed by an analysis of those reform projects that have been established and their economic performance to date. From this experience, a number of policy implications are drawn out, at both micro and macrolevels. In conclusion, the potential role of foreign assistance in supporting Brazil's agrarian reform is discussed, with recommendations relating particularly to institution-building and community mobilization.

Land Tenure, Rural Poverty, and Agrarian Policy in Brazil

Land Concentration and Landlessness

Brazil has one of the most concentrated structures of landownership in the world. Its roots lie in the Portuguese Crown's policy of making large land grants (*sesmarias*) to colonizers as a reward for military and political services rendered or to prospective export crop producers. These practices gave rise to the original sugar plantations, coffee estates, and cattle ranches of the northeast and south-central parts of the country. In contrast to the strong homesteading tradition of the small pioneer farmer in the United States, land in Brazil was, by and large, not given to the majority of settlers who were, instead, expected to provide the estate and plantation labor. This monopoly was reinforced in 1850 by the Land Law (*Lei de Terras*), which attempted to reserve public land for the estate system by prohibiting squatting. Significant changes came during the late nineteenth century when the geographical mobility of the Brazilian peasantry increased as a result of several factors: the catastrophic drought of 1877–1879 drove thousands of northeasterners to work as laborers in the rubber boom of Amazonia; the abolition of slavery in 1888 freed rural workers, at least nominally, facilitating the generation of an independent, self-provisioning peasantry in the north and northeast; and, crucially, during the early part of this century, the arrival of hundreds of thousands of poor immigrant farmers, from Europe and Japan, opened up the agricultural frontier of southern Brazil.

These historical factors, coupled with recent government agricultural policies (discussed below) have produced an agrarian structure characterized by extreme polarization in landownership, a high degree of landlessness, intensive rural violence arising from conflict over access to land, and growing environmental degradation, particularly in Amazonia. Official data gathered in 1985 by the National Institute for Colonization and Agrarian Reform (INCRA) shows that overall in Brazil the 2 percent of rural properties with more than 1,000 hectares occupy 57 percent of the agricultural land (see Table 7.1). At the other end of the scale, the 30 percent of farms smaller than ten hectares account for only 1 percent of farmland. INCRA classes almost 70 percent of all farmland in the country as latifúndia,[1] most of which are not put to productive use but held principally as a real estate investment and as a speculative hedge against inflation. Although *minifúndia*[2] occupy only 8 percent of Brazilian farmland, they provide 45 percent of farm employment.

Table 7.1   Distribution of Landownership in Brazil, 1985

Farm Size (ha)	Percentage of Total Number of Farms	Percentage of Total Area of Farmland Occupied
less than 10	30	1.0
10–100	53	13.0
100–1000	15	29.0
more than 1000	2	57.0

Source: INCRA, *Estatísticas Cadastrais Anuais*, Brasília, 1986.

Land concentration in the northeast is slightly higher than the national average. Seventy-five percent of northeast farmland is classified as latifúndia. Holdings tend to be more polarized in the semi-arid interior, or *sertão*, which is devoted largely to extensive cattle-raising, and in the coastal zone, where sugar plantations predominate. In the south and southeast of Brazil, land concentration was originally less intensive due to extensive colonization by largely European small-holder populations during the late nineteenth and early twentieth centuries, although polarization has become worse in the last two decades with the spread of large-scale commercial farming.

Table 7.2   Farming Population in Brazil with Insufficient or No Land, 1978 and 1984

Type	Numbers (thousands)	
	1978	1984
Minifundistas		
Owners	1,469	1,872
Squatters	505	644
Sharecroppers	273	433
Tenants	122	180
Permanent wage-workers	1,104	2,147
Temporary wage-workers	2,560	4,260
Other non-waged workers	713	1,104
Totals	6,746	10,640

Source: Proposta para a elaboração do 1ᵃ Plano Nacional de Reforma Agrária da Nova República-PNRA, Brasília, 1985.

Brazil's highly concentrated landownership pattern is paralleled by high indices of landlessness (see Table 7.2). According to official INCRA data, almost 11 million cultivators are classified as having either insufficient land to support their families or no land at all. Although there are some 2.5 million economically active cultivators with land of their own (1.87 million owners with title and some 650,000 squatters with no legal title), there are also more than 6 million landless wage-laborers, whose numbers almost doubled between 1978 and 1984. Sharecroppers and tenant farmers, with little security of tenure, also saw their numbers rise by a marked proportion, to reach a level of more than 600,000 by 1984. Numbers of small-holders (including legal owners and squatters) rose more slowly over the same period, however, from 2 million to 2.5 million. The disproportionately large increase in less stable forms of tenancy suggests, therefore, that insecurity of tenure within Brazilian agriculture is growing. Dispossessed producers are turning increasingly to wage-labor, squatting, and other temporary arrangements in order to earn a livelihood.

Successive Brazilian governments, especially since 1964, have pursued aggressive policies of encouraging immigration to the new frontier zones of Amazonia, in order to fulfill a variety of objectives. Amongst others, these included exploiting the region's natural resources for generating export revenue (minerals, timber, and other forest products) as well as the wider geopolitical aim of integrating the Amazon Basin firmly under national control. However, a parallel goal has clearly been to syphon off "excess" rural populations from the northeast and south of the country. Thus, Amazonia has been used as a "safety-valve," making land available for small farmers who could no longer be accommodated in their regions of origin. At the same time, it was hoped that these policies of colonization and resettlement would obviate the need to undertake structural reforms, at least in the short run. In the northeast, a combination of cyclical drought, agrarian stagnation, and land concentration has made the situation of the peasantry increasingly desperate. In south-central Brazil, the expansion of mechanization for soybean and wheat farming has led to growing land polarization and, for that minority who did not choose the urban route, the quest of dispossessed small cultivators for new lands and a new life elsewhere.

Some direct encouragement was given by the government to would-be migrants through the setting up of official colonization projects in the early 1970s along the Transamazon highway but these were a relative failure. For a variety of reasons, but mainly because of poor soils, bad INCRA organization, and a severe lack of official support for settlers, only 8,000 of a projected 100,000 families were relocated in this way. Other INCRA colonization ventures were more successful (in terms of total numbers attracted) in the western states of Rondônia and Acre in the late 1970s. Rondônia had, by 1985, absorbed some 60,000 migrant families in officially backed schemes of various kinds; this process was assisted by the World Bank–funded Northwest Integrated Development Program (POLONOROESTE). Similar policies were implemented in Acre, but only about 1,400 families had been resettled by 1980 on two directed colonization projects. As on the Transamazon, official colonization in western Amazonia has been beset by bad project design and serious problems of poor farmer support in terms of credit, extension, and marketing as well as conflicts with encroaching cattle ranches. This has led to high rates of settler turnover and a process of reconcentration of landownership on the frontier. Private colonization schemes, funded by corporations that purchased land from the government at heavily subsidized prices for resale to wealthier small farmers from the south rather than impoverished northeasterners, gained momentum. From 1969 to 1984 INCRA approved over seventy such schemes in Amazonia, although they have met with mixed economic success and have absorbed far fewer people altogether.

However, induced resettlement never accounted for more than a small proportion of migration to the north, west-central, and northwest of Brazil. The vast majority of hopeful settlers went of their own accord and with no government help, although access to the region was facilitated by the rapid expansion of the highway network across Amazonia. The major thrust of government policy throughout the 1970s and 1980s, despite brief but well-publicized episodes of "social colonization" such as the Transamazon, has been to support large landed and corporate agribusiness interests such as lumbering and cattle ranching. These priorities were clearly spelled out in the National Development Plans (PND I, 1970–1974 and PND II, 1975–1979) as well as through regional development programs such as POLAMAZONIA.

Generous financial support has been provided through the whole structure of subsidies and fiscal incentives channeled through the regional development agency, SUDAM, set up in 1966. Investment tax credits have allowed registered Brazilian corporations to offset up to 50 percent of their income tax liabilities against SUDAM-approved projects in Amazonia and receive fifteen-year exemptions from payment of federal taxes. According to the latest World Bank study, subsidized livestock schemes in the region now occupy some 8.4 million hectares and have benefited from incentives amounting to US$700 million. In addition, these enterprises were favored by subsidized rural credit from the early 1970s until 1987. Such policies have also received strong private backing from the road-building and construction company lobby, as well as through the specially created Association of Amazonian Businessman (AEA). More recent schemes, such as the Greater Carajás Program (PGC) set up in 1980 with the aid of $1.7 billion in foreign bilateral (from Japan and the EEC) and multilateral (World Bank) loans, reinforce the bias. Development activities in the PGC rural sector are heavily oriented toward large estates and toward lumbering, agro-livestock, and related agribusiness activities allied to industrial developments arising from the extraction and processing of iron ore and other minerals in a large part of eastern Amazonia.

This development pattern has had profound consequences for land tenure in Amazonia and for the rural population, which had placed its hopes in being able to establish a stable livelihood on the new frontier zones. Instead of allowing land-hungry peasants expelled from longer-settled agricultural regions to consolidate their positions as small-holders, the same polarized landownership structure witnessed elsewhere has been re-created on the Amazon frontier. INCRA data for 1985 show that in the north (Amazonia) nearly two-thirds of farmers have less than 100 hectares but occupy only 13 percent of the land, whereas the 6 percent of landowners with more than 1,000 hectares have 80 percent of the farmland. Figures for the west-central states show an even greater degree of polarization. Amazonia has at least eight estates with more than a million hectares and one, the Manasa Madeira Internacional SA, with 4.3 million hectares (about the same size as the Irish Republic). The largest 152 Amazonian estates occupy 40 million hectares, or the equivalent of about half of the total area of cultivated land in Brazil. In Rondônia and Acre, despite relatively intensive small farmer colonization strategies, most farmland has been taken over by large landed interests; by 1985, 60 percent of farmland in Rondônia and 90 percent in Acre were concentrated in estates of more than 1,000 hectares.

Both INCRA and agricultural census statistics clearly indicate an exacerbation of this phenomenon of land concentration over time. A greater percentage of Brazilian farmland is being concentrated into larger units, while peasant farms are becoming more fragmented and peasant farmers squeezed out, a trend particularly evident since latifúndio-biased agricultural modernization and resettlement policies were adopted starting in the 1960s. For example, during the decade 1974–1984, while holdings of less than ten hectares saw their share of farmland fall from 1.2 to 1.0 percent, the area occupied by estates with more than 1,000 hectares rose from 48 to 57 percent. The average size of small farms with less than ten hectares fell from 4.0 to 3.4 hectares from 1960–1980, while the average size of large estates of more than 10,000 hectares expanded from 24,000 to greater than 26,000 hectares. In particular regions, where mechanized production and/or land speculation have been proceeding rapidly, the pace of land concentration is even more pronounced than these figures suggest.

Some observers have commented on agricultural census figures for 1980 and 1985, which appear to show an anomaly of a reduction in land concentration in some regions of the country and an increase in the number of people occupying the land. However, this is probably due to temporary causal factors, which do not affect the major direction of change, including the 1980 northeastern drought, the general economic recession and lack of urban employment opportunities, and the reduction in subsidies to larger, commercial producers. Rather than signifying a growth in job opportunities in the countryside, the latest data are more suggestive of an expansion in rural underemployment. It was suggested above, for example, that there has been a particularly marked growth of insecure forms of tenure such as sharecropping. Although such groups are remarkably resilient in the face of these pressures and will remain a critical productive force in the Brazilian economy for the foreseeable future, adapting to changing circumstances and even actively resisting expulsions from the land, they have come under sustained attack in recent years. The issue of land reform is, therefore, even more critical within this evolving context.

There are other disturbing aspects of the trend toward land concentration in Brazil; these are manifested in the form of (1) growing landlessness; (2) escalating rural violence in the countryside due to the struggle over access to land amongst competing groups (small farmers, indigenous groups, and large-scale individual or corporate landowners); and (3) increasingly serious environmental destruction in Amazonia and elsewhere. Due in large measure to a hostile policy environment, small-holder farming in Brazil is becoming increasingly difficult to sustain. The monopolization of subsidized formal credit, extension, and other services by larger landowners has further exacerbated the position of small farmers denied access to more land. According to official INCRA figures (see Table 7.2), there has been a two-thirds increase in Brazil's squatter, sharecropper, tenant, and wage-laboring groups of cultivators within the space of only six years—from 5.2 million in 1978 to 8.7 million in 1984.

Historically, the customary route for those abandoning the land they had cultivated would have been to the towns and cities, contributing to Brazil's high level of urbanization, which is now officially put at more than 70 percent, one of the highest in the developing world. However, many larger urban centers in the south and northeast are reaching their saturation points, and neither the formal labor market nor the "informal" sector can absorb this potential influx. There is evidence of significant reverse migration—the return of aspiring migrants to their areas of origin in the face of long-term urban unemployment—especially during recent years of economic crisis. Thus, those who choose or are obliged to abandon farming the land directly, either as owners, sharecroppers, or tenant farmers, are increasingly drawn into wage-labor as the only alternative; on the sugar plantations of the northeast and São Paulo state, and the coffee estates and orange groves of southern Brazil. Circumstances permitting, off-farm activities such as gold-prospecting in Amazonia or work on large construction projects, may provide a complementary source of income due to the seasonality of farm laboring.

Rural Violence and Peasant Resistance

Closely related to this twin process of land concentration and growing landlessness in Brazil is the phenomenon of escalating rural violence. Since 1980 there have been more than a thousand killings of small farmers in Brazil. In 1986 alone, according to figures published by the Ministry of Agrarian Reform and Development (MIRAD), there were almost 300 officially registered deaths in land conflicts over the whole country, two-thirds of these occurring in Amazonia. Furthermore, there has been a dramatic increase in the number of nonfatal incidents involving the intimidation of small farmers by large landowners and their hired gunmen, including beatings, rapes, kidnappings, torture, and threats. In recent years, hardly a day has gone by without evidence coming to light either of numerous sporadic killings of peasants or of more systematically organized campaigns of persecution. The situation became so critical that in 1988 Amnesty International saw fit to publish a special report that roundly condemned what it called "authorized violence" in the countryside and expressed its concern over "evidence of inadequate State response to or even State acquiescence in these crimes."

The use of violence is nothing new and has historically, of course, been an integral part of Brazilian rural life, both for maintaining discipline amongst slave and quasi-slave laborers as well as advancing the agricultural frontier, usurping the lands of indigenous populations in the process. Since the 1960s, however, land-grabbing (*grilagem*) has become more widespread due to the incentives and subsidies provided by government to larger landed interests, whether in Amazonia, the northeast, or the south. Overwhelmingly, therefore, growing rural violence reflects the economic and political impetus given to land concentration in the face of weak or nonexistent opposition from existing pioneer populations of small farmers, which have traditionally had little option but to move out or suffer the consequences. Much of west, central, and north Brazil has been opened up in this way, with cattle ranchers and land speculators arriving in the wake of small settlers who have cleared the land for subsistence agriculture. Sometimes agreements are reached, the right to grow crops being granted by large landowners in exchange for limited usufruct rights, but on other occasions more forceful methods are employed.

However, if small farmers have in the past tended to be passive victims of such tactics, since the mid-1980s there has been a significant strengthening of peasant resistance to land-grabbing. This is reflected in several ways. First, those threatened with summary eviction have engaged in armed struggle against landowners and hired gunmen; as a reflection of this greater militancy, these two latter groups accounted for about 13 percent of the 300 or so deaths in land conflicts in 1986. Second, a further expression of the peasantry taking the initiative is exemplified by the growing number of estate occupations (*invasões*) by landless farmers in diverse regions of Brazil. In the south, the

Movement of Landless Rural Workers (MST) has become a well-articulated initiative which, by 1988, had organized more than eighty occupations involving some 13,000 peasant families. This represents an attempt by landless farmers to resist permanent "proletarianization" as agriculture in the region has become mechanized for large-scale soybean and wheat production and landownership itself increasingly concentrated. In eastern Amazonia, the single most violent rural area in Brazil, the occupation by some 20,000 farmers and their families of over 40 Brazil-nut estates has constituted a de facto land redistribution, which was subsequently ratified under the National Agrarian Reform Plan of the New Republic (PNRA-NR) of 1985. Similarly, in the western state of Acre, organized physical resistance, known as *empates*, by rubber tappers to encroachment by cattle-ranching and lumbering companies has led to the formation of protected "extractive reserves," the first (of more than 40,000 hectares) near Xapuri in February 1988. Since 1975, over 45 empates have resulted in the saving of more than 1.2 million hectares of rainforest. The National Rubber Tappers' Council (CNS) was set up in 1985 to sustain this movement. The sensitivity and inherent conflict of interests was highlighted in December 1988 by the murder of the rubber-tappers' leader, Francisco ("Chico") Mendes.

Environmental Degradation
Another major associated feature of this rural development pattern has been accelerating environmental destruction, principally in Amazonia. By the end of 1988 some 12 percent of the region had been deforested, with certain regions, notably in eastern Amazonia and Rondônia, witnessing much higher, exponential rates. During the latter half of the 1980s, an average of about 20,000 square kilometers (roughly 12,000 square miles, an area the size of Belgium) of rainforest was cut down every year, a rate that is likely to be maintained or increased unless corrective measures are implemented. Although the total area deforested is still relatively small compared with the much higher losses recorded for West Africa and southern Asia (72 percent and 63 percent of original forest cover, respectively), there is no justification for complacency. This is an increasingly grave problem with potentially disastrous social, economic, and climatic consequences. Although Brazilian policymakers have, in order to discredit peasant farming, frequently tried to apportion the entire blame for Amazonian deforestation to small, squatter farmers practicing slash-and-burn agriculture, they are responsible for only about 20 percent of the total. Independent observers agree that cattle ranching and pasture formation (both subsidized and nonsubsidized) are responsible for most deforestation—up to two-thirds according to the latest studies—with

other activities such as logging accounting for the remainder.

Pressure on the Amazonian environment is inextricably bound up with several wider issues: (1) polarization in the structure of landownership and occupation, both in migrants' areas of origin as well as in Amazonia itself; (2) growing landlessness as a result of this pattern; (3) the kinds of pro-latifúndia agrarian policies pursued by successive governments; and (4) the macroeconomic situation in Brazil. Land concentration and growing landlessness in the northeast and south of the country, coupled with the failure to undertake structural reforms in these areas, has led to high rates of out-migration to the new frontiers in Amazonia and resulting pressure on the rainforest. Coupled with this, the reconcentration of land in Amazonia and reproduction of the latifúndio-minifúndio complex has obliged small farmers to continuously seek new frontier zones, as they have been unable (with notable exceptions such as estate occupations) to establish themselves permanently in given areas.

Agricultural Policy
While small-scale, subsistence farming has exerted pressure on the rainforest, a far more important factor has been the role of government policy in subsidizing large cattle and lumbering enterprises with generous fiscal incentives channeled through SUDAM, the regional development agency. By the mid-1980s SUDAM had approved some 630 cattle enterprises, which benefited from tax breaks amounting to US$700 million. However, an official study published in 1985 showed that only 16 percent of these enterprises had achieved their production and sales targets, and that a large number were simply nonexistent, the funds having been diverted to other uses; only 92 of the 630 were awarded completion certificates by SUDAM. Most of these ranching enterprises in Amazonia existed only due to heavy official subsidy, a practice sustained by political patronage. Land was acquired for its speculative value as a hedge against rising inflation and not primarily as a productive asset, with real increases in value being recorded of up to 100 percent per annum. These activities have thus led to little economically productive output but, on the contrary, to widespread deforestation coupled with social conflict arising from clashes involving ranchers, small farmers, and Amerindian groups. Environmental destruction has been aggravated by Brazilian national and state laws that require a proportion of the land claimed to be cleared of forest cover as legal proof of occupation and subsequent ownership. Paradoxically, as discussed below, the 1985 agrarian reform law has further encouraged this process.

In other areas of the country also, agricultural policy has favored larger production units at the expense of small farmers, exacerbating the national trend toward land concentration. In the northeast, for example, fiscal incentives to the rural sector through the regional development agency, SUDENE, have been directed largely to the livestock industry and, more recently, to large-scale irrigated production of food crops for export. In the south, subsidized official rural credit has favored mechanized soybean and wheat production in large farms for export, with a disproportionately small amount going to staple-food crop producers, i.e., peasant farmers. Nationally, the alcohol program, PROALCOOL, has, since the oil crisis of the 1970s, given huge subsidies as incentives for the production of sugarcane and the distilling of ethanol as a gasoline substitute, with a large measure of success. These policies have had a dual and adverse impact on rural welfare and food security. First, they have diminished access to land for small farmers (initially in the longer-settled areas and later in Amazonia itself), thus increasing pressure on the rainforest. Second, they have probably had an adverse impact on rural incomes on the one hand and, on the other, contributed toward a national and regional decline in the production of staple food crops and, hence, nutritional status. Due to these structural changes, one researcher concluded on the basis of INCRA survey data that, from 1970 to 1980, the poorest 50 percent of the rural population saw its share of total income in the countryside fall from 22 percent to 15 percent, while the wealthiest 5 percent enjoyed an increase from 24 percent to 45 percent.

Although sheer poverty rather than food shortages is generally regarded as the main cause of hunger and malnutrition, in Brazil's case it does seem that prioritization of export crops together with a declining production of basic staple crops are major factors that help explain the worsening food security of large sections of the urban and rural population. Favorable world prices, subsidized credit, technological innovation, and exchange rates pegged to inflation have encouraged the growth of export crops. From 1960 to 1980 the area planted to soybean jumped from 0.2 million to 9 million hectares. The area planted to sugarcane more than doubled under PROALCOOL from 1.5 million hectares in 1972 to 3.8 million hectares in 1985. Over the same period, output of beans and cassava, the two most important staples in Brazil, fell by 8 percent and 14 percent, respectively. By 1983, per capita food production in the country had fallen to three-quarters of the 1977 level, reflecting a switch from food crops to nonfood crops. In Amazonia, there has been a disproportionately rapid increase in the area planted to long-cycle or permanent crops for export, and a much slower growth in short-cycle or temporary crops such as rice, corn, cassava, and vegetables. Many larger urban centers in the region fly these staples in from São Paulo, more than 2,000 miles away. Brazil has had to import an increasing proportion of its domestic food requirements.

Largely as a result of falling production levels, food prices in Brazil have risen on average in recent years by more than twice the overall rate of inflation. A major recent social survey commented that food production should be increased by 40 percent of its 1983 level to keep prices down and "have a powerful impact on labour productivity and income distribution . . . in view of the deteriorating nutritional levels among Brazil's low-income population." Various studies have testified to the worsening nutritional situation in areas of Brazil as a result of a combination of land concentration and landlessness, agricultural modernization, and food shortages. In the northeast, for example, almost 80 percent of the population suffers from calorie deficiency, contributing to high rates of infant morbidity and mortality. Even in the more "developed" south, malnutrition amongst the rural population has increased significantly as areas previously planted to staple foods have been converted to production for export. Problems of illness and malnutrition are especially pronounced among the growing population of landless rural workers (*boias frias* or *volantes*) and their families. It is no coincidence that it is precisely in these southern states where land invasions have been most widespread, as rural workers attempt to retain access to land as a source of livelihood.

Land Reform in Brazil

The Period of Military Government, 1964–1985

The issue of land reform in Brazil merited official mention for the first time in 1946, when the National Constituent Assembly declared the need to "promote the just distribution of property, with equal opportunity for all." However, it was only with the passing of the 1964 Land Statute (*Estatuto da Terra*, Law 4,504 of November 30) by the new military government headed by General Castello Branco, that a systematic plan was adopted. Potentially quite far-reaching in the Brazilian context, the 1964 Land Statute provided for the expropriation in the "social interest," with compensation, of latifúndia—over 600 times the regional farm "module" size[3]—as well as landholdings put to speculative use, where environmentally damaging practices were adopted and of areas destined for resettlement projects. *Minifúndia* were also liable for consolidation. Those categories exempted from the statute were, however, significant: they included (1) all farms classed as "rural enterprises," regardless of size, generously defined as those that "exploit the land economically and rationally . . . [including] pastures, natural and artificial forests and areas occupied by improvements"; (2) "family farms"[4] with less than three times the regional land module; and (3) farms outside of the areas decreed priority zones for agrarian reform. The law's expressed aim was the "gradual extinction of the minifúndia and the latifúndia." However, in practice, little redistribution took place under the 1964 Land Statute, which was usually applied in cases of colonization schemes and irrigation projects, as well as public works projects such as dam construction. Also targeted were areas of land conflict where property ownership had to be "regulated"; this almost inevitably meant that existing heavily polarized landownership stuctures were legalized, and contending small-holders or *posseiros* were resettled elsewhere.

The first and second National Agrarian Reform Plans (PNRA) of 1966 and 1968, respectively, achieved little, resorting to taxation as the principal means of discouraging "antisocial" land use. Not only was this insignificant in terms of revenue generation, but the structure of land tenure in Brazil, unsurprisingly, remained unaltered. Throughout the 1960s and 1970s, solutions to the growing problems of polarization, landlessness, and rural conflict in Brazil were thus seen primarily in terms of nonconfrontational policies, particularly through both directed and "spontaneous" forms of resettlement, private and public, on the Amazon frontier. This was epitomized by the creation, in 1971, of the *Instituto Nacional de Colonização e Reforma Agrária* (INCRA), which replaced the *Instituto Brasileiro de Reforma Agrária* (IBRA). The emphasis was now placed on colonization rather than on agrarian reform as such. Furthermore, it was mistakenly assumed that the regulation of land titles would defuse land conflict by stabilizing tenure.

The most notable example of this approach was the Executive Group for the Araguaia-Tocantins (GETAT), set up in 1980 to try and defuse serious land conflict in the Marabá region of eastern Amazonia. By the time GETAT was abolished in 1987, it had demarcated 7 million hectares and legalized more than 60,000 property titles. However, such intervention served largely to consolidate the existing highly unequal structure of land tenure in the region; for example, a mere 8 percent of properties occupied 51 percent of the titled land, whereas 70 percent of the plots involved (less than 100 hectares in size) accounted for only 21 percent of the legalized lands. Unless strong peasant resistance was encountered, the official policy was one of resettling small farmers to alternative areas. Furthermore, intervention was confined to land distribution, with no additional support for farming activities being provided. Tensions in the area continued at a high level throughout this period.

Agrarian Reform Legislation Under the New Republic

In an apparent attempt to stem the tide of rural conflicts generated by the ongoing struggle over access to land, the Democratic Alliance government of President José Sarney introduced the proposal for a National Agrarian Reform Plan of the New Republic in May 1985, only two months after the change of regime. The newly created Ministry for Agrarian Reform and Rural Development was headed by an outspoken Minister, Nelson Ribeiro. He was appointed with the backing of the Brazilian Catholic church and designed the reform proposals with the assistance of a strongly committed group of advisors. Based on the 1964 Land Statute, the main objective of the PNRA-NR is the redistribution of underutilized public and private lands to Brazil's estimated 10.6 million poor cultivators with insufficient or no land (see Table 7.2). It was hoped that nationally, from 1985 to 2000, a total of 7.1 million cultivators would be resettled, with 1.4 million being accommodated on 43 million hectares in the short term, from 1985 to 1989. Supporting measures would include a special credit program, agricultural research and extension inputs, and the organization of cooperatives. Regional plans drawn up at the state level would highlight priority areas for reform, where land concentration was severe and where land conflicts and rural violence were particularly acute. The average cost per family was estimated at about US$6,000, which the government considered reasonable when compared with other rural and industrial job-creation schemes.

These original proposals were quite radical when set against the cautious and piecemeal land policies applied in Brazil since 1964. By following the 1964 Land Statute in choosing as its main policy instrument the notion of land expropriation "in the social interest," the new PNRA harked back to the radical debates of the period immediately before the coup, and stressed the need for a "global strategy for changing the agrarian structure." The military government's poor record on land issues was condemned, and the need was highlighted for compulsory expropriations with compensation, rather than relying on amicable land purchases at market prices. Not surprisingly, reaction from the landed oligarchy to the May 1985 draft plan was intense. The recently formed landowners' pressure group, the *União Democrática Ruralista* (UDR), mounted a strong and well-organized lobby in defense of their interests. In little more than two years, from 1985 to 1987, the UDR had set up more than 150 branches throughout Brazil and recruited some 230,000 members. Private militias were strengthened, often with the unofficial assistance of off-duty policemen. An extensive campaign of rural violence and intimidation against farmer groups was complemented by an effecive publicity campaign through demonstrations and via the media. In July 1987, for example, the UDR organized a demonstration in Brasília of 30,000 landowners, costing an estimated US$600,000. This was designed to put pressure on the Constituent Assembly, which was then in the process of drafting a new Brazilian constitution, to soften future provisions for land reform.

The UDR, however, came into increasing conflict with a peasantry that itself had become more radical and predisposed to taking the initiative in securing access to farmland. In the south, the landless peasants' movement, the *Movimento dos Trabalhadores Rurais Sem Terra* (MST), stepped up its occupation of large estates. Likewise, in Amazonia, the Brazil-nut estates of southern Pará came under pressure from landless farmers or *posseiros*. The rubber-tappers of Acre started their own movement to protect the rainforest, their source of livelihood, through collective action, preventing incursions by cattle ranchers and pressing for the establishment of "extractive reserves." Yet the lack of effective representation at the national level in Congress on behalf of potential agrarian reform beneficiaries, that is, the mass of poor rural producers, meant that, politically speaking, the UDR held the upper hand in the debate over land reform.

As a result of massive pressure on the government from the landowners' lobby, the PNRA-NR was redrafted no fewer than twelve times in the ensuing months, becoming law on October 10, 1985, via Decree 91,766. The reformulated plans made many properties that would have previously qualified ineligible for expropriation. Following the 1964 Land Statute, rural enterprises (*empresas rurais*) were exempted from the PNRA-NR, as were all family farms smaller than three times the INCRA regional farm module size. Publication of the more detailed regional agrarian reform plans for each state was also delayed by UDR pressure until April 1986. The first minister of agrarian reform, Nelson Ribeiro, resigned the following month in protest at the dilution of the PNRA-NR, and was succeeded by Dante de Oliveira. The new head of MIRAD faced a similarly uphill task and he, too, resigned little more than a year later. UDR pressure for further changes to the PNRA-NR continued throughout this period, culminating in another major concession, announced by the new minister for agrarian reform, Marcos Freire, in a nationwide television and radio broadcast only a week before he and his team of advisors were killed when their plane crashed upon takeoff from the Carajás project airport in Amazonia.

This concession was formalized by Decree-Law 2,363 of October 21, 1987, which exempted from expropriation two major categories of landholding. First, all "small" and "medium-sized" properties were made ineligible, thus introducing a retention limit that varied from 1,500 hectares in Amazonia, to 1,000 hectares in west-central Brazil, 250 hectares in the south, and 500 hectares in the northeast. This measure was subsequently revoked by Congress, in March 1989, and retention limits remain to be defined by law following publication of the new Constitution. Second, all "productive" farms, regardless of size, were exempted. Whereas the PNRA law of October 1985 had, following the 1964 Land Statute, defined "rural enterprise" in vague terms as any farm that was using the land "economically and rationally," the notion of "productive" properties, although offering a wider scope, nevertheless remained unclear and is still to be specified. This is a major bone of contention between pro- and anti-reform groups because such a definition will go a long way toward determining the potential scope of the reform. This clause represents a major reinterpretation and extension of the 1964 Land Statute provisions for exemption because it legitimizes the notion (first introduced under Decree 84,685 of May 6, 1980) of ineligible "productive latifúndia," which would previously have qualified for expropriation by virtue of sheer size. Further concessions granted in 1987 included a limit of 75 percent on the area of property expropriated, with the owner able to choose which 25 percent to keep. Agrarian debt bonds (TDAs) were transformed into highly liquid assets, which could be used as capital investment in financial transactions, for payment of property taxes, and for the purchase of public lands, amongst other things. The government took pains to quell landowners' apprehensions; a series of advertisements in the Brazilian press stressed that the vast majority of landowners would not be affected and that "those who produce have nothing to fear."

Implementation of the PNRA-NR overlapped with the deliberations of Brazil's 556-member Constituent Assembly, which was drawing up a new national constitution, approved in October 1988. Although the basic principle of agrarian reform is maintained in the final text, the landowners' lobby managed to ensure that its provisions were significantly watered down when compared with the original constitutional proposals. Eleven of the twenty-four members of the Subcommission for Agrarian Policy and Land Reform were recognized representatives of the UDR, federal deputies who were themselves all large landowners, including an ex-minister of agriculture, Alysson Paulinelli. In addition to making sure that the constitution's provision for agrarian reform should be as weak as possible, this group within the subcommission brought about amendments to specific clauses that threatened to strengthen the reforms. Such was the case of a defeated draft clause that would have allowed the immediate distribution of land titles following expropriation (*imissão imediata de posse*) without the right of appeal, a provision that would have eliminated a major obstacle to execution of the program.

Brazil's new constitution (Articles 189–196) provides for the expropriation of properties that are not "fulfilling their social purpose," a criterion vaguely defined in terms of rational land use, environmental conservation, adherence to labor legislation, and the well-being of owners and workers. Following previous amendments to the PNRA-NR discussed above, "productive" farms are exempted, although, as already stated, this term has yet to be defined. Complementary legislation is currently being debated in Congress to formalize procedures and clarify these constitutional provisions regarding, for example, an appropriate definition of the "social purpose" of land and what constitutes "productive" property. This arena will allow competing groups to exert pressure so that, in the future, agrarian reform laws will serve their particular interests. Potential land reform beneficiaries, as represented by the Confederation of Rural Workers (CONTAG) in its own Agrarian Law proposal published in June 1989, are pressing for a broader and more demanding definition of the "social" function of land that will facilitate expropriation and redistribution, prioritizing job creation and the increased production of staple food commodities. INCRA, by contrast, in its own proposals of the same date, adopts a narrower, economistic definition of agrarian reform and introduces a commercial bias. In common with the Constituent Assembly, the Commission for Agriculture and Rural Policies of the Chamber of Deputies is dominated by large landowners and it remains to be seen what legislation will emerge from the ensuing congressional debates.

The Record of Agrarian Reform to Date

Predictably, these changes in the original PNRA-NR proposals (in terms of properties exempted), coupled with landowners' strong opposition and Brazil's political hiatus surrounding the drafting of a new constitution and the presidential succession, have imposed severe constraints on the resulting law's ability to act as a redistributive tool. This is clearly reflected in the limited progress toward the plan's ambitious goals. Once again, this illustrates the strength of political reaction in Brazil to the very notion of land reform, which is seen by landowning groups as a threat to the principle of private property and even national stability itself. The sensitivity of the issue is illustrated by the fact that none of the center or right-wing parties in the 1989 presidential race addressed the question of land reform, with only Luís Inâcio da Silva ("Lula") of the Workers' party (PT) adopting it as a campaign issue. The winner and successor to President Sarney, Fernando Collor de Mello, of the National Reconstruction party (PRN), made little or no mention of the subject. This does not auger well for the land-reform program after the new president takes office in March

1990.

Although INCRA expropriated 30 percent of the 4.6 million hectare target for 1986, it took possession of only 10 percent; and just 2,000 (1.3 percent) of the 150,000 families to be accommodated that year were benefited, utilizing part of the land acquired by the government. One observer calculated that at this rate it would take over 1,000 years to cater to the 1.4 million families targeted in the initial phase. The government's questionable commitment to land reform was illustrated in 1987 when INCRA received only 30 percent of its budget for the program and, in tacit recognition of the PNRA-NR's lack of progress, targets for 1987–1988 were cut by up to 70 percent. The Plan of Government Action (*Plano de Ação Governamental*, PAG), published in 1987, cut the total number of first-phase land-reform beneficiaries from 1.4 million to 1 million and extended the deadline from 1989 to 1991.

At mid-1989, the shortfall continued, and only about 2.5 million hectares (representing considerably less than 1 percent of all land in farms) were then available for reform projects, a similar area being under negotiation with landowners. This represented less than 10 percent of the revised land expropriation target of 27 million hectares for 1991. According to official INCRA figures, by the end of July 1989, 450 agrarian reform projects were at varying stages of implementation, involving some 4.2 million hectares, with an eventual settlement capacity of 81,000 families. Farmers receive individual plots ranging from four to thirty hectares, depending on the region, as well as access to collective farming and grazing areas. Land can be redistributed either in the form of family-sized plots or as collective units to farmer associations. Beneficiaries would initially be granted the right to cultivate (*concessão de uso*), and receive legal title later on, a clause designed ostensibly to help prevent resale of land in a speculative fashion. Execution of many of these schemes has been seriously delayed through legal disputes. It is hoped (somewhat optimistically perhaps) that 6 million hectares will eventually be expropriated in this first phase to 1991—far from the 42 million hectares initially projected.

Paradoxically, the PNRA-NR has had counterproductive impacts in the countryside, almost since the moment it was announced. Although the plan, following the 1964 Land Statute, professes a concern for preserving the environment, the reform has had a negative impact in this regard. The PNRA-NR has unwittingly helped to speed up Amazonian deforestation as landowners have cleared their properties and planted grass in an effort to demonstrate that their farms are "productive" and therefore exempt from expropriation. There has also been a marked increase in rural violence over the period 1985–1988, as larger claimants have sought to expel small *posseiros* and these, in turn, have resisted attempts at eviction in the hope that the reform program will legitimize their claims to ownership.

The fate of the PNRA-NR as a force for radical change appears to have been sealed by the abolition of MIRAD in January 1989 and the transfer to INCRA (under the jurisdiction of the Ministry of Agriculture) of full responsibility for implementing the agrarian reform program. This move is entirely consistent with the gradual weakening of the plan since its publication in May 1985, and reflects an attempt to further depoliticize the whole issue of land transfers in Brazil. The abolition of the agrarian reform ministry places greater control over the reform process in the hands of more conservative government groups. The National Security Council (CSN), arguably the single most important agrarian policymaking body in Brazil, had originally been excluded by MIRAD from preparation of the agrarian reform by the radical-minded planners involved. The replacement of MIRAD by INCRA, subordinated to the Ministry of Agriculture, reasserted the influence of the military-dominated CSN (now renamed the President's Advisory Secretariat on National Defense, or SADEN), which has traditionally adopted a strategy of land occupation for geopolitical purposes, especially in Amazonia. This policy stood in stark contrast to the tradition of "expropriation in the social interest" established by the 1964 Land Statute and embodied, although ineffectually, within the agrarian reform of the New Republic. INCRA, with its historical emphasis on nonconfrontational colonization policies and voluntary agreements rather than agrarian reform in the radical sense of the word, would prioritize voluntary land sales for land-reform purposes, in line with the changing content of the PNRA-NR itself. Another consideration was the fact that during its relatively short lifetime some more radical sectors within MIRAD had established close links with the rural trades union movement (CONTAG), and it was feared that this influence would undermine the government's ability to dictate the nature and direction of agrarian reform.

Preliminary Conclusions and Policy Implications

Had even the downgraded agrarian reform plan been executed, it would have had a significant impact on the distribution of landownership in Brazil. For example, if the PNRA's first phase was fully implemented, including the modifications to the original law made in 1987, some 7 percent of all Brazilian farmland would have been redistributed; in the northeast the figure would have risen to 13 percent, and to 12 percent in the north or Amazonia, with much smaller impacts in the west-central, southeastern, and southern parts of the country. Yet, as this discussion has shown, results so far have been relatively disappointing. The very nature of the country's highly polarized structure of landownership, together with the accompanying concentration of wealth and power, impose severe limits on the political feasibility for redistributing private property on any significant scale. Furthermore, pro-latifúndia agrarian policies, which have predominated since the 1960s, have tended to result in the monopolization of subsidized inputs by larger, commercial producers and made it difficult for resources to be channeled toward reform beneficiaries. This bias has been clearly reflected in the strength of political opposition to the PNRA-NR, both within the Constituent Assembly and the Congress, and in the steady watering down of its original content since 1985. The relatively high short-term political payoff arising from distributing land (notwithstanding the opposition from propertied interests), as opposed to providing funds for project maintenance, together with a situation of financial austerity related to the foreign debt problem, have also contributed to the relatively slow pace of implementation.

Surprisingly, even within these limits, some progress has been made toward a partial land reform. By July 1989, as mentioned before, 450 projects were at various stages of execution, involving 4.2 million hectares, with a resettlement capacity of over 80,000 families, according to official INCRA figures. Although this is a small contribution compared with the dimension of agrarian problems in Brazil, it is, nevertheless, a promising start. There is a strong regional variation in the implementation of resettlement projects, performance depending in large measure upon the commitment to reform of individual state governments. In the northeast, for example, Bahia and Ceará lead the field, with 37 (283,000 hectares) and 38 projects (93,000 hectares) under way, respectively; in Amazonia, Pará has 33 projects under way (covering almost a million hectares).

Many of these involve latifúndia that had already been occupied by peasant farmers carrying out their own informal, de facto redistribution. In southern Pará, for example, some 200,000 hectares of Brazil-nut estates had been seized in this fashion through "land invasions" before the area was legally expropriated under the PNRA-NR and titles were distributed. There are many similar cases in the southern states of Paraná and Santa Catarina, where the MST, with the backing of the Catholic church and the Workers' party, had by 1988 organized over 80 estate occupations involving some 13,000 families. The strength of localized and regional organized peasant estate interventions is thus also a key factor in acting as a catalyst, providing a fait accompli in the majority of cases, which INCRA has little option but to legalize under the agrarian reform.

By definition, agrarian reform must involve not only land redistribution but also the provision of complementary support services and inputs in order to render the new structures economically viable. Following the 1964 Land Statute, the PNRA-NR thus envisages the provision of support programs of rural credit, extension, marketing facilities, cooperative organization, agricultural research, and manpower training. The most important such instrument to date in this respect has been a credit program (PROCERA) created in January 1986 for reform beneficiaries. In this program, managed by the National Bank for Social and Economic Development (BNDES), each family is eligible to receive the equivalant of about US$1,200 altogether in funding, with an annual rate of interest of 30 percent, an eight-year repayment period, and three years' grace with no collateral required. The degree of subsidy is illustrated by the fact that in early 1990 Brazil's inflation rate was at over 1,000 percent per year. PROCERA had, by the end of 1988, benefited some 28,400 families with initial loans of about US$250 each. PROCERA departs from the conventional criteria used to grant rural credit in Brazil by being far cheaper and more flexible and by making funds available for a variety of purposes ranging from land clearing to the purchase of farm animals, implements, and fertilizers. This last category is particularly important because most lands acquired under the agrarian reform are generally considered to be of poor quality.

PROCERA's main objectives in providing agrarian reform beneficiaries with support services have been to provide stability of tenure while raising levels of agricultural production and farmer incomes through an emphasis on collective forms of organization. Although individual plots are distributed to reform beneficiaries, the official aim has been to encourage informal associations for the purpose of work sharing (*mutirão*), the hope being that, in the longer term, more permanent cooperative groupings will be established for production, marketing, and other purposes. INCRA maintains that the best results in the PROCERA program have been obtained in those settlements that are collectively organized, and that these have been used as demonstration models. The relative value of collective versus individual forms of production and farmer organization is bound to provide a controversial area for discussion as the PNRA-NR develops. Another critical area of debate surrounds the issue of whether reform projects will simply reproduce the polarized income distribution and landownership structures found in the countryside and in many traditional colonization schemes; in such schemes, lack of support for settlers in terms of production inputs has tended to result in high turnover, with wealthier farmers, either from within or outside of the project, being able to buy out the economically weak.

Starting from the premise that an agrarian reform of the type that has emerged in Brazil since 1985 does indeed have the potential for improving the livelihoods of significant numbers of the rural poor, a key question revolves around the nature of the process through which, in the post–land distribution phase, these new farmer-settlers are integrated into the wider agrarian economy. The first systematic field research into the performance of land reform projects under the PNRA-NR was carried out by the BNDES, based on data for 1986, and surveys of 1,500 farmers in twenty-six settlements. Its conclusions were cautiously pessimistic: most agrarian reform beneficiaries were experiencing considerable difficulties in raising farm incomes beyond a basic minimum level. Unequal access to critical inputs such as modern technology, seeds, fertilizers, extension assistance, and official rural credit had resulted in a strong concentration of income, with one-third of farmers earning on average less than the legal minimum salary. A minority of producers were becoming modernized and well integrated into the market economy, but the majority were obliged to continue with traditional forms of semi-subsistence farming. For many semi-subsistence farmers, however, the acquisition of a plot, in itself, represented significant progress compared with their previous situation of landlessness.

Other research along similar lines has yielded somewhat different conclusions. The BNDES research was carried out on pre-reform, long-standing resettlement schemes, which were subsequently placed under the PNRA-NR umbrella, where rural inequalities had been reinforced through conventional social and economic mechanisms. Another independent survey of 400 farmers in six new agrarian reform projects in different regions of the country found, on the other hand, that despite some concentration of income during the initial phase, at least 50 percent of beneficiaries had enjoyed a significant improvement in their standard of living. In spite of the relatively short project lifespan of only two years or so, the proportion of settlers who had successfully integrated into the agrarian economy (defined as earning more than three minimum wages, or about US$120 per month) ranged from 6 to 100 percent.

All of the schemes practiced some form of community organization such as the sharing of farm implements, collective purchase of inputs, and use of communal irrigation facilities, although the form of organization (collective versus individual) was not found itself to be a critical factor in explaining differential settler outcomes. Neither were individual differences in performance found to be related to farm size.

The most critical factor in determining the degree of farmer success was the use of modern agricultural techniques related to differential initial resource endowments of settlers, including the possession of capital, and educational levels. Unequal access to credit facilities and hence other modern inputs purchased in the marketplace were also crucial factors. The extension of PROCERA facilities, it is thought, will help to equalize access to such key resources and facilitate a more balanced performance amongst beneficiaries. Thus, it is not necessarily the case that Brazil's agrarian reform settlements are bound to reproduce the country's global pattern of rural wealth and poverty and are, therefore, doomed to fail as instruments of redistribution. In order for such projects to enjoy a relative degree of success, however, the limited research carried out to date indicates that certain prerequisites must be met. Land reform is, in itself, no panacea for solving problems of rural poverty and low productivity. In designing appropriate interventions, policymakers must bear in mind a number of relevant considerations at both national and local levels.

Agrarian Reform at the Macrolevel

Ideally, there should be a firm political commitment to the redistributive principles of agrarian reform within both the legislative and executive arms of government, strong enough to withstand anti-reformist pressure, both civil and military, and backed up by an independent judiciary. The problems of seeing through such reforms are heightened when there is strong opposition from powerful landowning and military groups, either within or enjoying close links to the government. These groups exert a strong influence on policymaking and, in Brazil's case, conceive agrarian reform in rather narrow terms as operating against their sectional interests, namely, those of private property and national security, both domestic and international. Extensive land reform is perceived by these groups as a strategy that would lead to political instability—on the one hand challenging the power of landed groups and, on the other, shifting the focus of settlement policy away from frontier consolidation as a major priority to a more radical or redistributive emphasis. Whether and precisely how such commitment may be achieved will depend on the political and economic interests of the government, the nature of its political alliances, and the degree of support it can count upon at all levels to see through such measures. Without an overall political commitment to reform in the countryside, there is the likelihood that, as has happened in Brazil's case, initial legislation is steadily watered down to the point that agrarian reform becomes little more than an ad hoc process of crisis management in areas of acute land conflict, the benefits of which accrue primarily to landowners in the form of generous compensation. In such circumstances, the land-reform institute loses its expropriatory powers, suffers from severe underfunding, and becomes little more than a glorified real estate agent, taking possession of targeted landholdings only on the basis of voluntary agreements with the owners. Land reform is possible on this basis, but its scale and pace are bound to be drastically reduced. The land resources undoubtedly exist to meet the basic requirements of poor Brazilian cultivators without undue sacrifice for the remainder of rural society. A redistribution of, say, ten hectares to each of 5 million landless or landpoor households would involve a total of 50 million hectares. This would be equivalent to less than one-third of the area currently under pasture and only 21 percent of existing farmland in Brazil.

Redistribution of land is, of course, a necessary but not sufficient condition for ensuring the material progress of large numbers of poor cultivators within a reform program. Thus, a genuine agrarian reform is dependent on the provision of supportive measures to facilitate agricultural production, marketing, and income generation. Notwithstanding the need for special programs of support at the project level (see next section), there must also, therefore, be a certain compatibility between macroeconomic agrarian policies and the goal of benefiting small farmers, providing the conditions for their fuller integration into the market economy. In particular, there must be a more equal distribution of access to basic inputs such as subsidized credit, seeds, fertilizers, extension services, and price support, which in Brazil have traditionally been monopolized by or worked in favor of larger commercial and agribusiness interests. A conscious policy of creating a favorable economic environment, which generates incentives for small farmers to stay on the land rather than migrate to the cities, is also one that, apart from stimulating rural development in general, will similarly be conducive toward successful agrarian reform.

Agrarian Reform at the Microlevel

The acquisition of sufficient land is merely the first stage in the process of agrarian restructuring. Provision of support services to ensure continuity of possession and agricultural production by project-holders is a sine qua non of any successful agrarian reform. Thus, a basic injection of rural credit on favorable terms for both investment and working capital is usually essential because most beneficiaries are undercapitalized. Similarly, technical guidance from specially trained extensionists, seeds, fertilizers, pesticides, and other complementary production inputs are also necessary.

A stable and cohesive community organization is probably as important as the provision of physical inputs and technical services in ensuring the viability of agrarian reform projects of the type undertaken in Brazil. Research undertaken so far indicates that practices such as work-sharing, communal decisionmaking, and other forms of mutual support (without the need for collective farming, as such) may help improve the livelihoods of larger numbers of beneficiaries (compared with settlements where these forms are absent) and be conducive toward a more balanced income distribution within projects. The minimization of large inequities within projects undoubtedly helps to increase security of tenure and reduce the incidence of plot abandonment and land reconcentration in the hands of more successful farmers, which is typical of land-reform experiences in Brazil. The organization of project beneficiaries into political units, linked to the rural trade union movement, will also help settlers to ward off more direct attempts by counter-reform interests to repossess distributed lands. Likewise, in the pre-reform period, as comments made above on estate invasions and subsequent redistribution make clear, the organization of potential beneficiaries can strengthen the reform process by applying social and political pressure on the authorities.

The Role of Foreign Assistance

In the Brazilian context, it is unlikely that foreign assistance could exert significant direct influence upon the economic or political macropolicy environment within which agrarian reform is conceived. Policy statements from major aid bodies regarding the virtues of agrarian reform, together with campaigns by nongovernment organizations, may have some very indirect impact on policymaking in this field. By and large, however, this is the exclusive domain of domestic institutions, and the interplay amongst internal economic and political interest groups will determine policy priorities, especially in countries such as Brazil, which are not heavily dependent on foreign aid in order to finance these interventions. This does not mean, however, that foreign aid programs are powerless to influence the nature and direction of agrarian reform in such cases. In Brazil and similar developing countries, where there is a (variable) commitment to reform but execution is held up by strong landed groups within a nominally democratic context, opportunities are present but they have to be carefully selected. Given the size and cost of Brazil's reform program, it is unlikely that foreign aid donors would be prepared to directly pay for a large proportion of major items such as land or credit, although some significant contributions could be made in this respect to get the process moving in the initial stages.

In a situation such as Brazil's, foreign assistance could play a perhaps more important role in two other major areas: (1) institution-building at national and regional levels, and (2) community mobilization at the local level. As far as the first option is concerned, a shortage of adequately skilled personnel is a major bottleneck to the implementation of agrarian reform. Programs of training and technical assistance, such as that set up by the United Nations Development Program (UNDP) in 1987 for Brazil's ten northeastern states, are thus critical in equipping staff with the basic skills needed to provide support for settlement projects. In this case, courses in agricultural planning and cartography have been given to technicians from institutions directly involved in the implementation of agrarian reform, including regional offices of the land-reform agency, state-level extension bodies, and the Federation of Rural Workers. However, the success of such assistance is strongly dependent on the degree of political commitment to the reform program at the state level. Significantly, the most progressive states in terms of the numbers of projects implemented (Bahia and Ceará) are also those with the most trainees within this UNDP scheme. Other serious problems are the lack of interinstitutional coordination, nonrecruitment of essential staff, and the lack of beneficiary participation in the planning of settlement projects.

The absence of effective channels through which small farmers may exert some influence on the planning and execution of reform settlements in Brazil is perhaps the major bottleneck. A second area in which outside assistance could be constructively applied is, therefore, that of providing financial and technical support to incipient forms of community organization amongst reform beneficiaries under the PNRA-NR. This would, in the first instance, facilitate economies of scale through labor cooperation. More important in the longer term, however, it would aim to encourage community mobilization both within and across communities, so that such groups acquire a collective voice and a degree of bargaining power to be able to negotiate with land-reform institutions. Such "bottom-up" participation and a certain autonomy of decisionmaking are thus essential if land reform settlements are to avoid being either totally neglected or manipulated by technocrats for their own ends. To the extent that participation in project implementation can build upon pre-exisiting forms of community activity rather than attempting to "create" such involvement from scratch, so much the better.

This kind of assistance is, by its very nature, probably best given by nongovernment organizations (NGOs) working through local intermediary voluntary institutions that deal directly with affected communities. Even more important, as already mentioned, well-organized local communities of reform beneficiaries could, in cooperation with NGOs, political parties, and the rural trade union movement, provide essential grassroots pressure in support of wider and more effective land reform, either before, during, or after its implementation. If such overseas aid is to have an impact, however, NGOs themselves need to overcome their own traditional lack of mutual communication and establish more effective channels of interagency cooperation to define common policies and working methodologies in this and other fields. Similarly, mechanisms must be found for improving collaboration amongst all the formal organizations involved in lobbying central government for land reform, including NGOs, political parties, unions, and the church. Without the combination of physical inputs, technical skills, and political organization suggested here, it is unlikely that Brazil's limited experiment with agrarian reform will expand significantly. If this proves to be the case in the longer term, a major opportunity for alleviating rural poverty and boosting agricultural production will surely have been wasted.

Notes

The author would like to thank Merilee Grindle, Roy Prosterman, and the other contributors to this volume for their valuable comments on an earlier draft.

1. Latifúndia are defined in the 1964 Land Statute as properties larger than 600 times the regional land "module" (see note 3 below).

2. Minifúndia are defined in the 1964 Land Statute as holdings smaller than the "family farm" (see note 4 below) size established for a particular region.

3. Regional farm modules were defined by the 1964 Land Statute. These vary in size according to population density, land quality, and the type of agricultural or livestock activities pursued, ranging from two to twelve hectares. Thus, areas with intensive farming that are heavily populated have small modules, whereas regions with a low demographic density and extensive farming or cattle-ranching, for example, are characterized by larger modules.

4. Family farms are defined by the 1964 Land Statute as those farms worked by the cultivator and his or her family, providing them with the means of subsistence, as well as "social and economic progress." Rural enterprises are classed as those farms, publicly or privately owned, that cultivate the land "economically and rationally . . . within the regional context."

Selected Bibliography

Barbosa, T. "O Plano Nacional de Reforma Agrária e o Latifúndio Produtivo." In E. Contini, A. Flavio Dias Avila, and M. Tollini (eds.), *Alimentos, Política*

Agrícola e Pesquisa Agropecuária, Brasília: EMBRAPA, 1989.
————. "A Reforma Agrária Brasileira e Seus Impactos Redistributivos." In E. Contini, A. Flavio Dias Avila, and M. Tollini (eds.), *Alimentos, Política Agrícola e Pesquisa Agropecuária,* Brasília: EMBRAPA, 1989.

Gomes da Silva, J. *Buraco Negro: A Reforma Agrária na Constituinte de 1987/88.* São Paulo: Paz e Terra, 1989.

Graziano da Silva, J. *Para Entender o Plano Nacional de Reforma Agrária.* São Paulo: Brasiliense, 1985.

Guanziroli, C. "Income Generation in Brazilian Land Settlements," mimeo. Dept. of Economics, University College, University of London, 1989.

Hall, A. *Developing Amazonia: Deforestation and Social Conflict in Brazil's Carajás Program,* New York: St. Martin's Press, 1989.

Mahar, D. *Government Policies and Deforestation in Brazil's Amazon Region,* Washington D.C.: World Bank, 1989.

Ministry of Agrarian Reform and Development. *Proposta para a elaboração do 1ª Plano Nacional de Reforma Agrária da Nova República-PNRA.* Brasília: MIRAD, May 1985.

————. *Plano Nacional de Reforma Agrária-PNRA.* Brasília: MIRAD, October 1985.

Monteiro de Castro, M. H. "Reforma Agrária-Um Estudo Preliminar." *Reforma Agrária* 18, no. 1 (April-July, 1988): 5–37.

Ribeiro, N. *Caminhada e Esperança da Reforma Agrária.* São Paulo: Paz e Terra, 1987.

part three

The Soviet Union and Eastern Europe

chapter eight

Land Tenure in Collectivized Agriculture: The Soviet Union, Poland, and Hungary

Karen M. Brooks

Summary

The Soviet Union has embarked on an attempt to reform its costly agricultural sector. In 1989 a radical rhetoric of fundamental reform replaced earlier timid attempts to make the inherited institutions of collectivized agriculture work better. Changes in land tenure are among the most far-reaching components of the agrarian reform. A new Land Law, released in draft form in November 1989 and modified in the winter of 1990, incorporates "land to the tiller" language granting limited ownership to producers who work the land, whether collectively or individually. The law brings private ownership of agricultural land, albeit limited, back to the Soviet Union for the first time since 1917. Earlier attempts to change tenurial relations by introducing lease contracts without ownership have been disappointing.

Changes in land tenure are fundamental to reform of collectivized agriculture, but, as the Polish and Hungarian experiences demonstrate, they are not enough. Private ownership is not enough if the structure of marketing and restrictions on labor and credit characteristic of centrally planned economies are not changed. If the most damaging constraints on the economic environment in which collective farms operate are released, collective farms can be viable organizations, although they are still not efficient enough to compete well on world markets. Changes in land tenure must be part of a comprehensive agrarian reform that reaches from farms to final consumers.

The high costs of inefficient agriculture in socialist countries, reflected in consumer shortages, farm debt, and the budget deficit, have motivated the current effort toward fundamental reform. Its success or failure will be one of the major developments shaping the lives of rural people in these countries and the world agricultural economy in the twenty-first century.

One-third of the world's population lives in the countries of Eastern Europe, the Soviet Union, and Asia in which agrarian institutions were abruptly and forcibly recast during collectivization in the middle decades of the twentieth century. Collectivization markedly changed world patterns of production, consumption, and trade in food, and affected producers and consumers far removed from its political and economic upheaval.

The effects have been most directly felt in the centrally planned economies themselves. Collectivized agriculture has been unable to deliver food and fiber to match the growth in demand in the Soviet Union and Eastern Europe at constant or declining real costs. The commitment of labor and capital to agriculture has remained high, but even with the remarkable increase in imports since the early 1970s consumers cannot purchase the foods they seek at prices they can afford to pay.

The political and economic implications of a worsening food economy led in 1988 to public recognition that the problem lies at the very heart of collectivized agriculture, the system of land tenure, and incentives for effective management. Gorbachev's call that "the land needs a master" and the discussions surrounding the Law of Cooperatives in July 1988 signaled a new and serious commitment to a change in land tenure.

The first approach was official endorsement of lease contracting, and the campaign in favor of lease contracting launched earlier that year intensified in the summer of 1988. Under lease contracting, an individual or small group of people manage a portion of the collective or state farm's assets, and earn residual profits generated from the leased assets.

Land tenure refers directly to rules governing the ownership and management of land, but tenurial arrangements in all societies are affected by the rules for other inputs, particularly labor, credit, and purchased inputs, and by marketing procedures for output.[1] By late 1989 it was clear that the lease contract system would not spread quickly or spontaneously in the Soviet Union, largely because arrangements in closely related markets for inputs and products did not support it. Lease contracting came to be viewed not as the final outcome of tenurial reform, but as a first step in a prolonged process that would yield a mixed system of commercial agriculture with land under state, cooperative, and private ownership. Profound changes in land law and input and product markets would be necessary for the tenurial reforms to proceed.

Realization that lease contracting is not a panacea for the tenurial problems of Soviet agriculture has had a major effect on the new Land

Law. The law was passed from the drafting committee for consideration by the Supreme Soviet in late October 1989. Earlier versions retained state ownership of land with mixed forms of management consisting of traditional state and collective farms, cooperative units, and individual leaseholders. The retention of full state ownership was rejected in the final draft and replaced by ownership by the people (*narod*). The principle of people's ownership is to be implemented through ownership by those who work the land: individual farmers or peasants, collective and state farms, cooperatives, and, under particular conditions, the state. The final Land Law of March 1990, offers a restricted ownership, under which the owner cannot sell or mortgage the land. Laws restricting the sale of agricultural land are not uncommon in the developing world, but in the Soviet Union, where fundamental changes in farm organization are underway, this restriction on activity in land markets may be quite costly.

In July 1989, Lithuania passed the Law on Peasant Farming in Lithuania, which legalizes private ownership of land of up to fifty hectares if the land is used for a family farm. The land cannot be sold, rented, or mortgaged, and there are a number of ambiguities in the law about terms of ownership and inheritance. In the nine months following its passage, about 1,500 farmers (or 1.5 per state or collective farm) set up small farms of from 10 to 50 hectares under the new law.

Tenurial arrangements in Eastern Europe have been diverse in the postwar period despite almost universal collectivization. Polish agriculture was never fully collectivized; approximately 80 percent of land remains privately owned and operated by small-holders. The profitability and productivity of private agriculture in Poland has been constrained even though private ownership has been tolerated. Polish private farmers have been severely limited in the quantities of inputs they can purchase and have had to pay higher prices than state farms. The Polish case holds one lesson for Soviet reformers: "privatization" of landholding is not enough. Private operators have incentives to manage their land well, but with limited access to modern inputs and efficient marketing they do not perform well.

Hungary's collectivization was comprehensive and largely completed by 1961. In the first period, coercion was the primary instrument, but after 1956 the process was completed through incentives encouraging voluntary membership in collective farms. After 1965, Hungarian collective farms could produce and market as much as they chose. Central planners in Hungary set prices, exchange rates, taxes, and credit rather than input and output quotas. Greater tolerance for activity in the private sector after 1965 provided opportunities for agricultural entrepreneurs, but the collective farms remain the dominant institution of landholding. Their economic performance under decentralized planning exceeds that of agriculture in other countries of Eastern Europe, but rising costs of production in the 1980s suggest that in Hungary, too, pressures for tenurial change may increase.

The decline of dogmatism in the Soviet Union has led to greater tolerance for the diversity of land tenure that has existed in recent years in Eastern Europe, but was not officially recognized. Eastern European countries are now encouraged by Moscow to forge their own agrarian institutions to improve agricultural performance and reduce the burden of agriculture on their economies. They and individual republics within the Soviet Union are searching for tenurial forms that work and that are acceptable to their own rural people. The politics of *perestroika* have removed the old limits and forced all parties to engage in a search to discover where the new bounds lie.

Resource Endowments

The poor performance of agriculture in Eastern Europe and the Soviet Union is striking because the resource endowments over much of this vast region favor agriculture. In the northern countries of Eastern Europe and northwestern republics of the Soviet Union—Poland, East Germany, Czechoslovakia, Latvia, Lithuania, Estonia, Belorussia, and northwestern non–black-soil provinces of the Russian Republic, where dairy, hogs, feed grains, potatoes, sugar beets, and flax predominate—land-to-labor ratios are in many places roughly similar to those of Western Europe, although productivity is lower. South of this region lie Romania, Hungary, Bulgaria, Moldavia, the Ukraine, and the black-soil region of the Russian Republic where climate and soils favor both wheat and feed grains, hogs, poultry, oilseeds, and fruits and vegetables. Small areas of this region are suitable for subtropical products. Rural areas are somewhat more densely settled than in the more northern region.

South and east of this region are the Caucasian republics and transcaucasian provinces and autonomous regions of the Russian Republic, with traditional advantage in viticulture, herding, and fruits and vegetables. Beyond this to the east stretches the spring wheat area of the steppe in the Russian Republic and Kazakhstan, with land comparable to the northern plains of the United States and prairie provinces of Canada. Land-to-labor ratios here are much higher than in the regions to the west, but lower than on comparable wheatlands in North America.

South of the steppe is the large, very densely settled area of irrigated desert of Central Asia, where cotton has been king since Stalin imposed it as a near monoculture, but where the ecological and economic advantages of a more diversified agriculture are now gaining adherents. East of the Urals to the north and Central Asia to the south lies Siberia, vast in territory and natural resources, but less important agriculturally than the rest of the country. The northern part is very sparsely settled and yields furs and meat. The southern part is suitable for grains, dairy, some oilseed production, and fruits and vegetables for local consumption.

Each of the diverse agricultural regions has within it a plethora of ethnic groups with distinctive traditions of land use. Collectivization in the Soviet Union resulted in a remarkable uniformity of agricultural organization across regions and ethnic traditions, testifying to the degree to which it was imposed from the outside and above, rather than molded by local conditions and needs. As the strictures of collectivized land tenure ease under the current reform, diverse forms of contracts and new units of production are appearing in different regions.

Within this diversity, the problems of Soviet Central Asia stand out as distinct from those of other regions. High rates of population growth, linguistic and cultural barriers to outmigration, and low levels of rural development, education, and public health have brought increased pressure of population on land. Generous subsidies to collective farms in the past allowed them to absorb much, but not all, of the growing rural labor force. As a result, both underemployment and unemployment have increased over the last several decades.

The new forms of land tenure, if implemented in Central Asia, will encourage farms and small groups of producers to keep fewer workers more fully and productively employed. Unemployment and landlessness common in densely settled developing countries may increase. Tenurial arrangements consistent with development of rural Central Asia may be quite different from those of the rest of the country, reflecting the atypical factor endowment of this area.

Sixty Years of Collectivized Agriculture

Collectivized agriculture emerged from the political, economic, and ideological turmoil of the Soviet Union in the 1920s. The decision to collectivize was most immediately a response to a marketing problem—peasants in the late 1920s reduced production and marketing of grain in response to poor relative prices and weakened incentives. Collectivization took decisions about production and marketing out of the hands of individual peasants and transferred them to the government and the party.

The short-term control over marketed output came at a cost of progressively reduced efficiency in the sector. Low efficiency has brought high and rising costs of production, exacerbated by the growth in demand and outmigration from agriculture that accompanied the transition of the Soviet Union from a low-income to a middle-income country.

Many aspects of agricultural development in the Soviet Union are particular to the geography and historical experience of its people and cannot be generalized to other countries. The brutality of forced collectivization should properly be laid to Stalin and the thousands of collaborators who implemented his orders. The extraordinary losses of the Red Army during World War II contributed to demographic problems of the postwar agricultural labor force. Yet the high costs of collectivized agriculture are embedded in the form of land tenure and resource management, rather than in particular Soviet experience.

High costs of collectivized agriculture in the Soviet Union have collided with decreased ability to pay the bill. Gorbachev's industrial modernization effort diverts resources from agriculture to heavy and light industry. Oil and gas have become more expensive in rubles to extract and earn fewer dollars on world markets.

What specific features of collectivized agriculture have caused it to perform so poorly in the Soviet Union despite a massive inflow of resources since 1965? Which of these features can be remedied by changes in land tenure? The following sections discuss the nature of the agrarian problem in the Soviet Union to provide a context in which to evaluate changes in land tenure as an instrument for agrarian reform. The Polish and Hungarian experiences offer perspectives on varying tenurial regimes in agrarian sectors of centrally planned economies.

Land Tenure in Collectivized Agriculture

Land on collective and state farms is owned by the state and leased to the farms in perpetuity. Prior to the 1960s, there were significant differences in taxation, pricing, and wages on state and collective farms, but these differences no longer remain. Private ownership of land was abolished with the Land Decree of 1917, issued the day after the October Revolution. Collective and state farms have not in the past paid for the use of land, although under recent legislation they will begin paying user's fees as soon as a set of rates is devised. The average farm has about 6,500 hectares of land (3,500 of which are cultivated) and a work force of 450.

People who work on collective and state farms also live there and have the right to farm a small plot of land adjacent to their homes. They do not own the private plot, but have a well-defined use right.

The private, or household, plot traditionally could not exceed half a hectare, and livestock held on the private plot was both strictly limited in number and intermittently taxed. The farm family can use the output of the household plot for home consumption or for sale.

The household plot is an essential component of the system of collectivized land tenure. Under Stalin, earnings for work on the collective fields were low, and the household plot provided both subsistence and earnings for rural people. Those who did not work the minimum number of days in the collective fields could lose the right to farm their household plots, and hence their livelihood.

After 1966, earnings in the collective sector increased and the proportion of rural residents' incomes earned from the household plot declined. It remains high, however—collective farm members on average still receive one-quarter of total family income from the household plot, and the proportion is higher in some regions. The household plot provides an essential supplement to commercially marketed food from the collective sector. Household plots produce about 26 percent of all meat, 27 percent of milk, 26 percent of eggs, 54 percent of fruits, and 58 percent of potatoes.

How can household plots of half a hectare, comprising in total less than 3 percent of cultivated land, produce such a large proportion of output of major products? Do not these remarkably productive small plots show that privatization is the answer to the Soviet agricultural problem?

The answer, unfortunately, is no. The plots are not remarkably productive if all inputs are fully measured, although they are more productive than land managed collectively. The meat, milk, and eggs produced on the household plots use feed from the collective sector, in combination with household wastes. Little feed is grown on the small household plots. Young animals are purchased from the collective sector, or in recent years taken on contract and fattened. The fertilizer and machine power are also usually purchased from the collective sector. The farm family provides labor, management, and structures. Thus much of the apparent high productivity of land in household plots derives from inputs that originate in the collective sector. Household plots are an integral part of traditional collectivized land tenure; independent private farms would not be.

If given the option, Soviet farm families may choose to expand household plots into mini-farms, but keep the security of wage work on the collective and state farms. This would be an alternative to the independence and risk of lease contracting or full private farming, but would still offer greater scope for entrepreneurial talent and hard work. The Hungarian experience suggests that workers associated with well-managed, solvent collective farms choose to remain with them and expand household minifarms, and rarely become full-fledged independent operators. The Soviet agrarian structure of the future will probably include a mix of collective and private different from the current period and recent past. This is particularly likely if owners of minifarms or their immediate family members will be allowed to work for wages on collective and state farms, or in off-farm employment. The performance of such a mixed system might be fairly good, although conclusions cannot be drawn by extrapolating from the productivity of private plots under current conditions.

Supply Side: The High Costs of Production

The sources of high costs of production on collective and state farms are diverse, but can be grouped into three general areas: poor labor incentives, weak economic links among farms and between farms and the rest of the economy, and limited autonomy for farms to run their own economic affairs. Each of these sources of high cost can be linked to particular characteristics of collectivized agriculture. Each also affects the prospects for implementation of new forms of tenure. One lesson from the disappointing experience with lease contracting to date is that changes in land tenure cannot be implemented if changes in corollary markets do not support them.

Labor Mobility and Labor Incentives

In the 1930s most farms were collective farms; state farms existed but were few in number. People who lived and worked on collective farms were members of the farm, not employees of the state, and constituted a separate class of Soviet citizens. They did not have rights to social security, pensions, standardized wages, and occupational choice granted state employees. Collective farm members did not have the right to internal passports until 1974, and those who lacked passports needed special documents to leave the farm.

The special legal status of collective farm members raised the costs of leaving agriculture, despite working conditions and standards of living that lagged considerably behind opportunities in the growing industrial enterprises. Workers were not tied to the farm, but neither were they fully free to quit. For work on the collective fields they were paid according to a work point system used to divide up profits after all obligations to the state and suppliers of nonlabor inputs had been met. Since procurement prices were low, profits were low, and work points were often worth little and paid in kind.

In 1939, 47 percent of the population within the Soviet borders were collective farm members or their minor children, and 3 percent of the population were uncollectivized peasants or craft workers. Many of these people, fully half of the Soviet population, supported themselves on the proceeds from their half-hectare private plots, and were only tenuously linked into the monetary economy.

A number of changes were made in the wage system after Stalin's death. Khrushchev raised farm purchase prices in an effort to raise residual profits and the value of work points. Under Brezhnev after 1966 the collective farm work point system was phased out and replaced by a standardized wage scale linked to wages on state farms. Wages for work on collective fields (excluding earnings from private plots) for collective farm members increased from one-third of average wages of state employees in all sectors in 1960 to 71 percent in 1989. When earnings from private plots are included, agricultural earnings do not lag significantly behind those in other sectors requiring comparable skills, although agriculturalists work longer hours.

The increase in wages under Brezhnev increased agricultural incomes, but did little to improve incentives. Its effect was to transfer to agricultural workers a large portion of the rent formerly collected by the state as landowner, and even to augment the transfer with subsidies from the state budget. Since Stalin's death the wage and payment system in agriculture has been the object of constant tinkering in an effort to discover a successful formula to motivate people to work more responsibly. None of the changes brought a noticeable improvement in labor productivity or costs of production.

Poor labor incentives and an inefficient distribution of workers geographically explains much of the current concern about a labor shortage when 19 percent of the work force is still employed in agricultural production, and a worker on average cultivates only eight hectares. Low labor productivity is an important source of high costs in agriculture, and one that a country with declining birth rates and high demand for labor in the industrial economy can ill afford.

Costs of production have increased markedly since 1965, and much of the increase is due to wage hikes unmatched by growth in productivity. Payments to labor and returns to land are intimately linked. The current search for better tenurial arrangements is motivated by a need for higher labor productivity, as well as better stewardship of the land.

Links Between Agriculture and the Rest of the Economy

The economic function of collectivized agriculture in its early years was to facilitate extraction of resources from the sector through taxation, low purchase prices, and reduced standards of living of agricultural workers. The state monopoly on supply of inputs and purchase of output was the mechanism for resource collection. The state monopoly on trade was thus an integral part of the system of collectivized land tenure.

Whether collectivization succeeded in transferring resources out of agriculture is a subject of debate. The loss of life and destruction of livestock and buildings, plus the lower productivity of resources that remained, may have made the net transfer nil or negative. For example, the number of horses and cattle on farms was halved between 1928 and 1933, and tractors produced in the 1930s were needed to replace slaughtered draft animals.

By Stalin's death in 1953 it was clear that agriculture was in a shambles, and the cause of that distress was thought to be the policy of taxation and disinvestment. Khrushchev, and later Brezhnev after 1965, initiated a massive reinvestment program. For most of the period since 1965 agriculture has received 20 percent of annual total investment in the entire Soviet economy; only recently has the proportion fallen to 17 percent.

With reinvestment, the marketing function that linked farms to the rest of the economy on both the input and output sides became more important, yet the modernization campaign did not include institutional innovations to assure that the investments went to the right places at the right times or were used well. Major and minor decisions about new projects and flows of current inputs reflected political jockeying of powerful local party officials. Without functioning markets or economic accountability the return to resources could affect their allocation little.

The input supply organizations through which much of the reinvestment was channeled were state monopolies. Most input prices are centrally set, and the organizations had and still have little of the traditional monopolist's power to set prices. But they engage in a number of practices that increase the real prices farms pay, such as restricting availability of inexpensive items in high demand and forcing substitutions of more expensive models, inflating repair bills, and failing to make contracted deliveries. Farms denied alternative suppliers were forced to accept late shipments of fertilizer or feed, and pay high prices for unnecessary repairs.

The losses due to monopoly in the input supply industry increased as more inputs moved through these organizations with the modernization campaign. The state monopoly in marketing is counterproductive when the goal of policy is to inject additional physical and financial resources into agriculture, rather than to take them out. Retention of this inappropriate marketing institution throughout the reinvestment campaign substantially reduced the return to investment.

Monopoly power in the input supply industry restricts the potential gains from alternative forms of land management, such as contract farming, proposed as part of the reform, and limits the attractiveness of new tenurial arrangements. Soviet producers need access to purchased inputs; land and labor is not enough. Yet small producers working under contract are even more poorly served by the input monopolies than are the larger state and collective farms.

Farm Autonomy

Farms in collectivized agriculture as it developed in the Soviet Union have little autonomy. Decisions about what, when, and how to plant, when to hay and weed, and when to harvest and deliver are made by party bureaucrats who know about conditions on the farm, if at all, by telephone.

Now, in this period of reevaluation of the experience of sixty years of collectivized agriculture, the existing severance of decisionmaking and implementation is a subject of anguished reflection. One expression of this is a populist sentiment that collectivization broke a mystical link between the peasant and the land, and that Soviet agriculture has gone downhill ever since. Gorbachev does not fully espouse the populist view, but frequently argues that the agricultural worker must again become "master" (*khoziain*) of the land—that is, a manager who not only has incentive to work well, but power to make responsible decisions.

The agricultural worker is twice removed from mastery of the land. The collective farm chairman (through the brigade leader) tells him or her what to do, but, in turn, receives orders from local party officials. One of the sources of high cost in Soviet agriculture is the fact that decisions about the use of expensive resources, such as fertilizer and labor, are made by people who have poorer information than those who are in the fields and barns. Successful tenurial reform will increase the autonomy of primary producers, making better use of inputs both possible and advantageous.

Demand Side:
Constant Prices and Rising Incomes Exacerbate Shortages

Assurance of inexpensive food for the industrial working class was one of the primary economic objectives of collectivization. Whether collectivization delivered inexpensive food even in the earlier period is debatable. Prices in the state stores were low, but quantities were limited, and excess demand spilled over to the collective farm market, where peasants sold output from private plots at market prices that were much higher due to the poor supply in the collective sector. This dual system on the demand side is still functioning today.

Many developing countries pursue policies intended to supply inexpensive food to the urban working class. By contrast, most middle- and high-income countries protect their agricultural sectors. Many pass a portion of the cost on to consumers in the form of prices higher than those in international trade, although some also invest in productivity-enhancing research that ultimately reduces international prices. The Soviet Union is unusual in that it has kept the rhetorical commitment to inexpensive food for urban people, but has simultaneously committed itself to costly protection and subsidies for many producers that usually characterize countries with per capita incomes higher than those in the Soviet Union. Only recently, with the rapid inflation in the ruble, rise in world trading prices, and control of farm level prices do Soviet producers again appear to be taxed, rather than subsidized, for many commodities.

Paradoxically, despite the enduring commitment to low and stable food prices in the Soviet Union, food absorbs a large share of family disposable income in comparison with middle- and high-income countries today. Families with per capita earnings twice the official poverty level spend on average one-third of disposable income on food. The high proportion of disposable income spent on food makes price increases politically sensitive. Official retail prices for most food items have not increased since 1962, when sporadic riots accompanied an attempt to increase meat prices. Nominal wages have more than doubled in the interval. Consumers are encouraged by distorted official prices to empty the shelves, and they then feel resentful that items they formally can afford (again at official prices) are not available. They then turn to collective farm markets, where products not owed to the state under the quota system are sold at market clearing prices. Prices on the collective farm markets are approximately three times the official prices in state stores.

Most Soviet consumers, and many economists as well, view the ubiquitous shortages and lines as purely supply-side problems. Rising money incomes and constant nominal prices would keep the stores empty even if supply were growing well, which it is not. Tenurial reform, such as the contract system or more radical variants including private ownership of land, have their greatest impact on the supply side of the agricultural economy. They cannot, by themselves, solve problems that originate on the demand side with distorted prices. Lack of attention to the demand side can subvert attempts to implement tenurial reform.

The most highly subsidized items are meat and dairy products. Income elasticities for these foods are high, and the distribution system channels the subsidy toward high-income consumers. The current control of retail food prices is thus both inefficient and regressive. Yet the beneficiaries of the subsidy are people whose political and economic support for perestroika is essential. The Soviet Union belongs to the growing group of countries that have found the economic imperative to change retail food subsidies thwarted by the political imperative not to.

The severity of disequilibrium in food markets and distortions evident on the demand side obscure the fact that the Soviet diet on average is adequate in calories and nutrients and reasonably diverse in the sources of these dietary components. It fares fairly well in international comparisons and is improving slowly. For example, despite chronic shortages, Soviet consumers eat more meat than do Portuguese or Japanese, and do not lag too far behind British and Italian consumers. The Soviet Union lags considerably behind the United States in consumption of meat, but so do most countries of the world, including Western Europe. The Soviet diet is simply not one that Soviet consumers, with their current incomes and current prices, would choose to consume.

The Subsidy: Large and Growing

Contradictions between supply and demand policies have caused a growing subsidy burden and farm debt problem, which together constitute a financial crisis of major proportions. The state pays the difference between high producer prices and lower retail prices as a direct subsidy from the budget. With declining sales of alcohol (a highly taxed item) and rising food production, payments from the budget rise faster than contributions, and the subsidy grows. It is now approximately 90 billion rubles, compared to the total budget deficit of 120 billion rubles.

The subsidy does not include farm indebtedness unless bad debts are written off the bank accounts by transfers from the budget. Farm debt has increased in the 1980s despite the price increase of 1983. In 1988, fully half of the outstanding agricultural debt was rescheduled (72 billion rubles). Of this, 62.8 billion was rescheduled over a long horizon, suggesting that a very large portion is of questionable recovery. Inclusion of uncollectible debts would appreciably increase the already large subsidy.

Farm indebtedness and delayed repayment contribute to the financial constraints that agriculture places on the rest of the economy. The direct subsidy fuels inflation through its contribution to the budget deficit. The indirect subsidy—continued rescheduling of bad debt—also adds to inflation by permitting monetary flows in excess of real flows. The inflation seriously undercuts efforts to introduce better labor incentives throughout the economy; people are reluctant to work harder for rubles that are worth less.

Land Tenure and Soviet Agricultural Reform

Advocates of land reform and tenurial change are often interested in two main issues: improved efficiency of land use and improved access for the poorest rural people to the economic and political power associated with landownership or secure tenure. The current discussion of land tenure and use in the Soviet Union is centered on the former. Distributional issues are important, as they have been throughout the post-Stalin period, but they are secondary to the search for alternative forms of land tenure that are technically more efficient and require fewer subsidies. Changes in land tenure proposed as part of the reform must address the problems of inefficiency, shortage, and financial overextension. Simply transferring title or use rights of land will make little difference unless changes in input and output markets make it both possible and attractive for rural people to become "masters of the land."

The initial proposal for a change in tenure came in the summer of 1988 and again at the March Plenum in 1989 with official promotion of a lease contracting system somewhat similar to the household responsibility system in China. Individuals or small groups of workers negotiate with the manager of a state or collective farm to use a portion of the farm's lands and working capital in exchange for delivery of output to the farm. Workers on lease contracts give up their guaranteed wages and agree to work for residual profits. After the contract is signed, those with leases are to be left alone to make their own managerial decisions.

Contract farming had been in existence before 1988, and even had roots back to the failed reforms of the 1960s. The official blessing in 1988 and 1989 was new, and it was initially expected that endorsement would guarantee implementation. Some farm families are taking out contracts, and attention in the press is lavished upon them. The exodus of people from poor regions of central and northern Russia, Belorussia, and the Baltics now has a small counterflow of homesteaders returning to reclaim abandoned fields and buildings. The sense that finally, after sixty years, there are economic opportunities for ambitious people in the Soviet countryside is tremendously important.

Yet many people are not persuaded that the leasing system is either here to stay or in their interests. Enthusiasm at the grassroots level has been much less than expected. Despite official pressure to show high rates of participation, in 1989 only 6–9 percent of workers in the Russian Republic were working under leases, and many of these appeared to be pro forma contractual arrangements that differed little from traditional payment procedures.

The reservations that many farm workers have about leasing are both legal and economic. Those entering into contracts need assurance that they are legal and that contract enforcement will be more effective than it has been in the past. The decree adopted after the March 1989 meeting improved the stature of the contracts, but ambiguity remains. A new law on contract leasing was issued in draft form for discussion in the summer of 1989. Even with stronger legal guarantees, producers may hesitate to seek contracts because enforcement of disputed commercial contracts in Soviet courts has been historically very weak. Producers well acquainted with the history of contract enforcement put greater stock in the attitude of the local party secretary and the interests of the state or collective farm chairman than in legal guarantees.

The power of the parties entering into leasing agreements is very asymmetric. Many agreements are simply verbal between a farm manager and workers and cannot be legally enforced. Until a legal precedent is established that workers have the right to written contracts, agreements will remain at the discretion of the farm manager.

The Lithuanian Law on Peasant Farming stipulates that citizens of Lithuania who want to establish family farms should apply to the executive committee of the local Council of People's Deputies and request a land allotment. The allotment will be chosen and assessed by a special commission, and the commission's decision will be legally binding. Priority in assignment of particular parcels goes to descendents of those who owned and worked the land prior to collectivization.

The potential landowner or proprietor has more power relative to the current landholder than does a lease applicant. The potential lessee must apply directly to the farm manager and request an allotment, but no third party participates in the negotiations. The draft Land Law at the national level provides for implementation of the redistribution by the deputies of the rural soviet, with consideration of the opinions of the managers of state and collective farms in question. The valuation and distribution of land both through leases and titles of ownership will have a tremendous impact on the distribution of wealth in rural areas and the economic and social viability of tenurial reform.

Leaseholders earn residual profits and give up the right to guaranteed subsidized wages. Workers on poor and indebted farms are unlikely voluntarily to trade secure subsidized wages for earnings both riskier and lower on average. Higher productivity due to better labor incentives alone is not likely to compensate for the foregone wage subsidy. On the wealthier farms, where both earnings and capital stock are higher, many workers could earn more under the leasing system, but farm managers are reluctant to relinquish control over farm assets. Leasing is in this early stage promoted most for poor farms. On some poor farms all land and assets have been leased out to teams and individuals as part of a financial reorganization of chronically weak farms. The parent farm becomes a cooperative of the constituent leaseholders. The few farms that have been reorganized in this way report much improved earnings, but details of the financial restructuring are vague.

There are several different kinds of leasing that differ in the degree of independence the lessee enjoys, how output is marketed, and how the rent is paid. The first is sometimes called targeted leasing. This is the main form for major commercial crops and animal products. It is also the form that gives the lessee least independence and differs least (and sometimes in name only) from early forms of labor organization. The contract stipulates what the lessee will grow. All output is marketed through the parent farm. Machinery and purchased inputs are leased or bought in the same way. The lessee gets credit by borrowing from the parent farm, and does not have an independent account. Rent is usually paid on a share basis, either as a share of the gross value of output or a share of net profits. The shares are established in the bargaining when the contract is drawn up.

The lessee on a targeted contract has as much autonomy as the collective or state farm chairman chooses to grant. It is difficult to see how this kind of contract could be meaningfully negotiated over a long horizon, such as the recommended twenty-five years. The substance of the contract is not the lessee's right to use the land, but the conditions attached in the form of prices, input supplies, and marketed quantities. These cannot be set for twenty-five years, and this contract, even at its best, would be a renewable short-term contract.

The other kind of contract now in discussion and rare use is called a free contract. This is more common in production of fruits, berries, vegetables, flowers, and livestock products on lands distant from densely settled areas. Producers with a free contract usually pay a fixed rent per hectare and per head of leased livestock. They market their output directly, although they may sell to collective or state farms as well as to other outlets. They carry their own accounts for credit at the state agricultural bank and have more autonomy to manage their own affairs than do producers on targeted contracts. They also accept more risk. These leases can meaningfully be written for long periods, although the rate of the fixed rent may change at given intervals. The maximum period allowable for a contract is now fifty years.

Setting the rental rate is important and controversial for both targeted and free contracts. Under the targeted contract, the price at which the lessee sells output to the farm is less than the price at which the farm resells it, and the difference is the rental payment. The higher productivity expected from leasing is split between the workers and the parent farm. The percentage split depends on who pays for investment and how social overhead costs, such as schools and cafeterias, are covered. Alternatively, lessees on targeted contracts can sell output to the farm at the same price at which the farm will resell it, and then pay a share of net profits (suggested as one-third) as rent.

Fixed rents for free contracts are reported to range from 100 rubles per hectare in the poor non–black-soil regions of the northwest to 2,000 rubles per hectare for irrigated land in Central Asia. The fixed rents are in fact determined simply by bargaining between a farm manager who has land he is willing to lease and a potential leaseholder. Recommended methodologies for calculating rents have not been useful, either because the procedures are wrong, or because they are based on uncertain quantities such as potential yield or profit. Confusion and uncertainty about how to value assets in a lease contract have contributed to the general reluctance to pursue them, and the agricultural economics profession has contributed little advice on this subject.

Contracting in the Soviet context differs from the Chinese experience in the early years of the household responsibility system. Soviet farms are specialized in their output and dependent on purchased inputs. The marketing function that the parent farm fulfills or does not fulfill for the lessee can make or break the contract independently of the diligence of the operator. Input markets are more important for Chinese producers today than they were in 1978 because use of yield-enhancing purchased inputs has increased. However, efficient delivery of inputs is even more critical for Soviet lessees because of their greater specialization.

Although the contracting system may be more difficult to implement in the Soviet Union than in China, the Soviets may have some advantages as well. The land-to-labor ratios in most parts of the Soviet Union are much better than in China, and individual leaseholds or private holdings can be assigned that are not fragmented strips. Labor mobility in the Soviet Union is very high except in Central Asia.

Many rural workers displaced by higher labor productivity in agriculture will find jobs in growing middle-sized cities and towns, although the ease of transition will depend on location and conditions in the urban labor markets. The collective and state farms will remain for the near future, at least, and can oversee maintenance and expansion of rural infrastructure and input supply if they withdraw in part or whole from production. The Soviet state does not have a clear political and social agenda for rural people, such as the Chinese emphasis on family planning and limitations on geographic mobility, with which to encumber the contract system or land redistribution. On the other hand, years of Soviet investment in the technology of large-scale production limit the divisibility of existing capital stock.

The leasing system, or the more radical privatization, if implemented, can address one major source of high costs of collectivized agriculture—poor labor incentives. Both will work best if monopoly in marketing, both of input and output, is reduced. The monopolies were put in place as part of the auxiliary set of economic relations supporting collective land tenure in its earlier form and function. Unfortunately, the decision to allow greater diversity of land tenure and management does not automatically undo the monopolization of marketing channels. This continues to be a source of high cost and a limitation on the extent of tenurial reform.

Financial Remedies: Few Options

High costs of production and stable retail prices have created a large and growing subsidy. The subsidy, in turn, and concern about its growth, have increased reliance on indebtedness to keep poor farms in business, rather than giving them still higher prices or outright grants, because both higher prices and grants would appear immediately in the subsidy accounts. Supply-side improvement that brings down costs of production will ease the financial crisis, as will the eventual and inevitable increase in retail food prices. These are both, however, medium- or long-term solutions to an immediate crisis. What can be done to improve finances at the farm and macrolevels now?

Farms that are bankrupt are to be given two years grace in which to improve their finances. According to a recently announced timetable, if they remain insolvent in 1991, they may be declared bankrupt, and their assets offered on lease to anyone who will take them. If full privatization is allowed, bankrupt farms could be sold off, and the proceeds might offset a good portion of the accumulated debt. Conservatives who seek to defend collectivized agriculture against reforms denounce bankruptcy as a violation of the social contract with the agricultural work force. The emphasis on regional self-sufficiency adds fuel to the controversy over bankruptcy; local leaders will fight to keep high-cost farms operating if the rhetoric of regional or republican autarky prevails.

In his speech in March 1989, Gorbachev ruled out a large-scale write-off of farm debt, arguing that a budget already in deficit could not afford it. In December 1989, however, a massive write-off of 73.5 billion rubles was announced. This is approximately half of the total farm debt.

Changes in procurement prices will affect supply and finance at the farm and aggregate level. Prices and credit have been the instruments for delivering the subsidy to farms, and output prices have been so finely differentiated as to differ on a farm-by-farm basis. Farms have traditionally not paid land rent, and differentiated output prices were intended to incorporate a land tax or rent. With the deterioration of farm finances in the 1970s and 1980s, a number of special premiums were added onto the differentiated base prices. In the current reform, output prices are to be raised to compensate for removal of the input subsidies, although the timing of the change is now unclear. Price zones are to be expanded, and uniform prices reflecting marginal costs of production within zones are to prevail. Farms will pay a land tax or land-use fee differentiated according to the quality of land, but the tax rate and methodology for its calculation are not yet determined.

Once prices are set in the procurement price revision, they are to be adjusted over time with a parity price index incorporating changes in prices of a basket of inputs. The revised procurement prices will apply to commodities purchased by the state under quota. Sales outside of quota will flow through expanding wholesale trade at negotiated prices. If the reform is successful, quotas will be reduced and wholesale prices as well as state procurement prices will affect producers' decisions.

The price reform is intimately linked to contract farming and tenurial reform. Land rents, valuation, terms of contracts, and profitability of contract or other individual farming will vary according to decisions made about the new price structure, both relative prices and price levels, and the timetable chosen for its implementation. The new price structure will also influence the pace of expansion of wholesale trade and marketing channels outside the state monopolies.

International Trade in Food

The maturation of collectivized agriculture in the Soviet Union after 1965 had a number of profound effects on world trade in food. Rising incomes and stable retail prices stimulated demand for food. The postwar generation reached adulthood in the late 1960s, and they were less willing than their parents and grandparents to sacrifice current consumption for past calamities or future promises. Brezhnev and his colleagues embarked on the modernization campaign in recognition that growth in demand was outpacing that of supply.

The performance of the agricultural sector in the late 1960s was good, in part because the additional fertilizer, machinery, and higher wages boosted output, in part because weather was unusually favorable, and in part because Khrushchev's peripatetic campaigns gave way to steady and relentless investment. In 1971 Brezhnev and his colleagues decided to increase domestic herds and meat production, temporarily importing grain for feed until domestic grain production grew to match the new higher feed requirements. Large Soviet purchases in 1972 and 1973, when world supply was tight, marked the entry of the Soviet Union into grain markets as a large net importer.

By the mid-1970s the modernization campaign had faltered, although investment continued. The Soviets, unable to exit from grain markets without abandoning the goal of higher domestic meat consumption, became regular purchasers of large and variable quantities of grain. Grain imports were followed by imports of sugar, oilseeds, dairy products, and meat, as domestic demand outgrew supply in these markets as well. From a position of roughly balanced agricultural trade in the 1960s, the Soviet Union ranked in the 1970s and 1980s among the world's largest net importers of agricultural products.

The trading behavior of the Soviet Union was an outgrowth of the performance of collectivized agriculture in a middle-income economy. Demand for agricultural products grew rapidly with income growth and urbanization, but growth in supply was slow and expensive. The Soviets turned to world markets to cover part of the gap, and paid for purchases with earnings from energy exports. The surge in energy prices allowed the Soviet Union to retain institutional barriers to more efficient agriculture into the late 1980s.

Several Eastern European countries, notably Poland, followed a similar course of import expansion during the 1970s. The emergence of the Soviet Union as a major hard-currency food importer meant that countries in Eastern Europe and the developing world that had followed the Soviet model of agricultural development could not rely on the Soviet Union for major shipments of food aid or soft-currency trade in food. Many of these countries, too, became net importers of commercial or concessionary food.

Comparison of the Soviet Reform
and Developments in Poland and Hungary

Poland and Hungary are important agricultural countries of Eastern Europe, and developments in their food economies influence the food balances of the region. Moreover, each holds significant lessons for understanding the potential for and problems with tenurial changes in the Soviet Union.

Eighty percent of Polish agricultural land is privately owned and farmed in smallholdings averaging approximately ten hectares for full-time farmers, and less than half that for part-time farmers. There are few constraints on ownership, sale, rental, and inheritance of land. Until recently, private farms in the eastern part of the country could not exceed fifty hectares and in the western part one hundred hectares, but few farms approached that size, and the restriction has been rescinded. Compulsory deliveries to state procurement organs were dropped in the early 1970s, and producers can choose whether to market their products to the state procurement organs or on the private market.

State procurement prices have in recent years been linked to farm incomes through a formula, the intent of which is to achieve a measure of income parity between agricultural and nonagricultural workers. Products sold to the state are processed and offered to consumers at subsidized retail prices. State procurement prices are lower than prices farmers receive if they sell on the private market, but the gap between state and market prices at the farm level is much smaller than the gap at the retail level.

The state has used a number of instruments to induce farmers to deliver products to the procurement organs instead of the free market. Most important among these has been the state monopoly on input supply. Private farmers pay higher prices for inputs than do the state farms, and delivery even at higher prices is often tied to sales of output to the state. Pensions for private farmers are also linked to sales to the state over the farmer's working lifetime. Beginning in 1990, the state will make its purchases at market prices.

Polish private farmers have the microeconomic incentives of private utility maximizing producers. The incentives to work hard and reduce costs are those that would obtain under the most radical proposals for tenurial reform in the Soviet Union—full private ownership and long-term fixed rent leaseholds. A tenurial system with incentives promoting efficiency has not been adequate to promote high productivity in Polish private agriculture, and the Polish experience illustrates the limits of tenurial reform within the agricultural sector of a centrally planned economy.

Although most Polish farmers have private ownership of the land they farm, private farmers have had limited access to purchased inputs and credit, and have faced high marketing costs if they chose to market outside the state channels. The large number of private farmers and a well-developed private market make output markets relatively competitive, whereas input markets are highly concentrated. Most proposals for price reform in the Soviet Union and Eastern Europe imply increased discretion in price setting for enterprises that produce agricultural inputs, but do little to reduce monopoly in these industries. Private producers will be caught in the middle, and the result may be a combination of lower farm income, higher rates of exodus from farming, and transfer of resources out of products that use more expensive inputs intensively.

Hungary fully collectivized between 1949 and 1961 through both coercion and voluntary incentives, but after 1965 encouraged diversity of landholding, including large state and cooperative farms and expanded private plots and auxiliary farms. The diversity of landholding after 1965 was combined with a large degree of farm autonomy. In fact, the emphasis was on autonomy and improved incentives for the collective farms, and only secondarily on changes in land tenure, such as contract farming and private enterprises.

Lessons from the Hungarian experience should be drawn cautiously. Hungary is a small country for which trade is essential. It can benefit from specialization in products for which it has a comparative advantage only if exchange-rate policy does not greatly inhibit trade. Trade is also important for the Soviet Union, but many advantages of regional agricultural specialization can be realized even prior to liberalization of exchange-rate policies. The transition to more decentralized agricultural management and diversity in landholding began fifteen years after the first wave of collectivization in Hungary, and sixty years after collectivization in the Soviet Union. Moreover, Soviet leaders have taken an interest in the Hungarian experience, but shown little inclination to emulate it.

Nonetheless, with these caveats, several observations on the Hungarian experience may be relevant to reform in other centrally planned economies, including the Soviet Union. Introduction of diversity in landholding and various forms of contracting has not led to rapid and near total privatization, as was the case in China. Most agricultural workers are still employees of state or collective farms, and these large units are autonomous firms regulated indirectly through tax, credit, price, and exchange-rate policy. Ivan Szelenyi has studied the career paths of people who chose in the 1980s to leave cooperative and state farms and operate market-oriented entrepreneurial minifarms.[2] This is a special group of people, and not a large one, although their numbers increased in the 1980s. Many more people, according to Szelenyi, combine employment in the state sector, including in nonagricultural work, or on collective farms with family sideline minifundia.

These small part-time farms are increasingly oriented toward production for the market. They differ from the tiny "victory garden" plots that Soviet nonfarm workers are encouraged to maintain, because Hungarian employees, unlike Soviet workers, more often live in the countryside and commute to nonagricultural jobs. Soviet workers, in contrast, trek long distances to their tiny plots, and cannot keep livestock with no one to tend the animals over the work days.

Hungarian agricultural workers have for more than a decade been able to choose between the risk and hard work of individual entrepreneurship and employment on a reasonably competently managed, economically autonomous collective farm. Many choose to stay with the collectives. They use the more liberal policies toward private activity to expand their own household subsidiary operations, and market more of their output, but rarely become full-time independent operators. Another group of agricultural workers has not only stayed with the state and collective farms, but abandoned household production for the market altogether, despite the greater legal opportunity to engage in private activities.

Hungarian aggregate statistics show a decline in the proportion of total output originating in the private sector over the 1970s and early 1980s, and an increase in the share originating in the collective sector. Szelenyi argues that complex shifts in the structure of private agriculture give the sector a dynamism masked by the aggregate statistics, as more production comes from explicitly market oriented minifarms and auxiliary plots rather than from the rare private producers who resisted collectivization. Moreover, costs of production in the collective sector for both crops and livestock products have risen in the 1980s. If this trend continues, Hungarian collective farm managers could feel some of the same pressures that their Soviet counterparts now face to hold down wages and adopt tenurial forms embodying better incentives. If that happens, workers may shift more labor to their family operations, or become full-time entrepreneurs.

The increased autonomy of Hungarian collective farms has allowed some to specialize in applied research and extension, offering packages of new technology to client farms on a commercial basis. The packages often include purchased inputs as well as advice, and this development has introduced a degree of competition into the marketing of inputs. The legacy of state monopolization of input supply remains, however, and private farmers and those working on contract complain about access to inputs and credit.

Despite the undisputed success of the Hungarian decentralization since 1965, costs of production, particularly for animal products, remain high, and until recently the state subsidized retail food prices substantially to cover the difference. The subsidy is a smaller share of the Hungarian state budget than is the case in the Soviet Union. Moreover, Hungarian output is adequate to meet domestic demand even at subsidized prices, so that the chronic excess demand and shortages evident everywhere in Eastern Europe are notably absent in Hungary. However, as argued above, rising costs of production may put pressure on the Hungarian land-tenure system.

Conclusions

The maturation of collectivized agriculture in Eastern Europe, the Soviet Union, China, and the developing world has significantly altered the geographic pattern of production, consumption, and trade in food. This is one of the more important developments in the world agricultural economy in the postwar period. Agricultural reform in the centrally planned economies, if successful, can be expected to have a correspondingly large impact on world agriculture. The effect will be a complex one, as flows of commodities, technology, and processing equipment and services adjust to changes in production and markets in these countries.

An important component of successful reform in the Soviet Union will be new forms of landholding and management embodying incentives for efficient use of land and labor. These will include various forms of contract leasing and full private ownership, along with more autonomy and financial responsibility for collective and state farms. Leaseholders have widely varying degrees of autonomy from the parent farm, and accept varying degrees of risk. At one extreme are contract teams that are simply old production brigades renamed to suit the rhetoric of perestroika. At the other are genuine agricultural entrepreneurs working under a tenurial form almost like private ownership of land, were the property right to be formalized and legally defended. Full-fledged private operators can be expected to begin to appear in 1990, if momentum for change in the Land Law continues. The demand for privately owned land may be much greater than the demand for leased land, although the economic conditions for agricultural production under the two forms differ little. The current excess supply of money and excess demand for other assets can be expected to create a very active land market. Restrictive conditions limiting the ownership right can reduce the speculative demand for land, but will also limit its efficient use. Expansion of credit for private purchasers will be necessary if a large group of farm employees are to have opportunities to expand private holdings or become full independent operators.

The attractiveness of newer forms of tenure and their productivity advantage over the old system depend on changes made in the markets for other agricultural inputs, particularly labor, credit, and purchased inputs. Workers will be less enthusiastic about opportunities for leases if they can continue to earn subsidized wages for indifferent work on state and collective farms and have trouble spending even those earnings on consumer goods that appeal to them. Ambitious, energetic, and skilled workers who could best take advantage of leasing will be dissuaded if the progressive form of land tenure is tied to the most backward and decrepit technology, as is the case when contract farmers are denied modern inputs suitable for small-scale operations.

The Polish, Soviet, and Hungarian experiences demonstrate that land tenure is important, and that improvements in efficiency of land use and labor incentives can be achieved only with corollary changes in interlinked agrarian markets. Poland has managed to hobble its large private sector, and has forgone many of the potential gains of land tenure embodying better incentives. Hungary has granted a large degree of autonomy to state farms and cooperatives, and has shed some of the most dysfunctional aspects of collectivized agriculture. The state and collective farms appear to have survived in the changed economic environment without pressure either from their members and employees or from the state budget adequate to force them into a different form of tenure with incentives for lower costs of production. Rising costs of production on collective farms in the 1980s may disturb this balance, and bring a new round of tenurial reform in Hungary in the 1990s.

After sixty years of collectivized agriculture in the Soviet Union, the country has entered a transition to a set of as yet unknown postcollectivist institutions. Their emergence is of considerable import both to those who seek to understand how and why institutions change and to those who will live in the world shaped in part by postcollectivist agriculture.

Notes

1. See Pranab Bardhan, *The Economic Theory of Agrarian Institutions* (New York: Oxford University Press, 1989).

2. Ivan Szelenyi, *Socialist Entrepreneurs: Embourgeoisement in Rural Hungary* (Madison: University of Wisconsin Press, 1988).

Selected Bibliography

Alchian, Armen A., and Harold Demsetz. "Production, Information Costs, and Economic Organization." *American Economic Review*, 62 (1972): 777–795.

Bardhan, Pranab. *The Economic Theory of Agrarian Institutions*. New York: Oxford University Press, 1989.

Boev, Vasillii R. *Razvitie arendnykh i podriadnykh otnoshenii v agropromyshlennom komplekse*. Moscow: VNIESKh, 1989.

Currie, J. M. *The Economic Theory of Agricultural Land Tenure*. Cambridge: Cambridge University Press, 1981.

Davies, R. W. *The Socialist Offensive*. Cambridge, Mass.: Harvard University Press, 1980.

Johnson, D. Gale, and Karen McConnell Brooks. *Prospects for Soviet Agriculture in the 1980s*. Bloomington, Ind.: Indiana University Press, 1983.

Lewin, Moshe. *Russian Peasants and Soviet Power*. Evanston, Ill.: Northwestern University Press, 1968.

Lin, Justin Yifu. "The Household Responsibility System in China's Agricultural Reform: A Theoretical and Empirical Study." *Economic Development and Cultural Change* 36, no. 3S (1988): 199.

Marrese, Michael. "Hungarian Agriculture: Moving in the Right Direction." *East European Economies: Slow Growth in the 1980s*, vol. 3. Joint Economic Committee, Congress of the United States, 1986.

Medvedev, Zhores. *Soviet Agriculture*. New York: W. W. Norton, 1987.

Millar, James R. "Soviet Rapid Development and the Agricultural Surplus Hypothesis." *Soviet Studies* 22 (July 1970).

Miller, Robert F. *100,000 Tractors*. Cambridge, Mass.: Harvard University Press, 1970.

Nove, Alec. "The Contribution of Agriculture to Accumulation in the 1930s." Economic History Workshop Paper #8384-15, University of Chicago, 1984.

———. *An Economic History of the Soviet Union*. New York: Penguin Books, 1976.

Ofer, Gur. "Soviet Economic Growth: 1928–1985." *Journal of Economic Literature* 25, no. 4 (1987): 1767-1833.

"Polozhenie ob ekonomicheskikh i organizatsionnykh osnovakh arendnykh otnoshenii v SSSR." *Ekonomicheskaia gazeta*, no. 19 (May 1989): 7.

Rembisz, Wlodzimierz. "Some Constraints on Introducing Free Market Regulation Into Private Farming in Poland." Department of Agricultural and Applied Economics, University of Minnesota, Staff Paper P89-13, 1989.

Semenov, V. "Sovershenstvovanie finansogo mekhanizma agropromyshlennogo kompleksa." *Ekonomika sel'skogo khoziaistva*, no. 9 (1987): 31–39.

———. *Prodovol'stvennaia programma i finansy*. Moscow: Finansy i statistika, 1985.

Sertel, Murat. *Workers and Incentives*. Amsterdam: North-Holland, 1982.

Szelenyi, Ivan. *Socialist Entrepreneurs: Embourgeoisement in Rural Hungary*. Madison: University of Wisconsin Press, 1988.

Vanous, Jan (ed.). *PlanEcon Report*, 4, no. 41 (November 4, 1988).

"Vokrug problemy potrebitel'skikh tsen." *Ekonomika i organizatsiia promyshlennogo proizvodstva* 12 (1986): 140.

Volin, Lazar. *A Century of Russian Agriculture.* Cambridge, Mass.: Harvard University Press, 1970.

Wadekin, Karl-Eugen. *The Private Sector in Soviet Agriculture.* Translated by K. Bush. Berkeley: University of California Press, 1973.

part four

Southern Africa

chapter nine

Ten Years After: Land Redistribution in Zimbabwe, 1980-1990

Michael Bratton

Summary

Ten years after political independence, the Zimbabwe government has undertaken a creditable measure of land redistribution but has yet to achieve a thorough land reform. Large areas of commercial farmland, far more extensive than in Kenya, have been transferred to peasant small-holders. Some of these small-holders have been able to intensify agricultural production, particularly of maize, calling into question dire predictions that land resettlement in Zimbabwe will result in a loss of national food security. On the negative side, resettlement has been implemented mostly in ecological zones of intermediate or marginal agricultural potential. Commercial farmers continue to own the prime farmland in the northeast of the country and to produce the export commodities, notably tobacco, upon which the government and economy depend for foreign exchange. Peasant farmers, for their part, have yet to obtain secure and enforceable land rights on settlement schemes that are owned and controlled by the state.

This chapter summarizes the history of land distribution and the current debates on land reform in Zimbabwe. To this well-known material the author contributes new analysis on: (1) the extent of landlessness in Zimbabwe's peasant farming areas; (2) the reemergence of the land issue as a political and policy issue in the late 1980s; (3) the legal, financial, administrative, and political factors constraining the land redistribution program; and (4) policy proposals implementable under an amended constitution after April 1990. The author argues for accelerating land acquisition, implementing more intensive land-resettlement models, and guaranteeing secure tenure rights to resettled family farmers.

Ten years of political independence have not assuaged the hunger for land among peasant farmers in Zimbabwe. If anything, population pressure and land degradation in the rural areas are more severe in 1990 than they were in 1980. To date, the government of Zimbabwe has responded in an ambiguous fashion to a widespread problem of landlessness. Its program to reallocate agricultural land from white commercial farmers to black peasant farmers has resulted in the transfer of substantial tracts of land and the planned movement of large numbers of people. But to date the land redistribution program in Zimbabwe has fallen far short of the transformation of property rights and agricultural production structures that was envisioned by many of Robert Mugabe's supporters.

As the first decade of independence draws to a close, the time is ripe to reflect on past constraints and future opportunities in Zimbabwe's land-resettlement program. What has been achieved to date? Why has progress been so mixed? How does Zimbabwe's record appear in comparative perspective, particularly in relation to Kenya, another former white settler colony? What can now be done?

In endeavoring to answer these questions, this chapter reviews and engages the current debates about land policy in this southern African country. First, there is the issue of economic growth versus social equity. Is it possible to redistribute land from commercial to peasant producers without incurring a negative impact on national food surpluses and agricultural export revenues? Second, there is the issue of political interests. Has the land acquisition and settlement program been impeded by international diplomatic and donor pressures, and by large-farm interests—white and black—within the domestic political arena? And finally, there is the issue of timing. Will the anticipated removal in 1990 of constitutional prohibitions on certain forms of land transfer enable the Zimbabwe government to breathe new life into a land-reform program? The chapter concludes with a discussion of the policy options presently before the government and some suggestions as to which are desirable, feasible, and likely.

Before we begin, a note on terminology. In this chapter, the term "land redistribution" is used in a limited sense to refer to programs of land acquisition, transfer, and settlement. It is distinguished from the term "land reform," which includes all of the above programs, but also involves changes in land-tenure laws to enable agricultural producers to obtain secure and enforceable rights in land. "Agrarian reform" is the most comprehensive term of all, embracing not only land reform but also the implementation of support services for agriculture and rural development.

Background: Agricultural Performance

Zimbabwe stands out as an agricultural success story among African countries because of the productivity of its small farmers and a regular ability to feed itself. The government imported maize, Zimbabwe's staple grain, only once over the past decade: in 1984, in the wake of the longest sustained period of drought on record. Since 1985, Zimbabwe has enjoyed the security of a domestically produced maize stockpile, amounting at peak to 1.6 million metric tons, or approximately two years' consumption. By 1986, agricultural planners, concerned with overproduction, cut price incentives to discourage large-scale farmers from producing maize and to steer them toward export crops. Because Zimbabwe is the largest agricultural exporter in the Southern Africa Development Coordination Conference (SADCC), it has been chartered by its fellow member-states to take responsibility for planning for food security for the region.

Agriculture is the engine of Zimbabwe's economic development. Although it accounts for only 12 percent of total production in a diversified economy, the agricultural sector sets the pace for growth in the manufacturing and service sectors. This reflects the critical export contribution of cash crops, which account for over 40 percent of total foreign exchange earnings, almost half of which come from tobacco. Moreover, the base of the agricultural sector is broad, with approximately 70 percent of the population gaining their primary means of livelihood from the land. Rural dwellers are primarily agriculturalists, but they also obtain significant amounts of household income from off-farm and nonagricultural employment.

It is perhaps surprising that Zimbabwe's farmers have performed as well as they have, for the country's natural resource endowment is unexceptional. Like other parts of southern Africa, Zimbabwe has a dry climate with rainfall inadequate or too variable for crop production over much of the land area. In general, Zimbabwe's rainfall decreases from north to south, from east to west, and from high to low altitudes. The prime agricultural land, which receives over 710 mm of rainfall per year and is suitable for intensive mixed farming, is located in the northeastern highlands. This land—known as Natural Regions I and II in the official agro-ecological classification—constitutes a mere 17 percent of the total area available for agriculture. The remaining agricultural land receives lower rainfall and is susceptible to severe dry spells in the middle of the growing season (Natural Region III) or to frequent droughts (Natural Regions IV and V). Land-use potential over most of Zimbabwe is therefore intermediate, being limited to the semi-intensive cultivation of drought-resistant crops, or marginal, suitable only for low-intensity grazing of livestock.

Background: Land Distribution

The distribution of land at the time of independence was a product of the British imperial strategy to set aside Southern Rhodesia as a haven for permanent European settlement. Once it became apparent that the colony did not possess mineral wealth on the same glittering scale as neighboring South Africa, the British and settler authorities sought to develop Southern Rhodesia as an agricultural exporter. Land was divided on racial lines, and Africans were legally prohibited from acquiring or occupying real estate in the well-watered highlands. Through a series of statutes—the Southern Rhodesia Order in Council of 1898, the Land Apportionment Act of 1930, the Native Land Husbandry Act of 1951, and the Land Tenure Act of 1969—Africans were evicted from their traditional landholdings and shunted into tribal reserves. Within these reserves, the colonial government used the coercive power of the state to create new patterns of production and exchange. Taxation was used to draw adult African males out of the reserves to serve as a labor force on large-scale European farms, and the population who remained behind, composed disproportionately of women, children, and the elderly, were subjected to compulsory regulations about the use of arable, residential, and grazing lands.

By the end of the colonial period, therefore, Zimbabwe possessed a deeply rooted agrarian structure with a dramatically dualistic form. In 1980, there were two major agricultural subsectors: a commercial subsector and a peasant subsector. The commercial subsector was governed by freehold land tenure and comprised 6,000 white farms on large-holdings averaging 2,500 hectares. The owners of these farms were either European settler families or agribusiness corporations, both domestic and international. Although these farm units accounted for 0.1 percent of total holdings, they covered some 15.3 million hectares, or 39 percent of the total land area. The peasant subsector was governed by usufruct tenure in which traditional authorities distributed cultivation rights to members of kinship communities. This sector contained about 750,000 households in 1980, or more than half of the national population, on small-holdings of 2 to 4 hectares of arable land plus common grazing. These parts of Zimbabwe, constituting some 16.3 million hectares or 42 percent of the land, are now known as the "communal areas." Arthur Hazlewood, recalling Zimbabwe's similarities to Kenya, describes "a striking contrast between the densely settled and farmed African land and the sparsely settled and underutilised European areas."[1]

Land was unevenly distributed between the races on the basis of quality as well as quantity. Whereas 30 percent of the commercial farmland was situated on the well-watered highlands (Natural Regions I and II), only 9 percent of the peasant farming areas (communal areas) were so favorably located. Indeed, almost all the land allocated to peasants was in the semiarid lowlands that make up the zones of lowest agricultural potential (Natural Regions III–V). The meager natural resource base of these areas was reinforced by their remoteness from the country's physical and institutional infrastructure. Peasants were unable to obtain access to the sophisticated network of agricultural services—research, extension, credit, transport, and marketing—that was established to encourage white commercial farmers to adopt modern farming techniques and to produce commodities for sale.

Because of the advantages bestowed by colonial agrarian policy, the commercial farm subsector came to dominate agricultural production in Zimbabwe. By 1980, commercial farmers produced an estimated 75 percent of total agricultural output and 96 percent of agricultural sales. Combining high technology with cheap labor, commercial farmers were able to obtain impressive yields of maize, averaging 4.2 metric tons per hectare, and to establish market niches in world trade for their high-quality, hand-picked cotton and tobacco. They generated over a quarter of a million agricultural jobs, almost one-third of the work force employed by the formal sector of the economy in 1980.

But alongside with profitable commercial operations, peasant farmers found increasing difficulty in eking a livelihood from the overcrowded reserves. On marginal land and in dry years, peasant producers were unable to meet household subsistence requirements; only if the rains were good might some farmers have small surpluses of maize or groundnuts to sell on local markets. Among the many constraints to increased production was the lack of facilities to store water for crops and livestock. Despite colonial efforts at land-use planning, the status of the peasant farming areas of Southern Rhodesia deteriorated badly between 1950 and 1980. With a human population growth rate above 3 percent and faster increases in livestock numbers, soil erosion and declining soil fertility were widespread. The population-carrying capacity of land under existing agricultural practices was exceeded in approximately two-thirds of the total peasant farming area. This ecological imbalance further impaired the natural potential of land that was marginal from the beginning for agricultural purposes.

Land therefore became a hot political issue. The organizers of nationalist political parties found that they could easily exploit peasant grievances over lands lost to white settlement. This is not to say land was the only concern driving the nationalist movement—the need for education and employment and resistance to agricultural regulation also were important—but land was a potent symbol that conveniently summarized the indignities of colonial rule. Ultimately, when all avenues of peaceful protest were closed, the nationalist parties adopted a strategy of armed struggle. During the 1970s, the peasant population bore the brunt of the convulsive civil war between the Rhodesian regime and the guerrilla fighters of the Zimbabwe African National Union–Zimbabwe African People's Union (ZANU-ZAPU) Patriotic Front. By the end of the colonial period, a rapidly expanding peasant population was bitterly estranged from the central government and precariously balanced on an eroded and deteriorating natural resource base. Clearly, once a majority African government could come to power, something would have to be done about land reform.

Landlessness

The extent of landlessness in Zimbabwe is difficult to estimate, due not only to a paucity of comprehensive and reliable data, but also to the complex structure of Zimbabwean society. In the context of labor migration and nonagricultural employment, individuals may have more than one occupation and households may have several sources of income; therefore, it is not always clear as to who should be counted as an agriculturalist, or who is actually landless.

One measure of landlessness covers "those who cultivate land without having . . . ownership or ownership-like rights."[2] In practice, this means tenant farmers and agricultural laborers. In effect, however, there are no tenant farmers in Zimbabwe; the strict laws of racial segregation in land allocation prohibited white farmers from subdividing their land and leasing it to black tenants in return for rent or a share of the crop. There are, however, large numbers of agricultural wage-laborers who work on white-owned farms: their numbers peaked in 1974 at 210,000 permanent workers and 110,000 temporary workers. But it would be misleading to assume that all these workers are landless because an unknown proportion are migrants with families and landholdings in the communal areas. Moreover, a large proportion of agricultural workers, perhaps as many as one-third, are not Zimbabwean nationals but migrants from Mozambique and Malawi who should not be counted in any calculation of the numbers of landless people in Zimbabwe.

Most important, the essence of landlessness in Zimbabwe is missed by a definition that excludes persons living in the overcrowded communal areas who have no land, little land, or poor-quality land. According to a national household survey, between 6 percent and 12 percent of the peasant population are entirely without access to assets in land, with the variation in these figures due to differences in the degree of landlessness in different administrative provinces. Landlessness is most severe in Mashonaland East in the northeastern highlands, and least severe in Midlands and the Matabeleland provinces of the southwest. The landless are either young men above school age who have not inherited a plot from their families, or widows and divorcees who have been deprived of access to the holdings of their former husbands. The true extent of landlessness in the communal areas may be partially disguised because young people now remain at home longer and delay setting up their own farms. And the problem will be exacerbated when the postindependence generation comes of age and begins demanding its own plots.

Already the parcels of land held by peasant households may be too small or too degraded to provide a decent livelihood. People in such households may be described as the "near-landless." Their economic needs and political grievances are substantially similar to those who are entirely landless. It is commonly claimed that peasants in Zimbabwe need 5 hectares of arable land to meet subsistence and basic income requirements; more than half of rural households have less than this amount. Actually, the minimum size of a viable holding varies markedly by agro-ecological zone: a two-hectare plot may provide surpluses above subsistence in the highlands, but much more than five hectares may be required simply to survive in the lowveld. A hectare of virgin red soil in Mashonaland will have far greater productive potential than a hectare of overgrazed sandy soil in Masvingo. Thus, detailed data on holding size and land quality by household are required in order to estimate soundly the extent of near-landlessness nationwide.

Indeed, any figures that purport to record the extent of land hunger in Zimbabwe must be treated with extreme caution. One can do no more than provide a "guesstimate" of households needing land in 1980 by adding together the truly landless—meaning households of agricultural laborers, peasant farmers with less than one hectare of arable land, and households displaced by the independence war—and the near-landless. By this method we can derive guesstimates of 180,000 truly landless households and 150,000 near-landless households. In total, 330,000 households had an objective need for at least some land in 1980. This amounted to 36 percent of the total agricultural population and 32 percent of the total national population.[3]

Landlessness among peasants in Zimbabwe is accompanied by shortages of other factors required for agricultural production. In many communal areas, farmers cite factors other than land, such as shortages of draft power, tools, inputs, or labor, as their main production constraints. Thus, the agricultural productivity and welfare of rural families also hinges critically on the availability of wage remittances from towns and the size of the household cattle herd. Especially in households where the adult male is away and the children are in school, women farming alone do not have enough labor to make use of a bigger plot. Finally, those farmers with at least some land are interested principally in gaining access to pasture, forests, and other "common" holdings. They may seek a "better"—meaning not overworked, or closer to market—piece of arable land for household crop production, but they do not always seek a larger one.

Issues in Land Redistribution

The starting point for the debate about land reform in Zimbabwe is whether to transfer white-owned commercial farms to black peasant farmers, and, if so, how much land? The logic of land redistribution is compelling in a situation where peasant holdings are denuded and overworked, and where tracts of commercial land are unused or used to less than full potential.

Analysis of land-policy options therefore has come to hinge on two technical questions. First, what is the extent of land utilization? In other words, what is the proportion of the land in each agricultural subsector that is actually cropped or grazed? Second, how efficiently is this land used? What returns can be obtained from investments in land under commercial, peasant, or other production systems?

The opponents of land redistribution in Zimbabwe argue that the utmost caution should be exercised in transferring land from commercial farmers to inexperienced operators because of the risks posed to aggregate agricultural output.[4] They typically warn that national food self-sufficiency could be lost and export revenues curtailed if land is taken out of commercial production. They argue that land in the northeast highlands has already been put into a sustainable program of cropping and fallow, and that the remainder is required for livestock production to meet Zimbabwe's beef quota to the European Economic Community. Intensive patterns of production are said to prevail on prime farmland, with little margin for increased productivity. In sum, the opponents of reform pose an ineluctable trade-off between the goal of equity in land distribution and the goal of economic growth.

The proponents of land redistribution argue that the goals of growth and equity do not necessarily conflict.[5] They accept that the commercial subsector will continue to contribute to national agricultural production for the foreseeable future. But they see opportunities to transfer substantial portions of commercial farmland without impairing that contribution. They demonstrate that only one-third of the net arable land in Mashonaland (Region II) is being used for cropping and fallow, and they suggest that the proportion of cropped land is even lower in the zones of intermediate agricultural potential (Region III), where many commercial farms are inefficient and financially unsound. The total area of underutilized land therefore could be as high as 2 million hectares nationwide. The proponents of land reform see unexploited opportunities to target this land for mixed farming by resettled peasant farmers. Much of the disagreement between the two sides hinges on whether commercial beef production amounts to "full" utilization of a scarce land resource.

Moreover, a case can be made that small-scale peasant production is not automatically less efficient than large-scale commercial production. Evidence, for example, from India and Kenya indicates that small-holders can make more economical use of land and other resources than their larger counterparts.[6] On average, peasant farmers in Zimbabwe reap far lower crop yields than commercial farmers—for example, about one-fourth the yield of maize per hectare. But once disadvantages of land quality and access to scientific inputs are corrected, selected small-holders are able to match large-scale farmers in obtaining maize yields in excess of four metric tons per hectare.[7] What is far less certain, however, is whether in the near future small-holders can match commercial yield levels of export commodities such as beef and tobacco, which generate the foreign exchange required by the government and the economy as a whole.

Land Redistribution Policy

With these considerations in mind, the new government of Zimbabwe headed by Robert Mugabe launched a development strategy marked by economic moderation and racial reconciliation. Its stance on major policy issues was determined by balancing two concerns: (1) the need to bring immediate and tangible benefits to members of the majority black population in line with the government's professed socialist direction, and (2) to sustain the confidence of the white minority population and to forestall a mass emigration of the skills necessary to operate the modern economy.

Within this calculus, there was clearly room for quick and bold action to redistribute land. At first, land redistribution was given high priority. As will be shown here, the Zimbabwe government transferred more land in the first ten years of independence than did the Kenya government, which Africanized its own "white highlands" between 1963 and 1975. Indeed, the Zimbabwe land distribution program may well be the most extensive such program in Africa to date. The resettled land in Zimbabwe is of poorer quality than in Kenya, but is being spread among approximately the same number of peasant households. There are also other important differences between the two countries: the government in Zimbabwe was hobbled by inadequate flows of international financial assistance, and it chose to forgo the options of privatizing land tenure and recovering the costs of resettlement from beneficiaries.

The Zimbabwe government promptly inaugurated a land resettlement program in September 1980, just five months after independence, with several objectives: (1) to reduce civil conflict by transferring land from whites to blacks, (2) to provide opportunities for war victims and the landless, (3) to relieve population pressure in the communal lands, (4) to expand production and raise welfare nationwide, and (5) to achieve all of the above without impairing agricultural productivity or aggregate production. By 1979, the outgoing regime had already removed the most egregiously discriminatory legislation by opening up commercial farmland to persons of any race who could afford to pay for it.

At first, the Mugabe government was able to obtain land for purchase readily, either from farms that had been abandoned during the war or from whites who wished to liquidate their assets in the face of perceived uncertainty. All transactions took place voluntarily with compensation at full market rates. The government was scrupulous in observing the Lancaster House independence agreement, which stipulated that land could change hands only on a "willing seller–willing buyer" basis and that payment had to be made in an exchangeable currency. Indeed, these provisions were entrenched within the Constitution of Zimbabwe and could only be changed by a unanimous vote in the House of Assembly for a period of ten years after 1980.

The government created a Ministry of Lands, Resettlement and Rural Development headed by political appointees to implement its objectives for land redistribution. The ministry's target, through implementation of intensive and accelerated programs, was to relocate 162,000 households by 1985. This figure closely approximates the number of truly landless people estimated earlier in this chapter (180,000), but the scope of the plan did not extend to cover the needs of the near-landless (150,000). At first the ministry selected settlers from among ex-combatants, refugees, displaced persons, and the landless in the communal areas. Most of these settlers lacked agricultural assets like oxen and tools, and they were short on farm management experience. The ministry also addressed the land needs of agricultural laborers, encouraging them to remain on the redistributed commercial farms on which they had previously worked.

Resettlement in Zimbabwe is planned according to a variety of production models. Government planners select a model they consider appropriate for a given block of land, and peasants apply for available positions on the land settlement scheme. On Model A schemes, commercial farms are subdivided into five-hectare arable plots for occupancy by peasant families with common grazing lands for seven to twenty-two cattle. On Model B schemes, commercial farms are retained intact as a single unit, and settlers are organized into a collective to manage mechanized production. Model C schemes combine a core commercial estate with individual small-holdings, and Model D schemes feature planned rotational grazing on fenced rangeland.

In every case, however, legal ownership of the land is vested in the state, and settlers have to make do with an occupancy permit that falls well short of a title or even a lease. Land cannot be sold, subdivided, or inherited; and farm management practices—including land use, crop choice, and husbandry methods—are mandated by the government extension services under threat of expulsion from the scheme. In addition, undercutting the diversified survival strategies of peasant households, members of settler families are prohibited from engaging in nonagricultural employment.

The accomplishments and results of resettlement will be discussed below, but for the moment let us complete the description of the evolution of land redistribution policy during the 1980s. With a few noteworthy exceptions, this is a story of the decline in prominence of land distribution as a policy issue and shortfalls in the allocation of supporting resources.

The portents emerged early. The Transitional National Development Plan of 1982, for example, devoted remarkably little attention to the land question. Instead, the government's strategy of "growth with equity and transformation" placed primary emphasis on educational and manpower development programs and on the provision of infrastructure in the communal areas. Land settlement schemes were presented in the context of an overall rural development strategy that stressed the reduction of differentials in service provision between the commercial and peasant subsectors. Budgetary allocations nonetheless favored land settlement, with 65 percent of the anticipated investments in agriculture earmarked for settlement during the plan period.

By 1985, it was possible to discern a clear shift of agricultural policy priorities in Zimbabwe from redistributing commercial lands to providing services for peasant farmers in the existing communal areas. Planned spending levels were undermined by economic adjustment reforms, and the budget of the Ministry of Lands was slashed by 53 percent in 1983, the largest cut that year for any ministry, and by a further 33 percent in 1989 for the Ministry of Agriculture. The criterion of admitting settlers by need was modified to allow experienced agriculturalists with private means to apply for resettlement. In 1986 the Ministry of Lands was abolished and its staff was absorbed back into the Ministry of Agriculture. Thereafter, as will be documented below, land purchases essentially ground to a halt and the flow of new settlers slowed to a trickle.

Two policy initiatives in recent years seemed to promise to put land resettlement—even land reform—back onto the national political agenda. In 1985, frustrated by the inability to obtain sufficient land under the Lancaster House arrangements, the government promulgated the Land Acquisition Act. This provided that all land for sale had to be offered to the government first, that underutilized land would be identified for possible involuntary appropriation, and that the state could seize derelict land. However, the final version of the act dropped proposals that would have permitted the designation of large blocks of contiguous land for mass resettlement. And, in practice, the act has never been enforced to full advantage: to date no land has been forcibly seized, and in some cases public officials have not acted swiftly enough to secure available land before the period for the state's "right of first refusal" expires.

In 1986, at the request of the government, the Food and Agriculture Organization of the United Nations submitted a major report on *Policy Options for Agrarian Reform in Zimbabwe*. This report was debated by officials from all levels of government at two symposia, in Nyanga in 1987 and Harare in 1988. The participants recommended that land resettlement should be integrated within a comprehensive strategy to address land shortage, upgrading of land, and reorganization of land use in all areas of the country simultaneously. This strategy would be implemented by a new Agrarian Reform Agency, which would be charged to speed up land acquisition, establish ceilings (size unspecified) on commercial holdings, and restore a settlement rate of 15,000 households per year. In addition, it would also be mandated to "rationalize" the use of land in communal areas. The minister for local government, rural and urban development has announced that this would involve the consolidation of peasant populations into planned villages, and the introduction of land tenure permits for communal and resettlement areas to "guarantee succession, prevent subdivision, [and] ensure protection of the environment and acceptable husbandry practices."

Since these policy recommendations were first submitted to the cabinet in late 1987, and until the time of writing, there has been no offical response. Despite a broad preference within the bureaucracy to move ahead on agrarian reform, the minister has been blocked from new initiatives by other cabinet and party leaders. As a senior government official opined in March 1989: "Zimbabwe currently has no clear policy on land reform; we are waiting for the politicians to come out and tell us what they want to do."

Accomplishments

The state of play in official programs for land acquisition, transfer, and settlement is presented below. Figures are drawn from an official report as of August 31, 1987, the latest date for which detailed breakdowns are available, and from recent summary statements from the Office of the President published in Zimbabwe's national press.[8]

From 1980 to 1989, the government of Zimbabwe acquired or set aside almost 3 million hectares of private (2.4 million hectares) and public (0.54 million hectares) land for purposes of transfer and settlement. This constitutes about four times the land area (746,500 hectares) transferred in Kenya. Of this land, some 2.7 million hectares, or about 90 percent, has been transferred to settlement schemes, with the remainder awaiting such transfer.

On the land that had been settled by 1987, the types of settlement scheme were distributed as follows:

Table 9.1 Types of Settlement Schemes in Zimbabwe, 1987 (Cumulative)

	Area Settled (ha)	Percentage of Total
Model A (individual)	2,164,832	91.0
Model B (collective)	135,982	6.0
Model C (core estate)	11,902	0.5
Model D (grazing)	57,997	2.5

As can be seen, the Government of Zimbabwe has opted decisively for a family farm model of agricultural production rather than for collectivization. Individual family holdings have also been favored by the peasant farmers who have elected to relocate and by the international financiers who have contributed to program costs. Of the area settled, 91 percent has been devoted to family small-holdings, and only 6 percent of the resettled land has been assigned to units of collective production. It is important to note, however, that wherever family farming prevails in Zimbabwe, peasant farmers have actively engaged in collective agricultural marketing through private farmer organizations and official cooperatives.

After ten years, other resettlement production models remain experimental. Just three Model C projects have been launched, all in Manicaland province, based on flue-cured tobacco, dairy, and cotton. On the land set aside for Model D resettlement in Matabeleland South, the rejuvenation of grassland under rotational grazing has yet to prove technically feasible.

The contribution that resettled farmers can make to national production does not depend only upon the quantity of land that is transferred, but also critically upon its quality. The distribution of settlement schemes by agro-ecological zone is presented in Table 9.2.

Table 9.2   Agro-Ecological Distribution of Settlement Schemes, 1987 (Cumulative)

| | Natural Region | | | | |
	I	II	III	IV	V
All land (%)	1.8	15.0	18.7	37.8	26.7
Models A/C (ha)	19,049	438,738	919,242	583,009	216,695
Model B (ha)	2,403	70,545	54,728	8,306	—
Model D (ha)	—	—	—	—	57,997
Resettled land (ha)	21,452	509,283	973,970	649,312	216,695
Resettled land (%)	0.9	21.5	41.1	27.4	9.1

Less than one-quarter of the resettlement effort has occurred on the prime agricultural land in the northeast of the country (Natural Regions I and II). The bulk of the land acquired, transferred, and settled—some 78 percent—is in intermediate or marginal rainfall areas of uncertain agricultural potential. Moreover, planners have chosen to concentrate the family farm schemes in drier regions: whereas only 21 percent of Model A schemes are located on prime farmland, some 54 percent of Model B collective production units are so located. The establishment of Model A schemes on better land after 1984, however, has eased an even more serious earlier discrepancy. It is nonetheless true that the national policy to restructure land-holding patterns in favor of peasant small-holders has yet to thoroughly penetrate Zimbabwe's commercial agricultural subsector in the northeastern heartland.

The numbers of households that were planned for existing settlement schemes, and the numbers actually relocated by 1987, are indicated in Table 9.3.

Table 9.3   Households Resettled, 1987 (Cumulative)

	Planned Resettlement Capacity	Actually Resettled
Models A, C, and D	39,824	37,168
Model B	6,700	2,842

The slack capacity to absorb settlers on family farm schemes was taken up after these figures were published, making a total of 40,000 households resettled by 1988. In August 1989, the government revised the total figure upward to 52,000, but did not provide detailed breakdowns by scheme type. This more optimistic total figure would constitute 32 percent of the official target for the resettlement program, 28 percent of the number of households estimated in this chapter to be truly landless, 16 percent of the estimated number of households needing land in 1980, and just 7 percent of the peasant farming population as a whole.

Apart from documenting the substantial scope but attenuated impact of the land-distribution program in Zimbabwe, official figures provide empirical verification of observations made earlier. First, the resettlement program made extensive use of land: with the resettled 52,000 households occupying some 2.7 million hectares, the average family has access to 51 hectares, of which a minimum of 80 percent is used for grazing. Had planners allocated holdings of smaller average size, the program would have been able to absorb many more people. Second, the pace of resettlement has slowed markedly in recent years. Up to 1985, the resettlement rate was about 7,000 households per year, but in the latter half of the decade the annual rate appears to have been 4,000 households or less. Third, the family farm model of resettlement has been more popular among prospective settlers than the collective model. Whereas all the available places on Model A schemes are currently filled, more than half the places on Model B schemes remain vacant. These schemes have encountered not only wariness from initial applicants about arrangements for sharing assets and incomes, but also defections by established settlers due to internal social conflicts and inadequate economic returns. The membership of collective cooperatives has recently stabilized, but at lower levels than planned.

The economic effects of land redistribution on agricultural production in Zimbabwe are now beginning to appear. Redistribution of land in Zimbabwe has not led to economic decline or collapse, and the dire predictions that it would do so no longer seem very plausible. In particular, the family farm model of resettlement has shown encouraging signs of economic viability: it has enabled an intensification of land use and a reduction in the costs of production on land of intermediate potential (Natural Region III); and, in years of good rainfall, the average maize yield on Model A resettlement schemes now surpasses 2 metric tons per hectare, an increase of more than 50 percent over yields in similarly situated communal areas.[9] Moreover, the provision of improved producer prices and agricultural services has benefited small-holders throughout Zimbabwe, to the point that they increased production of maize by 400 percent and cotton by 200 percent between 1980 and 1985. Small-holders now contribute almost one-half of national marketed production of these vital food and export commodities.

This positive news is offset by several qualifications. First, the performance of settlers on Model A schemes has been highly variable, depending on the agro-ecological location of the scheme itself and the movable agricultural assets brought by each family. It remains doubtful whether poorer settlers and those in the marginal zones can generate an adequate income from family-farm agriculture alone. Second, the growing contribution of small-holder production to aggregate national output emanates mainly from the communal areas, rather than from the resettlement areas, which accounted for just 11 percent of small-holder output in 1988. Production increases have been due to an expansion of land area under cultivation as well as improved yields per hectare, and gains remain to be made both from deploying unused land and intensifying land use within the communal areas. Third, the Model B collectives have failed to make full use of high-quality highland holdings. An analysis of twelve Mashonaland collectives in 1983 indicated that only 4 percent of the total land allocated was cropped, in part due to the fact that the farm operations were undercapitalized.

Constraints

There is no simple way to account for the Zimbabwe government's performance on the land issue. Instead, a tapestry must be woven out of several strands of analysis in order to discern a pattern of explanation. A number of factors—legal, financial, administrative, and political—interacted during the 1980s in Zimbabwe to constrain a more meaningful reform program.

Most commonly cited is the legal factor. Public officials repeatedly claim that the government was prohibited from acquiring as much land as it wanted by the provisions of the Lancaster House constitution. The "willing seller–willing buyer" clause ruled out the forced seizure of any land. The first few years of independence saw the emergence of a buyers' market, as commercial farmers scrambled to take advantage of generous terms of market-rate compensation. Most of the land offered at this time was on farms abandoned or run down during the independence war, principally in marginal or intermediate agricultural zones of Manicaland on the eastern border. As a result, this province is now home to 23 percent of the settlement schemes and 33 percent of the resettled households in Zimbabwe.

By 1983, however, the white exodus ebbed, the size of the commercial farming population stabilized (at about 4,400), and—with the exception of Matabeleland, where guerrillas were still active—the flow of commercial farmland onto the market dried up. Now that sellers held the initiative, the government discovered that the land was never available in the right location, as and when required, or in consolidated blocks. Thereafter, the government was able to acquire only the occasional pocket of land in odd parts of the country, leading to a slowdown in land acquisition and to a fragmented dispersal of settlement schemes.

There were also financial constraints. The estimated cost of the planned land-distribution program was US$364 million at constant 1981 prices. In practice, the government of Zimbabwe was never able to raise funding at anything near this level. Actual expenditure on land acquisition up to 1987 was US$38.6 million (Z$64.4 million), not an exorbitant amount when calculated on a per hectare basis of about US$15. But these costs had to be met essentially from domestic resources because the major international donors, with the exception of the United Kingdom, held back from supporting land purchases. Either they were unwilling to be seen to be making funds available to buy out white farmers or they did not favor an acquisition scheme of the scale proposed by the Zimbabwe government. This story contrasts starkly with the experience of Kenya, where 95 percent of the financing came from overseas. Moreover, the constitutional requirement that land purchases be set by the market meant that the government had to pay rising prices for land as a result of a real estate boom during the 1980s.

As for settling and developing acquired land, costs amounted to at least US$70 million by 1984. In this case, however, there was substantial donor support led by the United Kingdom and the European Economic Community, and including the African Development Bank, the government of the Netherlands, and several international nongovernmental organizations. The United States was noticeably absent as a contributor to any aspect of the land redistribution effort. And, in a context where the Zimbabwe government was beset with multiple competing demands, land redistribution was always accorded a lower priority in the national public budget than education, health, and defense. Under bilateral aid agreements, the government was expected to "match" donor funds for land purchase and resettlement, but—even when paying half the cost—it could not sustain its contribution.

The administrative constraints on a more extensive redistribution program derived in part from the inadequate funding base, but also separately from the paucity of professional human resources in a newly independent country. The Ministry of Lands was understaffed and inexperienced, and, in practice, much of the planning work and support services for resettlement was provided by the Ministry of Agriculture. The United Kindom and European Economic Community, among other donors, provided modest amounts of equipment, training, and technical assistance, for which there were delays in procurement and implementation. Most importantly, with limited resources, the bureaucracy fell back on conservative planning premises and settlement models derived by the previous government. For example, despite evidence that official stocking rates seriously underestimated the livestock-carrying capacity of land, resettlement models were put into practice with overly extensive provision for grazing land.

But political considerations are perhaps most important in accounting for the blunted thrust of land redistribution. As a vital productive asset, commercial farmland has become the object of intense political competition among vested, arriviste, and aspirant interests.

Even before independence, the Commercial Farmers' Union (CFU) lobbied hard and successfully with the British government to ensure the adoption of constitutional guarantees against the nationalization or confiscation of land. Since 1980, the CFU has persuaded the Zimbabwe government to evict squatters who illegally occupy private farms, to provide security services to commercial farmers in conflict zones, and to drop a proposal for the block purchase of land under the Land Acquisition Act of 1985. The CFU's strategy of persistent behind-the-scenes pressure, although publicly never appearing to disagree with the government, must be counted as a powerful element in shaping land distribution policy.

At the same time, a new segment of the African elite has entered into private transactions to purchase commercial land. Reliable information on this form of land transfer is sketchy. Perhaps 600 of the 4,400 commercial farmers are now black Africans. As many as a dozen cabinet ministers, as well as other senior party and government officials, are rumored to have bought farms. President Mugabe's leadership code, which stipulates that political leaders may not "own or have beneficial interests in more than 50 acres of land," is easily evaded and is effectively a dead letter. One hypothesis about the delay in strengthening land-redistribution policy is that political decisionmakers have a direct personal interest in maintaining the status quo. In particular, as absentee owners, they may benefit from a lack of clarity in the definition of the underutilization of land. To this group, the stringencies of Lancaster House may simply provide a convenient excuse as to why the government cannot do more.

Outside the elite, the peasant masses in Zimbabwe have generally lacked the economic or organizational means to influence land policy. One exception is the National Farmers' Association of Zimbabwe (NFAZ), a federated union representing some 200,000 of the market-oriented small-holders in communal and resettlement areas. In 1984, the NFAZ was active in obtaining a ruling that its members would be eligible for selection to land resettlement schemes, and in August 1989 it submitted a comprehensive position paper on land policy to the minister of agriculture. As for the landless, there are occasional instances in which "squatters" and "trespassers" have persuaded the government to recognize their rights to illegally occupy or graze livestock on commercial farmland. Otherwise, the landless have been a weak force in the postcolonial politics of Zimbabwe because they lack a national advocacy organization with which to formulate and press demands.

Politicians, nonetheless, have seized upon the potent symbol of land as a means to remobilize political support for the 1990 general election. To the alarm of the commercial farmers, President Mugabe has called publicly for "uninhibited land redistribution."[10] Joshua Nkomo, senior minister in the president's office, has noted that the demand for land in his home region of Matabeleland has escalated since the 1988 unity accord between Zimbabwe African National Union and the Zimbabwe African Peoples' Union. Edgar Tekere, of the opposition Zimbabwe Unity Movement (ZUM), has charged that land redistribution should begin with the holdings of government leaders themselves. All parties are seeking to associate themselves with a renewal of *chimurenga* (revolutionary war), this time "to win economic independence." Such rhetoric taps into strong popular sentiment that land acquisition should be accelerated, if necessary, by seizing back, without compensation, lands lost under colonial conquest. By 1989, land reform had undoubtedly reemerged as the most vital and volatile topic in the national politics of Zimbabwe.

Policy Options

The resurgence of public debate on land reform is timely, given the impending expiry in April 1990 of constitutional restrictions on the mode of land acquisition. The government has an opportunity to take five major policy initiatives:

1. Accelerate land acquisition. The government should amend the Constitution of Zimbabwe and the Land Acquisition Act by replacing the "willing seller–willing buyer" clause with legislation enabling the mandatory acquisition of underutilized commercial farmland. In order to facilitate this task, the government should appoint a public-private sector task force to define unambiguously the meaning of "underutilization" of land in the commercial areas. The task force should also define "landlessness" in the communal areas. Special attention should be given to variations in these definitions by agro-ecological zone. The data would inform the establishment of new priority targets for land purchase and population resettlement. International donors should indicate willingness to assist the government with financial or human resources to enable data collection, data analysis, and legal drafting.

Before undertaking any forced seizures of land, the government should attempt to release commercial farms onto the market by means of taxation. A land tax should impose penalties on a sliding scale for land that is underused, misused, or entirely unused. The treasury should earmark and segregate such taxes from other general revenues and apply them to a special fund from which to finance land purchases. During this interim period, the government could also lengthen the time for exercising its right of first refusal on land offered for sale and seek donor support for strengthening administrative capacity for timely land purchases.

To address the problem of the geographical fragmentation of resettlement schemes, the government should pay full market value for land only if it is consolidated into blocks above a certain minimum size or accessible to existing rural infrastructure. Otherwise, the government should institute controls on land-purchase prices, perhaps cued to the cost of developing the land for purposes of small-holder settlement. All payments should be made in Zimbabwean currency, in the form of long-term government bonds, and subject to prevailing rules of remittability in foreign currency.

If, within three years, tax and financial incentives fail to generate enough land for accelerated resettlement, the government should then implement mandatory acquisition of unused, misused, and underused land. A ceiling on landholdings should not be necessary, so long as large holdings are used to full capacity. In order to minimize a loss of business confidence, the government should announce its intentions well in advance and reiterate that compensation will be paid for any land acquired.

2. Intensify land settlement. Land redistribution would appear to be a relatively inexpensive proposition in Zimbabwe. On the basis of available information (admittedly sketchy and incomplete), it seems that about US$112 million has been spent to settle 52,000 families, a reasonable cost of just over US$2000 per family. International donors should therefore renew and expand their commitments to financing the costs of land acquisition and settlement. The British government, which has already indicated a willingness to consider renewed support, should actively encourage the World Bank, the European Economic Community, and U.S. Agency for International Development to follow suit.

Under any circumstances, the Zimbabwe government will have to channel budgetary resources away from education, health, and defense and toward land redistribution. Even with more resources, however, the concentrated coverage of agricultural services in resettlement areas will have to be reduced in favor of a more even distribution across the peasant farming population. In selected places, the government may wish to selectively acquiesce to spontaneous settlement by squatters, allowing an independent, "bare bones" model of resettlement to emerge, which could be serviced by the nongovernmental sector.

Most critically, the number of beneficiaries must be increased. The initial target of resettling 162,000 families has been rendered irrelevant by time, and the current de facto target of 15,000 families per year will not make a meaningful impact on the problem of landlessness. To address this problem, the government should design new and more intensive models of settlement.

For example, the size of landholding on the Model A family farms in the better rainfall areas (Natural Region II) could be radically reduced. In comparison with Kenya, where the average small-holding on settlement schemes is twelve hectares, the Zimbabwe average of fifty-one hectares, including grazing, seems extravagant. Of course, in Zimbabwe as opposed to Kenya, the generally lower quality of land transferred and the need to accommodate animal traction must be taken into account. Even so, several options are available to reduce the proportion of resettlement land allocated to grazing: reevaluate outmoded estimates of the livestock-carrying capacity of land, design crop rotations to produce livestock fodder, limit herd size to two oxen per family, or introduce mechanized tillage. Under such circumstances, and with high-input crop production, it should be possible for peasant households to thrive on two to five hectares in the highlands. Such intensification of production models is essential if more people are to be accommodated in a national program of land redistribution.

3. Guarantee security of tenure. The full productive potential of resettled lands will be released only when small farmers feel it is truly theirs. Farm operators make long-term investments to maximize land productivity only when they possess "ownership or an ownership-like right." At present, participants in settlement schemes in Zimbabwe enjoy precarious tenure at the pleasure of the state. They may even be thought of as Zimbabwe's first tenants, growing cash crops under public supervision on state-owned land. Although there is little evidence that farmers would rather leave Model A resettlement schemes than submit to the climate of overregulation that prevails there, there is a disturbing dependency among some settlers to sit back and wait for the state to deliver services rather than provide for themselves through entrepreneurship or collective action.

There is, therefore, an urgent need to replace the current occupancy permit with a more permanent, legally enforceable right. Planners in Zimbabwe are hesitant about freehold tenure, fearing that the commoditization and trade of land could lead weaker settlers to lose control of their holdings. It should not be beyond the bounds of creative policymaking, however, to devise protective mechanisms—for example, preventing owners from subletting, prohibiting transfer within a given period, or disallowing sale to anyone other than another small-holder. Alternatively, the government might promulgate a right that is tantamount to ownership, such as a ninety-nine–year lease of state land, transferrable within the family but not beyond it. Such an arrangement would free the household to make long-term investments in land improvement and to produce agricultural commodities as it sees fit, while at the same time protecting the family from landlords and speculators. Most importantly, settlers themselves should enjoy access to local government institutions through which they can register their own preferences on these matters.

4. Upgrade farm management. The resettlement program can contribute to national goals of growth with equity only if new settlers are at least as productive as the commercial farmers they replace. This requirement may not be stringent if future resettlement occurs principally on underutilized land. Even so, settlers must have, or obtain access to, relevant farm management skills. In order to salvage those Model B collectives that are failing, the government should move quickly to install resident farm management advisers and to devise procedures for making these officials accountable to the membership of the collective. The government should also create smaller, and more manageable, Model B settlements by subdividing large farms, and expand the Model C implementation by combining collective estates with a "household responsibility" sector.

As for Model A family farms, settler selection should include both the truly landless and those among the near-landless who have demonstrated a capacity to manage a productive small-holding. Special preference should be given to those in the latter category who are members of farmer organizations, who can obtain support services through private and collective efforts. Donor funds should provide establishment grants for poorer settlers who lack agricultural tools and equipment.

5. Protect communal lands. A rational allocation of scarce land resources and an intensification of agricultural production within the existing peasant farming areas is clearly desirable because much of the demand for land will have to be satisfied in this subsector. But memories of the reaction of peasant farmers to agricultural regulation in the colonial period should dissuade planners from formulating plans that are too rigid or compulsory. In the period 1950–1980, peasants boycotted services and resisted regulations handed down by a distant central government; they are quite capable of doing the same in the 1990s. Rather than rushing to prepare a national blueprint for "communal lands reorganization," the Zimbabwe government would stand to gain by allowing a longer period of gestation for the emergence of a flexible policy. A decentralized and participatory process should be set in motion to allow local communities to devise their own solutions to problems of sustainable agriculture—soil erosion, the shortage of grazing land, the scattered pattern of rural residence—in each locality.

There is no popular consensus on the critical issue of land tenure in the communal lands: whereas a majority of peasant farmers in Zimbabwe seem to favor a modified usufruct system, the richest and most vocal small-holders in the National Farmers' Association of Zimbabwe now opt for private ownership. Ideally, land-reform debates would focus on policy options that would allow consistent patterns of land tenure to emerge across communal and resettlement areas. The acceptability and sustainability of any tenure arrangements, however, depends upon the extent to which local communities impose such arrangements on themselves. It is quite appropriate for the time being that local authorities should retain powers of land allocation in the communal areas, and that the central government focus its attention on tenure reform on the resettlement schemes.

Overview and Prospects

Ten years after independence, Zimbabwe has undergone a measure of land redistribution, but it has yet to experience land reform. Large numbers of peasant farmers have been moved onto extensive tracts of commercial farmland, but they do not yet enjoy secure and enforceable rights of land tenure.

In purely quantitative terms the government's accomplishments are impressive. Within the short span of a decade, it purchased about 19 percent of the commercial farmland in Zimbabwe, a favorable comparison with the 10 percent purchased by the government in Kenya. It resettled about 16 percent of the population estimated to need land in 1980. These results surely constitute a creditable physical performance by a fledgling government faced with multiple competing demands and hamstrung by limited financial and administrative means.

From a qualitative perspective, however, the land redistribution program has not brought about a transformation of inherited patterns of ownership and production in Zimbabwe's agricultural sector. Commercial farmers still control one-third of the total land area, much of it prime farmland in the high rainfall zones. And the commercial subsector is still dominated by a few large-scale owner-operators, though some are now black Africans. As an alternative model of ownership and production, the large-scale production collective remains unproven, with unimpressive early results.

Also, the commercial and peasant subsectors are still clearly distinguished by differences in land-tenure arrangements—freehold in the former, varieties of usufruct in the latter. To the extent that ownership rights have changed at all, the state has been the main beneficiary. The government of Zimbabwe now owns the land that has been acquired for settlement, and the rights of the new settlers to retain access to land are probably less secure under the Ministry of Agriculture than they were under a traditional or local authority in the communal areas.

As for the structure of production, the case that Zimbabwean agriculture is dualistic is now more difficult to make: too many peasant farmers have rushed to join agricultural markets since independence. The line between "commercial" and "subsistence" agriculture is shifting and blurring. Yet the peasant farmers who remain behind in the communal lands are the major cause of the happy problem of overproduction of staple grain. The mere presence of new settlers on redistributed land cannot be credited as a significant component of Zimbabwe's agricultural success story.

Above all, the hard truth is that the land redistribution in Zimbabwe has not solved the problem of landlessness. In the ten years since independence, the peasant farming population has grown at an annual rate of 3.6 percent to an estimated 7.5 million persons, an increase of some 318,000 households. In other words, despite the government's success at moving 52,000 households onto settlement schemes, the number of households needing land actually increased between 1980 and 1990. Whereas there were 330,000 households needing land when the redistribution program began, there were some 370,000 such households just ten years later.[11] As in Kenya, the land redistribution program as presently designed is woefully inadequate to the scale of landlessness in Zimbabwe. The best that can be said is that the redistribution program has reduced the severity of the landlessness problem that would have existed otherwise.

Will the Zimbabwe government therefore recommit itself in earnest to redistribution, even reform? On both economic and political fronts, the prospects do not seem bright.

The government will have to make special appeals to key donors if outside resources are to be mobilized for land reform in the 1990s. Although donors will give proportionally more of their aid budgets to Africa in the 1990s, overall levels of concessional assistance will continue to decline. Now that Namibia is about to gain independence, Zimbabwe will no longer be the darling of the international aid community. Donors are likely, therefore, to play a less influential role in land policy formulation in Zimbabwe in the 1990s than in the 1980s. The Zimbabwe government will have to set the policy agenda and the financial pace. With a growing government budget deficit—projected at 15 percent of public revenues for 1989—domestic resources will have to be carefully husbanded if land purchase is to be accelerated and land settlement intensified. A peaceful end to South African destabilization and the Mozambican civil war would surely help to reduce the drain of defense spending.

In the final analysis, however, the future of land reform depends on political will. A meaningful land-reform program requires far more than a disposition to reallocate budget resources at the margin. It requires the government to redistribute the land assets of vested interests in the commercial agricultural subsector—namely black and white large-scale farmers—with whom it has already shown a willingness to coalesce. It requires political leaders to find alternative sources to commercial agriculture for the flows of foreign exchange that underpin the maintenance of regime power. For example, if land in the highlands is reallocated from beef production to small-holder cropping, the government must find alternative export crops to replace its profitable beef quota with the European Economic Community. In the face of these realities, the politicians will be reluctant to sever the lifeline to hard currency.

The government seems already to acknowledge that land alone can never solve the problem of rural poverty in Zimbabwe. There is no rational redistribution plan that can take all of the steam out of the population kettle. Land-reform policies will always have to be coupled with other policies to create alternative forms of employment that involve people leaving the land altogether. But land reform is surely an irreplaceable arrow in the quiver of development strategy. In both material and symbolic terms, it can help address the pressing needs of the majority rural population. For this reason, a program to accelerate land acquisition, intensify land settlement, and guarantee security of land tenure should be elevated to high priority as the government of Zimbabwe plans its development strategy for the 1990s.

Notes

1. Arthur Hazlewood, "Kenyan Land-Transfer Programs and Their Relevance for Zimbabwe," *Journal of Modern African Studies* 23, no. 2 (1985): 456.

2. Roy L. Prosterman and Jeffrey M. Riedinger, *Land Reform and Democratic Development* (Baltimore, Md.: Johns Hopkins University Press, 1987), pp. 10–11.

3. The figure for households needing land in 1980 was calculated as follows. (1) For agricultural workers, assume that one-third were foreign migrants and one-sixth were domestic migrants with landholdings; therefore, approximately one-half of all agricultural workers (320,000 adult persons) required land, or 160,000 persons or 80,000 households (assuming both husband and wife were on the farm). (2) For landless peasants we take the average nationwide figure of 9 percent of communal area dwellers (750,000 households), to arrive at a figure of 68,000 households. (3) The number of persons who lost land in the war is calculated from the number of refugees and displaced persons reported by the Zimbabwe government (Republic of Zimbabwe. *Zimcord: Let's Build Zimbabwe Together* (Salisbury, March 1981), p. 25): 250,000 persons in other countries plus 400,000 persons who fled to towns. Assume that half of the town dwellers returned to farming (200,000 persons) and that half of these had land to return to (100,000 persons). Assume that all refugees returned to farming and that half of these had land to return to (125,000 persons). This would leave 225,000 people needing land, or (dividing by seven persons per household) 32,000 households. Taken together, these three categories (80,000 + 68,000 + 32,000 households) give a total of 180,000 truly landless households in 1980.

For the near-landless, we refer to the finding of the Zimbabwe Energy Accounting Project survey (Daniel Weiner, "Land and Agricultural Development," in Colin Stoneman (ed.), *Zimbabwe's Prospects: Issues of Race, Class, State and Capital in Southern Africa* (London: Macmillan, 1988), p. 71) that 20 percent of the peasant households on medium-potential land had less than one hectare of arable holding. Using this admittedly crude standard, we can guess that a minimum of 20 percent of all peasant households (750,000) had insufficient land to produce all their own food; in other words, about 150,000 households were near-landless in 1980.

Adding together the landless (180,000 households) and the near-landless (150,000 households), we arrive at a total figure of 330,000 households needing land in 1980.

The total national population in 1980 was 7.2 million persons. The total agricultural population was estimated as follows: peasant farmers (750,000 households) plus all agricultural laborers (160,000 households) plus commercial farmers (6,000 households) multiplied by seven persons per household equals 6.4 million persons.

4. Commercial Farmers' Union, *Zimbabwe Agricultural and Economic Review* (Harare: Modern Farming Publications, 1982); Whitsun Foundation, *Land Reform in Zimbabwe* (Harare: Whitsun Foundation, 1983); Bill H. Kinsey, "Forever Gained: Resettlement and Land Policy in the Context of National Development in Zimbabwe," in J. D. T. Peel and T. O. Ranger (eds.), *Past and Present in Zimbabwe* (Manchester: Manchester University Press, 1983).

5. Dan Weiner, Sam Moyo, Barry Munslow, and Phil O'Keefe, "Land Use and Agricultural Productivity in Zimbabwe," *Journal of Modern African Studies* 23, no. 2 (1985): 251–285; Sam Moyo, "The Land Question," in Ibbo Mandaza (ed.), *Zimbabwe: The Political Economy of Transition* (Dakar: CODESRIA, 1986); and Weiner, "Land and Agricultural Development," pp. 63–89.

6. A. K. Sen, "The Size of Holding and Productivity," *The Economic Weekly*, annual number, 1966; Michael Lipton, "Towards a Theory of Land Reform," in D. Lehmann (ed.), *Agrarian Reform and Agrarian Reformism* (London: Faber, 1974); Diana Hunt, *The Impending Crisis in Kenya: The Case for Land Reform* (Aldershot: Gower, 1984).

7. Michael Bratton and Kate Truscott, "Fertilizer Packages, Maize Yields and Economic Returns: An Evaluation in Wedza Communal Land," *Zimbabwe Agricultural Journal* 82, no. 1 (1985): 1–8; Enos Shumba, "An Agronomic Study of Appropriate Maize Tillage and Weed Control Technologies in a Communal Area of Zimbabwe," D. Phil. dissertation, Department of Agricultural Economics, University of Zimbabwe, 1988.

8. Republic of Zimbabwe, Ministry of Local Government, Rural and Urban Development, *Resettlement Progress Report* (Harare: Government Printer, 1987); *The Herald* (Harare), August 4, 1989.

9. For communal areas, estimates are derived from Central Statistical Office, *Statistical Yearbook*, 1987, and Crop Forecasting Committee reports, 1984-1989. For resettlement areas, the source is the Ministry of Lands, Agriculture and Rural Resettlement, *Monitoring and Evaluation Section*, 1988. The author is grateful to Stephen Burgess for collecting these figures.

10. *The Herald* (Harare), August 12, 1989.

11. The same assumptions used in Note 3 are employed to calculate the number of households requiring land in 1990. Of the 318,000 households added to the communal lands population, 9 percent are conservatively estimated to be entirely landless and 20 percent near-landless. From these 92,000 households, we deduct the 52,000 households that were resettled in the 1980s. We add the remaining 40,000 households to the 1980 estimate of 330,000 households needing land in 1980 to arrive at the 1990 figure of 370,000 households.

chapter ten

The Land Question in South Africa

Daniel Weiner

Summary

Land is the pillar of grand apartheid. Apartheid legislation forbids black ownership of land in white areas and perpetuates mass poverty in ten designated "homelands" in South Africa. These bantustans, totaling 17 million hectares, function as cheap labor reserves and as dumping grounds for blacks illegally located in white territory. Overcrowding, landlessness, and decades of economic discrimination have reduced the productive capacity of black small-holders and increased the rate of urbanization. Nevertheless, some bantustan farmers are productive and there is strong grassroots demand for more and better land.

White farmers control 85.7 million hectares of white territory and account for over 90 percent of gross farm income. Many white farms, however, are not financially viable. Historically, government policies attempted to maximize the white farm population through agricultural subsidies. Foreclosure rates have been high in the 1980s, when there was a rapid concentration and centralization of white-farm capital. Farm workers and tenants, who are dismally poor and often ill treated, have farming skills and must be a primary concern of future land-reform initiatives.

Presently, it is politically premature to propose specific land-reform measures because the nature of the post-apartheid state is very unclear. Immediate efforts, therefore, must be geared to ending apartheid and replacing it with truly democratic political and economic institutions . In regard to land, economic democracy will likely require, at a minimum , the following four initiatives: (1) repeal of apartheid legislation, (2) selected expropriation of white-owned land, (3) land reform within the bantustans, and (4) the development of a mix of farming systems. Existing proposals for a free market in land are actually attempts to reform political apartheid through the maintenance of economic apartheid, and are therefore unacceptable.

Land is the pillar of grand apartheid.[1] The 1913 Native Land Act and the 1936 Native Trust and Land Act solidified white control of 87 percent of South Africa's territory, and transformed Africans into suppliers of cheap labor to the white economy. To this day, apartheid legislation forbids black ownership of land in white areas and perpetuates mass poverty in ten designated "homelands," or *bantustans*. Within the bantustans, over 12 million people inhabit 17.1 million hectares of mostly medium- to low-potential land. On the other hand, approximately 59,000 farms occupy 85.7 million hectares of white territory, and most of the limited high potential land in the country.

The successful transition to a nonracial and democratic South Africa will require dramatic changes in current patterns of land use and control. At the present time, however, it is politically premature to propose specific policy initiatives for land reform because the nature of the post-apartheid state is very unclear. Hence, this chapter focuses on the various issues and ideologies that are emerging about the land question in South Africa and outlines important objectives for future policy formulation. Relevant empirical information is also presented. We begin with a summary of the structure of South African agriculture.

The Structure of South African Agriculture

In South Africa's mature industrial economy, agriculture contributes only 5 percent of the gross domestic product and 15 percent of formal employment. At least one-quarter of the black population, however, is dependent on agricultural and rural resources for subsistence. More than 90 percent of gross farm income and 97 percent of agricultural export commodities are produced by white settler farmers and agricultural corporations. More than 80 percent of white farmland is used for livestock grazing. Only half of the 10.6 million hectares under cultivation are used for basic food crops.

In contrast, the bantustans are net food importers; only one-quarter of the food consumed is produced internally. An estimated 30,000–50,000 people die each year from hunger or hunger-related disease. The vast majority of the bantustan population are dependent on off-farm income for survival. Approximately 10 percent of household income is earned through crop production, although regional variations are significant. Wilson and Ramphele document bantustan regions where 25–50 percent of total income is earned through agriculture.[2] They also demonstrate that households dependent on agriculture tend to be poorer than households receiving steady wage remittances. In all bantustan regions, inequality between households is very pronounced.

There is also significant uneven development within white

agriculture, with a tendency toward uneconomic farming units, land concentration, and centralized control over production. In the mid-1980s, 6 percent of white farm units produced 40 percent of total income in the subsector. Data for the 1981/1982 agricultural season show an average net income of R146,200 (US$124,270, using March 1982 exchange rates) for the top 20 percent of white farms as compared with R9,100 (US$7,735) for the remaining 80 percent. Many farmers are absentee landlords. Others are located in strategic border areas and receive large subsidies to remain there. Some farms are located in low-potential agro-ecological zones. The average size of white farms increased from 722 hectares in 1950 to 1,193 hectares in 1978. In 1978, however, only 28.5 percent of all farm units were over 1,000 hectares. The pace of land concentration has accelerated during the last twenty years, and there has been increased corporate and company investment into the subsector. The number of company-owned farms increased from 2,293 in 1971 to 5,590 in 1981. Large corporations are also diversifying into agriculture; Anglo-American Corporation owns large maize, beef, fruit, and vegetable farms, sugar plantations, and forestry projects. Recently, with the rapid devaluation of the rand, there has been some foreign purchase of land. Corporate and company farms presently own approximately 8–10 percent of all white farm land, but a higher proportion of the high potential land resources.

A 1984 survey by the South African Agricultural Union found that approximately half of all white farms were financially viable. In 1988, the National Maize Producers Organization estimated that at least 40 percent of (white) grain producers would be forced into liquidation if state aid was suddenly withdrawn.[3] The profitability and viability crisis on white farms is linked to a restructuring process within the sector, which will have important implications for future land-reform initiatives. Maintaining white farmers on the land (and removing blacks) has been an important policy objective for the Nationalist party since it came to power in 1948. Government subsidies to white farmers (which include cheap inputs and credit, price supports, and tax breaks) created an incentive to produce more, rather than more efficiently. Inappropriate yield-enhancing inputs were adopted in environmentally marginal farming areas, and large debts were accumulated on land and equipment purchase. Current farm debt now stands at R14 billion (US$5.2 billion, using 1989 exchange rates); interest on agricultural debt is currently the largest financial burden for white farmers.

In the 1980s, the combination of drought, high interest rates, and inflated input costs (exacerbated in part by a slow transition toward "free-market" agricultural policies) hit indebted farmers hard. Foreclosures increased, and the historical process of concentration and centralization of farming land and capital accelerated. Along with fewer numbers of larger farms, there was a rapid displacement of labor for capital; 250,000 jobs were lost in agriculture between 1977 and 1985 alone. Mechanization and job displacement have been most pronounced in the grain industry. Presently, there are approximately 800,000 African and 100,000 Coloured farm workers (using South African terminology). The total population of farm workers and their families living in white rural areas is more than 5 million.

Farm workers are forced to work long hours at very low pay. They suffer from high rates of undernutrition, particularly amongst children, who are an important source of casual labor. Living conditions generally are very poor. Violence against workers is not uncommon. Most farm workers are wage-laborers, who are tied to the farm because of limited alternatives for work and shelter. Some workers are tenants, who have access to "white" land through labor contract. White farmers still use prison labor. According to Marcus, white farm restructuring has not significantly improved the real wages and living conditions for blacks working on white farms.[4] Rather, restructuring has "modernized superexploitation." In core white farming areas, and particularly on corporate farms where some unionization is beginning to take place, some small improvements are observable, however. The dismal conditions of black farm workers is one of the more shocking human elements of apartheid and must be central to future agrarian reform concerns.

To summarize, although inequalities are most pronounced between the races, South Africa's agricultural sector features uneven development between and within the dominant farming subsectors. The process of rural class formation in the bantustans and the concentration and centralization of white farming capital are important structural features to consider in future land-reform initiatives. Specific aspects of land potential, use, productivity, and tenure are now addressed.

South Africa's Land Resource

Land Potential

There is presently some controversy regarding the relative production potential of white versus black agricultural land in South Africa. Some studies assume that the bantustans generally have low production potential. Other research concludes that some of the region's best arable land resources fall in the bantustans, and that, on average, white land is no better than black land. Such generalizations about agricultural potential are misleading. Approximately half of the country receives less than 400 mm of rain annually, and is, therefore, unsuited for dryland cultivation. A disaggregated analysis of the eastern (well-watered) half of the country reveals that designated white farming areas have significantly greater agricultural potential than adjacent bantustans.

Approximately 15 percent (2.6 million hectares) of the total bantustan land area is potentially arable, and most of this land is classified as medium to low potential. Kangwane has a relatively high level of arable land potential (29.4 percent), and Transkei has the second highest potential (17.4 percent). Of the ten bantustans, Ciskei has the lowest percentage of potentially arable land (8.2 percent). There are an estimated 10.7 million people living in rural areas of the bantustans; therefore, there are only 0.24 hectares of potentially arable land on a per capita basis.

In white farming regions, there are approximately 15.9 million hectares of potentially arable land—over six times the amount in the bantustans—of which more than two-thirds are medium to high potential. Percentages of potentially arable land are much higher than in adjacent bantustans, ranging between 28 and 43 percent in the eastern half of the country. These numbers point to gross inequalities in both land *quantity* and *quality* between white and black farming regions.

Agricultural Land Use
There is no reliable data on land use in the bantustans. An examination of selected case studies, however, reveals a complex pattern of land use. Pressure on land is acute, and environmental degradation is well documented. Some households, however, do not farm some or all of their land due to severe capital and labor constraints and the poor quality of the resource base. Economically, it also makes more sense to look for off-farm employment; given current prices, poor quality land, and limited marketing opportunities in most regions, the opportunity cost of agricultural labor is high despite generally low wages. However, with rapidly rising unemployment, agriculture is slowly becoming more attractive to bantustan households with access to land and farming capital. The number of households in this category, however, is rather small. There is little cash available to purchase inputs, and most households have no draft animals. Landlessness is acute, ranging from 20 to 85 percent in rural bantustan regions. Nationally, less than half of all bantustan residents have access to land. The problem of landlessness is exacerbated by large-scale South African government-sponsored agricultural projects which appropriate the bantustans' most fertile arable land resources; these state farms currently utilize at least 15 percent of all the potentially arable land in the bantustans.

Future land-reform initiatives will have to address current land-use problems within the bantustans and, of course, expand black production onto existing white territory. An overview of white farm land-use and ownership patterns suggests that hard choices will have to be made. Approximately three-quarters of the potentially arable white farm land is cropped or fallowed in any given year; more than 4 million hectares of potentially arable area has not been cleared for cultivation. There are also important regional variations in the intensity of agricultural land use. Cropping intensities are high in the Eastern and Western Cape, Orange Free State, and Western Transvaal, where arable land is mainly medium- to low-potential. There is little room for horizontal expansion in these regions, where land overuse is a problem. Ninety percent of the 3.2 million hectares of high-potential land and more than 20 percent of the 7.2 million hectares of medium-potential land in white areas is located in Natal and the Eastern Transvaal. Only half of the land in these regions is cleared for agriculture. In Natal, 46.6 and 24.1 percent of the high- and medium-potential land, respectively, is cultivated; two-thirds of the total cropped area is under sugar and forestry crops. Commercial forests alone occupy one-third of all the high-potential land in the region.

Is much medium- to high-potential land in Natal and the Eastern Transvaal underutilized, and therefore a prime target for land resettlement? Although good data are not available, it is known that some of this land is being held for speculation or has been bought by coal companies for mineral rights. The region also has locations with poorly drained soils that flood, making tractorization difficult. A significant portion of the arable land in the region is also used for livestock grazing. The extent to which this represents land underutilization needs to be further examined. Just as important, however, is the question of landownership. Medium- and high-potential land is being purchased by companies and corporations for industrial crop production. Before exploring landownership and tenure, we briefly examine the relative productivity of black and white agriculture.

Land Productivity

Conventional wisdom in South Africa assumes that most rural black people do not wish to engage in agricultural production, and would rather live and work in town if given the opportunity. This argument assumes that there is substantial black agricultural deskilling, and that white farm productivity is overwhelmingly superior. There is limited data to engage in this debate; more research is certainly needed. But in the case of maize, where data are available, some bantustan farmers appear to be remarkably productive, given the numerous constraints they face. Maize yield data in the bantustans suggest an average of around 0.4 to 1.5 metric tons per hectare. This is consistent with other low-input farming systems in the world; only 10 percent of bantustan farmers use commercial fertilizer.

In the 1950s, before the adoption of fossil fuel inputs, white farm maize yields averaged only 0.72 metric tons per hectare. They now average between 1.0 and 3.0 metric tons per hectare. The difference between white and black maize yields is mostly a reflection of levels of technology employed. When Zimbabwe became independent, the superior yields achieved on white farms were also broadly advertised and successfully used to argue against agrarian reform. In less than a decade, however, black farm maize yields in high-potential zones are comparable, with less inputs used, to those achieved by adjacent large-scale white settler farmers.

South Africa is not Zimbabwe, where a frustrated peasantry led the liberation struggle. Agricultural marginalization in the bantustans is more pronounced than in Zimbabwe's communal areas. It is also true that a large proportion (probably at least one-third) of bantustan inhabitants are functionally urbanized. But this does not mean that no potential for black agricultural development exists. Quite to the contrary, high levels of structural unemployment are increasing the incentive and necessity for rural blacks to engage in agricultural production; landlessness and poor land quality are major constraints, however. A state committed to providing the resources and opportunities for black agricultural development would likely reveal the productive potential of many black farmers.

Land Tenure and Farming Systems
The discussion so far has focused mainly on the differences between white and black agriculture. These two subsectors, as suggested earlier, are not homogenous. There are important differences in farming systems and forms of land tenure within white and black agriculture that are central to emerging land reform debates.

White agriculture features freehold title where land is bought and sold (by whites only) in the marketplace. Within the subsector, however, there are differences in ownership patterns that are important. About 90 percent of white agricultural land is owned by individuals and partners. Within this broad category, Cooper has identified a core and a periphery according to farming viability; core farmers control the bulk of the land resources and are accumulating capital whereas peripheral farmers often have indebtedness problems.[5] Core farmers have moved closer to a full wage relation with their laborers, whereas tenancy is still found on peripheral farms. Core farmers are more productive and occupy better land.

Most of the remaining 10 percent of agricultural land is owned by companies and corporations. Although good data are not available, within South Africa it is widely known that companies and corporations (both private and public) are increasingly investing in agriculture. The concentration and centralization of agricultural capital is relevant to future land-reform efforts because core farmers are politically powerful, with increasing ability to steer the policy debate (partially through control over information) and manipulate land prices. In the case of a negotiated settlement, company/corporate and white settler interests will be well represented; this was certainly the case in Zimbabwe.

Bantustan land-tenure arrangements and farming systems are more complex and very political. There are three primary types of land tenure in the bantustans: tribal, private, and trust land. Tribal land—reserved for blacks in the late nineteenth century—was formally classified as reserve land with the 1913 Native Land Act. Land is administered by South African government-controlled "Tribal Authorities." Private land dates back to the early part of the twentieth century, when some blacks purchased land; it accounts for a small percentage of total bantustan land. Trust land was established as part of the 1936 Native Land and Trust Act. The land is effectively owned by the state in "trust" for the use of black farmers. Most bantustan arable land is used for small-scale production. Increasingly, however, land is allocated for large-scale agricultural projects. The South African government has also supported the establishment of individual large-scale black farm units for the bantustan elite.

There is evidence that land tenure is not linked to productivity differences in the bantustans. This is partially because most tenure arrangements ensure low levels of security of possession. Bantustan land tenure is a mechanism for social, economic, and military control of the black population. Repressive bantustan land-tenure arrangements have far-reaching consequences for any future land reform program.

Current Thinking About Land

The conditions associated with rural apartheid—landlessness, poverty, hunger, violence, and so forth—point to the human tragedy of the grand apartheid plan. The bantustans are not viable economic units. They cannot absorb South Africa's cheap and redundant labor (and family members). After decades of forced removals from white territory involving approximately 3.5 million people, reverse migration is rapidly accelerating. Squatters living in Soweto are considered "lucky," having escaped the genocidal poverty and politics of the bantustans.

These realities on the ground have done little to alter the grand apartheid visions of segments of the South African state. This is illustrated in a 1984 white paper on agricultural policy, which closely corresponds with the views of the South African Agricultural Union. The document states as a primary objective, "the pursuit of a maximum number of [white] well-trained and financially sound owner-occupant farmers."[6] Conservatives in the government are concerned about the white depopulation of the "platteland." Black agricultural development is viewed as the concern of bantustan administrations. There is no discussion of the dismantling of territorial apartheid.

It is also important to note that the South African state is deeply fragmented. The massive development problems of apartheid and the viability crisis afflicting parts of white agriculture are two primary reasons why segments of the government and private sector are beginning to address the politically sensitive question of land. For example, a leading government rural development institution recently said the following about the land question in South Africa:

> The opening of access to all farmers in Southern [South] Africa will inevitably direct attention towards the present availability and distribution of agricultural land resources. Regardless of the political sensitivity of this issue, it must be appreciated that individual restrictions in access to land would jeopardise the long-run economically optimal utilisation of land resources while effectively undermining private sector initiatives in agriculture. Land issues will receive increasing attention in future and should be put on the agenda.[7]

Of particular importance to South African land-reform debates is the emergence of free-market ideology within government policymaking institutions. As part of South Africa's "reform" process (not to be confused with the use of the term in this chapter), the market is increasingly viewed as a mechanism for dismantling apartheid. In the case of land, this would allow elite blacks to purchase rural resources while having little impact on the black majority. Using the "free" market as a mechanism to maintain racial privileges is an important objective of current government policy thinking. After generations of government subsidy and support to white agriculture, it makes little sense to propose that blacks do it on their own, particularly in the context of the poverty most rural blacks presently face. There would be nothing free about the market in a post-apartheid South Africa.

Land has always been on the agenda for the main liberation movements, although concrete proposals have yet to be formulated.

Since its conception in the 1950s, the Freedom Charter set the agenda
on land with the broad statement that "the land shall be shared
amongst those who work it." Recent African National Congress (ANC)
constitutional guidelines call for a land-reform initiative that abolishes
racial restrictions on the ownership and use of land and an affirmative
action program that gives special consideration to the victims of forced
removals. Other ANC documents call for selected nationalization of
land combined with production reorganization. The Pan Africanist
Congress (PAC) has recently argued that "to free the land which has
been usurped by the white minority regime, the African working class
must relentlessly wage labour war."[8]

On all sides of the political spectrum, the land question is being
addressed in the abstract; concrete proposals have yet to be formulated.
This is not a reflection of the relative unimportance of future land-
reform initiatives. Rather, it stems from the political reality that the land
question is only one component of the overall struggle for state power
and control. Until this latter question is resolved, specific policy
initiatives regarding land will have limited meaning. It is in this context
that issues and options for post-apartheid land reform are addressed in
the final section of this chapter.

Post-apartheid Land Reform: Issues and Options

Summary of Main Points
This chapter has focused on the structural realities of South African
agriculture today as well as emerging ideologies specific to the land
question. Because the empirical base is weak, more research is
necessary for the development of future land-reform initiatives.
Nevertheless, important empirical realities are presently discernible.

1. White farming areas have significantly more productive potential
than black farming areas. Although most low-potential arable land is
under crops, the same cannot be said for high-potential arable land;
much high-potential land is used for timber and livestock production,
and is possibly being underutilized. A large (but unknown) percentage
of all corporate and company land is in the high-potential Natal and
Eastern Transvaal regions. There appears to be little potential for
horizontal expansion of cropping in the bantustans (although this is not
true in all regions), where South African government-supported tribal
authorities, agrocorporations and private black farmers control the best
land. The current crisis in the bantustans is linked to land quantity,
quality, and tenure arrangements.

2. There is uneven development between and within white and

black agriculture. The concentration and centralization of white farming capital is part of a generalized restructuring process that has left at least half of all farm units severely in debt, and a rapid substitution of capital for labor. Within the bantustans, there are very large differences in individual household access to productive resources associated with a more generalized process of class formation.

3. In the case of maize, the land productivity gap between white and black farming is not as large as normally assumed; in similar agro-ecological zones some bantustan farmers have recorded maize yields approximately 50 percent lower than on adjacent white farms with considerably less inputs. There is growing evidence that some wealthier bantustan households with access to good-quality land are slowly experiencing agricultural intensification. However, this group is a small percentage of the total bantustan population.

What Can Be Done?
Assuming the objective of a democratic resolution of the land question in South Africa, the following issues and options stand out.

1. Repeal of apartheid legislation. The two agricultural land acts and the Group Areas Act ensure racial territorial division. Certainly, these acts must be repealed before any meaningful land reform can take place. In the case of the Group Areas Act, it is important to realize that residential land must also be part of any land-reform program; this important point has not been addressed here. But repeal of apartheid legislation alone will not stimulate equitable economic growth. Market-oriented solutions, which are increasingly part of official government policy, will benefit only the existing black elite who can afford to purchase land. Empowering the powerful should not be the objective of a land-reform program.

2. Expropriation of white-owned land. Because most blacks will not have the resources to purchase land, the post-apartheid government will come under pressure to expropriate white farmland. Daphne recently identified four possible mechanisms to do this short of wholesale nationalization: (1) nationalization of land owned by big business; (2) nationalization of land owned by absentee owners; (3) placing a ceiling on individual land ownership; and (4) controlling the sales of agricultural land.[9] One should add nationalization of underutilized land as a further possiblility. These options need not be mutually exclusive: some combination of them might be used. The exact mechanisms for land expropriation will be affected by the relative influence of specific social classes during the transition period. It is most likely, particularly in the case of a negotiatied settlement, that some form of compensation would be forthcoming. In this case, foreign assistance in purchasing land would become vital. (This continues to be the case in Zimbabwe today.) The process of land expropriation is, of course, complex and will require a data set on the relative prevalences and productivities of specific farm types in targeted regions.

3. Bantustan land reform. Land reform within the bantustans is also necessary.[10] Presently, land tenure in the bantustans is repressive, geared to the perpetuation of white hegemony through the empowerment of black puppets. It must again be stressed that purely market-driven privatization, which is supported by some bantustan administrations, is not a viable solution. Where desirable, there are numerous ways to provide individual rights in the absence of a land market (see Zimbabwe, for example). Within the bantustans, land redistribution must be community based and popular amongst the rural population. There are many community projects in the bantustans involving people with limited access to productive resources. These projects must be identified and funded.

4. The development of a mix of farming systems. Once land is made available, a fundamental question concerns the type of farming systems that should be supported. Different farming systems will be appropriate in different agro-economic and social contexts. It is important that future rural production organization absorb rather than displace labor. Land reform (and agrarian reform) cannot stop the flow of people to urban areas but should, as an objective, slow rural outmigration. Conversely, land/agrarian reform can only succeed in the context of an urbanization strategy for blacks. There certainly are many black small farmers and landless households who should be resettled, as small-holders, onto white land or given more access to bantustan land. A land/agrarian reform program geared solely toward re-peasantization, however, would not be logical for South Africa's mature industrial economy. Massive subdivision of large farms is not economically practical due to strong agro-industrial linkages and the current reliance on agricultural commoditites from this subsector. It is also politically imperative that a stable supply of (relatively) cheap food continues to be available to the urban working class and underemployed. In this context, some productive and politically cooperative white farmers should be part of the post-apartheid landscape; farm workers must be unionized and their standard of living greatly improved. There should also be limits set on the size of white farms to reverse the trend of large capital-intensive megafarms.

To achieve a better balance among farm size, productivity, and levels of capital and labor employed, alternative forms of medium- to large-scale farming will also be necessary. For example, cooperatives and pre-cooperatives might be appropriate for some farm workers and landless/marginalized bantustan households. Some white farms and bantustan projects will likely be appropriate sites for state farms and training schemes for worker self-management. Ultimately, the range of farming systems must incorporate the genuine desires of rural people so as to be more than a combination of the ideological tendencies of agricultural development planners and distorted political powers of specific farming constituencies (which is what happened in Zimbabwe). All post-apartheid farming systems, however, will require the expertise of South Africa's sophisticated agricultural institutions and support from the international community.

To conclude, farming systems are not simply products of planning institutions. They are forms of rural social organization. The mix of farming systems in a post-apartheid South Africa will ultimately result from the forms of popular struggle that overthrow the apartheid state. Hence, at the present time, drawing up plans for post-apartheid farming systems is secondary to supporting communities and organizations who are fighting for economic democracy and the end of apartheid in South Africa. In this task, there is much more that we can, and must, do.

Notes

1. Some of the data and arguments in this chapter are more thoroughly presented in Daniel Weiner, "Agricultural Transformation in Zimbabwe: Lessons for South Africa After Apartheid," *Geoforum* 19, no. 4 (1988): 479–496; and in Richard Levin and Daniel Weiner, "The Agrarian Question and the Emergence of Conflicting Agricultural Strategies in South Africa," paper presented at the SAERT policy workshop, University of Wageningen, The Netherlands, November 12–14, 1989.

2. Francis Wilson and Mamphela Ramphele, *Uprooting Poverty: The South African Challenge* (Cape Town: David Philip, 1989).

3. For an excellent study of the crisis in white agriculture, see Michael de Klerk, "The Accumulation Crisis in Agriculture," Labour and Economic Research Center, The University of Cape Town, 1988.

4. Tessa Marcus, *Modernizing Super-Exploitation: Restructuring South African Agriculture* (London: Zed Books, 1989).

5. David Cooper, "Ownership and Control of Agriculture in South Africa," in John Suckling and Landeg White (eds.), *After Apartheid: Renewal of the South African Economy* (Trenton, N.J.: Africa World Press, 1988).

6. "White Paper on Agricultural Policy of the Republic of South Africa," Pretoria, Republic of South Africa, 1984, p. 6.

7. C. J. Van Rooyen, "Agricultural Development in Southern Africa and DBSA as a Source of Funding," unpublished mimeo, Development Bank of Southern Africa, 1987, p. 56.

8. See Levin and Weiner, "The Agrarian Question," for a more detailed discussion of emerging ideologies regarding the land question.

9. Paul Daphne, "Agrarian Reform in a Post-Apartheid South Africa: Issues and Options," *South Africa Economic Research and Training Project Working Papers* 1, no. 2 (1989): 41–65.

10. For a thorough presentation of this complex issue, see Catherine Cross and Richard Haines, *Towards Freehold: Options for Land and Development in South Africa's Rural Areas* (Cape Town: Juta and Co., Ltd., 1988).

Selected Bibliography

Beinart, William. "Agrarian Historiography and Agrarian Reconstruction." In John Lonsdale (ed.), *South Africa in Question*, Portsmouth: Heineman, 1988, pp. 134–153.

Cobbett, Matthew. "The Land Question in South Africa: A Preliminary Assessment." *The South African Journal of Economics* 55, no. 1 (1987): 63–77.

Cooper, David. *Working the Land: A Review of Agriculture in South Africa.* Johannesburg: Environmental and Development Agency, 1988.

———. "Ownership and Control of Agriculture in South Africa." In John Suckling and Landeg White (eds.), *After Apartheid: Renewal of the South African Economy*, Trenton, N.J.: Africa World Press, 1988, pp. 47–65.

Cross, Catherine, and Richard Haines. *Towards Freehold: Options for Land and Development in South Africa's Rural Areas.* Cape Town: Juta and Co., Ltd., 1988.

Danaher, Kevin. "Bantustan Agriculture in South Africa: Obstacles to Development Under a Post-Apartheid Government." Paper presented at the Conference on The Southern African Economy After Apartheid, University of York, September 29–October 2, 1986.

Daphne, Paul. "Agrarian Reform in a Post-Apartheid South Africa: Issues and Options." *South Africa Economic Research and Training Project Working Papers* 1, no. 2 (1989): 41–65.

de Klerk, Michael. "The Accumulation Crisis in Agriculture." Labour and Economic Research Center, The University of Cape Town, 1988.

Fenyes, Thomas, Johann van Zyl, and Nick Vink. "Structural Imbalances in South African Agriculture." *The South African Journal of Economics* 56, no. 2 (1988): 181–194.

Harsch, Ernest. *Apartheid's Great Land Theft: The Struggle for the Right to Farm in South Africa.* New York: Pathfinder Press, 1986.

Letsoalo, Essy. *Land Reform in South Africa: A Black Perspective.* Johannesburg: Skotaville Publishers, 1987.

Levin, Richard, and Daniel Weiner. "The Agrarian Question and the Emergence of Conflicting Agricultural Strategies in South Africa." Paper presented at the SAERT policy workshop at the University of Wageningen, The Netherlands,

November 12-14, 1989.

Lipton, Merle. "South Africa: Two Agricultures?" In Francis Wilson, Alide Kooy, and Delia Hendrie (eds.), *Farm Labour in South Africa*, Cape Town: David Philip, 1977, pp. 72–85.

Mabin, Alan. "Land Ownership and the Prospects for Land Reform in the Transvaal." In Catherine Cross and Richard Haines (eds.), *Towards Freehold: Options for Land and Development in South Africa's Rural Areas*, Cape Town: Juta and Co., Ltd., 1988, pp. 137–144.

Marcus, Tessa. *Modernizing Super-Exploitation: Restructuring South African Agriculture*. London: Zed Books, 1989.

Platzky, Laurine, and Cherryl Walker. *The Surplus People: Forced Removals in South Africa*. Johannesburg: Ravan Press, 1985.

Seidman, Ann, Kamima Mwanza, Nomcebo Simelane, and Daniel Weiner (eds.). *Transforming Southern African Agriculture*. Trenton, N.J.: Africa World Press, 1990.

Viljoen, M. F. "Structural Changes in Respect of Ownership and the Right of Use of Land in Commercial Agricultural Production Units—Causative Forces and Influence on Social Welfare." *Agrekon* 27, no. 3 (1988): 21–30.

Weiner, Daniel. "Agricultural Transformation in Zimbabwe: Lessons for South Africa After Apartheid." *Geoforum* 19, no. 4 (1988): 479–496.

"White Paper on Agricultural Policy of the Republic of South Africa." Pretoria, Republic of South Africa, 1984.

Wilson, Francis, and Mamphela Ramphele. *Uprooting Poverty: The South African Challenge*. Cape Town: David Philip, 1989.

part five

Conclusion

chapter eleven

Issues for the Near Future

Roy L. Prosterman
Timothy M. Hanstad
Mary N. Temple

Land tenure has been one of the leading social and economic issues of the twentieth century. At least twenty-five countries have experienced sweeping reallocations of land since the beginning of the century, including such major countries as Mexico, the Soviet Union, Japan, China, and Egypt. Six of these significant redistributions have occurred since 1970: South Vietnam, Ethiopia, and Kerala state in India in the 1970s; and Nicaragua, El Salvador, and China's decollectivization in the 1980s. Prospects for the 1990s may be for the most active period of tenure reform since the immediate postwar era of 1946–1954,[1] with several of the prime candidates having been identified in this volume.

What are the issues that we should bear in mind as we enter the next decade? A review of the preceding ten chapters of this book suggests seven "thematic" questions that are vital to understanding what has happened in the field of land reform in recent years, and what may happen—or needs to happen—in the 1990s and beyond:

- What are the goals of land reform?
- What are the variables that lead a government to the decision to carry out significant land reform?
- What are the issues relating to the specific land-reform process of decollectivization?
- What are the key program-design issues, in light of the past decades of experience?
- What supporting measures are needed to build on land reform and turn it into complete agrarian reform?
- Where may we expect the issue of land reform to be addressed next?
- What are the implications for U.S. policy, and that of other industrialized democracies?

What are the Goals of Land Reform?

Land-reform programs can simultaneously serve a number of purposes. Sometimes agricultural productivity is the only goal considered, but as a number of the chapters and the authors' one-and-a-half days of roundtable discussions have indicated, there are other equally important goals.

Even apart from potential increases in production, land reform makes beneficiary families, which are typically among the poorest of the poor, better off by letting them keep—to consume or sell—a significant portion of the production that would otherwise go to the landlord or plantation owner. This is true even if the beneficiaries are required to make some repayment to the government for the land received, since the level of repayment is typically substantially less (rightfully so) than the ex-landowners would otherwise have received or kept.

Land reform can generate increased overall economic activity, including the creation of nonagricultural jobs. As a broad base of agricultural families benefiting from land reform receive higher incomes, they enter the marketplace for a range of locally produced goods and services, from improved housing to schoolbooks, from bicycles to sewing machines. Development theory has rediscovered agriculture, recognizing that a dynamic agriculture has significant forward and backward linkages to broader societal development.

As articulated so well by Ronald Herring in Chapter 2, beneficiaries achieve dramatic improvements in status and dignity. They are, as campesinos interviewed in El Salvador put it, "independent of the *patron*, and no longer in the service of the rich."

This accession of power at the local level has, in turn, significant consequences for participation in effective political activity. Initially, the peasants may be enabled to make demands for a fairer share of government-administered programs and services. Real democracy means real responsiveness by states. Land reform creates new configurations of secure and self-confident producers who are willing to challenge the inertia, elitism, and neglect that frequently characterize the politics of underdevelopment. These changes will eventually have impact above the village level.

The elimination of the basic grievances arising out of the relationship with the erstwhile landowner has fundamental consequences for reducing political instability, as seen in settings such as Mexico (where, as Merilee Grindle notes in Chapter 6, land reform has contributed to the long tenure of the *Partido Revolutionaria Institucional*), or El Salvador (where, as Rupert Scofield points out in Chapter 5, land reform may well have averted full-scale civil war in

1980–1981). Kerala offers a caveat, though, showing that it is important that more than a minority of those with a substantial relationship to given parcels of land receive initial benefits under a land-reform program. In Kerala, rights went to tenants but not to laborers who worked the same land. "Political stability" is a double-edged sword. Excessive instability means constricted development, violence, and human misery, whereas the professed goal of "stability" is sometimes used to justify human-rights violations, and excessive stability means stagnation. An optimum balance is achieved when the real grievances of the population are addressed. Land reform addresses the most basic rural grievances and optimally increases commitment to a system in which new demands are energized and negotiated.

In specific settings such as Brazil, distribution of unutilized and underutilized land may also have an important environmental impact by preventing desperate, landless peasants from descending on, cutting down, and burning the tropical forest in the search for a piece of land to farm, no matter how marginal. Also in Brazil, as Anthony Hall's account in Chapter 7 makes clear, land reform could play an important environmental role by permanently removing incentives given to large cattle ranchers, who do even more of the cutting and burning of the Amazon forest. Many other landless families are driven by their desperation into the cities. In a wide range of settings, effective land-reform measures give landless peasant families a stake in their village society, and keep millions from descending upon the bursting cities of the Third World.

On the agricultural-productivity side, there appears to be cogent evidence on four points. (1) Smaller holdings generally outproduce larger ones, hectare for hectare (thus supporting the desirability, from an agricultural-productivity standpoint, of subdividing all but the most efficient large plantations and large collective farms). (2) On any given holding, a cultivator with ownership or an equivalent owner-like tenure will be far more likely to make long-term capital and "sweat-equity" investments that improve and conserve the land, and that take a number of years to recover their cost and yield a profit, than will a cultivator with insecure tenure (thus supporting the desirability, from an agricultural-productivity standpoint, of providing ownership or equivalent tenure to those who are merely tenants, squatters, or insecure users). (3) A cultivator with ownership or owner-like tenure is also more likely to use improved (and more expensive) seeds, fertilizer, and other inputs than will a tenant in the typical tenancy arrangement where the tenant pays for all inputs and receives only a portion of the output. (4) Small-scale, owner-operated farms are more likely to substitute labor and on-farm inputs for hard-currency-intensive alternatives, thereby lessening foreign-exchange bottlenecks to growth.

Related to the productivity issue, it would appear that any given amount of production, in the hands of the cultivators rather than substantially in those of landlords or plantation owners, has a generally greater chance of contributing to the kind of investment and consumption patterns that will further increase agricultural productivity, meet basic human needs in the villages, and help via broad-based demand to create nonagricultural jobs in a range of goods-and-service–providing enterprises.

What are the Variables that Lead a Government to the Decision to Carry Out Significant Land Reform?

Building effective grassroots support for land-reform measures and forming linkages to political parties clearly have been important factors in determining whether land-reform measures will be adopted and whether land reform, once legislated, will actually be implemented. Such grassroots support and political linkages played a significant role in the Keralan and Salvadoran reforms discussed in this volume, and are likely to become even more important to the extent that many of the countries where land reform is still needed are political democracies. These include India (where, as in Kerala, much of the effort will have to be at the state level), the Philippines, Brazil, and Costa Rica. These variables also may be of considerable importance where there are weak authoritarian governments that find it difficult simply to act by fiat from the center, such as El Salvador in 1980, and perhaps Bangladesh and Honduras today. Even in the Soviet Union, grassroots demands and action by elected legislative bodies—including those at the level of individual republics—may play a significant role in shaping specific land-reform measures, and the same may prove true in Romania and elsewhere in Eastern Europe.

The organizational impetus for such grassroots political activism may come from several sources: political parties that see land reform as an issue around which they can build broad peasant support; religious groups; indigenous nongovernmental organizations; or labor organizations. As to the latter, it is important that even urban unions may come to see land reform as providing several major benefits: political stability, the growth of rural demand that stimulates nonagricultural employment, and a slowing of the flow of desperate migrants from the countryside competing for jobs at virtually any wage. The possibility of technical and financial assistance via public or private foreign aid to such grassroots organizational efforts (easiest in the case of labor organizations or private voluntary organizations) should be kept in view.

The variable of political will in a strong central authority, such as MacArthur in Japan or Chiang Kai-shek in Taiwan, has been important in the past, and may still play a dominant role in settings such as Indonesia. But in the future, the variable of political will in a strong central authority seems more likely to operate in a mode in which a resolute center acts in conjunction with local mobilization and cooperation.

The variables of fear, compensation, education, and outside support have played important roles as well. The willingness to consider land reform seriously in the Philippines seems to have varied over time to a considerable degree in tandem with the fortunes of the Huks and the New People's Army, and clearly the guerrilla threat was a factor in El Salvador (as it had been in the 1970–1973 land reform in South Vietnam[2]). Future guerrilla movements with an agrarian agenda might well stimulate land reform by the government in power in Bangladesh, Guatemala, or elsewhere.

The prospect of credible compensation for privately owned land, supported by either internal or external resources, has also been an important variable. The lack of resources for compensation (as seen in Zimbabwe) may limit land-reform efforts that would otherwise be possible. Compensation, by reducing the opposition of the landowners, as well as by helping to legitimize the reform in the eyes of significant sectors of public opinion, may substantially reduce the amount of grass-roots pressure or central-authority determination that would otherwise be necessary to carry out a given degree of reform.

Education is likely to be an important variable also. The clearly held knowledge both that land reform can bring extensive benefits to the society and that specific solutions to the technical issues of land reform are at hand may help, in turn, to crystalize the will to carry out such a program.

Support and encouragement from outside played an important role in the South Vietnamese and Salvadoran land reforms, as it did in the postwar reforms in Japan, Taiwan, and South Korea. External assistance, governmental or private, may be of significance for both the education and grassroots organization variables, and official foreign aid can have a vital role with respect to landowner compensation. This issue of external support comes up later, when we discuss implications for U.S. policy and for the policies of other industrialized democracies.

The decision to adopt and implement an effective land reform can be thought of as the "vector resultant" of all these interacting variables, and perhaps of others as well. There are those who suggest that effective land redistribution cannot occur through any of these variables, alone or in combination, but only through radical social change, most likely via the violent overthrow of the existing order. The land reform of Kerala, as well as those of Taiwan, South Korea, and a number of others, should stand as adequate counterexamples to this proposition. Moreover, extensive redistribution of the asset—land—on which most of the people in agrarian societies largely rely for their livelihood, security, and status is in itself a major step toward radical social change, with ramifications affecting the entire fabric of the society.

What are the Issues in the Process of Decollectivization?

Some of the most dramatic land-tenure reforms have recently come, or are in prospect, in settings of collectivized agriculture. The virtually universal decollectivization of China's agriculture in the early 1980s affected one out of every three agricultural families on the planet. Arguably, it was the largest land reform yet. The Soviet Union is seriously considering the option of individual farming. Decollectivization is already an issue in the wake of the Romanian revolution, and may become an issue in other parts of Eastern Europe, beyond Poland and Yugoslavia, which have kept a system of predominantly individual farming. It is currently a significant issue as well in other countries that have either adopted, or previously been committed to, collectivization—in Nicaragua and El Salvador (on Phase I cooperatives) which are discussed in Chapter 5, as well as in Ethiopia, Mozambique, Cambodia, Laos, and Vietnam.

Several important issues or potentially important lessons arise for those who are considering decollectivization, as Karen Brooks makes clear in Chapter 8 on the Soviet Union, Poland, and Hungary; and Roy Prosterman and Timothy Hanstad show in Chapter 4 on China.

Long-term tenure security is important if maximum productivity increases are to be achieved, although more modest increases that are achievable without substantial "sweat equity" or capital improvements to the land may be realized with somewhat less security. But the provision of long-term tenure security faces a significant ideological obstacle in many of the countries where decollectivization has been, or will be, an issue. Such long-term security, with considerable freedom from the cadres or erstwhile collective-farm bureaucracy, implies a status approaching that of ownership, and "private property" has been anathema to some ideologues since the Communist Manifesto.

There are several possible responses to such ideological concerns: First, a number of Communist countries do allow private ownership of land. Second, the separable and legitimate underlying concerns—such as those over accumulation of large tracts of land or leasing out to tenants—can be dealt with effectively in prohibitory provisions of the land-reform law, as they have been in a number of major non-communist land reforms. Finally, some new way of characterizing such broad provision of landownership can be found: not describing it as the institution of "private property," as Karl Marx understood it in the social setting of 140 years ago, but as the institution, for example, of "universal asset endowment," or "labor ownership," or even as a "microcooperative" involving only the family unit.[3]

An issue in the Soviet Union will be the acceptability to the farm bureaucracy of what is done. (China may have largely avoided this issue because much control had already devolved down to the production-team level, and the production-team leader was essentially just another farmer, who also stood to benefit personally from decollectivization.) Karen Brooks suggests in Chapter 8 that a separate cadre might be given power over the making of the individual arrangements. And, to the extent there is still resistance from the farm bureaucracy, many of the variables that can help promote reform on private land in other countries may find their counterpart: growth of grassroots pressure, authoritarian will at the center, or even the possibility of finding some way of "compensating" the bureaucrats for their lost authority (land of their own? other duties? even some form of severance pay?).

But, especially in the Soviet Union, the issue of acceptability to the collectivized farmers also looms. Present-day Soviet farmers know no other mode of farming (with the important exception of the private plots), and are heavily subsidized on the poorly performing collective farms. Both the possibility of the "carrot" and the "stick" may arise. Incentives might take the form of ownership or something approaching ownership (now under active discussion) rather than a forty-nine–year lease, as well as greater assurance of inputs and marketing freedom on the individual holding; the "stick" might consist of the reduction or termination of the present wage subsidies to the collectives.

A further important issue, just adverted to, is the environment in which decollectivization occurs. This includes the question of availability of credit and inputs, access to extension services, and ability to market agricultural products at free-market rather than low state-set prices. The privatization or at least partial privatization of inputs and marketing may be of particular importance in settings such as the Soviet Union, in which there might be only partial decollectivization involving a minority of farmers from a given collective, who might otherwise be placed in the adverse position of having to rely on the managers of the continuing collective both for agricultural inputs and for marketing.

What are the Key Program-Design Issues in Light of the Past Decades of Land-Reform Experience?

The principal subissues may be summarized under the following topics: alternatives to expropriation of private land, achieving sufficient universality, defining the land available, compensation and financial viability, beneficiary rights, local-level administration, and the need for data.[4]

A threshold issue may be whether there are alternatives to the mandatory (but compensated) taking of private land as the basis for redistribution to nonlandowning agricultural families. The basic conclusion is that there are only rare settings where this may be the case. "Resettlement" or "colonization" of uncultivated public lands has sometimes been urged as an alternative source of land, but few countries with significant landlessness problems have substantial amounts of potentially cultivable public land available; and even where such land appears available, heavy costs often make it impossible to solve any large part of the landlessness problem by such means. Such costs are discussed in this volume in the contexts of the Philippines, Guatemala, and, most extensively, Brazil, and may include great social dislocation, heavy financial subsidies per family resettled,[5] and extensive environmental degradation as tropical forests are cleared—with the uncovered soil, paradoxically, often proving fragile and unsuitable to cropping needs.

Another often-cited alternative to mandatory, compensated takings of private land as the basis for a land-reform program is voluntary purchase of private land via a land-bank mechanism. But settings where such voluntary purchases are likely to affect appreciably the landlessness problem are rare. Rupert Scofield's account of such efforts in Central America in Chapter 5 suggests that only when the pressure on landowners to sell becomes extreme—as it is today in El Salvador for landowners whose holdings are in zones of military conflict—is there a prospect of significant amounts of land being made available by such means. Even then, great care must be taken in negotiating a per-hectare price low enough to permit replication. In the great majority of cases, such programs are likely to be a gesture, reaching little land and few beneficiaries over an extended period of time. The voluntary-purchase mechanism has never figured significantly in any major land-reform program.

Assuming that private lands are to be expropriated, an initial question relates to achieving sufficient scope, or universality, in the program to reach most potential beneficiaries. In the postwar land reforms of Japan, Taiwan, and South Korea, it was generally self-evident who the beneficiaries should be. In those settings it was the tenant farmers who actually cultivated the land, and who formed a far larger group of nonlandowning agriculturalists than did agricultural laborers. But the question of who is to be included as land-reform beneficiaries will be more complex in most settings in which land reform is likely to be an important issue today, as Ronald Herring's account in Chapter 2 of the Keralan land reform suggests. There, the question arose—as it would elsewhere on the Indian subcontinent and in such settings as Java—of whether or not agricultural laborers who worked in the small- and medium-holding sector would be accommodated as well as tenants. Alternatively, in many Latin American settings where land reform is needed, a large majority of beneficiaries may be laborers on large plantations, with a range of possibilities in the definition of the beneficiary group, including permanent and nonpermanent, resident and nonresident laborers.

A land reform is likely to be more successful in terms of assuring status and dignity and in reducing political instability—and no less successful in agricultural terms—to the degree it extends benefits (on a given amount of land) to as many as practicable of all those agricultural families in the society who do not have ownership or an owner-like interest in the land they till. This means that laborers as well as tenants, and nonpermanent laborers as well as permanent ones, should wherever possible benefit from the process. Benefits need not necessarily be uniform: for example, in the Keralan land reform, the minority of agricultural laborers who received ownership of even tiny garden plots of a few hundred square meters found themselves considerably better off. We have made parallel observations on the potential importance of garden plots to otherwise landless laborers in fieldwork on Java.[6]

On the question of defining land available, most of the successful programs involving tenanted lands either redistributed all tenanted land by employing a "zero retention limit" for such land (as in Kerala, and also South Korea, South Vietnam, and, for nonvillage absentee landlords, Japan) or, with somewhat greater administrative difficulty, redistributed the great majority of tenanted land by using a very low nonzero limit (landlords could keep three hectares of average land in Taiwan, resident village landlords could keep one hectare in Japan). The possibility of obtaining zero or very low retention limits remains a live issue in the Philippines—and will be elsewhere, to the extent that tenanted lands become the subject of land-reform efforts.

In most of Latin America, and also in southern Africa, there is greater flexibility in defining the land to be taken than was true in East Asia. In East Asia, ratios of arable land to population were low, large farms were atypical, and most landless agriculturalists were tenant farmers on small- and medium-sized holdings. In contrast, a common pattern in much of Latin America and southern Africa is higher ratios of arable land to population, with large farms cultivated by hired laborers (both permanent and temporary) and, in some cases, with significant areas of underutilized land. Rather than focusing on the taking of all or the great majority of tenanted lands for distribution to the tenants presently on such land, the issue here should generally be one of taking from large, unitary operational holdings land defined in one or more of three ways: (1) land in excess of a given ceiling or retention limit that is very high by Asian standards—for example, "all land held in excess of 500 hectares"; (2) land that is underutilized—for example, "all underutilized land on holdings that are above 500 hectares," ·or even better, "all underutilized land, regardless of holding size"; or (3) excessive holdings of pastureland that can be redistributed for small crop-farming enterprises—for example, with special application to countries such as Brazil, Honduras, and Costa Rica, which have great amounts of poorly utilized pastureland in large holdings, "60 percent of all pastureland in holdings that are above 500 hectares."[7]

The desirability of providing compensation for land taken has already been alluded to. Besides the political argument, there are good legal and ethical arguments for reasonable compensation, regardless of the de facto coercive power of the government. This need not, and probably should not, however, mean "full market value." Jeffrey Riedinger, in his discussion of the Philippines in Chapter 1, notes the recent Philippine Supreme Court decision in which the court recognizes the vital point that "just compensation" must be taken to have a different meaning in the context of a sweeping and essential social program than it would in a narrowly targeted eminent domain proceeding (e.g., acquiring land for a road or a post office).

Compensation should probably generally be based on either a multiple of crop value (the usual approach in East Asia—Taiwan, for example, paid two-and-one-half times the annual main crop yield, payable 30 percent in shares of four government-owned corporations, which were thus privatized, and 70 percent in inflation-adjusting bonds, which were redeemed in equal installments over 10 years) or landowners' public declarations (past tax declarations were used quite successfully in El Salvador), with a rule of thumb that compensation should not exceed what is required at prevailing rates of return on other investments to produce the same ongoing flow of income that had been produced by the land taken (with an exception for cultivable land that is not in production). Drawing on the Taiwanese model, deferred compensation should normally be inflation-adjusting (although this has seemingly not been the usual practice); and, apart from the possibility of privatizing government-owned businesses, a portion of the bonds issued to former landowners should perhaps be made usable with the banking system as preferred collateral for loans for various productive investments.

Turning to beneficiary rights, one important aspect is the choice between individual and collective farming. The organization of farming should in general follow the freely expressed preferences of the beneficiaries. In our experience, these preferences are usually for individual farming, but there may be special political or other circumstances (e.g., El Salvador today on the Phase I holdings) where the short-term preference of many of the beneficiaries is to hew together in joint or mixed farming operations for security reasons. Also, one does not have a true expression of such preferences if it is perceived that one form of agriculture will be discriminatorily either heavily subsidized or starved of support.

It is clear that individual holdings are generally more efficient and productive on a given piece of land. This is evident not only from comparisons between nations, but from the longitudinal experience of China under collectivization followed by decollectivization, as well as from the general experience of private plots on collective farms. However, cooperation in ancillary services of credit and marketing can be important complements to the individual producer.

There are other important aspects of beneficiary rights. A corollary of the proposition that benefits should go to as many nonlandowning families as possible is that the per-family quantity of land allocated should not greatly exceed the amount that a family can intensively farm with its own labor and modest capital. Asian experience underscores that even without a year-round growing season (as in Japan and South Korea), a full-size farm of less than one hectare can in many settings provide adequate annual nutrition and a surplus for a household, whereas, as in the Keralan or Javanese setting, even small garden plots can provide a significant increment to household nutrition and income. A tendency in some land reforms has been to provide per capita holdings far larger than necessary—indeed, considerably larger than a family is likely to be able to work. This is evident in the account of the Zimbabwean reform, where a massive fifty-one hectares was the average amount of land given to beneficiaries, whereas, as Michael Bratton points out in Chapter 9, two to five hectares should suffice. Rather than providing some idealized holding size, it is generally much better to use the area calculated to be available under the land-reform acquisition formula divided by the number of families needing land, and to use the resulting quotient as an approximate target for average per-family allocations, recognizing that every recipient family will thereby be made substantially better off than they presently are, even if they are not made "ideally" well off.

Finally, with respect to beneficiary rights, there is a question of what bundle of rights beneficiaries should receive in the land they do get. Where beneficiaries receive individual rights, these should clearly be sufficiently secure so that long-term investments will be made, and normally this means they must receive the local equivalent of fee simple ownership of the land. Certainly the state should not become the owner, or the manager, of the land taken. On the other hand, there are certain sensible restrictions. The new individual owners should normally have the power of sale of the land (in contrast, for example, to the ejido arrangement in Mexico) so that they can cash out on improvements if they want to leave agriculture or retire; but they should probably be restricted from selling for a modest initial period—perhaps until they have paid for the land, or for a flat period such as ten years. Also, they should only be able to sell to another small cultivator, whose total holding will not thereby exceed some reasonable size limit defining a small family farm. And, although they should be able to sell, they should generally not be permitted to rent out the land, which would put someone on the land who is not likely to be motivated to make long-term improvements. The latter restriction may be lifted later in the development process, as in Japan, after needed capital improvements in the land are likely to have been made, and when increased economic activity and job creation have led to a situation in which would-be tenants have reasonable status and bargaining power.[8]

As to questions of land-reform administration, it is clearly important, as Asian experience has particularly demonstrated (e.g., Japan, Taiwan, South Korea, South Vietnam, China, and Kerala), to involve beneficiaries in program administration. By contrast, the Philippine and El Salvador discussions provide examples of top-down administration. Determinations on such initial questions as who owns the land, who has been farming it and whether they farm it permanently or occasionally, and what it produces (important for many valuation formulas, as well as for determinations taking underutilized land) are best made by cultivator-dominated, local-level administrative committees, assisted by initial instruction and guidance from the land-reform agency. In some Latin American settings, grassroots campesino unions or organizations may also be able to play this role. Beneficiaries should not have to leave the village or the locale of the estate to complete simple applications for benefits; and the land-reform program, and their rights under it, should be correspondingly publicized in advance at the local level. Regular radio broadcasts can be effective in publicizing details of the land-reform program, as they initially were in El Salvador (although the Salvadoran government regrettably failed to allow significant local-level administrative participation).

There should probably be an analogous role for committees of collective workers where comprehensive decollectivization is the issue. The beneficiary-dominated process of delineating and allocating over half a billion separate parcels to roughly 150 million farm households in China's decollectivization, most of this during a two-year period, is an extraordinary demonstration of the effectiveness of local-level involvement in such a land reform.

Finally, good data are vital to program design, both in terms of initial preparation (How many agricultural families are predominantly dependent on cultivating land they do not own? How many are tenants, how many laborers, how many others? What is the distribution and concentration of existing ownership? What are production, rent, and land incomes?) and in terms of monitoring program implementation and making desirable administrative adjustments. Such data, where lacking, should be collected. Even before the land-reform issue is ripe, collecting preparatory data is important. Where decisions on land reform are imminent, it is crucial to collect essential data by the fastest possible means, such as sample surveys rather than complete censuses, because, typically, there are only constricted windows of time when land reform is possible.[9]

What Supporting Measures are Needed to Build on Land Reform and Turn it into Complete Agrarian Reform?

Provision of land under secure ownership or owner-like tenure may in itself move significantly toward the important goals of providing status and dignity to the beneficiaries and resolving political grievances, but it is generally insufficient, standing alone, to achieve the goal of sharply increased and diversified agricultural production. That lesson emerges most notably in Merilee Grindle's discussion of Mexico in Chapter 6. Its obverse—what *is* achievable with the addition of even modest credit and support in the context of ownership or owner-like tenure—is illustrated by the experience of both reform beneficiaries and the traditional small-holders with owner-like tenure in Michael Bratton's description of Zimbabwean agriculture in Chapter 9. Decollectivization has a parallel problem, seen in the concern over what kind of support the individual holders will have in the Soviet Union, and previously experienced in Poland's long-standing discriminatory withholding of support from the majority private-farm sector in favor of the limited collectivized sector.

Achievement of full agricultural benefits generally requires building upon land reform, to achieve what is sometimes called "agrarian reform." Essential complementary services should include availability of credit and inputs at a modest level, targeted on the beneficiaries; extension services similarly targeted; and a supportive marketing environment (including the absence of artificially determined low prices set by government fiat). As with the distribution of land, one should strive to avoid excessive benefits, both because the provision of too many services may lead to state paternalism and because giving excess benefits to a few usually means a sacrifice of benefits to the many. For example, as a rule of thumb applicable in many settings, production credit for basic food crops should not exceed US$100 per hectare or US$500 per family, whichever is less. In addition to providing these supporting services to land-reform beneficiaries, they should (as in Zimbabwe) also be made available to existing small owners who have previously been without such support.

Among the important complementary measures, we should also include family planning. Land reform combined with complementary agricultural measures can create both a form of old-age security on the land and a basis for ensuring the survival of those children who are born that can, together, contribute powerfully to the success of family planning. On the other hand, the economic effects of the bare transfer of land or of land transferred in a pro-natalist cultural setting, unaccompanied by effective measures to bring down birth rates, can be counterbalanced in a generation—as seen in Mexico—by the continuing explosion of the rural population. People will still be better off than they would have been with population growth and without the distribution of land, but they will not be nearly as well off as they might have been had land reform been coupled with a sharp reduction in the birth rate (as it has been, for example, in Japan, China, Taiwan, South Korea, and Kerala).[10]

Where May the Issue of Land Reform Be Addressed Next?

Land-tenure issues persist in many parts of the world where exploitative patterns of plantation agriculture and landlessness prevail, as well as in settings of involuntary and inefficient collectivization. However, the land-reform issue in its conspicuous form—not only where a severe land-tenure problem exists, but where a government appears to be keenly aware of the problem and about to do something about it—generally arises at discrete moments in time, probably in only three or four countries during a typical decade. In terms of awareness in the industrialized democracies, landlessness is unlike other major problems such as childhood diseases or the international debt, for which it is relatively easy to keep development banks, bilateral aid agencies, and other relevant actors focused continuously on the issues and the need for relevant responses.

But the issue *is* with us today, in its conspicuous form, in several countries—indeed, probably in more countries than at any time since the end of World War II—and is very much in prospect in a number of others. Projecting the problem forward over time (rather than waiting for each separate window of opportunity, and reacting only after it opens) may be helpful in confronting the land-reform question in ways that make relevant administrative and financial resources available to support timely and adequate responses.

Land reform is an immediate issue today in several of the collectivized or previously collectivized agricultures: in the Soviet Union, in China (where the issue whether to make further major changes—forward in the direction of more secure tenure or perhaps even backward in the direction of recollectivization—is a live one), and also in Romania, Nicaragua, Vietnam, Laos, Cambodia, Mozambique, and Ethiopia. Land reform continues to be an immediate issue in El Salvador under the new ARENA government, both in terms of the preservation and the extension of the 1980 measures. It is presently an issue in Paraguay, in the wake of Stroessner's departure (perhaps leaving behind, like Somoza in Nicaragua, significant amounts of personally owned and "crony" land), and it is virtually sure to be a key issue facing the newly elected government of Namibia in 1990. It could also be a major issue again in Zimbabwe, when the "entrenched" anti-expropriation provisions of the constitution expire in 1990. Nor has it been resolved under the recent weak land-reform law in the Philippines, although the government for the moment apparently does not plan any additional efforts.

Although not presently a "conspicuous" issue that the government actively addresses, severe land-tenure problems exist in a series of other countries. In many of these countries the issue seems likely to provide opportunities for action over the next decade: this applies to Bangladesh, to Pakistan, to several of the most populous states of India, to the island of Java, to Brazil, to all of Central America (beyond El Salvador and Nicaragua), and to South Africa. In addition, the issue could arise in other countries with high proportions of landless families, such as Iran, Turkey, Iraq, Sri Lanka, Colombia, and Ecuador. Moreover, the specific decollectivization issue could eventually come up widely in Eastern Europe. In short, land reform remains a global issue, one that we must learn to confront in a systematic, rather than ad hoc, way.

What Are the Implications for U.S. Policy and that of Other Industrialized Democracies?

The global nature of these issues leads us directly to the question of policy implications for the United States and other industrialized democracies. At the final session of the authors' conference, we concluded that the United States and other industrialized democracies can and should stand ready to provide important support affecting three of the major variables that are likely to determine whether land reform occurs in a given country setting.

1. Technical assistance and financial support should be provided, especially via the private sector, to indigenous nongovernmental organizations, labor organizations, or other broad-based groups, to do essential grassroots organizing on the land-reform issue. Perhaps one noteworthy example of such activity in the 1980s was the support of the AFL-CIO's technical-assistance affiliate for democratic campesino organizations in El Salvador, which played a key role in the initiation of the reform, although not in its ultimate administration.

2. Technical assistance from either public or private sources in aid-donor countries (or multilateral institutions) should provide education and comparative perspective to government policymakers on land-reform benefits and on the elements of program design and administration. One consequence of the discrete nature of land-reform decisions is that many of the countries where it is needed have little experience or knowledge of how to carry out an effective land reform, and even with appropriate political will may end up with a seriously flawed program unless they consult the experience of other countries.

3. Financial support and technical assistance—especially from public aid agencies, given the scale that is required—should be provided to land-reform programs actually being carried out. In the case of the United States, a 1985 amendment to Section 620(g) of the Foreign Assistance Act, following the unanimous recommendation of the Kissinger Commission on Central America, allows funding for land-reform compensation, thus installing it as a recognized principle of the foreign-assistance law. Also, from the authors' own experience, aid officials in many of the other industrialized democracies are highly sympathetic on the issue. But there are two important elements that can make such assistance work most effectively.

First, it should not just be made available on an ad hoc basis, after the land-reform attempt is under way, as the United States has recently done in El Salvador and the Philippines. Rather, it should involve resources identified in advance, so that a country seriously considering land reform knows that such resources are there to be called upon. For example, the U.S. administration or Congress should consider earmarking at least a modest amount of the foreign-assistance budget—perhaps $50 million a year, which was the amount made available on a one-time basis to the Philippines in 1988—on a continuing basis for land-reform support, to be used wherever the opportunity arises, and to cumulate until used if the opportunity does not arise in a given year. The United States should also seek parallel commitments from other donor countries, with the goal that at least a few hundred million dollars each year (perhaps something like 1 percent of the $33–36 billion in aid given annually by the industrialized democracies) should be dedicated to this important purpose. Concomitantly, the Agency for International Development might consider drawing together available technical-assistance resources in a small, continuing Office of Land Reform (or, perhaps, "Office of the Family Farm"), so that those resources are not simply scattered throughout the agency after each encounter with the land-reform issue.

Second, financial assistance should be made available on a "progress payments" basis, so that resources are actually released only according to an agreed formula in each case as land is actually redistributed to nonlandowning agricultural families. This is important both to the incentive effect of these resources in the recipient country, and to political support for their renewal or expansion in the donor country.

In all of these issues, the United States has a crucial role to play, and one that has proven to be very influential when used to address the land-tenure problem. In the past, the United States has used its resources, its technical know-how, and its links to both central governments and grassroots organizations to great effect in support of major land-reform programs. But the opportunity to support the initiation and implementation of land-reform programs is available to other countries as well, as Great Britain has done, for example, in the case of Zimbabwe.

The opportunity always exists for foreign-aid donors to assist in addressing land-tenure problems. Land reform has been a vital issue throughout the twentieth century, and promises to remain critically important in a score or more of countries in the years to come. But the fact that land reform, unlike issues such as childhood diseases and international debt, tends to arise in its conspicuous form only at discrete moments in time makes it difficult to keep the media, the public, and the aid agencies in the industrialized democracies focused continuously on the need for programmatic responses. Perhaps, paralleling the earlier UN/UNICEF aim of "universal child immunization by 1990," we should articulate the goal of "land for the landless by 2010." Whatever is to be done, elaborating a sufficient response in the democracies must begin with a process of self-education. That, ultimately, is the reason for this volume.

Notes

1. This period included major land redistributions in Japan, Taiwan, North and South Korea, China, Bolivia, Poland, and Yugoslavia.

2. The South Vietnamese reform has been little written about, but was highly successful. Between 1970 and 1973 approximately one million tenant families received title to their land. While it was being carried out, indigenous Vietcong recruitment dropped about 80 percent, and rice productivity increased some 30 percent. The reform could not, of course, deal with other critical problems, such as the army divisions coming down from the North, the nepotism in the South Vietnamese army, or the understandable war-weariness in the United States. From all accounts, the reform sector has not been collectivized by the Communist government.

3. Compare the recently enacted land-reform law of Lithuania, which appears to take this last approach, although it prohibits the sale and mortgaging of family-"owned" land. *Pravda Litvy*, July 9, 1989.

4. For further discussion of program-design issues, see Roy L. Prosterman and Jeffrey M. Riedinger, *Land Reform and Democratic Development* (Baltimore, Md.: Johns Hopkins University Press, 1987), pp. 177–202.

5. Nicholas Guppy, in "Tropical Deforestation: A Global View," *Foreign Affairs*, 62, no. 4 (1984): 928, 939, indicates that, based on actual World Bank–financed resettlement schemes, costs per family ran between US\$5,000 and US\$20,000 per family even a decade ago. Comparable figures would probably be at least 50 percent higher today.

6. See Roy L. Prosterman and Jeffrey M. Riedinger, *Indonesian Development and U.S. Aid*, RDI Monographs on Foreign Aid and Development #3, January 1987, pp. 18–20; Roy L. Prosterman, Timothy Hanstad, and Erman Rajagukguk, "A Pilot-Project Test of a Possible Small-Plot Land-Asset Endowment Model for Landless and Nearly Landless Families on Java," February 27, 1990 (unpublished).

7. Investment by the original landowner of a portion of the compensation received in improvement of the remaining, poorly utilized pastureland could often result in as many cattle being grazed—and substantially as much net income being received—as is presently the case for the entire holding.

8. Some possible exceptions to this tenancy restriction may be to allow "frictional" tenancy, such as cross-renting of nonadjacent plots to rationalize cultivation, or short-term rentals during military service or by a sick or disabled

owner.

9. See also the discussion of "Rapid Rural Appraisal" in Robert Chambers, *Rural Development: Putting the Last First* (London: Longman, 1983).

10. Still another support measure that may be useful in some settings would be the provision, via external assistance, of food aid to the urban sector in order to overcome possible temporary declines in production due to sharp changes in the form of agricultural organization. This might be true, for example, in contexts in which beneficiary desires and mid- to long-term productivity considerations might lead to the subdivision of large estates into small family-size farms, but with concern being expressed over the possible short-term impact on food-crop production while the changeover is being made. (Daniel Weiner's discussion of South Africa in Chapter 10, for example, indicates that such concern may arise there.) This is, however, only likely to be an issue where a major part of the actual crop-producing land of large estates (as distinct from idle, underutilized, or pasture land) is to be taken.

Contributors

Michael Bratton is associate professor of political science and African studies at Michigan State University.

Karen McConnell Brooks is assistant professor in the Department of Agricultural and Applied Economics at the University of Minnesota.

Merilee S. Grindle is a political scientist at the Harvard Institute for International Development.

Anthony Hall is a lecturer in social planning in developing countries at the London School of Economics and Political Science.

Timothy M. Hanstad is the deputy director of the Rural Development Institute in Seattle, Washington.

Ronald J. Herring teaches political economy and politics of South Asia at Northwestern University.

F. Tomasson Jannuzi is professor of economics at the University of Texas.

James T. Peach is associate professor of economics at New Mexico State University.

Roy L. Prosterman is professor of law at the University of Washington.

Jeffrey M. Riedinger is a assistant professor of politcal science at Michigan State University.

Rupert W. Scofield is a partner with the consulting firm of Rural Development Services, Inc. of Bethesda, Maryland.

Mary N. Temple is the executive director of the Curry Foundation.

Daniel Weiner is assistant professor in the Department of Geology and Geography at West Virginia University.

Acknowledgments

Index